THE COMPLETE
BOOK OF TRUSTS

THE COMPLETE BOOK OF TRUSTS

Martin M. Shenkman, CPA, MBA, JD

96 - Estate Planning book
113 - Establish trust - tasks
23 - Transferring assets
132 - Stepwise tfr of inheritance
212 - Phone no: fee-only finan planners
9 - Execute trust prior to will
92 - Allowable deductions
25, 27 - Amend insurance policies to reflect trust as new owner
49 - Limitations on trustee's discretionary authority
54 - Note on reason for selection of trustee
67 - Trustee powers - questions on
122 - Transaction of trust assets must be done in trust's name
126 - Documents to create
225 - S corporations
244 - Trustee fee waived = trust income (re. IRS)
258 - 6 mo. alternate valuation date
278 - Power of appointment / GSTT
129 - Rename beficiary of pension & insur.

John Wiley & Sons, Inc.

New York • Chichester • Brisbane • Toronto • Singapore

Library of Congress Cataloging-in-Publication Data

Shenkman, Martin M.
  The complete book of trusts / by Martin M. Shenkman.
      p.   cm.
    Includes index.
    ISBN 0-471-57447-3 (acid-free paper). —ISBN 0-471-57448-1 (pbk. :
  acid-free paper)
    1. Trusts and trustees—United States—Popular works. I. Title.
  KF730.Z9S53 1992
  346.7305'9—dc20
  [347.30659]   92-12059

Printed in the United States of America

10 9 8 7 6 5 4 3 2 1

PREFACE

Of all estate and financial planning tools trusts are the most flexible. A trust can be made to perform almost any legal act you wish. It can provide for you and your loved ones in the event of sickness and disability. It can continue to care for your family after your death. A trust can provide for management expertise for your assets. It can attain significant tax benefits. It can protect your assets from creditors. In accomplishing all of these important goals, the trust often can remain confidential.

Most importantly, trusts are not only tools for the very wealthy. When properly used, trusts can benefit everyone.

However, the first step is to assess your overall financial position and objectives. Only within the context of an overall estate and financial plan can you properly use trusts. Readers are referred to my book, *The Estate Planning Guide* (John Wiley & Sons, Inc., 1991), for additional background. With your basic plan in place, this book will help you select the right trust arrangements, make informed decisions about what assets should be transferred to your trusts, decide what provisions should be included, understand the limitations of what trusts can do for you, and know the tax implications of different trust arrangements. The proper use of trusts often will be a key to the financial security of your loved ones and you, and this book will help you work with your lawyer to achieve these important goals.

MARTIN M. SHENKMAN

Teaneck, New Jersey

B"H

ACKNOWLEDGMENTS

I would like to thank a number of people who were of considerable assistance in the preparation of this book. Michael Hamilton of John Wiley & Sons, whose support and encouragement were outstanding, as usual; Richard Feld, partner with the Teaneck, New Jersey, accounting firm Feld, Marks & Co., for numerous ideas and suggestions; Herman M. Eisenstein and Gerald Parkoff, of Financial Benefits Research Group, Roseland, New Jersey, for comments concerning insurance and pension planning insurance funding examples; Gail Cass and Raymond Berberian, Trust Officer, First Fidelity Bank, N.A., New Jersey, for valuable ideas on trustee powers and selecting an institutional trustee; Asher Schechter, of Comp-Acct Fiduciary Software, Inc., of Merrick, New York, for suggestions concerning fiduciary accounting and trust accounting; Terry Theisen of Brentmark Software, a division of Commerce Clearing House, 4025 W. Peterson Avenue, Chicago, Illinois, for providing the *Charitable Financial Planner* and *Estate Planning Tools* software and for his assistance in discussing the program and planning for charitable giving and other tax calculations appearing throughout the book; Cal Feingold, Esq., of the Hackensack, New Jersey, law firm Deener, Feingold & Stern for his review of the manuscript; Sanford I. Ruden, of the New York City law firm of Ruden & Cramer for his assistance on special needs trusts; Mark Goldsmith, Esq., of the New York City law firm Herrick Feinstein, for his comments on the manuscript; Gary Greenbaum of Greenbaum and Associates, Inc. of Oradell, New Jersey, for his assistance on investment matters.

M.M.S.

CONTENTS

PART ONE
UNDERSTANDING THE BUILDING BLOCKS OF
A TYPICAL TRUST

1   **What Is a Trust?**   3

2   **The Trust Document: Basic Building Blocks**   11

    For Your Notebook:
    Sample Application for Employee
        Identification Number   17
    Sample Signature Page   20

3   **Transferring Assets to Your Trust**   21

    For Your Notebook:
    Sample Schedule A: Property Transferred to Trust   29
    Sample Declaration of Gift   30
    Sample Bill of Sale   31
    Sample Assignment of Partnership Interest   32
    Sample Schedule of Ownership of the Asset   33
    Sample Consent of Shareholders   34
    Sample Stock Power   35
    Sample Assignment of Contracts   36
    Sample Pour-Over Will Provision   37

4   **Grantor's Rights and Powers**   39

5   **Beneficiaries' Designations and Rights**   47

6   **Trustees' Rights, Obligations, and Powers**   53

    For Your Notebook:
    Sample Trustee Provisions   58
    Sample Guidelines in Designating Trustee Powers
        Over Investment Matters   67

7   **Distribution of Income and Principal, and**
    Miscellaneous Provisions   69

    For Your Notebook:
    Sample Distribution Provisions   74
    Sample Miscellaneous Provisions   80

PART TWO
UNDERSTANDING THE TAX CONSEQUENCES
OF A TYPICAL TRUST

8   Planning for the Gift and Estate Tax   87

9   Planning for the Generation-Skipping Transfer Tax   95
     For Your Notebook:
         Sample GST Trust Provisions   104

PART THREE
TRUSTS FOR YOURSELF AND OTHERS

10   The Living Trust   111
     For Your Notebook:
         Schematic of Living Trust   112
         Sample Living Trust   127

11   Trusts for Your Spouse   145
     For Your Notebook:
         Sample Credit Shelter Provision   149
         Examples of the Benefits of Using a Credit
             Shelter Trust   150
         Sample Provisions for Your Noncitizen Spouse   151

12   Trusts for Nonmarital Partners   153

13   Trusts for Children   157
     For Your Notebook:
         Sample 2503(c) Minor's Trust Provisions   166

14   Trusts for Charities   167
     For Your Notebook:
         Sample Charitable Remainder Unitrust   176

15   GRATs, GRUTs, and Even PRITs   181
     For Your Notebook:
         Examples of the Benefits of Using a GRAT   185

PART FOUR
TRUSTS FOR ASSETS

16   Using Trusts to Protect Assets from Creditors   189

17   The Medicaid-Qualifying Trust   199
     For Your Notebook:
         Sample Medicaid Trust Provisions   206

18   The Life Insurance Trust   207
     For Your Notebook:
         Sample Life Insurance Trust Provisions   217

19 The Voting Trust, the Qualified Subchapter S
    Trust, and the Massachusetts Realty Trust   221
    For Your Notebook:
      Sample Corporate Resolution Authorizing
        Participation in the Voting Trust   232
      Sample Voting Trust Agreement   233
      Sample Qualified Subchapter S Trust Provisions   237
      Sample QSST Election   239

PART FIVE
TRUST TAXATION AND ACCOUNTING

20 How Trusts and Beneficiaries Are Taxed   243

21 How a Trust Is Taxed on the Sale or Distribution
    of Property   257

22 Terminating a Trust   263
    For Your Notebook:
      Sample General Release and Indemnification   272

Glossary   275

Index   283

Part One

UNDERSTANDING THE BUILDING BLOCKS OF A TYPICAL TRUST

1 WHAT IS A TRUST?

Trusts are among the most versatile and useful estate and financial planning tools. You don't have to be rich to use them, you only have to be realistic about what these complex instruments can, and cannot, do for you. Within limits, trusts can help you do the following:

- Manage your assets in the event you are disabled
- Manage assets for your children or family in the event of your death
- Avoid probate
- Avoid creditors
- Minimize or eliminate estate and other transfer taxes
- Protect loved ones
- Own your insurance policies
- Control businesses, and more

Unfortunately, there is a lot of misunderstanding about when and how trusts can be used. To address the misunderstandings, and to clarify the powers and benefits that trusts can offer you, the first step is to understand what a trust is.

DEFINITION

A trust, like a corporation, is a creature, or fiction, of the law. A trust is something you create by following the procedures required by the laws of your state. The simplest way to explain a trust is with an example.

EXAMPLE: Greta Grandmother has her lawyer prepare a legal document called a trust. Greta then transfers $10,000 to her daughter, Debby, as trustee of the trust. Debby is required by the terms of the trust document to invest the $10,000 in a certificate of deposit and use all of the interest each year to pay for dancing and music lessons for her two children, Greta's grandchildren. When the youngest of Debby's two daughters reaches age 21, Debby is instructed to divide the money in the trust equally and distribute it to each of them.

This illustration also contains the important time periods in a trust's existence. First the trust is formed by having a legal document prepared and signed. This trust document is a contract between the grantor, who sets up the trust, and the trustee, who administers the trust. Next, assets are transferred to the trust. This step completes the establishment and funding of the trust. Third, the trust is administered for its duration. Finally, when the trust has fulfilled its purposes, the money and assets it holds are distributed and the trust is terminated.

Trusts Separate Legal and Beneficial Ownership of an Asset

The key to using a trust is knowing that a trust arrangement separates the legal ownership of an asset from the benefit of that asset. The person holding the legal title, the trustee, has a fiduciary duty to the person or persons entitled to the benefits of the trust property. A fiduciary duty is a responsibility of care imposed on the trustee by the provisions of the trust document and state law. The trustee is charged with exercising certain care in carrying out the requirements and intent of the trust document. Court cases of your state, can also create certain obligations and duties on the trustee. The advantages of a trust arrangement come from this separation of ownership and benefit.

When the IRS is willing to recognize the trust, certain important tax savings can be available.

In a case where the persons intended to benefit cannot, or should not, be in control of the assets, a trust provides an ideal vehicle to provide for management. For example, a trust can permit a bank or a savvy family member to manage money for the benefit of children or incapacitated family members. When the separation of the ownership and benefit is recognized, assets may escape the clutches of creditors of the beneficiaries (asset protection trusts).

Five Key Elements of Every Trust

A trust is an arrangement in which a *grantor* transfers *trust property* to a *trustee* to hold for the benefit of the *beneficiary* in accordance with the purpose or *intent* of the trust.

Every trust requires the five elements highlighted in the above paragraph:

1. *Grantor.* The grantor is the person who transfers property to the trust. The grantor is also called the trustor, settlor, or donor. The grantor generally must be the owner of the property that he or she transfers to the trust. The grantor also must have the proper legal capacity to transfer assets. This means that the grantor must be of sound mind and have the intent to form a trust. This intent of the grantor to form a trust must be manifested—almost always, in the form of a written and signed trust agreement.

2. *Trust Property.* Trust property is the principal or subject matter of the trust—it is also called the *trust res*. The property must be

transferred to the trust. It can be transferred during life, after death through the grantor's will, through a gift, or by the exercise of a power of appointment. The property of a trust can be cash you contribute, a life insurance policy, stock in a corporation, or any other asset that serves your purposes for establishing the trust, and that can be owned in a trust. In most trusts, a formal legal description of the trust property is attached to the end of the trust as a schedule.

When you set up a standby trust you form the trust now, but it may not have the intended assets transferred to it until some future date, such as your death. In such situations you should probably transfer a nominal amount of money, say $100, to the trust in order to open a trust bank account.

3. *Trustee*. The trustee is the person responsible for managing and administering a trust. The trustee should make a declaration, often by signing the trust agreement, that he or she accepts the trust property as trustee. The trustee may be you (the grantor), a trusted friend, a family member, a bank trust department, or any combination of these and other persons. If you are a trustee you should generally name a second person to serve as a co-trustee with you. This will help avoid a technical problem called "merger" which is discussed below. The main legal requirement to serve as trustee is that the trustee have the legal capacity to accept title (ownership) of the trust property. For example, a minor or incompetent person cannot be a trustee. The grantor will specify the trustee, and should specify successor trustees in the event the first-named trustee is no longer willing or able to serve as a trustee. If the grantor fails to do this, a court may have to name a trustee.

The trustee generally will hold legal title to the assets in the trust but not beneficial title. "Legal title" means the trust assets are owned in the name of the trustee, the trustee has specific duties and responsibilities for the trust property, or has certain powers concerning the disposition of the trust property. "Beneficial title" to the trust property is held by the beneficiaries of the trust.

EXAMPLE: Tom Taxpayer establishes a trust for the benefit of his children. Tina Taxpayer is the named trustee. The stock that Tom transfers is owned by Tina, as trustee of the trust. Thus, Tina holds legal title to the stock "in trust" for the beneficiaries. Beneficial title, however, is held by the children, and only they have the right to benefit from the dividends and principal value of the stock.

NOTE: The above discussion indicates why the same person can't be the *only* trustee and the *only* beneficiary. There would be no split of legal and beneficial title, which is essential for a trust. If the legal and beneficial interests merge, or become one by law, the trust could be invalidated. The rules vary by state.

---

4. *Beneficiary*. The beneficiary is the person or persons who will receive the benefits and advantages of the property transferred to the

trust. In the above example, Tom and Tina's children are the beneficiaries. It is important that the persons who are beneficiaries can be determined—that is, the description should be clear and certain. For example, if you name "my descendants" as beneficiaries, there must be a time for making the determination of who your descendants are, otherwise, it is impossible to know when to make the decision. A typical issue is, are children or grandchildren born after you set up the trust to be included? Beneficiaries also can be charities (see Chapter 14).

5. *Intent of Trust.* Every trust has a purpose, or intent, which motivates the grantor to set up the trust in the first place. Apart from the obvious requirement that the intent be legal, there are few restrictions on what the trust should be for. The intent can relate to benefiting a particular beneficiary (yourself, spouse, or child) providing for the management of certain assets (real estate or stock in a closely held corporation), or achieving certain tax benefits (charitable remainder trust or marital trust), or a combination of all three. The intent of the trust should be spelled out in detail in the trust document. Many of the "canned" "fill-in-the-blank" trusts sold in bookstores fail to do this adequately. When the trust document is silent, state laws and court cases may fill in some of the blanks.

How Do Trusts Compare to Other Legal Arrangements?

A common legal arrangement is an agency relationship. The most frequently used agency relationship is a power of attorney, which is simply a legal document that authorizes another person to act as your agent in handling your financial matters. A limitation of this arrangement is that many powers of attorney automatically terminate when you become disabled. The solution is to use what is called a "durable power of attorney." When state law permits, and the appropriate language is included, the power of attorney will remain effective even if you become disabled.

No power of attorney, however, will remain effective after your death. Therefore, when you want to provide for the management of your assets even after death, a trust, and not a power of attorney is the appropriate vehicle. There are also advantages to using a trust instead of a power of attorney during your life. In a power-of-attorney relationship, a person is designated as your agent, to act on your behalf. But the trustee's relationship to the assets is clearer, and the trustee's powers over the assets are likely to be greater, for the trustee has legal ownership of the assets. Thus, if you are planning for potential disability, a trust arrangement is preferable to merely using a durable power of attorney. The only disadvantage of the trust approach is cost, which makes the durable power of attorney the more practical solution in many situations.

Another common arrangement is a transfer under your state's uniform gifts (or transfers) to minors act (see Chapter 13). There are important differences between such an account and a trust. The beneficiary (in this case, your child) owns the property, not you. A trust can offer substantially more control, since you can tailor the trust document to address any concerns you may have. With a trust the child won't automatically be entitled to all the money when he or she reaches the age of majority (often 18), also the assets can be protected from creditors. However, there will be legal fees required to set up the trust, and you may have to file annual tax returns. Assets can be placed in a uniform gifts or transfers to minors act account at no cost.

Privacy and Anonymity of Trusts

The opportunity to retain anonymity and privacy is often touted as an important advantage of establishing trusts, particularly when assets are placed in trust to avoid the probate process. The reason is that, unlike wills and many other documents, trusts do not have to be filed in the public record. However, privacy can be breached if the court orders that the trust be made part of the public probate record, or if the parties, beneficiaries, or others sue each other, forcing the trust into the court records.

Privacy also can be breached because of the legal steps necessary to transfer assets into the trust. For example, when real estate is transferred to a trust, a deed will have to be filed. A deed is a public record. So even if the trust document itself remains private, the fact that the real estate was transferred to the trust will be public knowledge. Certain other property transfers to the trust may be subject to public filing requirements under the provisions of the Uniform Commercial Code. Thus, while available in many situations, the privacy afforded by trusts is not as foolproof as many people believe.

DIFFERENT TYPES OF TRUSTS

Trusts can be as varied as the people who set them up. The reason to categorize trusts is to better explain their uses, and help you pick the right trust for your needs. Trusts can be categorized by numerous factors, including the following:

- *When Established.* You can set up a trust during your lifetime (an *inter vivos*, or living, trust). Common living trusts include a revocable living trust (sometimes called a "loving trust"), a charitable remainder trust, and a children's trust. Alternatively, you can establish a trust that only becomes effective on your death (called a "testamentary trust"). Testamentary trusts are frequently contained in your will. Common testamentary trusts include a trust for your spouse and trusts for minor children. This category is difficult to apply because many trusts can be set up either way—during your life or after your death.

- *Type of Beneficiary.* Trusts can be established to benefit any type of person or cause. As Chapter 10 demonstrates, a living trust is an excellent tool for planning for your own disability, in a living trust you are the beneficiary. Several different trusts can be set up for your spouse. Numerous trusts are used for children. For example, a special trust can be used to make gifts to children under the age of 21 and still qualify for favorable tax benefits. When a special child is involved, a trust can be used to protect the child while preventing the loss of governmental benefits. A trust can be set up for a charity.

- *Purpose of Trust.* Some trusts are organized according to the purpose for which they are established. For example, marital trusts are designed to qualify transfers of assets for the gift or estate tax marital deduction. A trust can be designed to avoid having assets used to pay for Medicaid benefits (called the Medicaid-qualifying trust).

- *Grantor's Control.* Trusts can be categorized according to the control exercised by the grantor. When the grantor retains the right to terminate or change a trust, the trust is called "revocable." Living trusts are, perhaps, the most common examples of revocable trusts. When the grantor relinquishes the right to change or terminate the trust, it is said to be "irrevocable." When tax considerations or asset protection are important, the trust is more likely to be irrevocable.

- *Assets Held.* The type of assets transferred—for example, insurance, real estate, and the stock of S corporations—can be used to characterize trusts. A voting trust can be used to hold stock of a closely held corporation.

- *Powers of Trustees.* Trustees can be given the power to appoint the assets of the trust, to pay the income of the trust to a single beneficiary or accumulate the income, or to sprinkle the income among various beneficiaries. Trustees can be given the power to buy, rent, or mortgage real estate, operate a business, or any other type of management control. Chapters 5 and 6 explain the issues and alternatives regarding trustees when designing a trust. Trusts are sometimes known by the powers given the trustees. For example, where the trustee can allocate income to various beneficiaries the trust is called a "sprinkle trust."

- *Powers of the Beneficiaries.* Although the beneficiaries are often passive and the trustees make most decisions, there are several powers that the beneficiaries can be afforded. For example, the beneficiaries may be given the right to require the distribution of certain amounts of principal each year from the trust. A beneficiary may be given the right to designate where the assets of the trust will eventually be distributed. This latter right is known as a power of appointment.

Choosing a Trust Must Be Part of Your Overall Planning

How will you decide what trust, or trusts, are necessary to meet your goals? You cannot do it in a vacuum. For a proper decision to be made, you must review thoroughly your present and anticipated future financial position. You must anticipate the health, education, and other needs of your family, yourself, and others for whom you feel responsible. You must coordinate the use of any trusts with your will; in fact, some or all of the trusts you choose may even be included in your will. If you use a pour-over will, which will transfer assets to one of your trusts, you obviously must coordinate that trust with your will. For example, the trust should have provisions permitting the trustees to accept assets from your will. The trust also should be executed prior to the will (otherwise the transfer may be invalid under certain state's laws).

You should coordinate the use of powers of attorney with your trust planning. As noted above, a power of attorney is a legal arrangement that permits others to take financial actions on your behalf, possibly when you're disabled. If you establish a trust, particularly a revocable living trust or another type of trust during your lifetime that may not be completely funded, the agent to whom you grant a power of attorney should have the specific authority to transfer assets to your trust.

You should evaluate your insurance needs and coverage and coordinate these with your selection of a trust or trusts. This is a critical point because a common use of trusts is to own your insurance policies.

If you want to use a trust as part of a plan to own or transfer ownership of business interests, you should consider the future growth of the business, the interests and wishes of any other partners or shareholders, and any restriction that a partnership, buy-out, or shareholders' agreement might contain preventing your transfer of partnership interests or shares to the trust.

The key point in properly planning for the use of any trust is to coordinate the process with your overall business, financial, tax, and estate plan. You should conduct this planning with *all* of your advisers, including your accountant, attorney, and insurance and investment advisers. Any attempt to plan without this coordination is dangerous.

Selecting the Right Trust

The myriad possibilities for different trusts and trust provisions make for a selection process that should be completed with professional advice. Nevertheless, this book can provide you with substantial help by introducing you to many of the trust arrangements available. Based on the kind of thorough review outlined above, you can devise a comprehensive estate and financial plan. Within the context of implementing this comprehensive plan, you can identify the trusts appropriate for you and then implement them. The following example illustrates the comprehensive selection of appropriate trusts.

EXAMPLE: Gary and Gail Grantor, a married couple, estimate their net worth at $1.4 million. Their estate planner recommends the use of credit shelter trusts so that each of their estates can benefit from the once-in-a-lifetime $600,000 exclusion (see Chapter 8). Each of their wills thus incorporates a credit shelter trust.

Gail has children from a previous marriage and wants to set up a trust for their eventual use containing any assets she owns above the $600,000 amount. A Q-TIP trust is selected. This trust will qualify for the estate tax marital deduction, eliminating any tax on Gail's death. Following Gail's death, Gary will be entitled to all of the income from this trust. Following Gary's death the assets from Gail's Q-TIP trust will be distributed to Gail's children from her first marriage. With this arrangement there won't be any federal estate tax due on Gail's death because the first $600,000 of her estate (her unified credit) will be tax free. The amounts above $600,000, included in a Q-TIP trust, will be exempted from tax on Gail's death by the unlimited estate tax marital deduction.

To protect his family, Gary has a $1 million term life insurance policy. If either Gary or Gail owns this policy, it will create a tax cost on the death of the second to die. The solution is to have an irrevocable life insurance trust own the policy (Chapter 18).

Because Gail and Gary's children are minors, the Grantors have provided trusts for their children in their wills. These trusts name a succession of close and trusted friends to handle the financial affairs of their children in the event that both Gail and Gary die while their children are still young.

If Gail and Gary were concerned about planning for disability and avoiding the expenses and delays of probate, they could transfer their assets to a revocable living trust. In such an event, the credit shelter and Q-TIP trust provisions discussed above could be included in each of their living trusts.

Gail owns 60 percent of the stock of a corporation that operates a manufacturing business. The corporation is organized as an S corporation. As her children grow, Gail plans to give them gifts of the stock to remove the value from her estate. However, she wants to retain control over the children's use of the stock and voting control for herself over the corporation. Gail establishes a qualified subchapter S trust (QSST) to hold the stock (Chapter 19). She can vote the stock as trustee of the trust.

CONCLUSION

Trusts are valuable and flexible tools that can provide substantial benefits for meeting estate, financial, personal, and business goals. They can be organized in many different ways, according to several different factors. This book will elucidate these principles and factors to give you a firm grasp of the possibilities available in using trusts.

2 THE TRUST DOCUMENT: BASIC BUILDING BLOCKS

Most trusts are made up of several similar components. If you are the grantor, knowing the basic building blocks of a trust will help ensure that any trusts you establish will be appropriate to meet your needs. If you are a beneficiary or trustee of someone else's trust, knowing the basic building blocks will make it much easier for you to understand your rights and responsibilities under that trust. The following schematic shows what these components are.

SCHEMATIC OF BASIC TRUST BUILDING BLOCKS

INTRODUCTORY PARGRAPHS

TRANSFERRING ASSETS TO YOUR TRUST

GRANTOR'S RIGHTS AND POWERS UNDER THE TRUST

BENEFICIARIES' DESIGNATIONS AND RIGHTS

TRUSTEES' RIGHTS, OBLIGATIONS, AND POWERS

DISTRIBUTION OF INCOME AND PRINCIPAL
(OPERATIVE PROVISIONS OF YOUR TRUST)

MISCELLANEOUS PROVISIONS

SIGNATURE LINES, EXHIBITS

BUILDING BLOCK #1: INTRODUCTORY PARAGRAPHS

Introductory paragraphs are only needed for trusts established during your lifetime (*inter vivos* trusts). Trusts established in your will (testamentary trusts) do not need these paragraphs because the provisions of the will and state laws substitute for many. Your trust typically begins by being named; this is followed by fairly simple introductory paragraphs.

SAMPLE TRUST CLAUSES:

NAME OF TRUST

WHEREAS, the Grantor desires to create a trust, and transfer the assets listed below to the trust, on the terms which are detailed below, and the Trustee has consented to accept and perform said trust in accordance with such terms;

NOW, THEREFORE, this Trust shall be effective as of the date and terms following:

DECLARATION OF TRUST.

THIS TRUST AGREEMENT dated as of MONTH DAY, YEAR, between, GRANTOR'S NAME, who resides at GRANTOR'S ADDRESS (the "Grantor"), and TRUSTEE1-NAME, who resides at TRUSTEE1-ADDRESS, and any successor Trustee appointed as provided in this Trust Agreement (the "Trustee").

The first step is selecting the name for your trust. You may want to avoid the use of a family name so that the use of the trust will not immediately convey to third parties the fact that you have a trust. However, you should find a name that is sufficiently descriptive to make it easy for you, your family, and professional advisers to work with the trust. This becomes particularly important when you have several trusts.

EXAMPLE: Tom Taxpayer sets up a grantor-retained annuity trust (GRAT) in 1991 (Chapter 15). The trust is called "The Tom Taxpayer 1991 Trust." If this were Tom's only trust, the name might be reasonable. However, in 1992, Tom sets up a second GRAT and calls it "The Tom Taxpayer 1992 Trust." In 1993, Tom sets up an irrevocable life insurance trust and calls it "The Tom Taxpayer 1993 Trust." Administration will become exceedingly confusing since the names are so similar. Tom could consider the following names instead: "Tom's 1991 GRAT," "Tom's 1992 GRAT," and "Tom's Irrevocable Life Insurance Trust." These names are more descriptive, and they don't advertise Tom Taxpayer's name to anyone seeing any trust-related documents.

After the name and intent to have a trust, the first paragraph lists the date the trust is established, the name of the grantor establishing the trust (if it's your trust, this probably will be you), and the initial trustee or trustees. This paragraph contains three of the five essential elements of a trust that were presented in Chapter 1—a grantor, a trustee, and the intent of the grantor to form a trust.

The date of your trust is particularly important. If you want to make gifts to a trust that qualify for your annual $10,000 per person gift tax exclusion, the trust must be established prior to the year's end. Every taxpayer is entitled to give away up to $10,000 to an unlimited number of other persons during each tax year without incurring a gift tax (and without using any of the $600,000 lifetime unified credit against the gift and estate tax to which each taxpayer is entitled). If the gift is for your children, grandchildren, or other minors, you may prefer to make the gift to a trust in order to provide some control over the child's use of the money. You'll need to set up this trust soon enough before the end of the year to open a bank account and make an initial deposit.

NOTE: You may need a tax identification number from the IRS before you can open the bank account. This can be obtained faster over the telephone (via facsimile) rather than through the mail. The form to complete is IRS Form SS-4. A sample form is presented in the "For Your Notebook" section following this chapter. Each district of the IRS has its own facsimile number for sending such forms. Call the main IRS office serving your area for additional information, or write the IRS forms center for Form SS-4 and instructions. Be sure to use the current form.

If you use a will with a pour-over provision, the trust should have a date prior to the date of the will. Rather than providing details about where your assets should go after your death, the pour-over simply transfers all assets to your trust. The trust contains the details regarding who gets what (see the "For Your Notebook" section following Chapter 3).

The introductory descriptive paragraph of your typical trust also illustrates the point noted in Chapter 1—that a trust is a contract between the grantor and trustees. (If the trust is a revocable living trust, however, you may be both the grantor and one of the trustees—see Chapters 4 and 10.) The introductory paragraph will name only the initial trustee (or trustees) for your trust. Successor, or alternate, trustees will be named in later provisions of the trust.

If one or more of your trusts is established under the provisions of your will, the preceding sections concerning date or effective date will not appear. The trust will simply become effective on your death.

BUILDING BLOCK #2: TRANSFERRING ASSETS TO YOUR TRUST

NOTE: Building blocks #2 through #7 are discussed in separate chapters, so that the discussion here will be merely by way of introduction.

As explained in Chapter 1, trust property—identification of assets transferred to the trust—is one of the five essential elements of a trust. Without assets there is little a trust can do. However, in some instances you may want to set up a trust now even though it won't have assets until a later date. This is called a "Stand-by trust." Identifying the assets to be transferred to your trust, however, represents only a small part of what is necessary in funding the trust. The legal ownership (called title) of these assets also must be transferred to your trustees. The steps involved in this process, as well as the decisions regarding what assets should be transferred, will be detailed in Chapter 3.

BUILDING BLOCK #3: GRANTOR'S RIGHTS AND POWERS

The grantor is the person setting up a trust—for our purposes, you. In many living trusts the grantor retains certain rights and powers over the trust and the property transferred to the trust. The nature and extent of these powers depends on the objectives of the trust. For example, if the trust is formed to remove assets from your estate, you will retain no powers over the trust. On the other hand, if you set up a revocable (you can change it at any time) living trust for purposes of administering assets in the event of your later disability, and to avoid probate, you will probably retain total control over the assets and trust.

When a trust is formed under a will, the grantor obviously cannot retain any rights or powers. These matters are discussed further in Chapter 4.

BUILDING BLOCK #4: BENEFICIARIES' DESIGNATIONS AND RIGHTS

Beneficiaries are another essential trust element. The provisions that affect a beneficiary can be quite simple, as shown in the following example:

SAMPLE TRUST LANGUAGE: I, Gary Grantor, hereby transfer $10,000 to Terri Trustee to hold in trust for the benefit of Mary Minor, as beneficiary. The Trustee shall pay the income from this money to or for the benefit of the beneficiary until the beneficiary reaches age 21, when any money remaining in this trust shall be given to the beneficiary.

In many trusts, however, the provisions concerning beneficiaries are far more complex. For example, if the primary beneficiary, Mary Minor in the above example, were to die, other persons could be named as beneficiaries. Some trusts give beneficiaries the right to demand that certain payments be made to them, or for their benefit. These matters are detailed in Chapter 5.

BUILDING BLOCK #5: TRUSTEES RIGHTS, OBLIGATIONS, AND POWERS

This is the longest and most complex section of a trust, discussing who should serve as trustee. Although you've named the initial trustee in the introductory paragraph of your trust, you should always name alternate or successor trustees in the event that the initial trustee cannot continue to serve. Instructions regarding how the trustee should serve, what rights the trustee has, what powers and authority the trustee can exercise over the trust property, and how the trustee should manage the trust all must be provided. These paragraphs are the "guts" of your trust, meaning they are what make your trust work. Although they are often skimmed quickly as "boiler plate" provisions, this approach can be a serious mistake. If you're named as a trustee, these are the sections you must read with the greatest of attention. These matters are further discussed in Chapter 6.

State law is also important because it may fill in where your trust provisions are insufficient.

BUILDING BLOCK #6: DISTRIBUTION OF INCOME AND PRINCIPAL (OPERATIVE PROVISIONS OF YOUR TRUST)

Most trusts are established to distribute income to, or for the benefit of, the trust's beneficiaries. Similarly every trust contains rules for when the principal of the trust can be distributed. In the most basic terms, principal is the asset transferred to the trust, and income is the money this asset earns. The provisions of your trust stating how and when income and principal should be distributed are extremely important. Further, the clearer your trust is about the rules for allocating receipts between income and principal, the less likely that your trustee will become embroiled in difficult problems.

EXAMPLE: You've just married for the second time. You establish a trust for the benefit of your second spouse during his or her lifetime. On your second spouse's death, the assets will be divided among your only children, who are from your first marriage. You name a close family friend as trustee. Any receipts that are characterized as income will be distributed to your second spouse. Any receipts that are characterized as principal will be allocated to your children from a prior marriage.

The provisions that govern how income and principal can be distributed are closely related to the provisions that make your trust a particular type of trust. Consider the following:

- *Qualified S Corporation Trust (QSST).* An S Corporation is treated in a manner similar to a partnership for federal (and some state) income tax purposes. It generally avoids the corporate tax level. However, all income must be distributed currently to a single beneficiary in order for a trust to be a shareholder in an S corporation. Thus, the provisions of your trust governing when income and principal can be distributed must meet these requirements (see Chapter 19).

- *Charitable Lead or Remainder Trust.* Both of these trusts are formed to achieve specific tax advantages. The provisions of the trust governing the distribution of income and principal must conform strictly to the applicable IRS requirements in order to attain the intended tax benefits.

- *Marital Deduction Trust.* The estate tax can apply at rates of 55 percent, and even higher. One of the exclusions from this tax is that every taxpayer can give away an unlimited amount of assets to his or her spouse. If you want to put these assets into a trust, you must use a qualified terminable interest property trust (Q-TIP trust) or qualified domestic trust (Q-DOT trust), and one of the tax law requirements is that all income from that trust must be distributed, at least annually, to your spouse (see Chapter 11).

Thus, the income and distribution provisions of your trust may have to address the specific character and nature of the assets transferred to your trust, the purpose of your trust, and other factors. These matters are addressed in detail in Chapter 7.

BUILDING BLOCK #7: MISCELLANEOUS PROVISIONS

Included in most trusts are definitions of key terms used in your trust document, specification of which state law should govern, and several technical legal provisions governing how your trust document should be interpreted in the event there are ever questions as to what should be done. These matters are reviewed in Chapter 7.

BUILDING BLOCK #8: SIGNATURE LINES, EXHIBITS

If your trust is created under your will, the final paragraphs, signature lines, and other formalities are governed by the state laws applicable to wills. If you set up a trust during your life, you may, depending on state law, need to provide for the proper signature (execution) of the trust, notarization of the signatures, and a schedule detailing the assets transferred to the trust upon its formation. For a sample signature page, see the "For Your Notebook" section following this chapter.

CONCLUSION

This chapter has summarized the key components of a typical trust. The chapters that follow will greatly expand on this summary and provide you with the tools to understand and work with your trusts. If you keep this summary in mind when reviewing any trust, it will help your understanding of the relevance of any particular part of a trust document to the overall purpose of the trust.

For Your Notebook:

Form **SS-4** (Rev. April 1991) Department of the Treasury Internal Revenue Service	**Application for Employer Identification Number** (For use by employers and others. Please read the attached instructions before completing this form.)	**EIN** OMB No. 1545-0003 Expires 4-30-94

Please type or print clearly.

1 Name of applicant (True legal name) (See instructions.)
TOM TAXPAYER IRREVOCABLE TRUST

2 Trade name of business, if different from name in line 1	**3** Executor, trustee, "care of" name SUE SMITH, CPA
4a Mailing address (street address) (room, apt., or suite no.) 123 MAIN STREET	**5a** Address of business (See instructions.) 123 MAIN STREET
4b City, state, and ZIP code SOME CITY, NEW YORK 00000	**5b** City, state, and ZIP code SOME CITY, NEW YORK 00000

6 County and state where principal business is located
COUNTY NAME, NEW YORK

7 Name of principal officer, grantor, or general partner (See instructions.) ▶
TOM TAXPAYER

8a Type of entity (Check only one box.) (See instructions.)
☐ Individual SSN _____   ☐ Estate   ☒ Trust
☐ REMIC   ☐ Personal service corp.   ☐ Plan administrator SSN _____   ☐ Partnership
☐ State/local government   ☐ National guard   ☐ Other corporation (specify) _____   ☐ Farmers' cooperative
☐ Other nonprofit organization (specify) _____   ☐ Federal government/military   ☐ Church or church controlled organization
☐ Other (specify) ▶   If nonprofit organization enter GEN (if applicable) _____

8b If a corporation, give name of foreign country (if applicable) or state in the U.S. where incorporated ▶ | Foreign country | State

9 Reason for applying (Check only one box.)
☐ Started new business   ☐ Changed type of organization (specify) ▶ _____
☐ Hired employees   ☐ Purchased going business
☐ Created a pension plan (specify type) ▶ _____   ☒ Created a trust (specify) ▶ IRREVOCABLE INTER-VIVOS TRUST
☐ Banking purpose (specify) ▶ _____   ☐ Other (specify) ▶

10 Date business started or acquired (Mo., day, year) (See instructions.)
1/1/92

11 Enter closing month of accounting year. (See instructions.)
DECEMBER

12 First date wages or annuities were paid or will be paid (Mo., day, year). **Note:** *If applicant is a withholding agent, enter date income will first be paid to nonresident alien. (Mo., day, year)* ▶ N/A

13 Enter highest number of employees expected in the next 12 months. **Note:** *If the applicant does not expect to have any employees during the period, enter "0."* ▶

Nonagricultural	Agricultural	Household
0	0	0

14 Principal activity (See instructions.) ▶ TRUST

15 Is the principal business activity manufacturing?   ☐ Yes   ☒ No
If "Yes," principal product and raw material used ▶

16 To whom are most of the products or services sold? Please check the appropriate box.   ☐ Business (wholesale)
☐ Public (retail)   ☐ Other (specify) ▶   ☒ N/A

17a Has the applicant ever applied for an identification number for this or any other business?   ☐ Yes   ☒ No
Note: *If "Yes," please complete lines 17b and 17c.*

17b If you checked the "Yes" box in line 17a, give applicant's true name and trade name, if different than name shown on prior application.
True name ▶   Trade name ▶

17c Enter approximate date, city, and state where the application was filed and the previous employer identification number if known.

Approximate date when filed (Mo., day, year)	City and state where filed	Previous EIN

Under penalties of perjury, I declare that I have examined this application, and to the best of my knowledge and belief, it is true, correct, and complete

Telephone number (include area code)

Name and title (Please type or print clearly.) ▶ SUE SMITH, CPA, TRUSTEE   (212) 999-9999

Signature ▶   Date ▶ 1/1/92

Note: *Do not write below this line.   For official use only.*

Please leave blank ▶	Geo.	Ind.	Class	Size	Reason for applying

For Paperwork Reduction Act Notice, see attached instructions.   Cat. No. 16055N   Form **SS-4** (Rev. 4-91)

Prepared by Richard Feld, CPA, Feld Marks & Co., Teaneck, New Jersey.

General Instructions

(Section references are to the Internal Revenue Code unless otherwise noted.)

Paperwork Reduction Act Notice.—We ask for the information on this form to carry out the Internal Revenue laws of the United States. You are required to give us this information. We need it to ensure that you are complying with these laws and to allow us to figure and collect the right amount of tax.

The time needed to complete and file this form will vary depending on individual circumstances. The estimated average time is:

Recordkeeping	7 min.
Learning about the law or the form	21 min.
Preparing the form	42 min.
Copying, assembling, and sending the form to IRS	20 min.

If you have comments concerning the accuracy of these time estimates or suggestions for making this form more simple, we would be happy to hear from you. You can write to both the **Internal Revenue Service,** Washington, DC 20224, Attention: IRS Reports Clearance Officer, T:FP; and the **Office of Management and Budget,** Paperwork Reduction Project (1545-0003), Washington, DC 20503. **DO NOT** send the tax form to either of these offices. Instead, see **Where To Apply.**

Purpose.—Use Form SS-4 to apply for an employer identification number (EIN). The information you provide on this form will establish your filing requirements.

Who Must File.—You must file this form if you have not obtained an EIN before and

● You pay wages to one or more employees.

● You are required to have an EIN to use on any return, statement, or other document, even if you are not an employer.

● You are required to withhold taxes on income, other than wages, paid to a nonresident alien (individual, corporation, partnership, etc.). For example, individuals who file **Form 1042,** Annual Withholding Tax Return for U.S. Source Income of Foreign Persons, to report alimony paid to nonresident aliens must have EINs.

Individuals who file **Schedule C,** Profit or Loss From Business, or **Schedule F,** Profit or Loss From Farming, of **Form 1040,** U.S. Individual Income Tax Return, must use EINs if they have a Keogh plan or are required to file excise, employment, or alcohol, tobacco, or firearms returns.

The following must use EINs even if they do not have any employees:

● Trusts, except an IRA trust, unless the IRA trust is required to file **Form 990-T,** Exempt Organization Business Income Tax Return, to report unrelated business taxable income or is filing Form 990-T to obtain a refund of the credit from a regulated investment company.

● Estates

● Partnerships

● REMICS (real estate mortgage investment conduits)

● Corporations

● Nonprofit organizations (churches, clubs, etc.)

● Farmers' cooperatives

● Plan administrators

New Business.—If you become the new owner of an existing business, **DO NOT** use the EIN of the former owner. If you already have an EIN, use that number. If you do not have an EIN, apply for one on this form. If

you become the "owner" of a corporation by acquiring its stock, use the corporation's EIN.

If you already have an EIN, you may need to get a new one if either the organization or ownership of your business changes. If you incorporate a sole proprietorship or form a partnership, you must get a new EIN. However, **DO NOT** apply for a new EIN if you change only the name of your business.

File Only One Form SS-4.—File only one Form SS-4, regardless of the number of businesses operated or trade names under which a business operates. However, each corporation in an affiliated group must file a separate application.

If you do not have an EIN by the time a return is due, write "Applied for" and the date you applied in the space shown for the number. **DO NOT** show your social security number as an EIN on returns.

If you do not have an EIN by the time a tax deposit is due, send your payment to the Internal Revenue service center for your filing area. (See **Where To Apply** below.) Make your check or money order payable to Internal Revenue Service and show your name (as shown on Form SS-4), address, kind of tax, period covered, and date you applied for an EIN.

For more information about EINs, see **Pub. 583,** Taxpayers Starting a Business.

How To Apply.—You can apply for an EIN either by mail or by telephone. You can get an EIN immediately by calling the Tele-TIN phone number for the service center for your state, or you can send the completed Form SS-4 directly to the service center to receive your EIN in the mail.

Application by Tele-TIN.—The Tele-TIN program is designed to assign EINs by telephone. Under this program, you can receive your EIN over the telephone and use it immediately to file a return or make a payment.

To receive an EIN by phone, complete Form SS-4, then call the Tele-TIN phone number listed for your state under **Where To Apply.** The person making the call must be authorized to sign the form (see **Signature block** on page 3).

An IRS representative will use the information from the Form SS-4 to establish your account and assign you an EIN. Write the number you are given on the upper right-hand corner of the form, sign and date it, and promptly mail it to the Tele-TIN Unit at the service center address for your state.

Application by mail.—Complete Form SS-4 at least 4 to 5 weeks before you will need an EIN. Sign and date the application and mail it to the service center address for your state. You will receive your EIN in the mail in approximately 4 weeks.

Note: *The Tele-TIN phone numbers listed below will involve a long-distance charge to callers outside of the local calling area, and should only be used to apply for an EIN. Use 1-800-829-1040 to ask about an application by mail.*

Where To Apply.—

If your principal business, office or agency, or legal residence in the case of an individual, is located in:	Call the Tele-TIN phone number shown or file with the Internal Revenue service center at:
Florida, Georgia, South Carolina	Atlanta, GA 39901 (404) 455-2360
New Jersey, New York City and counties of Nassau, Rockland, Suffolk, and Westchester	Holtsville, NY 00501 (516) 447-4955
New York (all other counties), Connecticut, Maine, Massachusetts, New Hampshire, Rhode Island, Vermont	Andover, MA 05501 (508) 474-9717
Illinois, Iowa, Minnesota, Missouri, Wisconsin	Kansas City, MO 64999 (816) 926-5999
Delaware, District of Columbia, Maryland, Pennsylvania, Virginia	Philadelphia, PA 19255 (215) 961-3980
Indiana, Kentucky, Michigan, Ohio, West Virginia	Cincinnati, OH 45999 (606) 292-5467
Kansas, New Mexico, Oklahoma, Texas	Austin, TX 73301 (512) 462-7845
Alaska, Arizona, California (counties of Alpine, Amador, Butte, Calaveras, Colusa, Contra Costa, Del Norte, El Dorado, Glenn, Humboldt, Lake, Lassen, Marin, Mendocino, Modoc, Napa, Nevada, Placer, Plumas, Sacramento, San Joaquin, Shasta, Sierra, Siskiyou, Solano, Sonoma, Sutter, Tehama, Trinity, Yolo, and Yuba), Colorado, Idaho, Montana, Nebraska, Nevada, North Dakota, Oregon, South Dakota, Utah, Washington, Wyoming	Ogden, UT 84201 (801) 625-7645
California (all other counties), Hawaii	Fresno, CA 93888 (209) 456-5900
Alabama, Arkansas, Louisiana, Mississippi, North Carolina, Tennessee	Memphis, TN 37501 (901) 365-5970

If you have no legal residence, principal place of business, or principal office or agency in any Internal Revenue District, file your form with the Internal Revenue Service Center, Philadelphia, PA 19255 or call (215) 961-3980.

Specific Instructions

The instructions that follow are for those items that are not self-explanatory. Enter N/A (nonapplicable) on the lines that do not apply.

Line 1.—Enter the legal name of the entity applying for the EIN.

Individuals.—Enter the first name, middle initial, and last name.

Trusts.—Enter the name of the trust.

Estate of a decedent.—Enter the name of the estate.

Partnerships.—Enter the legal name of the partnership as it appears in the partnership agreement.

Corporations.—Enter the corporate name as set forth in the corporation charter or other legal document creating it.

Plan administrators.—Enter the name of the plan administrator. A plan administrator who already has an EIN should use that number.

Line 2.—Enter the trade name of the business if different from the legal name.

Note: *Use the full legal name entered on line 1 on all tax returns to be filed for the entity. However, if a trade name is entered on line 2, use only the name on line 1 or the name on line 2 consistently when filing tax returns.*

Line 3.—Trusts enter the name of the trustee. Estates enter the name of the executor, administrator, or other fiduciary. If the entity applying has a designated person to receive tax information, enter that person's name as the "care of" person. Print or type the first name, middle initial, and last name.

Lines 5a and 5b.—If the physical location of the business is different from the mailing address (lines 4a and 4b), enter the address of the physical location on lines 5a and 5b.

Line 7.—Enter the first name, middle initial, and last name of a principal officer if the business is a corporation; of a general partner if a partnership; and of a grantor if a trust.

Line 8a.—Check the box that best describes the type of entity that is applying for the EIN. If not specifically mentioned, check the "other" box and enter the type of entity. Do not enter N/A.

Individual.—Check this box if the individual files Schedule C or F (Form 1040) and has a Keogh plan or is required to file excise, employment, or alcohol, tobacco, or firearms returns. If this box is checked, enter the individual's SSN (social security number) in the space provided.

Plan administrator.—The term plan administrator means the person or group of persons specified as the administrator by the instrument under which the plan is operated. If the plan administrator is an individual, enter the plan administrator's SSN in the space provided.

New withholding agent.—If you are a new withholding agent required to file Form 1042, check the "other" box and enter in the space provided "new withholding agent."

REMICs.—Check this box if the entity is a real estate mortgage investment conduit (REMIC). A REMIC is any entity

1. To which an election to be treated as a REMIC applies for the tax year and all prior tax years,

2. In which all of the interests are regular interests or residual interests,

3. Which has one class of residual interests (and all distributions, if any, with respect to such interests are pro rata),

4. In which as of the close of the 3rd month beginning after the startup date and at all times thereafter, substantially all of its assets consist of qualified mortgages and permitted investments,

5. Which has a tax year that is a calendar year, and

6. With respect to which there are reasonable arrangements designed to ensure that: (a) residual interests are not held by disqualified organizations (as defined in section 860E(e)(5)), and (b) information necessary for the application of section 860E(e) will be made available.

For more information about REMICs see the Instructions for **Form 1066,** U. S. Real Estate Mortgage Investment Conduit Income Tax Return.

Personal service corporations.—Check this box if the entity is a personal service corporation. An entity is a personal service corporation for a tax year only if

1. The entity is a C corporation for the tax year.

2. The principal activity of the entity during the testing period (as defined in Temporary Regulations section 1.441-4T(f)) for the tax year is the performance of personal service.

3. During the testing period for the tax year, such services are substantially performed by employee-owners.

4. The employee-owners own 10 percent of the fair market value of the outstanding stock in the entity on the last day of the testing period for the tax year.

For more information about personal service corporations, see the instructions to **Form 1120,** U.S. Corporation Income Tax Return, and Temporary Regulations section 1.441-4T.

Other corporations.—This box is for any corporation other than a personal service corporation. If you check this box, enter the type of corporation (such as insurance company) in the space provided.

Other nonprofit organizations.—Check this box if the nonprofit organization is other than a church or church-controlled organization and specify the type of nonprofit organization (for example, an educational organization.)

Group exemption number (GEN).—If the applicant is a nonprofit organization that is a subordinate organization to be included in a group exemption letter under Revenue Procedure 80-27, 1980-1 C.B. 677, enter the GEN in the space provided. If you do not know the GEN, contact the parent organization for it. GEN is a four-digit number. Do not confuse it with the nine-digit EIN.

Line 9.—Check only one box. Do not enter N/A.

Started new business.—Check this box if you are starting a new business that requires an EIN. If you check this box, enter the type of business being started. **DO NOT** apply if you already have an EIN and are only adding another place of business.

Changed type of organization.—Check this box if the business is changing its type of organization, for example, if the business was a sole proprietorship and has been incorporated or has become a partnership. If you check this box, specify in the space provided the type of change made, for example, "from sole proprietorship to partnership."

Purchased going business.—Check this box if you acquired a business through purchase. Do not use the former owner's EIN. If you already have an EIN, use that number.

Hired employees.—Check this box if the existing business is requesting an EIN because it has hired or is hiring employees and is therefore required to file employment tax return for which an EIN is required. **DO NOT** apply if you already have an EIN and are only hiring employees.

Created a trust.—Check this box if you created a trust, and enter the type of trust created.

Created a pension plan.—Check this box if you have created a pension plan and need this number for reporting purposes. Also, enter the type of plan created.

Banking purpose.—Check this box if you are requesting an EIN for banking purpose only and enter the banking purpose (for example, checking, loan, etc.).

Other (specify).—Check this box if you are requesting an EIN for any reason other than those for which there are checkboxes and enter the reason.

Line 10.—If you are starting a new business, enter the starting date of the business. If the business you acquired is already operating, enter the date you acquired the business. Trusts should enter the date the trust was legally created. Estates should enter the date of death of the decedent whose name appears on line 1.

Line 11.—Enter the last month of your accounting year or tax year. An accounting year or tax year is usually 12 consecutive months. It may be a calendar year or a fiscal year (including a period of 52 or 53 weeks). A calendar year is 12 consecutive months ending on December 31. A fiscal year is either 12 consecutive months ending on the last day of any month other than December or a 52-53 week year. For more information

on accounting periods, see **Pub. 538,** Accounting Periods and Methods.

Individuals.—Your tax year generally will be a calendar year.

Partnerships.—Partnerships generally should conform to the tax year of either (1) its majority partners; (2) its principal partners; (3) the tax year that results in the least aggregate deferral of income (see Temporary Regulations section 1.706-1T); or (4) some other tax year, if (a) a business purpose is established for the fiscal year, or (b) the fiscal year is a "grandfather" year, or (c) an election is made under section 444 to have a fiscal year. (See the Instructions for **Form 1065,** U.S. Partnership Return of Income, for more information.)

REMICs.—Remics must have a calendar year as their tax year.

Personal service corporations.—A personal service corporation generally must adopt a calendar year unless:

1. It can establish to the satisfaction of the Commissioner that there is a business purpose for having a different tax year, or

2. It elects under section 444 to have a tax year other than a calendar year.

Line 12.—If the business has or will have employees, enter on this line the date on which the business began or will begin to pay wages to the employees. If the business does not have any plans to have employees, enter N/A on this line.

New withholding agent.—Enter the date you began or will begin to pay income to a nonresident alien. This also applies to individuals who are required to file Form 1042 to report alimony paid to a nonresident alien.

Line 14.—Generally, enter the exact type of business being operated (for example, advertising agency, farm, labor union, real estate agency, steam laundry, rental of coin-operated vending machine, investment club, etc.).

Governmental.—Enter the type of organization (state, county, school district, or municipality, etc.)

Nonprofit organization (other than governmental).—Enter whether organized for religious, educational, or humane purposes, and the principal activity (for example, religious organization—hospital, charitable).

Mining and quarrying.—Specify the process and the principal product (for example, mining bituminous coal, contract drilling for oil, quarrying dimension stone, etc.).

Contract construction.—Specify whether general contracting or special trade contracting. Also, show the type of work normally performed (for example, general contractor for residential buildings, electrical subcontractor, etc.).

Trade.—Specify the type of sales and the principal line of goods sold (for example, wholesale dairy products, manufacturer's representative for mining machinery, retail hardware, etc.).

Manufacturing.—Specify the type of establishment operated (for example, sawmill, vegetable cannery, etc.).

Signature block.—The application must be signed by: (1) the individual, if the person is an individual, (2) the president, vice president, or other principal officer, if the person is a corporation, (3) a responsible and duly authorized member or officer having knowledge of its affairs, if the person is a partnership or other unincorporated organization, or (4) the fiduciary, if the person is a trust or estate.

For Your Notebook:

SAMPLE SIGNATURE PAGE

[CONSULT AN ATTORNEY BEFORE USING THIS FORM]

IN WITNESS WHEREOF, the undersigned Grantor and Trustee have executed this Trust as of the date first-above written.

WITNESSESS:

_____ (L.S.)
GRANTOR'S NAME, Grantor

_____ (L.S.)
TRUSTEE1-NAME, Trustee

State of STATENAME   )
) ss:
County of COUNTYNAME)

Before me, a Notary Public or Attorney of STATENAME, personally appeared GRANTOR'S NAME, personally known to me, or proved to me on the basis of satisfactory evidence to be such person, who acknowledged that such Grantor understood and executed the above instrument for the purposes of establishing the Trust therein described.

Subscribed and sworn to before me this MONTH DAY, YEAR.

_____
Notary

State of STATENAME   )
) ss:
County of COUNTYNAME)

Before me, a Notary Public or Attorney of STATENAME, personally appeared TRUSTEE1-NAME, personally known to me, or proved to me on the basis of satisfactory evidence to be such person, who acknowledged that such Trustee understood and executed the above instrument for the purposes of accepting as Trustee the Trust therein established.

Subscribed and sworn to before me this MONTH DAY, YEAR.

_____
Notary

3 TRANSFERRING ASSETS TO YOUR TRUST

The assets transferred to your trust (the trust property, or *res*) constitute one of the five key elements of any trust. The selection of the property to transfer to your trust can be complicated, and certain types of property (for example, insurance and stock in an S corporation) require special trust provisions to deal with them. Transferring stock in a closely held business may carry the need for a trustee with relevant business experience. A large securities portfolio could call for a trustee with investment expertise. The nature and quantity of the assets transferred is also critical. If you hope to use a trust to avoid probate, all of your significant assets that could be subject to probate should be transferred to your trust.

TRANSFER ISSUES AND TERMS

Funded or Unfunded?

A trust can be either funded or unfunded. A funded trust is a trust to which you transfer assets. For example, if you want to set up a trust for the benefit of your children, you will probably transfer assets to the trust each year. An unfunded trust is a trust that has no assets at present. However, you may transfer a nominal amount of cash, perhaps $100, to such a trust in order to activate the trust and open a bank account. The reason to establish an unfunded trust is so that it will be ready to receive assets at the proper time—for example, by means of a pour-over will at the time of your death.

How you fund your trust may be determined in part by the nature of the trust. If the trust is being established to provide management of your assets, it must be funded to meet its objective. If you are using a trust to avoid probate, then the trust must be funded to accomplish that objective, since only assets transferred to the trust will avoid probate. In the latter case, as a safety-precaution, you should also have a durable power of attorney that specifically authorizes your agent to transfer assets to your trust, as well as a pour-over will (for a sample pour-over provision, see the "For Your Notebook" section following this chapter). The benefits of avoiding probate, however, are not always as significant as what many people believe, as Chapter 10 will explain.

Ancillary Probate

If you have assets in more than one state, you may want to avoid what is called ancillary probate (probate in several states). You can do this by transferring the assets in states other than where you live (in legal terms, the state where you're domiciled) to your trust. For example, if you are a resident of one state and have a real property in another state (perhaps a vacation home), this property is ideal to transfer to a trust. This action may enable your estate to avoid an ancillary probate proceeding in the second state.

Identification of Assets

For a trust to have assets, the trust property must be designated and then transferred to the trust. In a typical trust, there are two parts that address this issue. First, there is the introductory section of the trust, which corresponds to basic building block #2 in the trust document and may be similar to the following:

SAMPLE TRUST CLAUSES:

I. *TRUST ASSETS*

A. *Transfer of Property to Trust*

The Grantor assigns and transfers to the Trustee, and the Trustee, by the execution of this Trust, acknowledges receipt from the Grantor of the property described in Schedule "A." This property, together with any Addition shall be the Trust Estate. The term Trust Estate shall also include any other property which the Grantor, the legal representatives of the Grantor's estate pursuant to the provisions of the Grantor's Last Will and testament, or any other persons transfer to the Trustees, as well as the proceeds from the sale or investment of such property, and the securities or other assets in which such proceeds may be invested and reinvested.

B. *Additional Assets Contributed to Trust*

The Grantor, or any other person, may assign or transfer after the date of this Trust Agreement, to the Trustees, securities or other property, whether real or personal, tangible or intangible, reasonably acceptable to the Trustees as an Addition to the Trust Estate. All Additions shall be added to the Trust Estate and the Trustees shall hold and dispose of any Addition as part of the Trust Estate subject to the terms and provisions of this Trust Agreement.

C. *Additions to the Trust Estate*

Following the death of the Grantor, the Trustees shall collect and add to the Trust Estate: (i) Amounts payable under insurance policies on the life of the Grantor held in this Trust; (ii) Amounts payable under insurance on the life of the Grantor in which the Trustee has been designated beneficiary which are not held in this Trust; (iii) Amounts payable under the Grantor's employee benefit plans in which the Trustee has been designated as beneficiary; (iv) Property payable to the Trustee by the legal representatives of the Grantor's estate pursuant to the provisions of the Grantor's last will; and (v) Property payable by any other persons, whether pursuant to the provisions of such person's Last Will or otherwise, to the Trustee. The Trustee shall then deal with and dispose of these additions as part of the Trust Estate as provided in this Trust Agreement.

The second part of your trust that is likely to address the transfer of assets to the trust is an attached schedule. This technique is often used simply as a matter of administrative or drafting convenience. The assets to be transferred are listed in detail on the attached schedule. Be aware, however, that this attached schedule merely identifies the assets transferred to the trust. Important, and often formal, legal steps must be taken to transfer many assets, such as real estate. Many of these steps are discussed below.

Where real estate, for example, is to be transferred to the trust, you may attach a copy of the deed to the trust agreement. This is because the deed will contain a full legal description of the property.

WHAT TYPES OF ASSETS SHOULD BE TRANSFERRED TO YOUR TRUST?

Almost any type of asset can be held in trust. The assets can be tangible (equipment, buildings), intangible (stocks, bonds, patents), real (buildings, land), or personal (equipment, paintings). The only requirements are that the assets can be separated and assigned.

Interplay of Factors

Deciding what assets should be transferred to your trust, or trusts (many people need more than one), is the hard part. The process should start with an assessment of your overall financial and estate planning goals, including an evaluation of your assets and their likely appreciation, and of your current and future cash needs. A few examples will illustrate:

EXAMPLE: You're a retired widower and are concerned about managing your money and financial affairs. Your estate, consisting of a condominium and marketable securities, is worth approximately $650,000. It may be advisable to transfer all of your assets into a revocable living trust. You will continue to manage your assets while you're able. When you are no longer able, the mechanism is in place for your chosen trustees to immediately assume management responsibility. Most of your estate should avoid probate, possibly saving your heirs expenses and delays. In this scenario, all assets could be transferred to your trust.

EXAMPLE: A couple in their forties have an estate valued at approximately $1.8 million, including approximately $800,000 of investment real estate, $250,000 of equity in their home, and $750,000 in certificates of deposit, bonds, and income stocks. Since the couple's estate is in excess of the amount that can be shielded by the $600,000 unified credit for each (or $1.2 million for both, see Chapter 8), the couple wants to begin a gift program. They will give gifts to trusts for their children to reduce their combined estate to approximately the $1.2 million level, on which no federal estate tax will be due. The investment real estate is the preferred asset to use for the gift. The parents still can retain significant control over the asset and real estate is the asset most likely to appreciate. Therefore, a gift of real estate will remove the most future appreciation from their estate, while real estate is also likely to be the least liquid of their assets.

EXAMPLE: A young couple in their thirties have an estate worth approximately $150,000, which requires no special treatment. However, the husband, the sole bread-winer, has a $1 million term life insurance policy. If the husband establishes an irrevocable life insurance trust and transfers the life insurance and all incidents of ownership in the insurance to the trust, the couple effectively will have eliminated any potential estate tax. The trust will provide for the management of the substantial insurance proceeds in the event of the husband's untimely death. The insurance trust, with a spendthrift provision, offers a measure of protection from creditors for the proceeds that direct ownership of the policy by the wife cannot provide.

Revocability

The selection process is also affected by the type of trust being established. For example, if the trust is revocable (you can change the trust at any time), you don't need to be as concerned about which assets you transfer, although if the objective of your trust is to provide for you in the event of disability, it may be advisable to fund the trust with some amount of liquid assets. Remaining assets can be transferred by someone named as your agent (also called an "attorney-in-fact") under a durable power of attorney.

Whenever an irrevocable trust is involved, exercise caution, since the transfer cannot be changed once it is made. Never transfer any asset to an irrevocable trust unless, even in the worst-case financial scenario, you will not need the asset.

Cost, Tax, and Time Factors

Always investigate the costs, and possible legal restrictions, on transferring assets to a trust. Real estate transfers may cause you to incur transfer taxes, recording fees, mortgage or deed taxes, and so forth. Business and investment interests may have restrictions on transfer. For example, investment limited partnership interests may only be transferable with the consent of a general partner, which may be withheld for any reason. Stock interests may be restricted from transfer. Interests in a professional corporation (say, medical or law practice) may be prohibited from transfer by law. Don't despair, however; there may be more creative ways to address the issue. For example, it may be possible to transfer the building in which the practice is located, as well as the equipment and perhaps other assets, to a trust.

EXAMPLE: A doctor is quite concerned about the risk of expensive and unwarranted medical malpractice claims. She makes a gift of all her equipment and the building in which she conducts her practice to an irrevocable trust for the benefit of her children. She then leases the equipment back from the trust at the current fair rental rate established by an independent appraisal. If the transfer is made sufficiently in advance of any claim, it may be possible for the assets held in the trust for her children to escape untouched. Further, this plan may be advantageous from an estate planning perspective by removing assets from the Taxpayer's estate.

For certain tax-oriented charitable or other trusts, the assets transferred may have to be income-producing in order to achieve the desired tax benefits. In these instances, careful selection of assets is vital. Raw land may be inappropriate, while leased property may be ideal.

Don't discount the importance of personal preferences. You may have a specific asset that you want to go to a particular beneficiary for purely personal reasons.

Finally, it is important to consider when your trust will be activated. If the trust is provided under your will (testamentary trust), no steps to form it will occur before your death. It can be left to your executor to decide what assets to transfer to the trust. This approach provides the maximum flexibility to make decisions, and it is often advisable not to specify in your will which assets are to be transferred to which trusts, unless special circumstances warrant it. Some testamentary trusts are funded by your will specifying a dollar amount. The amount to be transferred to other testamentary trusts may be based on a percentage of the assets in your estate, or in some portion of your estate.

HOW TO TRANSFER ASSETS TO YOUR TRUST

Once you've decided which assets to transfer to your trust, you and your attorney must complete the necessary steps and documentation to properly transfer the assets. The steps to be taken depend on the ownership arrangements and the nature of each asset. The following discussion highlights some of the considerations. Since custom, practice, and law can vary from state to state, it is important to consult with an attorney in your area.

- *Real Estate*. Real estate can be transferred to your trust by properly completing a quit claim or gift deed from you to the trust. It is important to review your prior deed to ascertain exactly who the present owners are and how their names appear. If you are not the sole owner, you will have to obtain the consent of the other owners. Also, if there will be owners other than your trust, you should carefully consider how this will affect the management or use of the property.

  There are several other responsibilities when transferring real estate. When there is a transfer of title to a new person, such as your trust, the title company may require that the trust purchase a new title insurance policy. Title insurance guarantees that you own the property, which protects you from claims by other persons who may not have been properly listed in the public property records. Make sure this matter has been properly resolved with the title company in advance and the costs considered. Also be certain that the liability and fire insurance policies are properly amended to reflect the names of the new owner, your trust. Mortgage recording fees and taxes, real estate transfer taxes, and recording fees for the deed should all be considered. In some situations, the costs will be so significant that your planning will change.

CAUTION: Ask whether the transfer of real estate to your trust could trigger a property tax reassessment. If your property is presently undervalued, this could result in a substantial increase in taxes.

If there is also a mortgage on the property, you should have your lawyer review the mortgage and note that were signed. They will likely require that the mortgage be repaid unless the lender consents otherwise. This may not be a simple matter to resolve. Many mortgages are sold, and resold, in the secondary markets. It may take some legwork just to identify the party to whom you should address the question. You should also review any potential tax consequences with your accountant prior to the transfer. If the property is being used by you personally and the trust is an irrevocable trust, you will have to sign a lease with the trust in order to have the legal right to continue using the property. You'll have to pay a fair market rental, too. If the trust is a revocable living trust for your own benefit, a lease won't be necessary since for tax purposes you will continue to be treated as the owner of the property.

- *Bank Accounts.* Simply contact the bank and ask for the necessary forms. The bank will probably ask to see the trust agreement. A federal tax identification number will be needed for the trust in order to open a trust bank account (see Chapter 2 for the information necessary to complete Form SS-4 and obtain the identification number). New checks with the name of the trust will be needed. Note that checks will have to be signed by the trustee after the transfer. Also, ask the bank for details regarding any formalities they may require.

- *Securities.* If you own stocks or bonds in your own name, you will have to contact the transfer agent for the securities and obtain the necessary transfer forms, such as stock powers. Complete the forms and return them with the stock or bond certificates. The transfer agent will reissue the stock or bond certificates in the name of the trust.

CAUTION: Never send any original stock or bond certificate through regular mail. Always use certified mail, return receipt requested, so that you'll have proper records in the event the securities do not arrive. Also, be certain to make photocopies of all documents before sending them.

For some transfers, you may be asked to provide a guarantee or verification of signature. This extra bit of red tape, which requires a separate trip to the bank, can be arduous for those who are infirm and seek to establish a trust to manage their assets.

TIP: If you have a considerable number of securities, open a brokerage account and transfer the securities to the account. Once the securities are in an account in your name, it will be relatively easy for your broker to change the name of the entire account to the name of your trust. The broker will likely require the same documents mentioned above for the transfer of bank accounts.

- *Partnership Interests.* Partnership interests are transferred by using an assignment of partnership interest form. A sample is reproduced in the "For Your Notebook" section at the end of this chapter. You must carefully review the partnership agreement prior to making any transfer. The agreement may prohibit any type of transfer. You may be required to get the approval of some or all of the other partners. If the structure is a limited partnership, you will probably have to receive the permission of the general partner. In some states, certificates of limited partnership must be filed at the state or county level. The partners, or the partnership agreement, may require that you pay the legal and filing fees to complete the necessary filings.

CAUTION: Carefully ascertain whether your attempted transfer of a partnership interest could trigger mandatory buy-out provisions contained in the agreement. This is critical because some buy-out provisions require that you sell the partnership interest to the other partners. Other agreements simply prohibit any transfer.

- *Business Interests.* Many of the considerations affecting the transfer of stock apply to the transfer of partnership interests. If the structure is an S corporation, your trust must meet the strict requirements of a qualified S corporation trust (QSST) to avoid jeopardizing the tax status of the corporation (see Chapter 19). The transfer of stock will be accomplished by signing a stock power authorizing the transfer of the particular stock on the corporation's books. You will have to surrender your stock certificates, which will be canceled and retained by the corporation. The corporation will issue new stock certificates in the name of your trust. The changes will be noted in the corporation's stock transfer ledger. In most closely held corporations you will also have signed minutes of the board of directors, or a unanimous consent of all shareholders and directors, to authorize the transaction. The trustee will probably have to sign a copy of the corporation's shareholders' agreement, agreeing to be bound by the terms in the agreement.
- *Furniture, Art, Jewelry, and Other Personal Property.* Ownership of these (documents) does not appear in title documents like a deed, stock certificate, and so forth. However, this makes it even more important that care be taken and documentation be recorded with the appropriate formalities. To be safe, you should sign and have notarized a bill of sale, and, when the transfer is a gift, a gift declaration. Also change the name on the insurance policies to reflect the trust as the new owner. These records are particularly useful when you want to prove to the IRS that certain assets were transferred to the trust at a certain time. These latter steps are *in addition to* the listing of assets

on a schedule attached to your trust agreement. Illustrative forms are provided in the "For Your Notebook" section following this chapter.

CONCLUSION

Selecting the right assets and then taking the proper steps to transfer them to your trust are critical aspects in making your trust accomplish the desired goals.

For Your Notebook:

SAMPLE SCHEDULE A
PROPERTY TRANSFERRED TO TRUST

[CONSULT AN ATTORNEY CONCERNING THIS FORM]

The fact that property held by the Trust, as part of the Trust Estate, is not listed in this Exhibit shall not affect the fact that such property is in fact held by the Trust.

1. Cash in the amount of $10,593.00, in XYZ, Bank, Account No. 12345-678.
2. 100 Shares of General Motors common stock, CUSIP No. 123456-00.
3. 152 Shares of IBM common stock, CUSIP No. 123456-78.
4. $5,000 Certificate of Deposit at ABC Savings and Loan, Account Number 00-00123.
5. Water-color of "Birds in Sunset," by Budding Artist, valued at $12,250.
6. Stock in Family Business Corp., Inc.—5 shares common stock, no par.

NOTE: Remember to investigate all transfer costs and requirements. The appropriate document to properly transfer each of the above assets should be completed, notarized, and witnessed. For insurance, you must contact your insurance company for the necessary forms. Note that if Family Business Corp., Inc. (asset #6), is an S corporation, its tax status could be jeopardized if the trust is not properly characterized as one permitted to be a shareholder of an S corporation (see Chapter 19).

For Your Notebook:

SAMPLE DECLARATION OF GIFT

[CONSULT A TAX AND ESTATE PLANNING ATTORNEY BEFORE USING ANY FORM]

I, Sandy Taxpayer, hereby state and declare that:

1. I am a resident of the State of New Jersey, residing at 111 West State Street, Sometown, New Jersey.

2. I, Sandy Taxpayer, have this day executed a Bill of Sale and stock power to transfer 200 Shares of XYZ Corporation, Inc., common stock to John Taxpayer, Trustee of the Sandy Taxpayer Irrevocable Children's Trust, dated December 13, 1992, c/o John Taxpayer, 123 Main Street, Anytown, New York, valued at $9,850.00, by way of gift and without any consideration.

3. I declare under the penalties of perjury that the foregoing is true and correct and further declare that this Declaration of Gift is being executed this 27th day of December, 1992.

_____
Sandy Taxpayer, Donor

State of New Jersey   )
) ss:
County of ABC   )

On this 27th day of December, 1992, before me personally came, Ms. Sandy Taxpayer, to me known and known to me to be the 111 West State Street, Sometown, New Jersey individual described in and who executed the foregoing instrument, and she duly acknowledged to me that she understood the meaning of the instrument and that she executed the same.

_____
                                    Notary Public

NOTE: When property of any nature is to be assigned to your trust for no consideration (that is, as a gift) you should prepare and sign a declaration of gift form similar to the one reproduced above to make clear your intent to make a gift. Consult with your tax adviser concerning any requirements to file a federal or state gift tax return. The federal form is Form 709, which can be obtained from any IRS office or forms distribution center.

For Your Notebook:

SAMPLE BILL OF SALE

[CONSULT A TAX AND ESTATE PLANNING ATTORNEY BEFORE USING ANY FORM]

KNOW ALL MEN BY THESE PRESENTS, that MS. SANDY TAXPAYER, an individual who resides at 111 West State Street, City of Sometown, County of ABC, State of New Jersey (the "Donor") for and in consideration of the sum of $1.00 and as a gift to John Taxpayer, Trustee of the Sandy Taxpayer Irrevocable Children's Trust, dated December 13, 1992, c/o John Taxpayer, 123 Main Street, Anytown, New York (the "Donee"), has granted, transferred and conveyed and by these presents does grant, transfer, and convey unto the said Donee, and said Donee's successors and assigns, property as hereinafter described:

ALL THE RIGHT TITLE AND INTEREST in the following asset ("Asset"):

Gold men's wrist watch

including all Donor's right, title, and interests in the Asset.

Donor hereby represents and warrants that she has good and marketable title to the Asset name hereinabove, subject to no liens, mortgages, security interests, encumbrances, or charges of any nature.

This Bill of Sale has been executed to complete the gift contemplated herein. Nothing herein contained shall be deemed or construed to confer upon any person or entity other than Donee any rights or remedies by reason of this instrument.

TO HAVE AND TO HOLD the same unto the said Donee and the Donee's successors and assigns forever; and the Donor covenants and agrees to and with the said Donee to warrant and defend the said described Asset against all and every person or persons whomsoever.

IN WITNESS WHEREOF, the Donor has set her hand and seal to be hereto affixed this 27th day of December, 1992.

Sworn, Signed, Sealed, and Delivered
Sandy Taxpayer

_____

in the Presence of:

_____
Witness

NOTE: When personal property (as opposed to real estate) is to be assigned to your trust, you should prepare and sign a bill of sale form similar to the one reproduced above. Legal publishers make standard forms available in office supply stores in most states. If the transfer is a gift, consider completing a declaration of gift form as well.

For Your Notebook:

SAMPLE ASSIGNMENT
OF PARTNERSHIP INTEREST

[CONSULT A TAX AND ESTATE PLANNING ATTORNEY BEFORE USING ANY FORM]

I, Sandy Taxpayer, who resides at 111 West State Street, Sometown, New Jersey, hereby assign by gift to John Taxpayer, Trustee of the Sandy Taxpayer Irrevocable Children's Trust, dated December 13, 1992, c/o John Taxpayer, 123 Main Street, Anytown, New York (the "Donee" or "Assignee"), a percentage interest in ABC Property Associates. The percentage interest hereby assigned is Twenty Two percent (22%) of the total interests in the partnership. The value of this partnership interest is $2,785.00.

ASSIGNOR/DONOR:

_____ Date: December 21, 1992
Sandy Taxpayer

STATE OF NEW JERSEY   )
) ss:
COUNTY OF ABC   )

On this 21st of December, 1992, before me personally came, Sandy Taxpayer, to me known and known to me to be the individual described in and who executed the foregoing instrument, and she duly acknowledged to me that she understood the meaning of the instrument and that she executed the same.

_____
Notary Public

[ATTACH APPRAISAL OF PARTNERSHIP INTEREST MADE NEAR DATE OF GIFT]

NOTE: When an interest in a partnership is to be assigned to your trust, you should prepare and sign an assignment of partnership interest form similar to the one reproduced above. If the transfer is a gift, consider completing a declaration of gift form as well. Always review with your attorney any additional requirements of state law or of the partnership agreement.

For Your Notebook:

SAMPLE SCHEDULE OF
OWNERSHIP OF THE ASSET

[CONSULT AN ATTORNEY CONCERNING THIS FORM]

The following parties hereby own the following ownership interests in the Asset described in the Bill of Sale to which this Schedule is attached:

1. Sandy Taxpayer	78%
2. Sandy Taxpayer Irrevocable Children's Trust, dated December 13, 1992	22%
Total	100%

STATE OF NEW JERSEY)
) ss:
COUNTY OF ABC)

On this 21st day of December, 1992, before me personally came, Ms. Sandy Taxpayer, to me known and known to me to be the individual described in and who executed this schedule of partnership interests, and she duly acknowledged to me that she understood the meaning of the instrument and that she executed the same.

_____
Notary Public

NOTE: When the asset involved is transferred over a period of more than one year, a schedule detailing the changing percentage of ownership should be attached. For example, if a partial interest in a family partnership were transferred, this schedule could be attached to the partnership agreement for the family partnership, and to the gift declaration forms. Each year in which new transfers are made, a new schedule of ownership should be prepared until the intended percentages of ownership are achieved. A major reason for partial transfers over several years is to make gifts within the available $10,000 per person annual exclusions from the gift tax (Chapters 13 and 22).

For Your Notebook:

SAMPLE CONSENT OF SHAREHOLDERS

[CONSULT AN ATTORNEY CONCERNING THIS FORM]

XYZ MANUFACTURING CORP. ACTION TAKEN BY UNANIMOUS WRITTEN CONSENT OF ALL SHAREHOLDERS AND DIRECTORS

The undersigned, being all of the directors and shareholders of the Corporation, hereby take the following action:

RESOLVED, The Corporation acknowledges receiving notice from a shareholder, Jane Doe, in the form of a Stock Power, requesting that certain Shares owned by such Shareholder, be transferred to John Doe.

RESOLVED, The officers of the Corporation are hereby directed to cancel the following stock certificates received from the above Shareholder:

Shareholder Name	Class of Stock	Number of Shares	Cert. No.
Jane Doe	Common—A	295	AC-1
Jane Doe	Preferred—A	23,600	AP-1
Jane Doe	Preferred—B	5,900	BP-1

and to issue the following stock certificates to the Shareholders listed for the shares indicated:

Shareholder Name	Class of Stock	Number of Shares	Cert. No.
Baby Doe	Common—A	45	AC-3
Baby Doe	Preferred—A	3,600	AP-3
Baby Doe	Preferred—B	900	BP-3
Jane Doe	Common—A	250	AC-4
Jane Doe	Preferred—A	20,000	AP-4
Jane Doe	Preferred—B	5,000	BP-4

RESOLVED, The officers of the Corporation are hereby authorized to take any actions necessary to effecting the above Resolutions.

Dated: November 2, 1992

_____
John Doe, Director and Shareholder

_____
Jane Doe, Director and Shareholder

For Your Notebook:

SAMPLE STOCK POWER

[CONSULT AN ATTORNEY CONCERNING THIS FORM]

FOR VALUE RECEIVED, I, Jane Doe (the "Donor"), hereby sell, assign, and transfer unto Baby Doe, who resides at 10 Main Road, Anytown, New York (the "Donee"), the certain Shares of stock in XYZ Manufacturing Corp. as set forth herein:

The following Shares, standing in my name on the books of said Corporation represented by the following Share Certificates:

a) 295 shares of Common Class A - Share Certificate No. AC-1.

b) 23,600 Shares Preferred Class A - Share Certificate No. AP-1.

c) 5,900 Shares Preferred Class B - Share Certificate No. BP-1.

I do hereby tender the Share Certificates set forth above to the Corporation herewith for cancellation, requesting that new certificates be issued to myself, the Donor, and to the Donee, to effect the transfer of the number of Shares set forth in the following paragraph to the Donee.

The following portions of said Shares, standing in my name on the books of said Corporation represented by the following Share Certificates, shall be transferred to the Donee set forth below:

a) 45 shares of Common Class B.

b) 3,600 Shares Preferred Class A.

c) 900 Shares Preferred Class B.

I do hereby irrevocably constitute and appoint Martin M. Shenkman, Esq., as attorney to transfer the said stock on the books and records of the Corporation with full power of substitution in same, to effect the transfers set forth herein.

Dated: November 2, 1992

SHAREHOLDER/TRANSFEROR

_____   Witness: _____

Jane Doe

For Your Notebook:

SAMPLE ASSIGNMENT OF CONTRACTS

[CONSULT AN ATTORNEY CONCERNING THIS FORM]

THIS AGREEMENT made as of the 3rd day of December, 1992, between JANE DOE, trustee of the BABY DOE CHILDREN'S TRUST, dated December 1st, 1992, who resides at 123 Main Street, Anytown, New Jersey ("Assignee"); and JOHN DOE, an individual who resides at 323 High Street, Sometown, New Jersey ("Assignor").

WHEREAS, the Assignor wishes to assign all his right title and interest in those certain contracts more particularly set forth and described in Schedule "A" hereto (hereinafter called the "Contracts"); and Assignee wishes to accept the assignment of the Contracts.

NOW, THEREFORE, THIS AGREEMENT WITNESSETH that the parties hereto covenant and agree as follows:

1. In consideration of One Dollar ($1.00) by way of gift, Assignor hereby assigns, transfers, and sets over unto Assignee the said Contracts and all rights, titles, and interests of Assignor therein and thereto, together with all rights, benefits, privileges, and advantages of Assignor to be derived therefrom, subject to the rights of certain third parties to approve, or consent to such assignments, as provided in the Contracts.

2. The Assignor covenants and agrees with the Assignee that Assignor shall, at the request of the Assignee, do and perform all such acts and things, and execute and deliver all such consents, documents and other writings as may be required to give full force and effect to the assignment herein contemplated.

3. Assignee accepts the within assignment to it of the said Contracts and agrees with Assignor to assume, carry out, observe, perform, and fulfill said Contracts in accordance with their terms.

4. This Agreement shall, subject to the terms and conditions of the individual Contracts, inure to the benefit of and be binding upon the parties hereto and their successors and assigns.

IN WITNESS THEREOF, the parties hereto have executed and delivered this Agreement as of the day and year first above written.

WITNESSES:

ASSIGNEE:
BABY DOE CHILDREN'S TRUST

_____

By: _____
Jane Doe, Trustee

ASSIGNOR
JOHN DOE

_____

_____

NOTE: Be certain that any contract rights that are assigned are assignable by their terms. Review the documents carefully and consult a lawyer.

For Your Notebook:

SAMPLE POUR-OVER WILL PROVISION

[CONSULT AN ATTORNEY CONCERNING THIS FORM AND YOUR ENTIRE WILL]

RESIDUARY

All the rest, residue, and remainder of my property and estate, both real and personal, of whatsoever kind and wheresoever situated, of which I shall die seized or possessed, or of which I shall be entitled to dispose at the time of my death (my "residuary estate"), I give, devise, and bequeath to the Trustee in office at the time of my death under a certain Trust Agreement entitled JANE DOE REVOCABLE INTER VIVOS TRUST made the 12th day of August, 1992, between me, as Grantor, and myself as Trustee, to be held, administered, and disposed of by the Trustee in accordance with the provisions of said Agreement.

NOTE: When you have a revocable trust designed to hold all of your assets (either currently or after your death), you still should properly sign a will that contains a "pour-over" provision. This pours over any assets passing under your will into your revocable trust. The trust should be in place before the will is signed. Be sure any requirements of your state's laws are complied with. In some situations where secrecy is a significant concern you may prefer not to have a pour-over provision since this could increase the risk of information concerning the trust becoming public knowledge. The safest approach is to include all the provisions directing how your assets should be distributed in your will, as well as in your living trust. The provisions in the will only would apply if your trust was terminated or invalid.

---

4 GRANTOR'S RIGHTS AND POWERS

Although many people tend to focus on who the beneficiaries are and how money will be distributed, your powers and rights as grantor are clearly some of the most important to consider when setting up your trust.

This book covers dozens of different types of trusts. The powers you should have over your trust will vary depending on your goals and the type of trust involved. Obviously, your power to revoke or modify your trust only applies to trusts set up in your lifetime (in tax jargon, *inter vivos* trusts). You cannot reserve any rights over trusts established under your will (testamentary trusts), although the loophole here is that, as long as you have sufficient awareness and ability (in legal jargon, "capacity"), you can always change your will. Thus, even testamentary trusts, except those included within an irrevocable trust agreement, can be changed prior to your death.

YOUR RIGHT TO REVOKE

Your right to modify or revoke your trust determines whether your trust is revocable or irrevocable. Revocability of the trust has profound tax and legal implications. Irrevocable trusts are mainly used to avoid estate taxes and to keep the trust assets out of the reach of creditors or Medicaid and health care providers. Revocable trusts are mainly used to provide protection in the event of disability, or to avoid probate.

Go First for Revocability

When first considering the type of trust you should have, begin with the assumption that a revocable trust is best. The flexibility of being able to change any provision of your trust, or to terminate it entirely, is of great importance. Tax laws change, financial situations change, and personal goals and needs change. If your trust is irrevocable, it can't be adapted to take advantage of the new circumstances. Only choose an irrevocable trust when, after considering all of the options, it is essential to do so.

If you want your trust to be revocable, make sure to have a specific provision stating that it is. Under the laws of many states, if your trust doesn't specify that it is revocable, it could be treated as irrevocable. The sample provision below includes a right of the grantor to amend or revoke the trust. A provision included in the miscellaneous portion of the trust will define the specific procedures required to give notice (see Chapter 7).

The following are illustrations of clauses that can be used to make it explicit that your trust is either irrevocable or revocable. Obviously, you would use one or the other of these clauses, but not both.

SAMPLE TRUST CLAUSES:

Irrevocable Trust

The Grantor has been advised with respect to the difference between revocable and irrevocable trusts and hereby declares that any trust formed under this Trust Agreement, and the Trust Estate created hereby, are to be irrevocable. The Grantor has no power to alter, amend, revoke, or terminate any Trust provision or interest, whether under this Trust Agreement, or any rule of law. Grantor shall not have any reversionary interest in this Trust or the Trust Estate.

Revocable Trust

The Grantor has been advised with respect to the difference between revocable and irrevocable trusts and hereby declares that any trust formed under this Trust Agreement, and the Trust Estate created hereby, is to be revocable, so that Grantor, during Grantor's life, may change, amend, or modify, in any manner and to any extent, the provisions of this Trust Agreement. The Grantor has retained every right and power to alter, amend, revoke, or terminate any Trust provision or interest, whether under this Trust Agreement, or any rule of law. Grantor may revoke this Trust, or amend any provision of this Trust, by giving Notice to the Trustee. Such revocation or amendment shall be effective Five (5) business days after such Notice is properly dispatched to the Trustee.

When determining the revocability of your trust, remember that on your death the trust always becomes irrevocable. Further, if you are disabled, you may no longer have the legal capacity to revoke your trust, which will make it irrevocable at that point. (It is important to have a provision in your trust defining when you should be considered disabled.) Finally, every trust you establish may have several trusts incorporated in its trust agreement. For example, if you establish a revocable living trust to manage your affairs in the event of disability, and to avoid probate, that trust may include a credit shelter trust, a Q-TIP trust, and so forth. Therefore, just because the main trust is revocable, this doesn't mean that it cannot include trusts that are more commonly considered irrevocable.

Caution Is Required in Choosing an Irrevocable Trust

Before agreeing to make your trust irrevocable, consider the following:

- Are you confident in the ability of the trustees and the successor trustees named in the trust agreement to carry out their duties in a professional manner?

- Have the needs of the beneficiaries adequately been provided for? If you have a trust that is only permitted to pay income, and not principal, to the current beneficiary, what will happen if that beneficiary suffers an unforeseen calamity, such as disability? When the trust is irrevocable, and adequate safeguards and discretion have not been built in, tremendous hardship can result.
- Can you and those under your care afford to live comfortably and handle any emergencies that may arise for the remainder of your lives if the trustees only distribute the least amount of money that the trust agreement permits (which may be nothing)?
- Will marriage, divorce, or other major family events require the trust to be changed in order for basic business matters to be conducted, or basic living needs to be provided for?

EXAMPLE: An obstetrician, concerned about malpractice risks, transfers every asset he owns except his practice to an irrevocable trust for his wife, who is a homemaker and doesn't face any particular risk of creditors or other claimants. He even transfers all of the equipment and the office building used by his practice to the trust. He then enters into a lease agreement to rent the use of the equipment from the trust. The trustee is an independent trust company. The trust, in addition to being irrevocable, does not provide any right to the trustee to distribute any income or principal to the obstetrician. Trust distributions can only be made to the wife, and after the wife's death to the children (and only for expenses that are not the obligation of the obstetrician-husband under local law).

The wife is pregnant with their third child when she and her obstetrician husband divorce. He has virtually no assets as a result of the trust arrangement. Unless the trust is broken, he may not be able to operate his practice or afford many basic expenses. To terminate the trust will require the consent of an independent trust company (which may view the premature termination as violating its fiduciary obligations to the minor children, not to mention its awareness that termination will result in the loss of all trustee fees), the wife (who, unless forced by the courts, is unlikely to be interested in providing assets to her ex-husband), and the children. How can minor children consent to termination of the trust? A court proceeding may be required in which the court appoints a guardian to act on behalf of the interests of the children. What about the interests of the unborn child? How can they be protected? Even if termination of this trust is possible, it will be an expensive and time-consuming task.

What can you do if you've created an irrevocable trust and circumstances change so dramatically that you really have to change the trust? It may be possible. The rule is that every person having any interest in the trust—grantor, trustees, current beneficiaries, remainder beneficiaries, and perhaps even certain contingent beneficiaries—must agree. This is not a simple matter to achieve, and it may require an expensive court proceeding. Terminating an irrevocable trust prior to the time the trust agreement permits is discussed in Chapter 22. Never rely on this approach. If you're not sure at the outset that the trust should be irrevocable, don't make it irrevocable.

HOW GRANTOR RIGHTS AFFECT TAXES

When a trust is revocable, or when your powers and rights are sufficient, the assets in the trust will be included in your estate for tax purposes. Further, when the powers you retain over your trust are sufficient, the income earned by the trust will be taxed on your personal tax return and not on a separate tax return filed by the trust. Then you have what is called a grantor trust.

NOTE: Don't let the tax results be the sole factor in determining the type of trust you set up. The "kiddie tax" (see Chapter 13) and the limited amount of trust income that can be taxed at lower tax rates (see Chapter 20) make the tax advantages of many trust arrangements less important than they used to be. Unless taxes are the primary motivation for setting up the trust, make sure that your personal, financial, and other goals are placed first.

What Powers Can Cause a Trust to Be Characterized as a Grantor Trust?

The extent of the rights you retain to control your trust can cause your trust to be characterized as a grantor trust, with the income taxable to you, instead of the trust. The key point in this discussion is that if you have any right to obtain the assets of the trust for less than their fair value, the trust will be treated as a grantor trust taxable to you.

- If you retain the right to remove and replace the trustee, you will probably be treated as if you retained the powers that the trustee had and be taxable on the trust.

- If you retain the right to revoke, terminate, alter, or amend the trust, you may be taxable on the income from the trust.

- If you have the power to appoint income to yourself or to your spouse, whether presently or in the future, the trust income could be taxable to you.

- If you can use trust income to discharge your legal obligations, such as paying for the education of your child, the trust income will be taxable to you.

EXAMPLE: You set up a trust for the benefit of your child. Your spouse is the sole trustee. All of the income from the trust is used to pay for your child's education in a private school and related expenses. The laws of your state make a parent responsible to pay for such expenses. The income from the trust used to meet these expenses should be taxable to you.

- These rules can apply to a portion of a trust. It isn't an all-or-nothing situation. If you retain the right to appoint the income, but not the principal, of the trust to anyone including yourself, the income will be taxable to you, but the principal may not be considered to be owned by you. Similarly, if you have the right to appoint one asset, such as a house or certain bonds in a trust, but not the other assets, only the asset that you can appoint will be considered yours.

- Any rights that your spouse has will be attributed to you for purposes of this power-to-appoint test.

- Even if you need the permission of another person to get benefit from the trust property, you will continue to be taxed on the trust assets, except when the person granting permission is an adverse party. Under this exception, the other person whose permission you need must have interests in the trust that are "adverse" to your interests. Someone who shares trust powers with you will only be considered to have adverse interests when that person has a substantial beneficial interest that would be adversely affected by your power to revoke the trust.

EXAMPLE: Jones sets up a trust for the benefit of Jones and Wright. The unanimous consent of the two trustees is required to make any distribution of income from the trust. If Jones needs the approval of Wright, the trust should not be characterized as a grantor trust because Wright is considered to have "adverse" interests to Jones. This is because for every dollar Wright authorizes for distribution to Jones, there is a dollar less in the trust that could be paid to him.

- An unrestricted right to remove existing trustees in your sole discretion will be interpreted as giving you complete control over the trust since you can dismiss any trustee who doesn't perform exactly as you wish. For tax purposes, your right to remove trustees without restriction will be treated as if you have retained the rights yourself.

- A trustee's right to fees and commissions alone is not sufficient to classify the trustee as an adverse party.

- When the trust principal may come back to you (in legal jargon, you have a "reversionary interest"), and when the terms of the trust agreement (or applicable law) provide that capital gains on the sale of trust assets must be allocated to the principal of the trust (rather than being allocated to the income of the trust and paid to the current beneficiaries receiving trust income), then you will be taxable on these capital gains (see Chapters 20 and 21). Any time you have a reversionary interest in the income or principal of a trust, with more than 5 percent of the total value of the trust (determined when the assets are first transferred to the trust) due back to you, you will be treated as the owner of the trust.

When your trust is treated as a grantor trust taxable to you, and the trust makes charitable contributions, you will claim the contributions as itemized deductions on your personal income tax return. The deductions will be subject to the same limitations as any other charitable contributions reported by an individual taxpayer.

Personal Taxation Can Be an Advantage

There are some very important advantages to the use of revocable trusts that remain taxable to you. For example, if you transfer your interests in your home to a revocable trust, when the home is sold, the special tax rules of rolling over a gain on the sale of a personal residence, and the ability to exclude up to $125,000 of gain for taxpayers age 55 and older, should continue to be available. If your home were transferred to any other type of trust, these benefits could be lost (because you would no longer be the owner of the house). This is important for taxpayers wishing to use a revocable living trust as a tool to manage assets, avoid probate, and so forth. Similarly, where you set up a revocable living trust you may prefer to report all of the income from a living trust on your personal tax return because of the simplification in the tax-reporting requirements.

Powers You Can Retain Without Having the Trust Characterized as a Grantor Trust

There are certain powers that you, as grantor, can retain over the trust, without having the trust's income taxable to you. For example, you can have the power to distribute the principal of the trust to any beneficiary in accordance with a reasonably definite standard. You can have the right to withhold income temporarily, in such event as when a beneficiary is disabled or a minor. If these are the only powers you have over the trust, the trust can be treated as a separate taxable entity.

SHOULD YOU SERVE AS A TRUSTEE OR CO-TRUSTEE?

When your trust is revocable, there is no particular disadvantage from a tax perspective in your serving as a co-trustee. A revocable trust probably will have no tax advantages in any event, and your serving as trustee gives you complete control over trust affairs and trust assets. When you are disabled, you will not be able to serve as a trustee and your successor trustees will take over management. If one goal of setting up your trust is to provide for current management assistance, you may want to have another person serve as sole trustee, or at least as co-trustee, to provide this assistance.

When your trust is irrevocable, and particularly when a goal of establishing your trust is to move assets beyond the reach of creditors or malpractice claimants, as indicated above, you generally should not serve as trustee or even as co-trustee. When it is inappropriate for tax purposes for you to serve as trustee, your spouse also should not serve as trustee. This is because your spouse is not considered an adverse party. There are exceptions, however, such as with certain trusts for minor children described in Chapter 13. It also may be possible for you or your spouse to serve as a co-trustee when the powers and rights are carefully restricted. For example, your rights to appoint trust income or principal may be limited to appointing income or principal to persons other than yourself, or they may be limited to a specified ascertainable standard, as discussed in the tax discussion above.

When legal rather than tax considerations are paramount, the conclusions can differ. Depending on the laws of your state and the goals of your trust, it may be possible to have your spouse serve as trustee of your trust and still achieve certain of your goals. Be sure to review the rules with your attorney before making any final decision since the risks can be substantial.

CONCLUSION

Always be sure that the trust you intend to establish meets your personal and other needs and goals before addressing tax issues. When your trust is revocable, you have more freedom to retain whatever rights you want without affecting the tax results. When tax consequences are important, you will generally be best served by severely limiting any rights you retain over your trust. When protection of assets is important, you will face rapidly changing laws and complex regulations that govern what rights you can retain. These laws should be reviewed with your attorney before completing your trust.

5 BENEFICIARIES' DESIGNATIONS AND RIGHTS

Although beneficiaries are generally passive and the trustees make most of the decisions, there are some powers beneficiaries can be afforded. For example, beneficiaries may be given the right to require that certain amounts of principal be distributed each year. This and other rights that can be given to beneficiaries, and the tax implications of these rights, are discussed below.

ISSUES IN NAMING BENEFICIARIES

It is often obvious who the beneficiaries of your trust should be. If you're setting up a revocable trust to provide for the management of your own assets if you become disabled, you will be the beneficiary. However, you will also name beneficiaries to receive the trust assets after your death. These can be your family, loved ones, friends, a favorite charity, or anyone else you select. If you're setting up a trust for your spouse, or other partner, as described in Chapters 11 and 12, that person will be the primary beneficiary. If you're setting up any of the trusts for children described in Chapter 13, your children or grandchildren will be the beneficiaries. If you're setting up a charitable trust, as described in Chapter 14, qualifying charities will be among your beneficiaries. Still, unusual situations can arise.

In naming and defining the beneficiaries of your trust, consider the following:

- Suppose you name your children as beneficiaries of a trust, but, years later, something totally unexpected happens and you have another child. Is that child also a beneficiary? It's possible if you're careful about the language used in the trust. You can specify "My children, Dick, Jane, and Tom, and any later-born children."

- Suppose you adopt a child after setting up a trust for your natural children. Is the adopted child going to benefit? Specify, "My children, Dick, Jane, and Tom, and any later-born or adopted children."

- Suppose you name a charity, ABC charity, as a beneficiary, but the charity ceases to operate. Specify, "The sum of $10,000 to the ABC charity located at 123 Main Street, City Name, State Name, for its general purposes, or to its successor. In the event that charity no longer exists, to the DEF charity located at 456 State Street, City Name, State Name, for its general purposes, or to its successor. In the event that charity no longer exists to a charitable organization that has a similar purpose named in the discretion of my trustee." A legal doctrine called "cy press" can act to preserve an intended charitable bequest. But it is always preferable to name alternatives.

- Suppose you leave $5,000 to your aunt, Kate. If Aunt Kate dies and no other beneficiary has been named, this $5,000 will probably be distributed as part of your residuary estate if included under your will, or else through a comparable provision under your trust (if one is provided). Perhaps you would prefer that Aunt Kate's husband or surviving children receive the money. Specify, "$5,000 to my aunt, Kate Smith, who resides at 555 Main Avenue, City Name, State Name. If she shall not survive Grantor's death, to her surviving spouse. If she has no surviving spouse, then to her living issue, *per stirpes* (for a definition, see Section XXVI in the living trust that appears in the "For Your Notebook" section of Chapter 10). If there are no living issue, then this legacy shall lapse."

TAX CONSIDERATIONS AFFECT RIGHTS YOUR BENEFICIARIES SHOULD HAVE TO WITHDRAWALS

Many trusts are set up for tax benefits. For example, the credit shelter trust (also called a bypass trust) discussed in Chapter 11 is designed to keep a portion of your estate out of the taxable estate of your surviving spouse. The objective is to use up as much of your $600,000 unified credit and give your surviving spouse as much interest in the trust as a beneficiary as possible without having the income from the trust included in your surviving spouse's estate. How much access can you give your surviving spouse to the trust monies without having the IRS consider the access sufficient to tax the proceeds in his or her estate?

When Your Spouse Is Both a Beneficiary and a Trustee

If your surviving spouse is to be the trustee, several of the principles discussed in Chapter 4 apply. For example, the right to be trustee should not apply to making decisions concerning the distribution of income or property to herself or himself. These same considerations apply when any trustee is also a beneficiary of your trust.

The following provision is illustrative of the restrictions that can be included in your trust to prevent tax and legal problems when a trustee is also a beneficiary of the trust.

SAMPLE TRUST CLAUSE:

Limitations on Trustee's Discretionary Authority

Notwithstanding anything in this Trust to the contrary, no single Trustee shall:

a. Have the authority to appoint income or principal of any trust formed under this Trust Agreement to himself or herself, his or her creditors, his or her estate, creditors of his or her estate; or to or for the benefit of any child to whom he or she owes a legal obligation of support and for which such appointment of income or principal would constitute a discharge of such legal obligation of support.

b. Participate in any decisions regarding the discretionary distribution of income or principal to himself or herself, or to or for his or her benefit.

c. In the event any Trustee is in a position where such a decision would have to be made, such Trustee shall not participate in such a decision and instead any co-Trustee shall make such decision. Further, if there is no co-Trustee, then the next named successor Trustee under this Trust Agreement who is willing and able to participate shall so participate in such decision.

As an additional precaution, the right to make distributions to your spouse can be limited to an ascertainable standard, such as to maintain his or her health, education, and welfare in accordance with the accustomed standard of living. This right can be given to a beneficiary also serving as a co-trustee without tax problems and should ensure that the beneficiary's standard of living is maintained.

The Five-and-Five Power

What if a person you've named as beneficiary needs additional money and the trustee decides not to provide it? To prevent that scenario, you can give the beneficiary the right to demand that some amount of principal be distributed each year. When tax considerations are not a concern, you can set any limit you feel will meet the beneficiary's needs without excessively depleting the trust. But when tax considerations are important, you will want to sufficiently limit the amount that can be distributed to avoid adverse tax consequences. One useful approach is to give a beneficiary what is called a "five-and-five power." This lets the beneficiary, even one who is a trustee, take the greater of $5,000 or 5 percent of the trust assets in any year. This power gives flexibility and will not alone cause all of the assets of the trust to be included in the beneficiary's taxable estate.

The following is illustrative of the type of right that a beneficiary, such as your surviving spouse, who is also serving as a trustee, can have without pulling the entire value of the trust into his or her estate.

SAMPLE TRUST CLAUSE:

Limited Annual $5,000/5 Percent Right of Withdrawal

In addition to the aforementioned payments of net income, the Grantor's spouse shall have the absolute right during such spouse's lifetime, at any time upon written request to the Trustee, to receive payment out of the principal of this Trust, in such amount or amounts as he or she shall desire. However, such amounts shall not exceed, in aggregate, in any one tax year of the Trust for federal income tax purposes, the greater of the sum of Five Thousand Dollars ($5,000.00) or Five percent (5%) of the value of the principal of the Trust Estate as determined on the last day of such tax year. The Trustee shall endeavor to make the payment of the amount requested by Grantor's spouse within Thirty (30) days after the receipt of such written request by the Trustee. This provision shall be noncumulative, so that if he or she shall not exercise the maximum right to invade principal under this Section prior to the close of the tax year of the Trust, all of such unexercised right to receive payment with respect to the tax year shall expire.

A beneficiary can be given the right as a trustee to make distributions to himself or herself to meet an ascertainable standard of living. The better approach, however, is to have a co-trustee make such decisions. One additional point is that when a beneficiary is given the right to demand $5,000 or 5 percent of the trust assets, this amount can provide funds for a limited amount of luxuries, above the standard-of-living distributions.

TAX TRAP: When your trust may accumulate income rather than distributing it to the beneficiaries (for example the trustee is given the right to sprinkle income to different beneficiaries), the beneficiary who has a five-and-five power could be taxed on the amount of income he or she could have demanded to be distributed, even if the demand for the money is not made.

TAX PLANNING FOR BENEFICIARIES' RIGHTS

When you're setting up a trust that may receive later contributions of property or cash, planning for the $10,000 annual gift tax exclusion can be critically important. You will want the trust to be structured so that gifts to the trust will qualify for the annual exclusion. Otherwise, any gifts to the trust will use up a portion of your once-in-a-lifetime $600,000 exclusion, and once that is used up, the remainder is subject to tax. These concepts are explained further in Chapter 8. One possible solution is to include in your trust an annual demand right called a Crummey power (named for the court case in which it was recognized). This power permits your beneficiaries a limited right to withdraw an amount each year, which allows the gift to the trust to qualify for the annual exclusion. There is more about the Crummey power in Chapter 13.

SAMPLE TRUST CLAUSE:

Beneficiary's Annual Demand Power

Immediately following any Addition to the Trust Estate, the Recipients (individually, the "Holder") shall have the right to withdraw up to the amount of such Addition. Notwithstanding anything herein to the contrary, the total withdrawals by any Beneficiary, under this provision, for any calendar year, shall not exceed the lesser of: (i) the maximum annual gift tax exclusion allowable under Internal Revenue Code Section 2503(b), as amended; or (ii) the proportion of the Addition during any year divided by the number of beneficiaries during such year who may make a demand that would qualify a portion of such Addition as a gift of a present interest. This demand power shall take precedence over any other power or discretion granted to the Trustee. This demand power shall not be interpreted to limit the income distributions that may be made by the Trustee to the beneficiaries.

With respect to this demand power, the following rules shall apply:

(1) The Holder can exercise this demand power by a written request delivered to the Trustee.

(2) If the Holder is unable to exercise this demand power because of a legal disability, including minority, his or her parent, guardian, or personal representative (including but not limited to committee or conservator) may make the demand on the Holder's behalf. However, in no event can Grantor make the demand for the Holder, regardless of Grantor's relationship to the Holder.

(3) The Trustee must reasonably notify the person who would exercise the Holder's demand power of its existence not later than November 30 of each year and of the amount of any Additions made to the Trust Estate that are subject to this demand power.

(4) The Holder's demand power is noncumulative and lapses on the earlier of: (i) the last day of the calendar year in which the Addition was made; or (ii) Thirty (30) calendar days following the Trustee's sending the Holder notice of such contribution.

(5) The Trustee may satisfy the Holder's demand for a distribution by distributing cash, other assets, or fractional interests in other assets, as the Trustee in his or her sole discretion deems appropriate.

Notwithstanding the foregoing, if upon the expiration of any right of withdrawal or any portion thereof the Holder of such right would be deemed to have made a gift for federal gift tax purposes, such right shall continue in existence to the extent of the amount that would have been a taxable gift until and to the extent that its expiration shall not result in a taxable gift by the Holder thereof.

The Trustee shall give reasonable advance written notice (but not less than ten days) to each Holder entitled to exercise the right of withdrawal of any Additions.

In the case of a large estate, where planning involves transfers to grandchildren, the generation-skipping transfer tax can be a major concern (see Chapter 9). When assets are transferred to a trust for which the only beneficiaries are grandchildren (in tax jargon, "skip persons") a substantial generation-skipping transfer tax (called GST tax) could be incurred. An approach to avoid the GST tax is to give your children (who are not skip persons for tax purposes) the right to appoint the principal of the trust under their wills. This general power of appointment will cause the assets of the trust to be included in your children's estate for estate tax purposes. This will prevent the transfer from being subject to the GST tax.

CONCLUSION

Naming the beneficiaries of your trust is usually a straightforward task since providing for these persons is often the major reason for setting up the trust. Always name sufficient alternate beneficiaries to address unforeseeable situations, such as the death of a primary beneficiary. If you give any rights or powers to your beneficiaries, be certain to review the tax implications to avoid unpleasant surprises.

6 TRUSTEES' RIGHTS, OBLIGATIONS, AND POWERS

Trustees are the persons or institutions (such as a bank or trust company) who manage your trust. Within the framework you give them in your trust document, the trustees are left with the task of carrying out your intent. Without their efforts, the trust would not work. Your selection of the trustees, and the successor trustees (those who take over when prior trustees are no longer able or willing to serve), is one of the most important and sensitive issues in setting up a trust. Although many of the trustees' functions and rights are specified by law, the list of trustees' rights, obligations, and powers are usually spelled out in full in the trust document. A sample trustee section appears in the "For Your Notebook" section following this chapter.

WHO SHOULD BE THE TRUSTEES OF YOUR TRUST?

In the case of a revocable living trust, naming the initial trustee is easy—it's you (though its often best to have a second person serve as a co-trustee with you). If you're setting up a trust for your children under your will and your spouse survives, while there may be complicating factors, it is likely that your spouse will be the trustee. In every other situation the decision to select a trustee is not an easy one. Many people have a close friend or family member whom they trust. Some fortunate people may even have several. For most people, however, once their first few choices for trustee are named, coming up with the next can be very difficult.
Consider the following situations:

- You're setting up a trust to manage your money in case you become disabled. Your trustees ultimately could have substantial control over your personal life and well being.
- You have three children (or substitute siblings, friends, or partners) and would have confidence in one or two of them as trustees, but not all. Will you create friction and other problems if you name only the one or two?

EXAMPLE: Sometimes, using a little tact in drafting the trust language can overcome this type of problem: "I select my youngest son, John, as Trustee. I have selected John prior to his older siblings as my first choice for Trustee, not out of any lack of love or concern for my other children, but in recognition of his background as an accountant, which makes him best suited for this role." In many situations, a personal note may be preferable. In some cases, the friction may be caused by desire to earn trustee fees. This can be resolved by providing that no trustee shall earn a fee. Alternatively, you could make larger gifts to the persons not serving as trustee to maintain equality.

- You are setting up a trust for your children that will be effective after both you and your spouse die, which means that your trustees will have important control over the welfare of your children. The trustees' distribution of money from the trust could affect the type of education your children receive, how well they live, and how much money they will ultimately have.

TIP: No matter how hard it is for you to name a trustee, and successor trustees, consider the alternative. If you name only one trustee and he or she can't serve as trustee (because of dying before you, becoming disabled, or for any other reason), who will serve? A court proceeding will be necessary so that someone can be designated to take over as trustee. Most likely someone you select, even if you're not 100 percent happy with the choice, will be a better choice than whomever a court may select. Also, name as many alternates as you can—the more the better. Don't be concerned that someone you name is old. The typical trust clause will provide that if that person is unable or unwilling, another successor trustee will take over.

Characteristics Desirable in a Trustee

After you and your spouse, additional trustees should be selected based on their skills, rather than on any perceived obligation on your part or concern about insulting someone who is left out. The job is far too important for such niceties to matter. In making your decisions, consider the following five criteria:

1. *Has the Ability to Manage Assets.* If there is an interest in a business or other difficult-to-manage asset, does the person have the specific skills necessary?

2. *Has Investment Acumen.* Even when people don't consider themselves particularly well off, a trust can accumulate substantial assets. Suppose an insurance policy is paid to the trust. This alone could add a significant sum. Will the persons you select be able to handle this much money properly? If they don't have the necessary investment skills themselves, will they consult proper advisers and use them effectively? One way to address these concerns is to set up your trust now and have your present brokers and investment advisers involved with managing the money. This way, your trustees can pick up where

you left off, with a qualified cadre of advisers in place. See the sample guidelines regarding providing investment authority in the "For Your Notebook" section following this chapter.

3. *Has Adequate Judgment to Determine the Needs of Your Beneficiaries.* Someone who is financially astute still may not exhibit the proper sensitivity you want shown to your beneficiaries. A solution to this dilemma is to name co-trustees. One trustee can be a person, or a company, with substantial business sense and financial expertise. The co-trustee can be someone who exhibits the personal sensitivity and skills you desire. Together they may do a better job than either would alone. This approach is frequently used with institutional trustees. You could select an institution, such as a bank's trust department, to serve as a co-trustee with a family member.

4. *Has No Conflict of Interest.* Your longtime business partner may be your most trusted friend and the most financially astute individual you know, but if her decisions about the business could adversely affect your family's interests, she may not be the best choice. An alternative is to name her as co-trustee and prohibit her from making any decisions concerning the voting of the stock in the company. Also, consider using a buy-out agreement to dispose of the stock. This could leave your trust with cash instead of business interests and eliminate the problem entirely.

5. *Has a Good Temperament.* Will the person be able to get along reasonably well with all of the beneficiaries?

Legal and Tax Considerations

When evaluating who the trustees should be, consider these additional points: If you name a person as trustee who is a beneficiary, several problems can be created. As noted in Chapter 1, legally, if the same person is the *only* trustee and the *only* beneficiary, there may be no trust. This won't happen if there are remainder beneficiaries (those who receive money or assets when the current beneficiary dies or ceases to be a beneficiary for any reason). A trustee-beneficiary can also be subject to tax claims; when a trustee can distribute all of the trust assets to himself or herself as a beneficiary, the entire amount of the trust could be included in the person's estate for tax purposes. Whether you or your spouse (or anyone the IRS considers not to be "adverse" to your interests) should be a trustee is discussed in Chapter 4.

NOTE: One solution to problems arising when a trustee is also a beneficiary is to have two co-trustees. Another one is to have the provisions of the trust that define the trustees' powers specifically prohibit any co-trustees who are also beneficiaries from participating in any decisions to distribute money to themselves.

Who Will Be the Last Trustee?

The duration of the trust is important to consider as part of your trustee decisions. A trust established for young children or grandchildren could be in existence for a long time, so that you want to name an institution, such as a bank trust department, as a trustee. Institutional trustees don't get old or die, and usually don't resign (they may just merge). Or, if you prefer, you could name the institution as a final successor trustee in the event that the individuals named cannot serve.

Another alternative is to give the trustee the right to name a successor trustee, which may include an institution. Then, if your last-named trustee realizes that there is a possibility of the trust agreement's not designating a trustee, he or she can appoint a successor. The "For Your Notebook" section following this chapter includes such a trust provision.

POWERS THAT YOUR TRUSTEES SHOULD BE GIVEN

Your trustees need a broad range of powers in order to effectively discharge their responsibilities. There is some debate regarding whether these responsibilities, which constitute a large portion of most trust documents, really need to be listed. This is because state law provides for certain powers that trustees shall have, and it may not be necessary for these details to be repeated. Nevertheless, the long, all-inclusive approach often wins out because few attorneys are willing to risk not providing the trustee with whatever powers they may need. Also, many trustees like the comfort of being able to look in the trust document for an explicit statement authorizing them to take the actions they are considering. The "For Your Notebook" section following this chapter includes, as an illustration, a detailed list of the types of powers given to trustees. The notes interspersed among the provisions highlight some of the central points to consider when reviewing the specific powers to include in your trust.

RIGHTS THAT YOUR TRUSTEES SHOULD BE GIVEN

Unless the trust agreement specifically says otherwise, every person serving as trustee is entitled to compensation. Beyond immediate family members, no person is likely to serve without compensation. In order to prevent abuse, state laws have set maximum fees that may be charged by trustees. Often, the trust agreement is silent and the permissible fees are charged. Or you may want to include a specific provision regarding fees in the trust agreement. If you're using an institutional trustee, they may require this.

In order to encourage the people or entities you've named as trustees to serve, you may want to exonerate them from liability when they have acted reasonably and in good faith, and many trust agreements include such a provision. An honest error or poor investment made as a result of reasonable analysis should not cause your trustee to be penalized. State law may affect the extent to which you can relieve a trustee of liability.

CONCLUSION

Choosing trustees is one of the most difficult and important decisions to be made when setting up any trust. Although often dismissed as "boiler plate," the powers and rights of the trustees are extremely important and should be reviewed with care to ensure that your trust will function as closely as possible to what you desire.

For Your Notebook:

SAMPLE TRUSTEE PROVISIONS

[DO NOT USE THESE PROVISIONS IN ANY TRUST AGREEMENT WITHOUT FIRST REVIEWING WITH YOUR LAWYER]

I. *TRUSTEE RIGHTS, OBLIGATIONS, AND POWERS*

A. *Trustee Selection*

NOTE: The first trustee is usually named in the preamble, or introductory paragraph, of your trust (see Chapter 2). The alternate or successor trustees are appointed in the section below.

---

1. *Additional or Successor Trustee*

a. The Trustee may appoint an additional or successor Trustee which may be an individual (other than the Grantor), or a bank or trust company. This appointment shall be by an instrument in writing executed by any other Trustee. It shall become effective upon the approval of the Trustee in accordance with the Section above Trustee Decision Making, and on the date or condition specified in such instrument. Prior to the specified date or condition, however, the appointment may be withdrawn by an instrument in writing delivered to the Trustee. In the event that there should be no Trustee acting hereunder for a period of Thirty (30) days, the Grantor appoints as a successor Trustee the individual (other than the Grantor) or the bank or trust company to be designated by an instrument in writing signed by the law firm of LAWYER'S NAME, or any successor firm, and delivered to the Grantor and the Trustee, or if the Grantor should then be deceased, to the legal representatives of the estate of the Grantor and the Trustee.

NOTE: The approach of having your lawyer's firm name a final trustee is merely a stopgap approach to ensure that the line of successor trustees does not end prior to the termination of your trust. An alternative is to name a particular institutional trustee, such as a trust company or bank trust department, or its successor in interest (in the event it merges or is bought out), as a final trustee. If you are concerned about your lawyer naming herself, or someone from her firm, you can provide that the appointment must be of a family member.

---

b. The acceptance of trusteeship by any Trustee <u>not a party</u> to this Trust Agreement shall be evidenced by an execution of a <u>counterpart</u> to this Trust Agreement delivered to the remaining Trustee hereunder. Should there be no remaining Trustee, to the Grantor, or if the Grantor should then be deceased, to the legal representatives of the estate of the Grantor, or to such person as designated by a court of competent jurisdiction.

2. *Trustee Resignation*

a. Any Trustee hereunder may resign at any time without obtaining prior judicial approval. Such resignation shall be deemed complete upon the delivery of an instrument in writing declaring such resignation to the Grantor, if the Grantor is alive, and to the remaining Trustee hereunder, or should there be no remaining Trustee, to the successor Trustee hereunder. Such resigning Trustee shall promptly deliver the assets of the Trust Estate to the remaining or successor Trustee hereunder.

b. The resigning Trustee shall, at the request of the remaining or successor Trustee hereunder, promptly deliver such assignments, transfers and other instruments as may be reasonably required for fully vesting in such remaining or successor Trustee all right, title and interest in the Trust Estate.

NOTE: A reasonably detailed description should be provided of the steps to be followed when a trustee resigns.

---

c. If any of Trustee named in the preceding Sections is, or becomes, divorced or legally separated from the NAME OF PERSON to whom such person was married at the date this Trust Agreement was executed, than such person shall cease to serve as Trustee of any trust created under this Trust Agreement, and such Trustee shall immediately be deemed to have tendered a resignation hereunder.

NOTE: If, for example, you name your son-in-law as trustee, you also may want to provide that should he divorce your daughter, his appointment as trustee will terminate. Be sure to discuss this provision with your lawyer.

B. *Trustee Rights and Obligations*

   1. *Trustee Compensation*

Each Trustee acting hereunder, except for NAME OF TRUSTEE NOT TO BE COMPENSATED, shall be entitled to withdraw from the Trust Estate, without obtaining court or other approval, the compensation which is allowed to a trustee under the laws of the State which govern compensation to the trustee, computed in the manner and at the rates in effect at the time the compensation is payable.

NOTE: You can be more specific and incorporate a fee schedule of your institutional trustee or any other fee arrangement. If the fee arrangement exceeds the maximum compensation permitted by state law, be certain that you review the matter with your attorney. It may suffice to include the arrangement and acknowledge that you are aware that it exceeds the maximum allowed.

---

   2. *No Bond Required*

No bond or security of any kind shall be required of any Trustee acting hereunder.

   3. *Accounting*

a. No Trustee acting under this Trust Agreement are under any duty to render a judicial accounting upon resignation or otherwise. However, the Trustee may submit any account to a court for approval and settlement.

b. The Trustee may render an accounting upon the termination of any trust created under this Trust, and at any other times which the Trustee may deem necessary or advisable. The written approval of all persons, who are not subject to a legal disability, and who are entitled to receive the net income of any trust created under this Trust Agreement, and of all persons not subject to a legal disability then presumptively entitled to the principal of any trust, as to all matters and transactions shown in the account, shall be final, binding and conclusive upon all such persons, and upon all persons who may then be, or thereafter become, entitled to any income or principal of any trust created under this Trust Agreement. The written approval or assent of the persons mentioned in this Section shall have the same force and effect in discharging the Trustee as a decree by a court of competent jurisdiction. However, any such written approval shall not enlarge or shift the beneficial interest of any beneficiary of any trust created under this Trust Agreement.

c. If the Trustee is accounting to another fiduciary, then the written approval of the other fiduciary shall be final, binding and conclusive upon all persons beneficially interested in the Trust Estate represented by such other fiduciary.

NOTE: See Chapter 22 concerning trust accountings.

---

4. *Trustee Responsible for Care of Assets Comprising Trust Estate*

The Trustee shall have the entire care and custody of all of the assets comprising the trust estate and shall keep the assets with the same care as given to other property held by him in a fiduciary capacity. The Trustee shall become responsible for the trust estate only when, as and if the same shall have been received by such Trustee. No Trustee shall be responsible for any act or omission of any prior Trustee, nor shall any Trustee be under a duty to take any proceedings against any prior Trustee, but shall be entitled to rely on the propriety of the actions of the prior Trustee as such actions appear from the records and accounts of the prior Trustee. In determining which assets constitute the trust estate, a Trustee shall be responsible only for the making of reasonable inquiry from records of the prior Trustee reasonably available to such Trustee.

5. *Limitation on Trustee Liability*

a. No Trustee shall be individually liable for any loss to, or depreciation in, the value of the Trust Estate occurring by reason of (i) the exercise or non-exercise of the powers granted to the Trustee under this Trust; or (ii) a mistake in, or error of, judgment in the purchase or sale of any investment or the retention of any investment, so long as the Trustee shall have been acting in good faith.

b. Every act done, power exercised or obligation assumed by the Trustee, pursuant to the provisions of this Trust Agreement, shall be held to be done, exercised or assumed, as the case may be, by the Trustee acting in the Trustee's fiduciary capacity and not otherwise, and every person, firm or corporation contracting or otherwise dealing with the Trustee shall look only to the funds and property of the Trust Estate for payment under such contract or payment of any money that may become due or payable under any obligation arising under this Trust Agreement, in whole or in part, and no Trustee shall be individually liable for such matter even though the Trustee did not exempt itself from individual liability when entering into any contract, obligation or transaction in connection with or growing out of the Trust Estate.

c. The Trustee shall be liable for gross negligence and for such acts, neglect and defaults which constitute a breach of trust and which are committed in bad faith.

NOTE: As discussed in the chapter, you will want to have some reasonable limits on the liability of the trustees so they are encouraged to serve. On the other hand, you do not want to give a trustee *carte blanche* to do wrong without liability. At the same time, state law, as a matter of public policy, may limit how broad an indemnification you can give.

---

6. *Trustee Consultation with Counsel*

The Trustee may consult with legal counsel (who may be counsel to the Grantor) concerning any question which may arise with reference to the Trustee's duties or obligations under this Trust Agreement, and the opinion of such counsel shall be full and complete authorization and protection in respect of any action taken or suffered by the Trustee in good faith and in accordance with the opinion of such counsel.

7. *Receipt by Beneficiary Discharges Trustee*

The receipt of any beneficiary upon distribution hereunder shall discharge the Trustee from any further obligation with respect to the property so distributed. Upon final distribution hereof, the Trustee shall be fully discharged, and this entire trust shall terminate.

NOTE: This provision is not necessarily required because state law may not hold your trustee liable for what a beneficiary does with the money or property distributed. It is often included to provide security to the trustees, for it may be impractical or impossible for any trustee to police what a beneficiary does with trust distributions.

C. *Trustee Decision Making and Authority*

1. *Trustee Decision Making*

Any authority, discretion or power granted to or conferred upon the Trustee by this Trust may be exercised by any such Trustee who shall be acting under this Trust Agreement at such time, or by such of them who shall be so designated by an instrument in writing executed by any other Trustee.

Where there are more than Two (2) Trustees at any time, the decision of a majority of them shall control and shall be binding on all of the Trustees.

Where no majority decision can be reached, then the first Trustee whose name appears in this Trust Agreement shall make the final decision which shall be final and binding on all Trustees.

NOTE: Many trust agreements have little discussion of how decisions should be made when there is more than one trustee. The above approach is merely a suggestion. However, this matter can be quite important, especially when several family members are named as co-trustees. If you have an institutional co-trustee and a non-institutional co-trustee (for example, a family member), discuss the trust provision with the institutional trustee. The preferred approach is to have the institutional trustee have final decision-making authority on such business matters as investments, and so forth, and to leave the more personal matters, such as the allocation of distributions among various permitted beneficiaries, to the family member serving as co-trustee. Another approach is to have the next named successor trustee cast the deciding vote.

2. *Trustee Decision Is Final and Conclusive*

The exercise by the Trustee of the discretionary powers herein granted with respect to the payment, distribution or application of principal or income of any trust created under this Trust Agreement is final and conclusive upon all persons and shall not be subject to any review whatsoever. Grantor intends that the Trustee shall have the greatest latitude in exercising such discretionary powers, and that the persons entitled to receive the principal of any trust created under this Trust Agreement shall upon the termination of such trust be entitled only to such principal as may remain after the last exercise of the Trustee's continuing discretionary powers.

3. *Trustee Decisions Are Non-Reviewable and Binding*

Any decision to be made by the Trustee is to be made in such Trustee's sole, absolute and non-reviewable discretion and shall be binding on all parties affected unless specifically provided to the contrary in this Trust Agreement.

4. *Court Approval of Trustee Acts Not Required*

No Trustee shall be required to obtain the approval of any court for any action of such Trustee unless such approval is required by law or by a specific requirement in this Trust Agreement.

NOTE: The preceding few paragraphs are typical. They are intended to give the trustees leeway to make the best decisions they can without challenge and court review.

5. *Limitations on Trustee's Discretionary Authority*

Notwithstanding anything in this Trust to the contrary, no single Trustee shall:

a. Have the authority to appoint income or principal of any trust formed under this Trust Agreement to himself or herself, his or her creditors, his or her estate, creditors of his or her estate, or to or for the benefit of any child to whom he or she owes a legal obligation of support and for which such appointment of income or principal would constitute a discharge of such legal obligation of support.

b. Participate in any decisions regarding the discretionary distribution of income or principal to himself or herself, or to or for his or her benefit.

NOTE: The above provisions are not always appropriate. For example, in a revocable living trust, you do want these rights. The main purpose of these provisions is to prevent the assets of the trust from being included in the trustee-beneficiary's estate.

---

c. In the event that any Trustee is in a position where such a decision would have to be made, such Trustee shall not participate in such a decision and instead any co-Trustee shall make such decision. Further, if there is no co-Trustee than the next named successor Trustee under this Trust Agreement who is willing and able to participate, shall so participate in such decision.

d. If Grantor's spouse, serves as a Trustee under this Trust, he shall have no incidents of ownership, rights, powers, privileges of any nature with respect to the life insurance policies purchased or acquired by the Trustee on the life of either Grantor or Grantor's spouse.

D. *Trustee Administrative Powers*

1. *Trustee Powers*

Except as specifically provided to the contrary in this Trust Agreement, the Trustee shall have in addition to, and not in limitation of, the powers granted elsewhere in this Trust Agreement, or the powers allowed by law, the following powers:

NOTE: The following provisions are designed to give the trustees the powers to deal with business, investment, and related matters. Also see the For Your Notebook section that follows for guidelines regarding investment policies of your trustees.

---

a. To invest and reinvest any assets comprising the Trust Estate in any securities or other property, whether real or personal, tangible or intangible, of any class, kind or nature (including an undivided interest in any one or more common trust funds), as the Trustee may deem advisable without regard to any restrictions of law on a trustee's investments.

b. To exercise voting rights in person or by proxy, rights of conversion or of exchange, or rights to purchase or subscribe for stocks, bonds or other securities or obligations which may be offered to the holders of any asset, and to accept and retain any property which may be acquired by the exercise of any such right with respect to any stocks, bonds or other securities or obligation included in the Trust Estate.

c. To employ or retain accountants, custodians, agents, legal counsel, investment advisers, and other experts as the Trustee shall deem advisable. To rely on the information and advice furnished by such persons. To fix the compensation of such persons, and in the case of legal counsel, who may also be acting as a Trustee hereunder, to take payments on account of legal fees in advance of the settlement of the Trustee's account without applying to or procuring the authority of any court.

d. To the extent permitted by the laws of the State, the Trustee may hold securities in the name of a nominee without indicating the trust character of such holdings, and may hold unregistered securities, or securities in a form that will pass by delivery.

e. To retain and continue for any period deemed appropriate by the Trustee, any asset, whether real or personal, tangible or intangible, included in the Trust Estate.

f. To sell at public or private sale and to exchange or otherwise dispose of any stocks, bonds, securities, personal property, or other asset constituting the Trust Estate at the time, price, and terms as the Trustee deems advisable.

g. To grant options for the sale or exchange of any asset comprising the Trust Estate, at times, prices and terms which the Trustee deems advisable, without applying to or procuring the authority of any court.

h. To sell, exchange, partition, convey and mortgage, and to modify, extend, renew or replace any mortgage which may be a lien on all, or any part, of any interest in real property included in the Trust Estate.

i. To lease any real or personal property, whether or not for a term beyond the period of time fixed by statute for leases by a trustee, and whether or not, extending beyond the termination of any trust established under this Trust Agreement, and upon such terms as the Trustee deems advisable, without obtaining the approval of any court.

NOTE: This provision is illustrative of the reason for a detailed powers statement in your trust. Some state laws do not permit a trustee to lease property for a period longer than the time remaining in the trust, a restriction that can hamper the trustee's ability to perform effectively. The inclusion of the above provision in the trust powers gives the trustee flexibility in this area.

---

j. To foreclose mortgages and bid in property under foreclosure and to take title by deed in lieu of foreclosure or otherwise.

k. To extend the time of payment of any bond, note or other obligation or mortgage included in the Trust Estate, or of any installment of principal thereof, or of any interest due thereon. To hold such instrument after maturity, as a past due bond, note or other obligation or mortgage, either with or without renewal or extension. To consent to the modification, alteration and amendment of any terms or conditions of such instrument, including those regarding the rate of interest, and to waive any defaults in the performance of the terms and conditions of such instrument.

l. To compromise, adjust, settle or submit to arbitration upon terms the Trustee deems advisable, in absolute discretion, any claim in favor of or against the Trust Estate. To release with, or without, consideration any claim in favor of the Trust Estate.

m. To participate in any refunding, readjustment of stocks, bonds or other securities or obligations, enforcement of obligations or securities by foreclosure or otherwise, corporate consolidation by merger or otherwise or reorganization which shall affect any stock, bond or other security or obligation included in the Trust Estate. To participate in any plan or proceeding for protection of the interests of the holders of such instruments. To deposit any property under any plan or proceeding with any protective or reorganization committee and to delegate to such a committee the discretionary power with respect thereto. To pay a proportionate part of the expenses of a committee. To pay any assessments levied under such a plan, and to accept and retain any property which may be received pursuant to any such plan.

n. To borrow money for the purpose of raising funds to pay taxes or for any other purpose deemed by the Trustee beneficial to the Trust Estate, and upon such terms as the Trustee may determine. To pledge as security for the repayment of any loan any assets included in the Trust Estate.

o. To make any distribution under any Trust, in cash or in property, or in any combination of cash and property. To make non-pro-rata distributions of cash and property then included in the Trust Estate.

p. To exercise for the benefit of the Trust Estate, and for any property included in the Trust Estate, all rights, powers and privileges of every nature, which might or could be exercised by any person owning similar property absolutely and in his own right. In connection with the exercise of any or all of such rights, powers and privileges, even where such right, power or privilege may not have been specifically mentioned in this Trust Agreement. To negotiate, draft, enter into, re-negotiate, or otherwise modify any contracts or other written instruments which the Trustee deems advisable, and to include in them the covenants, terms and conditions as the Trustee deems proper.

2. Trustee Authority to Operate Business Interests

Subject to the Trustee complying with the terms of any agreement which the Grantor may have executed concerning the management, operations, sale or other disposition of any business interests of which Grantor may die possessed, the Grantor directs that the Trustee may either dispose of any such business interests which the Grantor may die possessed, or may operate and exercise all powers with respect to the operation of such business interests, in whatever manner the Trustee deems to be in the best interest of the beneficiaries of any trusts created under this Trust Agreement.

No Trustee shall be disqualified from serving hereunder, or from exercising any powers vested in him or her under this Trust Agreement, because of any interest or connection such Trustee may have in or with any partnership, joint venture, association, business or other enterprises in which any trust formed under this Trust Agreement may also hold an interest, or by reason of being an officer, director or stockholder of any corporation, the stock, securities or debt of which is owned by any trust formed under this Trust Agreement.

NOTE: This is an optional provision that may be included, or modified, to address the situation of the trustee's holding stock in a closely held business. Be certain to have your lawyer review the shareholders' agreement or partnership agreement for the business for any possible conflicts.

E. Trustee Discretionary Powers

1. Accumulations of Income

The Trustee may accumulate any of the net income not paid or applied for the benefit of the Recipients, and add it to the principal of this Trust Agreement at least annually and thereafter to hold, administer and dispose of it as a part of the Trust Estate.

2. Distribution Standard for Changed Circumstances

Because of the possibility of changes in circumstances which cannot be predicted, and because of Grantor's desire to provide adequate funds for the education of the Children, to assist the Children in purchasing a principal residence, or in the Children establishing themselves in prudent business ventures, Grantor has authorized the Trustee, at any time that they deem advisable, to distribute so much of the principal of any trust created under this Trust Agreement for any of the Children, in advance of the time for distribution set forth in such trust, as the Trustee deems to be in the best interests of the Child for the purposes stated in this Section.

NOTE: You will want to give your trustee flexibility to distribute money to deal with an emergency.

---

3. Unified or Separate Accounts

For the Trustee's convenience in administering any of the trusts created under this Trust Agreement, the Trustee may administer as a unified account the assets of any trust created under this Trust, and Donee Property. The Trustee shall keep a separate record of all transactions.

NOTE: If you have separate trusts—for example, one for each of your children—formed under one trust, it may be easier for your trustee to administer them as a single trust to minimize paper work. As long as the trustee keeps accurate records of what each child's trust has, this should not present any problem.

---

4. Termination of Trust Where Uneconomical to Manage

Notwithstanding anything to the contrary contained in this Trust Agreement, if the Trustee shall determine that the aggregate value or the character of the assets of any trust created under this Trust, or the aggregate value or the character of the assets being held for a donee under a disability, makes it inadvisable, inconvenient or uneconomical to continue the administration of such trust or assets, then the Trustee may transfer the Trust Estate, equally or unequally, to or among one or more persons then eligible to receive the net income of such trust.

5. Merger of Trusts

In the event that Trusts have been created under this Trust Agreement and/or under a trust under Grantor's will or by Grantor's spouse for the same beneficiaries, then the Trustee shall be authorized to merge said trusts.

6. Distribution to Persons Under a Disability

a. Retention and Distribution of Income and Principal to a Person Under a Disability

Whenever pursuant to the provisions of any trust formed under this Trust Agreement, any Donee Property is to be distributed, title to that property shall vest in that person under a disability, but the payment or transfer of the property may be deferred until the disability ceases. If the transfer of property is deferred under this Section, that Donee Property shall be held by the Trustee, who shall apply so much of the principal and income as they deem necessary, and in accordance with the Standard For Payment, for the benefit of the person under a disability.

b. Transfer of Donee Property

When the disability ceases, the Trustee shall transfer to the person formerly under a disability the remaining Donee Property, and any accumulations of income or principal (collectively, both such items are referred to as the "Remaining Property"). If the person under a disability should die, the Trustee shall deliver the Remaining Property to the legal representatives of the estate of that person. Notwithstanding the foregoing provisions the Trustee may, at any time, deliver all or any part of the Donee Property which shall then remain, together with any accumulations, of income, to a parent, guardian, custodian under the Uniform Gifts to Minors Act or the Uniform Transfers to Minors Act, committee, conservator of the property, or an individual with whom such person under a disability resides, and the receipt by such person or entity shall constitute a full discharge of the Trustee for such payment or delivery. The powers granted to the Trustee shall be applicable to any Donee Property dealt with in this Section and shall continue until the actual distribution of such Donee Property.

NOTE: This common trust provision is used as a safety net in the event that anyone entitled to receive property is not in an appropriate condition to handle the money or assets distributed.

---

7. Transactions with Grantor's Estate

The Trustee is authorized and empowered, at any time and from time to time, (i) to purchase at fair market value from the legal representatives of the Grantor's estate any property constituting a part, or all, of the Grantor's estate, and (ii) to loan for adequate consideration to the legal representatives of the Grantor's estate such part, or all, of the Trust Estate, upon such terms and conditions as the Trustee deem advisable.

8. Modification of Trust Agreement by Trustee

Notwithstanding anything in this Trust Agreement to the contrary, the Trustee shall not have the power to use any of the Trust Estate for the benefit of Grantor's estate, as such term is defined in Treasury Regulation Section 20.2042-1(b). The Trustee, however, may modify or amend any trust formed under this Trust Agreement to facilitate the administration of the Trust Estate or to conform such trust to laws or regulations affecting trusts, the requirements of qualifying as a Qualified Subchapter S Trust, to meet the requirements of a Qualified Domestic Trust, or to properly implement the provisions affecting the GSTT set forth herein, as the same may be amended from time to time. No such modification or amendment shall affect the possession or enjoyment of the Trust Estate.

9. *Distribution of Trust Estate Where Amount Less Than Specified Sum*

In the event that subsequent to any of the principal distributions provided for above, the principal remaining in the trust for any beneficiary shall be less than _____ Thousand ($_____,000) Dollars, the Trustee may, in the Trustee's sole and absolute discretion, immediately distribute such remaining principal.

NOTE: When the amount left in the trust is too small to warrant the legal, accounting, trust, or other fees and costs, your trustee should have the right to terminate the trust. See Chapter 23.

For Your Notebook:

SAMPLE GUIDELINES IN DESIGNATING TRUSTEE POWERS OVER INVESTMENT MATTERS

The following document addresses one of the most important issues for many trusts: What latitude should be given to the trustees concerning investment matters? If you're extremely conservative—adverse to risk—and hope that your trust will remain intact for the benefit of your children for many years to come, do you want your trustee making highly speculative commodity investments? The following page will provide you with guidance.

GREENBAUM AND ASSOCIATES, INC.

496 Kinderkamack Road   Financial and Investment Counsel   Fax(201)261-9365
Oradell, NJ 07649-1523   Phone (201)261-1900

Investment Issues that should be EXPLICITLY addressed in every trust document

1. Are any of the trustees authorized to act individually, independently, and without the consent of other trustees? If so, is notice to the other trustees required? Must assets controlled individually by a single trustee, or group of trustees, be segregated in some manner?

2. How many of the trustees' signatures are needed to evidence sufficient authority? Are instructions communicated by telephone, fax, or verbally, equivalent to a written signature?

3. Can trustees delegate to others the authority to give trading instructions? Is this authority restricted to a limited power of attorney, also called a "discretionary trading authorization," or is a general power of attorney permitted?

4. Which types of securities and other investments are the trustees permitted to purchase, sell, hypothecate or rehypothecate, margin, hedge, pledge or repledge, use as collateral, or hold? What types of securities and other investments are not permitted?

5. Can the trustees open and maintain a margin account?

6. Can the trustees sell short?

7. Can the trustees trade in derivative securities? This includes options, futures, and commodities.

8. Do successor trustees have the same investment rights and limitations as the original trustees? Does some future event change the rights and limitations of the trustees? How will the advisor and the broker dealer be noticed of any change in investment rights and limitations?

9. What type of investment performance reporting is required by the trustees and the beneficiaries? Does the reporting have to comply with the Association for Investment Managements and Research (AIMR) standards?

10. Are the trustees required to prepare a written Investment Policy Statement periodically?

11. Are trustees required to adhere to some specific investment policy (i.e. "socially responsible investing" might not permit investment in South Africa or in nuclear weapons firms).

Exclusive FEE-ONLY Compensation

7 DISTRIBUTION OF INCOME AND PRINCIPAL, AND MISCELLANEOUS PROVISIONS

The manner in which income and assets (in legal jargon, "principal") are distributed will depend largely on the purposes for which your trust was formed. A lot depends on the degree to which tax planning is a consideration.

THE EFFECTS OF PERSONAL AND TAX CONSIDERATIONS

With a revocable living trust, you will have reserved every right to amend or revoke the trust; therefore, you will have total control over distributions. You can get what you want, when you want it. Typically, if you become disabled, other persons will take over as trustee, and then the provisions of your trust will govern how income and principal should be distributed. Following your death, the manner in which income and assets of your trust are distributed will depend on the various trusts or outright distributions for which your living trust provides.

The following is illustrative of the generous language typically included in a revocable living trust to govern trustee distributions for your benefit when you are disabled:

SAMPLE TRUST CLAUSE: It is the express desire of the Grantor that the Trustees apply income liberally, without concern for the retention of any monies for future or remainder beneficiaries.

With a credit shelter trust your surviving spouse will generally be provided the maximum income and certain principal invasion rights without the assets of the trust being taxed in his or her estate.

With a minor children's trust specific tax law requirements (either a Crummey or 2503(c) distribution provision) will be followed to qualify gifts to the trust for the $10,000 annual gift tax exclusion.

If your trusts are not set up primarily for tax benefits, the distribution provisions are more likely to be structured straightforwardly to meet the purposes for which you formed the trust. For example, under your living trust you can provide that on your death all of your assets are to be held in trust for the benefit of your children until the youngest reaches age 25, at which time the remaining assets will be distributed equally to your children. During the period before the final distribution, the distribution objectives probably will be to provide for the education and welfare of your children. The provisions will be drafted accordingly.

On the other hand, if tax considerations come into play, the distribution provisions start becoming complex.

EXAMPLE: When you or your spouse is the trustee, if you hope to keep the assets of the trust out of your estate, you will want to limit the powers of the trustees to distribute assets for the benefit of your children.

Tax considerations are the point of many trusts, and when this is the case, the distribution provisions will usually track the tax laws so that they do not defeat the estate planning goals. For example, a Q-TIP trust is designed to take advantage of the unlimited gift or estate tax marital deduction. There are specific restrictions and instructions on the distribution of income and principal from this trust if you are going to meet the goal of keeping assets out of your estate and the estate of your spouse (see Chapter 11).

These and other tax-oriented distribution provisions are explained in detail and illustrated throughout the remainder of this book. You generally will pick and choose the provisions appropriate for your trust and your objectives.

TRUSTEE POWERS GOVERN THE DISTRIBUTION OF INCOME AND ASSETS

Administrative Powers

Many of the provisions governing how income and assets can be distributed from your trust are included among the powers granted to your trustees (see the "For Your Notebook" section of Chapter 6). These include the right of a trustee to defer distributions to a beneficiary under a disability, the right to make emergency or special distributions of trust assets in the event of changed circumstances (such as to assist a beneficiary in purchasing a home), and the right to terminate the trust when the balance of trust assets is so small as to make it uneconomical to continue administering a trust.

In addition to these administrative powers of a trustee regarding distributions, several important discretionary powers may be given to a trustee, depending on the nature of the trust, which can affect distributions.

Discretionary Powers

Different standards can be provided for determining the trustee's authority to make distributions, depending on tax, legal, and personal considerations. For example, when the trustee is completely independent, you may feel confident in giving him or her the widest latitude "to distribute any amount of income earned by the trust, or principal of the trust, to the beneficiaries as could reasonably be necessary for the comfort and welfare of the beneficiaries."

When a beneficiary is a trustee, however, this language could result in having the trust assets included in that trustee-beneficiary's estate for tax purposes, because under such a vague and broad guideline the trustee-beneficiary could distribute the entire trust principal to himself or herself.

In such a case, you may prefer to use a narrower, ascertainable criterion for distributions from the trust, specifying that distributions be made only for the health, education, and maintenance of the beneficiaries in accordance with the current standard of living. This approach has the benefit of mitigating potential tax problems, and, for many people setting up trusts, the primary goal is precisely to provide for basic living needs rather than an extravagant lifestyle. Also, this more restrictive distribution standard can be combined with a right given to the beneficiary to withdraw the greater of $5,000 or 5 percent of the trust principal in any year. This limited withdrawal right won't create significant tax problems for the beneficiary, and it gives the trust arrangement a little flexibility (see Chapter 5).

Sprinkle Power over Distributions

One of the most helpful trustee powers is a sprinkle power—the power of the trustee to "sprinkle" income or assets wherever the trustee determines the funds are most needed. For example, you could require all of the income from a childrens' trust to be distributed each year to all of your children. However, your trustee could be given the power to sprinkle the income among your children in any manner deemed appropriate. If there were no unusual circumstances, the trustee could simply divide the proceeds equally. However, if one child has special medical needs or was pursuing a graduate degree while the others were working, the trustee could sprinkle the monies to the child in need. This is an excellent device to use in certain trusts since it builds in flexibility, enabling the trustee to address circumstances that may not have been foreseen when the trust was first formed.

At the same time, a sprinkle power can create a number of serious tax issues. If a trustee is also a beneficiary, it will be inappropriate for that trustee to exercise a discretionary sprinkle power. The standard trustee powers illustrated in the "For Your Notebook" section of Chapter 6 (see "Limitations on Trustee Discretionary Authority") specifically prohibit any trustee from participating in any decision concerning any distribution to that trustee. This approach requires that you have at least two trustees, which was also recommended in Chapter 6. If the grantor is a trustee, a sprinkle power could cause the assets of the trust to be included in the grantor's estate for tax purposes.

CAUTION: Carefully consider the type of trust involved before using a sprinkle power. For example, if you're setting up a Q-TIP trust for your surviving spouse, the use of a sprinkle power would disqualify the trust, and create a substantial tax cost if your estate were large enough. This is because all of the income from such a trust must be payable to your spouse at least annually.

PERSONAL CONSIDERATIONS SHOULD GOVERN FINAL TRUST DISTRIBUTION PROVISIONS

Your personal feelings and concerns should be a major factor in determining how assets will be distributed from your trust. You may want to have assets tied up in trusts for years to protect the ultimate beneficiaries from their own excesses, from creditors, and from other unknowns.

EXAMPLE: One parent, concerned about his daughter's erratic marital history after four divorces, decided to leave her share of his estate in trust until she is 55. Until that time, she will be entitled to the distribution of all of the income annually, and only so much of the principal as the trust company named as sole trustee deems necessary for her health and maintenance.

Other people setting up trusts take a different view. Perhaps they had their own assets tied up in a trust for many years and were uncomfortable with the arrangement. They may choose to have all assets remaining in their trust be distributed to each child upon reaching age 18. Neither of the above extremes is usually appropriate, however. In the "For Your Notebook" section following this chapter, various sample provisions illustrate the more commonly used distribution arrangements.

NOTE: It's your money and your estate. No rule of thumb or typical arrangement has to be used. No trust form is sacrosanct. As long as your goals are legal, they should be the primary determinant of how your trust assets ultimately should be distributed. If you're not satisfied with any of the examples in the "For Your Notebook" section, devise your own in consultation with your advisers.

MISCELLANEOUS PROVISIONS FOR YOUR TRUST

In addition to the main provisions of a trust governing the transferring of assets to the trust and the distributing of assets from the trusts, which state the rights and powers of the grantor, the trustees, and the beneficiaries, there are a few more, rather mundane and "boiler plate" provisions that help make the key provisions of your trust work. Although these provisions may be dull by comparison with those discussed thus far, they are still important. Often these provisions are ignored, and no one will ever notice until there is a problem. Therefore, be sure the provisions at the end of your trust agreement are properly dealt with.

These provisions are illustrated and annotated in the "For Your Notebook" section for this chapter.

CONCLUSION

Stating how and when income and assets of your trust can be distributed are vital to achieving your tax, financial, personal, and other goals. To accomplish your objectives, the distribution provisions of your trust must be carefully reviewed and coordinated. Don't overlook the miscellaneous provisions, which must also appear in proper form.

For Your Notebook:

SAMPLE DISTRIBUTION PROVISIONS

[DO NOT USE THESE SAMPLE PROVISIONS IN ANY TRUST AGREEMENT UNTIL YOU REVIEW THEM WITH YOUR LAWYER]

CAUTION: The provisions below illustrate many different types of distribution approaches. The notes indicate some of the appropriate uses. These provisions are *not* all appropriate to include in a single trust; they represent different options to use in different trusts. Thus, many are contradictory. These provisions are intended to provide a good starting point for evaluating the different distribution approaches. But remember, start with your personal goals and choose accordingly.

DISTRIBUTION OF INCOME AND PRINCIPAL; OPERATIVE TRUST PROVISIONS

A. *Distribution During Grantor's Life*

The Trustee shall hold the Trust Estate for the following purposes and subject to the terms and conditions of this Trust Agreement.

1. *Application of Trust Estate*

The Trustee shall hold the Trust Estate, in trust, to pay or apply to or for the benefit of any one or more of the following persons: Grantor's spouse, SPOUSE NAME, and Grantor's children, which shall include CHILDREN-NAMES, and any children born or legally adopted after the execution of this Trust Agreement (collectively "Children", individually "Child"), as shall be living during Grantor's life, or the issue of any deceased Child (collectively, the Children and the issue are called the "Recipients"). The net income of the Trust shall be applied in amounts, whether equal or unequal, as the Trustee, in the exercise of absolute discretion, may consider desirable for the maintenance and support of any one of the Recipients.

2. *Distributions to Grantor of Revocable Living Trust*

The Trustee shall hold, manage, invest and reinvest the Trust Estate. The Trustee shall collect any income from Trust investments. Upon demand by the Grantor, at any time and in any amount, the Trustee shall pay to the Grantor all of the income earned on the Trust Estate and any portion, or all, of the principal of the Trust Estate. Where the Grantor does not demand distribution of all of the income from the Trust Estate, the Trustee shall add such amount to the Trust Estate and administer as part of the Trust Estate.

NOTE: The above paragraphs illustrate the types of distribution provisions included in a revocable living trust. Since there is no tax benefit, and the assets are primarily intended for your benefit, the distribution standards are extremely liberal.

B. *Distribution Standards, Generally*

1. *Trust Self-Destruct Provision*

In addition to the powers conferred upon the Trustee under this Trust Agreement, during the life of the Grantor, the Trustee may pay out any part or all of the net income or principal, or both, in such amounts as the Trustee determines appropriate to such one or more persons and the Trustee determines from the class of persons consisting of: the Recipients [THIS TERM WOULD BE DEFINED ELSEWHERE IN YOUR TRUST, BUT WOULD EXCLUDE THE TRUSTEES]. In exercising this power, the Trustee shall be subject to the restrictions (set forth more fully elsewhere in this Trust Agreement) that no Trustee may participate in the decision to appoint assets to himself or herself.

NOTE: Use this type of clause when it is not clear that the trust should be kept in force—for example, in the event of a major change in circumstances, such as a divorce. This type of provision, however, can raise significant questions regarding the status of the trust and should only be used after consultation with an estate planning attorney. If there is considerable uncertainty about establishing a trust, the trust should be revocable, or perhaps it is simply not the appropriate time to establish a trust.

---

2. *Standards for Payment*
    a. *Ascertainable Standard for Payment of Income and Principal*

Unless specifically provided to the contrary in this Trust Agreement, any payment of principal or income by the Trustee shall be made in accordance with the standards contained in this Section ("Standards For Payment").

    b. *Standard of Payment for Principal*

The Trustee of any trust created under this Trust Agreement is authorized, at any time, with respect to any beneficiary of any trust formed under this Trust Agreement then eligible to receive the net income from such trust, to pay to, or apply for the benefit of such persons such sums out of the principal of such trust (including the entire principal amount), as the Trustee considers advisable to provide for such person's education, maintenance and support, according to the standard of living to which such person is accustomed at the time of Grantor's death, as well as any amounts necessary for expenses incurred by any beneficiary because of any illness, operation, infirmity, or emergency of any nature, irrespective of cause or need, as the Trustee shall deem to be in the best interest of that beneficiary.

NOTE: As discussed above, this is a narrow standard that can be important to use when tax consequences to trustees and others are important.

---

    c. *Standard of Payment for Income*

The Trustee shall pay any portion, or all of the income of any trust formed under this Trust Agreement to the designated beneficiaries of such trust in accordance with the instructions provided for in any such trust. Where no specific instructions are so provided, or such instructions are unclear, the amount of income distributed shall be payable in the discretion of the Trustee. The Trustee, however, is directed to liberally interpret this Section so as to provide for the expenses incurred by any beneficiary because of any illness, operation, infirmity, or emergency of any nature, irrespective of cause or need, as the Trustee shall deem to be in the best interest of that beneficiary.

    d. *Non-Ascertainable Standard for Payment of Principal*

The Trustee may, during the continuance of any Trust under this Trust Agreement, distribute to or for the benefit of the Beneficiary so much of the income or principal of such Trust as the Trustee, in such Trustee's sole and uncontrolled discretion, may deem necessary for the support, maintenance, comfort or welfare of that beneficiary, to aid the beneficiary in obtaining an education, including college, university, graduate or professional school; or to aid the beneficiary in meeting any illness, accident, emergency, unexpected contingency or extraordinary financial distress.

NOTE: This is intended to be a broad and liberal standard to provide the maximum funds to the beneficiary without restriction. If spendthrift concerns are important to you, or if the beneficiary is also a trustee, these broad provisions may be inappropriate.

---

e. *Divorce*

If a divorce judgment is entered into between Grantor and Grantor's spouse, SPOUSE NAME, then Grantor's spouse shall be deemed to have predeceased Grantor as effective on the date of such judgment, and all provisions of this Trust Agreement, and any trust formed hereunder, shall be interpreted accordingly.

NOTE: A concern for many people setting up an irrevocable trust is the risk of what a divorce could do to their planning. This provision should be carefully reviewed with an attorney. One solution is to address the divorce concerns in a prenuptial agreement, or to avoid establishing a trust until there is more confidence in the future of the relationship.

C. *Distributions Following Death of Grantor*

1. *Distribution of Trust Estate, Generally*

The Trustee shall hold the Trust Estate, in trust, for the following purposes: (i) To pay to, or apply for the benefit of, any one or more of the Recipients then living, the net income, in equal or unequal portions, which the Trustees consider advisable in accordance with the Standard For Payment (as defined below) of any one or more of the following persons: the Recipients; or (ii) To accumulate any net income which is not paid or applied and add it to the principal of the Trust Estate, at least annually, and thereafter to hold, administer and dispose of it as a part of the Trust Estate.

2. *Distribution to Multiple Children's Trusts*

NOTE: When there are sufficient resources, and when each child is to receive an equal amount, many people prefer to set up a separate trust for each child. However, when a child has special needs, or when resources are more limited, a single trust for the benefit of all children may be more prudent since it provides the trustee with flexibility to give the money where it is needed most, especially when combined with a sprinkle power.

Upon the death of SPOUSE NAME the remaining principal balance and any undistributed income, shall be distributed to Grantor's Trustee in trust for the use and benefit of Grantor's Children, to be divided into as many equal parts as there are Children then surviving and Children then deceased leaving surviving issue, and in respect of these parts, the Trustee is hereby directed to pay such amounts in the manner provided in this Section ("Distribution By Age"):

a. To pay One (1) of such parts to the issue of each deceased Child, per stirpes, according to the provisions of the Article governing Bequests and Devises to Persons Under Age Thirty Five (35).

b. To pay One (1) of such parts to each of the Children who has attained the age of Thirty Five (35) years.

c. To pay Two-Thirds ($^2/_3$) of One (1) of such parts to each of the Children who has attained the age of Thirty (30) years but has not attained the age of Thirty Five (35) years, and to hold the remainder of such part according to the terms and conditions of this Section.

d. To pay One-Third ($^1/_3$) of One (1) of such parts to each of the Children who has attained the age of Twenty Five (25) years but have not attained the age of Thirty-Five (35) years, and to hold the remainder of such part according to the terms and conditions of this Section.

e. To hold One (1) of such parts or the remaining portion thereof (whichever shall be applicable for each Child) as a separate trust fund in trust for the benefit of each Child who shall not have attained the age of Thirty Five (35) years, and to manage, administer, invest and reinvest the principal of such part, collect and receive the income and principal thereof, and pay over and distribute the income and principal as follows:

(1) Until the termination of the trust, the Trustee shall pay over to each Child who has reached the age of Eighteen (18) years all of the net income of such part, at convenient intervals but not less often than annually.

(2) Until the Child for whose benefit a part is held in trust attains the age of Thirty Five (35) years, the Trustee, at any time that they deem it advisable, may apply for the benefit of such Child, or pay over to such Child, so much, all or none of the principal of such Child's part, as the Trustee shall deem advisable to provide for such Child in accordance with the Standard For Payment, as defined elsewhere in this Trust Agreement.

(3) Upon any Child reaching the age of Twenty Five (25) years the Trustee shall distribute to that Child One-Third ($^1/_3$) of the remaining principal of that part. Upon any Child reaching the age of Thirty (30) years the Trustee shall distribute to that Child One-Half ($^1/_2$) of the remaining principal of that part. Upon any Child reaching the age of Thirty Five (35) years the Trustee shall distribute to that Child any remaining principal of that part, together with all undistributed income.

NOTE: The assumption is that if a child receives part (one-third) of the money free and clear at different intervals, rather than all at once, the child will have an opportunity to learn how to handle the assets. If the child becomes involved in a poor business venture, or an unsuccessful marriage, there will be future distributions. The ages can be any you feel comfortable with, but those illustrated above seem agreeable to many people setting up trusts.

---

3. Distribution to Single Children's Trust

Upon the death of SPOUSE NAME the remaining principal balance and any undistributed income, shall be distributed to Grantor's Trustee, in trust, for the use and benefit of Grantor's Children, to be held in a single trust of all of Grantor's Children then surviving and Children then deceased leaving surviving issue (the "Descendants"). The Trustee is hereby directed to manage, invest and reinvest the same, to collect the income thereof, and to pay over the net income to or for the benefit of such one or more of the Descendants living from time to time, to such extent, in such amount and proportions and at such time or times as the Trustee, shall determine. Any net income not so paid over or applied shall be accumulated, and added to the Trust Estate at least annually and thereafter shall be held, administered, and disposed of as a part of the Trust Estate. Upon the youngest of Grantor's Children then living reaching the age of DIVISION-AGE (_____) years, or upon the death of Grantor's youngest child living at any time if Grantor's other Children living shall all have then reached the age of DIVISION-AGE (_____) years, or upon the death of the last to die of all Grantor's Children if none of them shall reach the age of DIVISION-AGE (_____) years, whichever event is the first to occur, the Trust provided for under this Section shall terminate and the Trustee shall transfer, convey, and pay over the principal of the trust to Grantor's then living Descendants as provided in the preceding Section, Distribution by Age.

NOTE: Unlike the approach used when each child has his or her own trust, with a single trust for all of the children, monies may be kept in the trust until the youngest child reaches a certain age. If there is a big age disparity this approach can be unfair to the older children. However, if earlier distributions are to be made to the older children, the formula for determining distributions, especially when parents want overall distributions to be as equal as possible, becomes quite cumbersome.

---

4. Distribution Outright to Children and Issue of Deceased Child

a. Distribution to Children

Upon the death of the last of the Grantors the remaining principal balance and any undistributed income, shall be divided into as many equal parts as there are Children then surviving and Children then deceased leaving surviving issue. One such part shall be distributed outright and free of trust to each of Grantor's surviving Children, and one part in trust, as provided in the following section, to the issue of any deceased Child ("Descendants").

b. *Distribution to Issue of Deceased Child*

In the event that any of the Children predecease both Grantors, then upon the death of the last of the Grantors, the equal part for each deceased Child, as determined in the preceding Section, shall be distributed to the Trustee, to hold, in trust, and to apply as provided in this Section. In the event that more than one Child shall then be deceased, the Trustee shall maintain one separate trust for all of the Descendants of each such Child. The Trustee is hereby directed to manage, invest and reinvest the same, to collect the income thereof, and to pay over the net income to or for the benefit of such one or more of the Descendants living from time to time, to such extent, in such amount and proportions and at such time or times as the Trustee, shall determine. Any net income not so paid over or applied shall be accumulated, and added to the Trust Estate at least annually and thereafter shall be held, administrated, and disposed of as a part of the Trust Estate. Upon the youngest of such deceased Child's Descendants then living reaching the age of Twenty Five (25) years, or upon the death of the deceased Child's youngest Descendant living at any time if the deceased Child's other Descendants then living shall all have then reached the age of Twenty Five (25) years, or upon the death of the last to die of all the deceased Child's Descendants if none of them shall reach the age of Twenty Five (25) years, whichever event is the first to occur, the Trust provided for under this Section shall terminate and the Trustee shall transfer, convey, and pay over the principal of the trust to Grantor's then living Children as provided in the preceding Section.

5. *Alternate Distribution on Death of Beneficiary of Trust*

If any trust under the preceding Sections shall terminate as a result of the death of the Child who was the beneficiary of such trust prior to such beneficiary reaching age Thirty-Five (35) years, the Trustee shall transfer the Trust Estate of such trust, in equal parts per stirpes to that beneficiary's then living issue. If there are no living issue, then in equal parts per stirpes to the Grantor's then living issue. If any of Grantor's living issue is a beneficiary of a trust under the preceding Sections, then the amount such person is entitled to shall be added to the Trust Estate of that trust and shall be dealt with accordingly. If there are no living issue of the Grantor, then the Trustee shall divide the Trust Estate of that trust into the number of equal parts as there are parts in the following provisions, and transfer that Trust Estate to the following:

(1) One (1) parts to ALTERNATE ONE, who resides at ALTERNATE-1-ADDRESS, or such beneficiary's issue, per stirpes if such beneficiary is deceased.

(2) One (1) parts to ALTERNATE TWO, who resides at ALTERNATE-2-ADDRESS, or such beneficiary's issue, per stirpes if such beneficiary is deceased.

(3) One (1) parts to ALTERNATE THREE, who resides at ALTERNATE-3-ADDRESS, or such beneficiary's issue, per stirpes if such beneficiary is deceased.

NOTE: This is an alternate approach, which can be used as a safety net in the event that other distributions fail. The concept of dividing the total into parts can be much safer than using fixed dollar amounts because the value of the trust may be difficult to predict.

---

6. *Beneficiary Under Age Thirty Five*

a. If any individual under the age of Thirty Five (35) years, becomes entitled to any property under any Trust established under this Trust Agreement, or any property from any trust created hereunder upon the termination thereof, the share set aside for such person shall be held further in trust by the Trustee for the following uses and purposes: to manage, invest and reinvest the same, to collect the income thereof and, to distribute such principal and interest in accordance with the Distribution by Age provided for in the Section above.

b. If any tangible personal property shall at any time be held as part of such individual's trust, the Trustee shall have no duty to convert the same into productive property and the expenses of the safekeeping thereof, including insurance, shall be a proper charge against the assets of the trust.

c. If the Trustee shall determine at any time not to transfer in trust or not to continue to hold in trust any part or all of such property, they shall have full power and authority to transfer and pay over such property, or any part thereof, without bond, to such individual, if an adult under the law of the state of his or her domicile at the time of such payment, or to his or her parent, the guardian of his or her person or property, or to a custodian for such individual under any Uniform Gifts to Minors Act or Uniform Transfers to Minors Act, pursuant to which a custodian is acting or may be appointed, or to the person with whom such individual resides.

d. The receipt of such individual, if an adult, or the parent, guardian or custodian or any other person to whom any principal or income is transferred and paid over pursuant to any of the above provisions shall constitute a full discharge to the Trustee from all liability with respect to such transfer.

NOTE: It is common to include a provision in a trust stating that when distributions, for any reason, would be payable to a person under some specified age (25 or 35 are common), the trustee can hold the amounts in further trust.

---

7. *Distribution to Charity*

The Trustee shall distribute an amount equal to the lesser of _____ Dollars ($_____.00) to _____, or _____ percent (_____%) of the Trust Estate. The Trustee shall have full power and sole discretion to fund this gift wholly or partly in cash or kind, and to select the assets which shall constitute this gift. However, the Trustee shall determine the value all assets so selected, and assets comprising the Trust Estate.

NOTE: Many people like to leave some amount to charity. The percentage limitation is used when the contribution is more than a nominal amount because if the value of the trust fluctuates, the fixed charitable amount could excessively disturb other intended distributions (see Chapter 14).

For Your Notebook:

SAMPLE MISCELLANEOUS PROVISIONS

[DO NOT INCLUDE IN ANY TRUST
WITHOUT FIRST DISCUSSING WITH YOUR LAWYER]

I. *MISCELLANEOUS TRUST PROVISIONS*

A. *Third-Party Reliance*

No bank or trust company, corporation, partnership, association, firm, or other person dealing with the Trustee, or keeping any assets, whether funds, securities or other property of the Trust Estate, shall be required to investigate the authority of the Trustee for entering into any transaction involving assets of the Trust Estate. Nor shall such person be required to see to the application of the proceeds of any transaction with the Trustee, or to inquire into the appropriateness, validity, expediency or propriety thereof, or be under any obligation or liability whatsoever, except to the Trustee; and any such person, bank or trust company, corporation, partnership, association or firm shall be fully protected in making disposition of any assets of the Trust Estate in accordance with the directions of the Trustee.

NOTE: Banks, brokerage houses, and others will have to work with your trustees. A specific clause indemnifying them for relying on, and working with, your trustee may encourage their cooperation. However, if you know your trustee will have to work with certain institutions, discuss this in advance. Inquire about their requirements. They may wish to have a copy of the trust agreement on hand. They may request that specific language be added to your trust agreement. While a general indemnification provision can be helpful, nothing can substitute for careful advance planning.

B. *Further Assurances*

Grantor agrees to execute any documents reasonably necessary for the Trustee to implement such Trustee's duties under this Trust Agreement.

C. *Rule Against Perpetuities*

Notwithstanding any provisions of this instrument to the contrary:

1. If any Trust created under this Trust Agreement shall violate any applicable rule against perpetuities, accumulations or any similar rule or law, the Trustee is hereby directed to terminate such trust on the date limited by such rule or law, and thereupon the property held in any Trust under this Trust Agreement affected by this Section, shall be distributed to the persons then entitled to share the income from that property in the proportions in which they are then entitled to share such income.

2. No power of appointment granted under this Trust Agreement shall be so exercised so as to violate any such rule or law, and any attempted exercise of any such power which violates such rule or law shall be void.

NOTE: The rule against perpetuities is a technical legal provision that is designed to prevent trusts from lasting indefinitely. The above provision is intended to make any trust cease prior to the time at which it would violate this rule. The laws differ from state to state, so if you wish to have a trust last for an extended period of time (often more than 21 years after the death of certain key persons living at the time the trust was formed), consult an attorney specializing in estate planning. See the more detailed discussion of this rule in Chapter 23.

D. *Definitions*

The following terms when used in this Trust are defined as follows:

NOTE: It is often convenient to place all of the definitions in your trust in one location. This makes them easier to find and work with. The following are some commonly used terms in the trusts found throughout this book.

1. "Addition" means any cash or other assets transferred to the Trust after the date of the initial execution of this Trust Agreement, and which is to be held as part of the Trust Estate. The amount of any contribution is its federal gift tax value, as determined by the Trustee at the time of the transfer.

2. "Child" is an issue in the first degree.

3. "Children" is defined as CHILDREN-NAMES, and any children born or adopted after the execution of this Trust Agreement.

4. "Code" means the Internal Revenue Code of 1986, as amended. Any reference to any Code Section shall also include a reference to any successor statute of like import, and any regulations issued thereunder.

5. "Donee Property" is any net income of any Trust created under this Trust Agreement, and/or all, or any part, of the Trust Estate of any Trust created under this Trust Agreement, which is, or could become, distributable to a person under a disability.

6. "Income" and "Principal" are defined as follows. All cash dividends, other than those described hereafter, shall be income. All corporate distributions in shares of stock (whether denominated as dividends, stock splits or otherwise, and cash proceeds representing fractions thereof) of any class of any corporation (whether the corporation declaring or authorizing such distributions or otherwise) shall be principal. Dividends on investment company shares attributed to capital gains shall be principal whether declared payable at the option of the shareholders in cash or in shares or otherwise. Liquidating dividends, rights to subscribe to stock and the proceeds of the sale thereof, and the proceeds of unproductive or under-productive property shall be principal. There shall be no apportionment of the proceeds of the sale of any asset of the Trust Estate (whether real or personal, tangible or intangible) between principal and income because such asset may be or may have been wholly or partially unproductive of income during any period of time. Notwithstanding anything in this definition to the contrary, all income attributable to S corporation stock shall be distributed as required for the trust to retain its status as a qualified S corporation trust.

NOTE: It is important to define how income and other transactions should be characterized because different people may benefit depending on the definitions used. See the discussion in Chapter 20.

7. "In trust" is to manage, invest and reinvest the principal of a trust and to collect the income thereof.

8. "Issue" is a descendant in any degree, whether natural or adopted.

9. A "person under a disability" is a person who, for such period as the Trustee shall determine, is deemed by the Trustee to be physically or mentally incapable of managing such person's affairs. A judicial declaration is not required to be made with respect to such disability.

NOTE: This provision is intended to enable your trustees to prevent distribution of money or other trust assets to a beneficiary who is unable to handle the responsibility. This definition, and the definition of "donee property" above, work in conjunction with the trust provisions explained in Chapter 6 concerning the trustees' powers to defer distributions to such persons.

---

10. "Per stirpes" is a disposition of property whereby issue take a portion thereof in representation of their deceased parent, with division to be made into such number of equal shares at each succeeding degree of relationship from the common ancestor that there shall be one share for each person of such degree living at the time of such division and one share for the issue collectively then living of each person of such degree who is then deceased; such division to be made although there may not then be any person living within such degree.

NOTE: This concept can best be illustrated with an example. You have two children, John, who has one son, and Jane, who has two sons. One-half of your estate is to go to each child on your death. What happens if both of your children die first? If the deceased children's children (in tax jargon, issue) share equally in their deceased parents' shares, each grandchild would inherit one-third, then the distribution is per capita. If only Jane died, and her sons would each share in her 50 percent (one-half) share of the estate, they each would get 25 percent (one-quarter) each if the distribution is per-stirpes.

---

11. "State" means STATE NAME.

NOTE: You insert the name of the State where the trust is to be effective. This will almost always be the state where you reside. This definition ties into other provisions of your trust and helps to define which state's laws govern, and other matters.

---

12. "Trustee" is the trustee named in this Trust or appointed by a court or pursuant to the terms of this Trust and any and all successors, and may be masculine, feminine or neuter and singular or plural, as the sense requires.

13. "Trust Estate" is the property which Grantor assigns and transfers to the Trustee, the property described in Schedule "A," any Addition, any other property which the Grantor, the legal representatives of the Grantor's estate pursuant to the provisions of the Grantor's Last Will and Testament, or any other persons transfer to the Trustee, as well as the proceeds from the sale or investment of such property. The "Trust Estate" is the remaining principal of any Trust formed under this Trust Agreement, as then constituted, and upon the termination of any Trust any accrued and undistributed income.

E. *Construction*

1. *Governing Law*

The validity, construction and effect of the provisions of this Trust shall be governed by the laws of STATE NAME.

NOTE: This provision states which state law governs. This definition ties into the provision above where you define the state.

---

2. *Counterparts*

This Trust Agreement may be executed in more than one counterpart, each of which is an original, but all taken together shall be deemed one and the same instrument.

NOTE: This is a practical provision that permits the trustees and the grantor to sign different copies of the trust and still have the trust become effective. This should only be used in extreme emergencies, since banks and others your trustee will have to deal with won't like not seeing all signatures on the same document.

---

3. *Captions*

Captions, Section numbers and headings have been inserted for convenience only and such shall not be construed to affect the interpretation of any provision of this Agreement or to limit or broaden the terms of any provision.

NOTE: Many lawyers want to avoid titles fearing that in a lawsuit, the courts may be influenced by what the abbreviated terms in the captions say. The problem is that the trusts then will be organized by section number or article number only and will be very difficult to read. An alternate approach is simply to say that the captions used are for convenience but should not affect the meaning of any provision.

F. *Binding Agreement*

This Trust Agreement shall extend to and be binding upon the executors, administrators, heirs, successors and assigns of the Grantor and the Trustee.

G. *Partial Invalidity*

Any provision of this Trust Agreement prohibited by law shall be ineffective to the extent of such prohibition without invalidating the rest of this Trust Agreement which shall be interpreted to conform, to the extent permitted by law, with the original intent of the Grantor.

NOTE: If any provision in your trust is held to be improper, you probably will want the rest of the trust, to the extent possible, to remain intact.

Part Two

UNDERSTANDING THE TAX CONSEQUENCES OF A TYPICAL TRUST

8 PLANNING FOR THE GIFT AND ESTATE TAX

Trusts are a valuable tool for achieving a number of goals. Minimizing taxes is only one of these goals. Thus, even if your estate is not large enough for you to be concerned about gift and estate taxes (over $600,000 of assets for federal estate taxes, but much lower for some state estate taxes), trusts can be of important use, and Parts Three and Four of this book detail many of the nontax applications. For many people, however, the estate tax planning advantages that can be achieved through the use of trusts are vitally important. But the emphasis is on *planning*. When tax benefits are to be gained from transfers to a trust, the trust will almost always be irrevocable. This means that you will have to plan carefully for the gift and estate tax implications, because you will not have the right to change or revoke the trust.

THE GIFT TAX EXCLUSION

It is common knowledge that anyone can give away up to $10,000 in any tax year, to any person, without incurring a gift tax. Many transfers qualifying for the annual $10,000 gift tax exclusion also avoid the generation-skipping transfer tax, which is discussed in the next chapter. You can make this type of gift to as many people as you want during each year. It's an *annual* tax exclusion, so you can give away $10,000 to the same person every year (or to as many other people as you wish)—tax free.

NOTE: Few people realize the tremendous benefits that can be achieved in reducing the size of their taxable estate with a regular program of $10,000 tax-free gifts to their children and heirs. Too frequently, people buy large insurance policies or take other expensive, drastic, or unnecessary steps to deal with an estate tax cost when a simple program of giving assets, either directly or to trusts, can suffice.

The following example illustrates the tax results of a gift program by a couple for their joint life expectancy.

EXAMPLE: If you and your spouse have four children, each of whom are married, and if the two of you survive for 42 more years, you can give away nearly $7 million

---

in gifts, not counting the income earned on those gifts. If you count the income the gifts can earn after you've given them to trusts for the benefit of your children (and their spouses), the amount given would total more than $22 million.

VALUE OF ANNUAL GIFT PROGRAM
OF A COUPLE TO THEIR FOUR MARRIED CHILDREN

ESTATE TAX ADVANTAGE OF GIFT TAX EXCLUSION	
Donor's Age	40 Years
Donees' Annual After-tax Return on Gifts	0.050
Amount of Unused Annual Exclusion	$20,000
Number of Donees	8
Donor's Life Expectancy	42.5 Years
Total Amount of Gifts	$6,800,000
Donor's Projected Estate Tax Bracket	0.500
Potential Estate Tax Savings	$3,400,000
Projected Value of Gifts at Life Expectancy	$22,250,434
Potential Estate Tax Savings if Annual Gifts were Invested by Donees at Compound Interest	$11,125,217

Chart prepared using *Estate Planning Tools* software copyright Commerce Clearing House, Inc., Chicago, IL.

Gift Splitting

A basic, but important technique in estate planning is gift splitting. This enables either you or your spouse to make a gift and have the other spouse join in the gift; in other words, you can effectively double the gift. Gift splitting enables one of you to make a transfer of up to $20,000 to each person, with the gift deemed to be made one-half by each spouse. Each spouse's $10,000 annual exclusion is applied to eliminate any tax on the gift. The requirements to qualify for this valuable benefit include the following:

- You must be married.
- Both you and your spouse must be citizens or residents of the United States.
- The spouse making the gift must not remarry during the remainder of the year.
- Both of you must agree to this tax treatment for the particular gift, and for all gifts made by either of you while married during the calendar year.

Gifts to a Trust Can Cause You to Exceed the $10,000 Exclusion

It's important to note that when a gift is made to a trust, the beneficiaries of the trust, and not the trust, are considered to be the recipients.

EXAMPLE: You pay $20,000 to an insurance trust that purchases insurance on your life. Your two children are the beneficiaries. You can't, then, make direct gifts of $10,000 to each of your children and expect these to qualify for the annual exclusion as well. You will have given more than the maximum $10,000 to each child in that year. The fact that one gift is direct and the other indirect, through a trust, is not considered relevant.

The point here is that you can't expect to make yearly gifts both to a trust and directly for the benefit of the same person and qualify for the gift tax exclusion unless the combined total of the gifts is no more than $10,000 in any one year. In all cases consult your accountant concerning any requirements to file a gift tax return.

The Gift Must Be of a Present Interest

There is an important stipulation attached to the gift tax exclusion: It is only available for gifts of a present interest. This is an important technical term that should be carefully reviewed with your estate planner. The basic concept is that the recipient of the gift must have the use of and access to the gift. This means that direct gifts always qualify because the recipients have immediate use of the gift. But any gift to a trust of a remainder interest is characterized as a future interest and won't qualify for the annual exclusion. This can be illustrated by a simple example.

EXAMPLE: You transfer assets worth $50,000 as a gift to a trust for the benefit of your children and family members. If the children and other family members can't use or benefit from the gift until the money is distributed at some unknown future date (perhaps in the sole discretion of an independent trustee), the transfer may not qualify as a gift of a present interest. If this happens, you will have to pay a gift tax on the $50,000 value, or use up a portion of your remaining unified credit. Had you transferred the assets directly to the five beneficiaries, the gift would have qualified for the annual exclusion, and you would have avoided paying a gift tax or using up any of your unified credit.

As a general rule, a gift made in trust *will not* qualify for the annual gift tax exclusion unless it can be shown to be a gift of a present interest. There are three criteria for determining when a transfer to a trust does qualify as a gift of a present interest: (1) The trust must generate an income flow. (2) Some portion of the income must go to the trust beneficiaries. (3) The amount of income the beneficiaries will receive must be ascertainable.

There are exceptions and planning possibilities. A gift to a special trust for the benefit of a minor child, which meets certain requirements, can qualify for the exclusion (see Chapter 13). The other alternative is to use a Crummey demand power. This power is named after the tax case in which the court sustained the taxpayer's argument that when the beneficiary had an opportunity to withdraw the funds currently but did not elect to do so, a gift to a trust qualified as a gift of a present interest. (There is more about the Crummey power in Chapter 13.)

The Gift Must Be Complete

There are rules regarding the effective date (completion) of a gift and these rules vary for different assets. The general concept, however, is that you must part with sufficient control over the assets so that the gift is complete and you cannot retract it; the gift must be beyond your recall. When possible, you should complete every technicality required to consummate the gift (as in signed, sealed, and delivered) prior to the year's end. This can raise issues when the gift is made to a trust over which you have substantial control. If you are a trustee or have reserved significant powers, such as the right to appoint the principal of the trust, either for yourself or for any person who is not adverse to you (see Chapter 4), so that the property could revert back to you, the gift won't be considered complete.

NOTE: Incomplete gifts may be used as an intentional planning technique when setting up Medicaid-qualifying trusts. The idea is to transfer assets up to the point where they are not considered yours for local law purposes, which can put the assets out of the reach of creditors. At the same time, you retain just enough power over the trust so that the transfer of assets is considered incomplete for gift tax purposes, which enables you to avoid any gift tax on the transfer (see Chapter 17).

Which Property Should Be Gifted to a Trust?

Part Three of this book explores the use of trusts to protect and hold different types of assets. Insurance is an ideal asset to place in a trust designed to contain it, especially when the insurance has little current value and no loans outstanding (see Chapter 18). Gifts of stock in an S corporation raise special issues; if these are not properly addressed in your trust, the S corporation could lose its favorable tax status (see Chapter 19).

THE ESTATE TAX EXCLUSION

The estate tax is a transfer charge assessed on property owned by you on your death. However, you can give away up to $600,000 of this property, above the annual $10,000 amounts, as a once-in-a-lifetime exclusion. There are a number of other deductions to complicate matters (like the unlimited marital deduction). With estate tax rates as high as 55 percent (60 percent when certain phase-outs are in effect), planning to minimize the burden is essential if you want to pass on the maximum amount of assets to your heirs. When the trusts you use are revocable, the entire amount of assets included in the trust will almost always be included in your estate. Even irrevocable trusts can create estate tax problems for you. When you have a right to distribute income or hold any of the other prohibited powers (see the discussion in Chapter 4), all of the assets in an irrevocable trust still can be taxed in your estate.

A few basic concepts concerning the estate tax and the $600,000 unified credit are necessary to understand in order to discuss several of the common trusts. In addition to the so called unified credit which permits everyone to give away up to $600,000 of assets with no tax cost, married persons are generally entitled to give their spouse, by gift during their life, or at death under their will or a trust, an unlimited amount of money with no estate tax cost. This benefit is called the unlimited marital deduction.

The unlimited marital deduction can sometimes lull taxpayers into taking the wrong action. Since you can give an unlimited amount to your surviving spouse without tax, each spouse can simply complete a will leaving everything to the surviving spouse. By virtue of the unlimited marital deduction, there will not be any tax due on the death of the first spouse. However, on the death of the second spouse, any assets above the second spouse's $600,000 unified credit will be taxed. In effect, the $600,000 unified credit of the first spouse has been wasted. It was wasted because the assets were simply given to the surviving spouse. The solution to this dilemma could be to leave the assets to the children or another beneficiary. This approach, however, is seldom used. This is because each spouse wants to assure the maximum protection of the surviving spouse. The answer is the use of what is called a credit shelter trust. On the death of the first spouse, up to $600,000 of assets (i.e., the amount of the first spouse's unified credit) is placed in a special trust called a credit shelter, because the assets in the trust are sheltered from estate tax by the unified credit. The surviving spouse will receive the broadest income and principal distributions possible without causing the assets of the trust to be included in his or her estate.

This planning is not important for a single person since he or she will automatically use up his or her unified credit since no gift or other transfer could be treated as qualifying as a marital deduction (gifts to surviving spouse don't use up any of your unified credit of $600,000 since they don't create a tax). It is most critical to plan for with a married couple. Each of the people comprising the couple is entitled to a $600,000 credit. However, if all assets are in one spouses name, the second spouse's credit of $600,000 will be wasted because he or she has no assets to give.

What's Included in Your Gross Estate?

The first step in planning for the estate tax is to identify all property and interests that are included in your gross estate. Generally, your gross estate includes all property, whether real estate, personal property, or intangible property, to the extent that the estate tax rules require this property to be included in your estate. Assets in your gross estate also include any interest that you had in property at the time of your death that is included in your probate estate. For example, a bonus you were entitled to at the time of your death is included in your gross estate.

NOTE: Don't confuse taxable estate with probate estate. "Taxable estate" means assets that will be subject to estate tax on your death. "Probate estate" refers to assets that must pass through the probate process on your death. Thus, if you set up a revocable living trust and transfer all of your assets to the trust, your probate estate may be nonexistent. However, your taxable estate may be substantial, since it will include all assets in your trust.

Property interests to be included in your estate are very broadly defined. Even property that you gave away during your life can be required to be included in your gross estate, depending on the conditions of the gift. For example, if you transferred assets but retained the right to the income, these assets could be brought back into your gross estate. If you transferred property to another person, but this person could only obtain the right to use that property after your death, the entire value of this life estate property would be included in your estate. If you transferred property but reserved the right to change who would receive that property, this condition would result in the property's being included in your estate. If you had a general power of appointment over property (you could designate who would get the property and the recipient could include your estate or creditors), the value of that property would be included in your gross estate.

Valuation of the Property

Once the assets to be included in your taxable estate are identified, they must be valued. The sum of all properties you own, after reduction for certain expenses and other allowable adjustments, will be the base on which your estate's tax is calculated.

The criterion to be used in determining the worth of your gross estate is called the "fair market value." This is the price at which the property would change hands between a willing buyer and a willing seller, with neither being under any compulsion to buy or to sell, and with both having reasonable knowledge of the relevant facts. When a stock traded on a public exchange is included in your estate, the value is easily found in any major newspaper. For assets like real estate and closely held business interests, valuation can be a substantial point of contention between your estate and the IRS.

Your estate is allowed deductions for funeral expenses, estate administrative expenses, claims against your estate, debts relating to any property included in your gross estate, charitable bequests, which can include the value of assets in a charitable trust, and qualifying bequests to your surviving spouse such as Q-TIP and Q-DOT trusts (see Chapter 11).

Calculating the Estate Tax

The federal estate tax is calculated as follows: A tentative tax is calculated on the sum of your taxable estate, as determined above, increased by your adjusted taxable gifts made after 1976. This does not include most gifts made using the annual $10,000 exclusion. These are gifts made in most prior years on which you incurred a gift tax. The idea is that since a single tax structure is used for estate and gift tax purposes, all taxable transfers, whether made during your life or after your death, should be added and subjected to the same graduated tax rate schedule. There is no double taxation of the gifts, however, because a credit is provided for gift tax already paid on those amounts. Gifts included in this tentative tax calculation are based on their fair market value when the gifts were made. This tentative tax amount is then reduced by the gift taxes that would be payable on your gifts made after 1976. There are a number of credits that may also be applied to reduce your estate tax, including a credit for prior transfers, a credit for death taxes paid to your estate, and so forth.

CONCLUSION

The gift and estate taxes are complex and broad transfer taxes that can substantially affect the type and nature of trusts that you may choose to use. A properly planned gift and estate tax program is an essential step for any larger estate. The judicious use of annual exclusions, with particular attention to the problems created by gifts to trusts, can enable you to transfer substantial assets out of your estate at little or no tax cost. The careful planning of assets transferred to an irrevocable trust, using the proper restriction of the rights and powers that you retain, can provide outstanding opportunities for reducing your potential estate tax while still providing you with some comfort regarding the disposition of those assets. Considering the complexities and the substantial sums usually involved, always review gift and estate tax issues with your tax adviser, when setting-up any trust.

9 PLANNING FOR THE GENERATION-SKIPPING TRANSFER TAX

So few people are affected by the generation-skipping transfer tax (called GST tax) that a preliminary discussion of who can safely ignore the GST tax is provided before going into detail about the subject. This will enable most readers to skip the remainder of this chapter and proceed to "The Living Trust" (Chapter 10). For those who *are* affected by the GST, the planning will focus on the use of trusts. This is because the gifts that could trigger the GST are generally to young children, who are in no position to oversee their assets. Further, the nature of the GST tax is such that it is often advantageous to make the gifts in trust.

WHO DOESN'T NEED TO WORRY ABOUT THE GST TAX

The generation-skipping transfer tax, or GST tax, is an expensive and complicated tax that will affect very wealthy people only. Unless your assets are in the millions (not merely hundreds of thousands), the GST will not be relevant to you for the following reasons:

- The GST tax only applies to transfers that skip a generation, such as to your grandchildren. Most people prefer to give their assets to their children, and to entrust their children with the responsibility of caring and providing for their grandchildren.
- You can give up to $10,000 per year to any person, including every grandchild, without triggering the GST tax. If your spouse joins you in the gift, you can give $20,000 per donee. Thus, over a period of years, you can transfer substantial assets to your grandchildren with no tax cost whatever.
- If all of the above still is not enough, you can give away an additional $1 million to your grandchildren with no GST tax cost. Your spouse similarly can join in making a $1 million gift to the grandchildren for a total of $2 million.

EXAMPLE: You have four children, and nine grandchildren. You and your spouse set up trusts for each of your grandchildren. You jointly give $20,000 per year to each grandchild's trust. This amounts to $180,000 per year. Over a 10-year period (not even counting the earnings, which would have made the trust balances grow substantially), you will have given away $1.8 million to your grandchildren. This, of course, is in addition to any amounts you could have given to each of your children and their spouses (which could have amounted to an additional $1.6 million over the same 10 years). Finally, each of your wills provides for a $1 million GST-exempt trust (explained below). Thus, over a 10-year period, you have transferred $3.8 million to trusts for your grandchildren.

If the basic estate planning ideas discussed in *The Estate Planning Guide* (John Wiley & Sons, Inc., 1991) are used in making gifts to the trusts for your grandchildren, the amounts transferred can be increased substantially over what the above example indicates. For example, if stock in a closely held business rather than cash is given to the grandchildren's trusts, the gifts may qualify for a minority discount, which can enable the transfer of more economic value than the equivalent cash amount.

CAUTION: Exercise great care in undertaking gifts of minority interests in businesses. Be certain to obtain a proper appraisal, and have your tax adviser review the various gift tax valuation rules, including some complex rules under Chapter 14 of the Internal Revenue Code.

It's safe to say that most people need never worry about the GST, and of those who should plan for it, a modicum of planning can enable them to transfer substantial amounts to their grandchildren without any GST tax.

WHAT IS THE GST TAX AND HOW DOES IT WORK?

The purpose of the GST tax is to equalize intergenerational taxation of property transfers when planning is attempted to avoid the estate tax. The GST tax is charged on every gift or other transfer of property that can be classified as a generation-skipping transfer. The GST tax is calculated as a flat 55 percent tax rate on the taxable amount of a generation-skipping transfer.

EXAMPLE: A grandmother wants to give her grandchild a $1 million gift (this can be cash, an interest in a property, or another asset). Assuming she has used up her $1 million lifetime exemption, the GST tax is in the maximum tax brackets, $550,000! Further, if the GST tax is paid, the amount of GST tax is itself subject to tax! The tax laws treat the amount of GST tax paid as another gift to the grandchild. So the gift tax to be paid on the $1 million transfer is based on a total gift of $1,550,000 [$1 million actual gift + $550,000 GST tax, which is deemed to be a further gift]. At the 55 percent maximum gift tax rate, the grandmother will owe a gift tax of $852,500. To make the $1 million gift she will have had to pay taxes totalling $1,402,500 [$550,000 GST tax + $852,500 gift tax]. Thus, the total cost of making the $1 million gift will be $2,402,500!

What Triggers a GST Tax?

The GST tax can apply to a broad range of property transfers, including transfers of (1) property in trust (for example, a gift to a trust established for a grandchild, (2) life estates (for example, a child has the right to income from the property for life and on the child's death a grandchild receives the property), (3) remainder interests (for example, a grandchild receives the property after the death of a child and the termination of the child's life estate), and more.

For the GST tax to apply, a taxable event must occur, meaning a generation-skipping transfer must be made.

EXAMPLE: You're generation #1. Your child is in generation #2. Your grandchild is generation #3. Assume that your spouse sets-up an irrevocable trust for one of your grandchildren and makes a gift to the trust of $45,000 of stock. This gift would use up part of your spouse's remaining $1 million GST exemption (or if it was already used up cause a GST tax). This is because the gift is for the benefit of a member of a generation at least two generations below your generation. A gift from your spouse to your child of the same amount would not cause the GST tax to apply (but there could be a gift tax).

There are three events that can be classified as such a transfer: a direct skip, a taxable distribution, and a taxable termination.

- *Taxable Transfer #1—A Direct Skip.* A "direct skip" is a transfer that is made to a skip person. A "skip person" is someone two or more generations below the generation of the person making the gift. (This can be either your grandchild or a trust for the benefit of your grandchild.) A trust is also considered a skip person when no distributions can be made to nonskip persons. A "nonskip person" is someone less than two generations below the generation of the person making the gift. This can be your child or sibling, for example. When your child has died and a grandchild survives, your grandchild may not be considered a skip person, so that a transfer to your grandchild won't trigger the GST tax.

  A direct skip, then, is a transfer to a skip person of an interest in property that is subject to the estate or gift tax. The GST tax for a direct skip is to be paid by the person making the transfer (probably you).

PLANNING TIP: If you transfer property to an irrevocable trust for your grandchild, but you retain sufficient powers over the trust, or alternatively give sufficient powers to your children over the trust so that the trust will be taxable in their estates, the GST tax won't apply. If you transfer assets to a revocable trust, the gift will be incomplete for gift tax purposes and no GST tax can apply. These are two additional planning techniques for accomplishing personal goals while avoiding the GST tax. They are, again, (1) retaining powers over the trust or having the trust be revocable; or (2) giving your child (a nonskip person) sufficient powers over a trust.

Once it's been determined that a gift is subject to the GST, the GST tax must be calculated. For tax purposes, the property is generally valued at the time the generation-skipping transfer occurred. However, if the transfer was a direct skip and the property was included in your gross estate, the special valuation rules your estate uses will apply to the GST as well. Where the transfer also triggers a gift tax, the amount of GST tax paid by the donor is treated as a further gift subject to the gift tax. Once the tax has been calculated, a credit for taxes paid to your state may be available. This will occur where the GST tax transfer occurs by reason of a taxable distribution or a taxable termination at the time of your death. You're also entitled to a $1 million exemption, discussed below.

- *Taxable Transfer #2—A Taxable Distribution.* When there is a distribution of property or money from a trust to a skip person, the GST tax may apply.

EXAMPLE: Your spouse sets up a *single* trust for the benefit of your two daughters and their three children (your grandchildren). Any distribution by the trustee to any of your grandchildren will result in a GST tax. The grandchildren are all considered skip persons for purposes of the GST tax since they are two generations below you, the grantor of the trust.

PLANNING TIP: The result in the above example is not always bad, and your planning may encourage you to set up trusts for your children that can make taxable distributions to your grandchildren. This could occur when you've used up your $1 million exemption. If you set up a trust solely for the benefit of your grandchildren, the transfer would immediately trigger the GST tax. Since this tax is so onerous, it's always best to defer it; this will let the assets in the trust continue to grow and earn interest. If the trust names both your children and grandchildren as beneficiaries, and the trustee has the power to sprinkle income to any of these beneficiaries, the GST tax can be deferred until the trustee actually makes a distribution to one of the grandchildren (this is called a sprinkle trust). If you've set up a GST-exempt trust (see below) to use your $1 million GST exemption amount, your trustee could be making generous distributions to your grandchildren from that trust before tapping the expensive (from a GST tax perspective) money in the sprinkle trust described above.

The GST tax on a taxable distribution is charged against the property which was given, unless specific provisions are made for a different treatment. The tax is based on the fair value of the property transferred, reduced by any expenses incurred in connection with determining the GST tax. If the GST tax is paid out of a trust, the amount of tax paid is treated as an additional distribution subject to the tax. The transferee (your grandchild in the above examples), however, is liable to pay the GST tax.

- *Taxable Transfer #3—A Taxable Termination.* This occurs when the interests of a beneficiary of a trust (the person entitled to receive income from a trust, such as a child) terminate as a result of a death, lapse of time, or release of a power. This event will be considered a taxable termination resulting in a GST tax unless one of the following takes place: (1) Immediately after the termination, a nonskip person has an interest in the property; or (2) no distribution can be made to a skip person. The GST Tax on a taxable termination is payable by the trustee of the trust. The amount of tax is calculated based on the value of all property to which the taxable termination related, reduced by expenses, debts and taxes.

Ways to Minimize the Harsh Effects of the GST Tax

There are a number of planning techniques that can help you avoid the confiscatory GST tax:

- *Use of the Annual Gift Tax Exclusion.* As explained in the previous chapter, you can give up to $10,000 of assets ($20,000 if a spouse joins in the gift) in any given year to any recipient without triggering a gift tax. Many transfers that are exempt under this $10,000/$20,000 rule also avoid the GST tax. When a husband and wife elect to split their gift, the GST is deemed to have been made one-half by each. Over a number of years, this can result in a substantial transfer without incurring either gift or GST tax.

  The limitation of this technique is that the requirements for the GST are different from those applicable to the gift tax, so that some transfers that qualify for the annual $10,000 gift tax exclusion will not qualify for the GST tax exclusion. The $10,000 annual exclusion is only available for GST tax purposes on a direct-skip transfer (a direct gift to a grandchild or later generation, or to a trust for a grandchild). It doesn't apply to a taxable termination or a taxable distribution.

EXAMPLE: Grandmother has one child, a divorced daughter, with two children. Grandmother gives $30,000 of corporate bonds to a trust for the benefit of her daughter and two grandchildren. She may have a GST problem depending on the terms of trust. If the grandmother transfers $30,000 to the trust, each beneficiary should have a Crummey demand power in order for Grandmother to qualify for the annual gift tax exclusion on the entire transfer (see the previous chapter). After the demand power lapses (which occurs if the beneficiaries don't use it), the trustee can make distributions to the daughter and grandchildren, free of a gift tax. But if the trustee has a sprinkling power between generations, there is a potential GST tax problem.

Even without such a power, if distributions will skip a generation when the interest of the middle generation (the daughter) terminates (for example, upon the daughter's death, or upon her reaching age 35, when the trust instrument requires a distribution to the grandchildren), a GST tax will be triggered. A better approach to avoid technical tax problems would be to have a separate trust for each beneficiary. The trusts for each of the grandchildren then can use the trust provisions discussed in Chapter 13 for minors instead of the Crummey power.

- *Transfers for Educational and Medical Benefits.* This is a nontrust approach. You can gift unlimited amounts of money to pay for a grandchild's education or medical benefits. (A drawback is that this approach will not help you transfer investment property or properties or business assets to future generations.) A simple technique is for a grandparent with a substantial estate to set up a checking account. All children and grandchildren send any qualifying medical and tuition bills directly to the grandparent, who pays them directly. With a large family, considering the high cost of quality medical care and education, tremendous amounts can be transferred for the benefit of later generations with no GST tax implications. This technique should be considered and carefully reviewed before you incur the expense, and problems, of setting up grandchildren's trusts.

- *Use of the Million-Dollar Exemption.* A once-in-a-lifetime exemption is allowed that will permit you to transfer up to $1 million of property or other assets to grandchildren without triggering a GST tax. This $1 million exemption can be allocated by you or your executor. Many taxpayers plan for this exemption by setting up multiple trusts under their wills and granting their executors the authority to make certain decisions. This provides the maximum amount of planning flexibility. An expanded discussion of planning for this exemption appears below.

- *Certain Other Transfers.* Transfers that meet the following three requirements are also excluded: (1) The property transferred was subject to the GST tax before; (2) the transferee (recipient) in that prior transfer was a member of the same generation as the current transferee; and (3) the transfer does not have the effect of avoiding the GST tax.

ALLOCATING YOUR $1 MILLION GST TAX EXEMPTION

Every person is entitled to a once-in-a-lifetime $1 million exclusion from the GST tax. This exclusion must be irrevocably allocated to any property transfers you make. This allocation is generally made on your gift tax return, and the allocation method used can't be changed.

To understand the use of the $1 million exemption, another bit of jargon must be introduced, the "inclusion ratio." The GST tax exemption percentage, or inclusion ratio, is set when you make the gift and allocate your exemption. The inclusion ratio is: [1 − the applicable fraction]. The applicable fraction, when you make the gift to a trust, is determined as follows:

$$\frac{\text{Amount of GST Exemption Allocated to Trust}}{\text{Value of Property Transferred to the Trust}}$$

EXAMPLE: You set up a $1 million trust fund for your grandchildren and great-grandchildren. You allocate your entire $1 million GST tax exemption to the trust. The assets of the trust appreciate to $10 million before being distributed in a taxable distribution or termination. None of the transfers of the $10 million in trust property to your children and grandchildren is subject to the GST tax. This is because the applicable fraction is 1 [$1 million GST exemption ÷ $1 million property value], and the inclusion ratio is zero.

One approach to addressing the potential GST tax problem is to allocate some portion of the $1 million GST tax exemption to a trust. The problem is, how much should be allocated? Any portion of your GST tax exemption allocated to a trust is considered used, whether or not a GST tax is ever incurred. So, if you make the allocation, and no tax is incurred, you've wasted that portion of your exemption. If the trust in the above example declined to $600,000, rather than growing to $10 million, you would have wasted $400,000 of your exemption. The only course is to analyze all the relevant factors and estimate the likelihood of the trust's incurring a GST tax. If it appears likely, you should wager some of your exemption on the trust. If not, you should preserve your GST tax exemption for other planning opportunities.

EXAMPLE: Grandpa has one son, who has two children. He transfers $100,000 in trust with income to his son for life and the remainder to the two grandchildren on the son's death. Assume that Grandpa doesn't allocate any of his GST tax exemption on the gift tax return. When the son dies, the trust property is worth $500,000. The inclusion ratio is 100 percent. The IRS will collect a $275,000 tax at the flat 55 percent rate.

Assume a different scenario: Grandpa allocates $100,000 of his $1 million GST tax exemption against the $100,000 transfer to the trust when he makes the gift. Now the inclusion ratio is zero, and the entire $500,000 passes free of the onerous GST tax.

Under a third scenario, if Grandpa makes the same gift but allocates $50,000 of his exemption against the transfer, the inclusion ratio will be 50 percent. On the death of the son, the GST tax will be $137,500.

PLANNING FOR THE GST TAX THROUGH THE USE OF TRUSTS

Three Approaches

- One approach is to set up a GST tax-exemption trust. This is a trust designed to use your $1 million GST tax exemption. If this trust is structured as a Qualified Terminal Interest Property ("Q-TIP") trust, it will provide your surviving spouse with the right to receive all of the income, at least annually, and a limited right to invade principal for his or her benefit. However, any invasion of principal will reduce (and perhaps waste) the maximum GST tax exemption. In a very large estate it is preferable not to invade the principal unless absolutely necessary in order to preserve your full $1 million exemption. A sample provision to accomplish this GST-exempt Q-TIP trust is illustrated in the "For Your Notebook" section of this chapter.

- Another approach is to provide for the establishment of two GST tax trusts. The first trust will be equal to the amount of the unused unified credit (that is, a credit shelter trust for $600,000 if no unified credit is used prior to death). The executor then allocates $600,000 of the GST exemption to this trust without triggering any estate tax because of the unified credit. A second trust can be provided under the will to absorb the remaining, or excess, GST exemption amount (most likely $400,000 left of the $1 million exemption). This will be a Q-TIP trust, which will avoid any estate tax because of the unlimited marital deduction.

- A third approach is to establish two GST tax trusts, one wholly exempt, and one wholly nonexempt. Distributions to children can be made from the nonexempt trust so that none of the GST exemption amount will be wasted (gifts to the children will not trigger any GST tax since they are not a skip generation). This preserves the maximum GST tax-free amount for the later distribution to the grandchildren.

When planning for the GST tax, your attorney should also consider the tax allocation clause in your will or trust. Taxes should be paid out of a portion of the residuary (or other bequests), which won't result in wasting any of your GST tax exemption.

Sample Approaches for the Married and the Not (or No Longer) Married

The following examples illustrate several uses of trusts to plan for the GST tax, depending on your marital status.

EXAMPLE: You are a married person, and your GST $1 million exemption is going to be allocated by your trustee (or executor if the transfer is made under your will). It first can be allocated to each spouse's credit shelter or bypass trust (approximately $600,000). The trust will have an inclusion ratio of zero and will not trigger any GST. This means that the entire trust is GST-exempt since all of the assets transferred to it are covered by the GST exclusion. Securities most likely to appreciate should be allocated to this trust since it will not be included in the estate of the second spouse to die.

If neither estate is significantly larger than the maximum $1 million GST exemption each spouse is entitled to use, only one additional trust will need to be set up—a Q-TIP trust to which the remainder of the GST is allocated (approximately $400,000). Any remaining assets (above the $600,000 GST exemption used by the credit shelter trust and the $400,000 used in the Q-TIP/GST trust) are distributed outright to the spouse. This plan can avoid any GST tax, take maximum advantage of the $600,000 estate tax credit, and provide for the surviving spouse.

EXAMPLE: When you aren't married or there is no surviving spouse, the plan is somewhat different. There is no need for a Q-TIP or credit shelter trust because there is no spouse to provide for and no other estate qualifying for the unlimited marital deduction. Thus, your residuary estate (which is the entire estate after costs and taxes, and any specific distributions) can be dealt with in different ways, depending on the facts.

Assume you are a widow, who is survived by several children. One approach is to put the remaining estate into a trust. All of the income from the trust can be distributed to your children and the remaining assets eventually can be distributed to your grandchildren. This trust can be divided into two parts—one exempt from GST and one not. Distributions of income to the children during their lifetimes will be made out of the portion that is not exempt from GST as long as possible, so as to preserve the maximum GST tax-free portion for the grandchildren.

CONCLUSION

The GST tax affects very few people. However, if it can affect you, it is important to carefully plan any trust transaction in order to avoid, or at least defer or minimize, the GST tax impact. With proper planning, substantial assets often can be transferred with no GST tax burden.

For Your Notebook:

SAMPLE GST TRUST PROVISIONS

[THESE GST TRUST PROVISIONS ARE FOR ILLUSTRATION ONLY AND SHOULD NOT BE INCLUDED IN ANY WILL UNTIL THEY HAVE BEEN REVIEWED WITH YOUR TAX AND ESTATE PLANNING ADVISERS]

ILLUSTRATIVE GST PROVISIONS

PAYMENT OF TAX CLAUSE

Taxes shall first be paid out of the property, if any, transferred to my spouse, under ARTICLE FIFTH, outright and free of trust. Should such assets be insufficient, then taxes shall be paid from the other assets passing under ARTICLE FIFTH. The following taxes are excluded from this provision: taxes on the qualified terminable interest property included in my gross estate through the application of Code Section 2044 and taxes on any generation skipping transfer ("GST") which shall be charged against the property generating such tax as provided in Code Section 2603(b). In the event of any GST tax, such tax shall first be paid out of the GST-Exempt Q-TIP property, to the extent possible, prior to making payment of such tax out of the Unified Credit Shelter GST Exempt Sprinkle Trust.

RESIDUARY INCLUDING Q-TIP TRUST FOR SPOUSE

If my spouse survives me, all the rest, residue and remainder of my property, wherever situated, and all property which I shall be entitled to dispose of at my death after deducting all my debts, funeral expenses and any expenses of the administration of my estate (my "residuary estate") shall be disposed of as follows:

A. Provision for the payment of any death or similar taxes, as required under this Will shall be made.

B. Provision for Credit Shelter Trust provided in ARTICLE SIXTH, below shall be made.

C. My Executor shall divide the portion of my residuary estate governed by this ARTICLE FIFTH into Two (2) separate parts.

1. For the first such part, my Executor shall set apart a fractional share of my residuary estate governed by this ARTICLE FIFTH (the "GST-Exempt Q-TIP") which shall be determined with reference to the amount (if any) of my remaining GST exemption (within the meaning of Code Section 2631) that has not been allocated by me or my Executor to any other property during my lifetime or after my death, including but not limited to the amount of my GST exemption allocated to the Credit Shelter Trust provided for in ARTICLE SIXTH. I direct that the GST-Exempt Q-TIP shall be the largest fractional share of my residuary estate governed by this ARTICLE FIFTH that, given the amount of my GST exemption so allocated, will result in an applicable fraction of One (1) and an inclusion rate of Zero (-0-) (within the meaning of Code Section 2642) for all property comprised in the GST-Exempt Q-TIP. No descendant of mine who is an executor shall participate in the allocation of my GST exemption.

2. The remainder of my residuary estate governed by this ARTICLE FIFTH, if any, shall be allocated to a second part (the "Non-GST Part"). The Non-GST Part shall be the balance of the rest, residue and remainder of my estate which is governed by this ARTICLE FIFTH, after deducting therefrom the amount allocated to the GST-Exempt Q-TIP under Paragraph D.1. of this ARTICLE FIFTH.

3. The GST-Exempt Q-TIP (but not the Non-GST Part) shall be held, IN TRUST, NEVERTHELESS, and administered as provided in this ARTICLE FIFTH, Paragraph D, below. The Non-GST Part shall be distributed outright and free of trust to my spouse.

D. All of my property included in the GST-Exempt Q-TIP, I give, devise, and bequeath to the Trustee hereinafter named, IN TRUST, NEVERTHELESS, to hold, manage, and invest such property.

My Trustees shall collect the income from this trust, and to pay over the net income to my spouse, or to apply such income for the benefit of my spouse, in convenient installments but at least quarter-annually, during the lifetime of my spouse. This Section is intended to qualify as a qualified terminable interest property trust under Code Section 2056(b)(7) and shall be interpreted to so qualify. I direct my Executor to give consideration to the minimizing the federal estate tax due on my death, but to also consider the federal estate tax likely to be payable by my spouse's estate. Any decisions by my Executor as to whether to elect under Code Section 2056(b)(7) to qualify this trust, or any part of this trust, for the federal estate tax marital deduction shall be made in the Executor's absolute discretion and shall be final and conclusive.

E. Upon the death of my spouse, if my spouse survived me, the principal and any undistributed income not then added to principal of the GST-Exempt Q-TIP trust shall be distributed in accordance with the provisions of ARTICLE SEVENTH.

CREDIT SHELTER WHERE SPOUSE SURVIVES

A. If my spouse survives me, I give to my Trustee, IN TRUST, NEVERTHELESS, an amount equal to the largest amount which will not result in any federal estate tax payable after giving effect to the unified credit to which I am entitled, as well as any other credits applicable to my estate. In determining the credits applicable, state death tax credit shall only be considered to the extent that it will not increase the state death tax liability. The amount so calculated shall be reduced by the following: (i) the value of property transferred under previous Articles of this Will (other than ARTICLE FIFTH which is calculated after the application of this ARTICLE SIXTH; (ii) Property passing outside of this Will which is included in my gross estate and does not qualify for the marital deduction (or for which no marital deduction is claimed); and (ii) Administration expenses and principal payments on debts that are not allowed as deductions for my federal estate tax. For the purpose of establishing the amount disposed of by this ARTICLE SIXTH the values finally fixed in the federal estate tax proceeding relating to my estate shall be used. In making the determinations required under this ARTICLE SIXTH it is my intent that this Unified Credit Shelter GST Exempt Sprinkle Trust be funded so as to make the maximum use of my unified credit, even if the result is a reduction in the amount to be included in a Q-TIP Trust, if one is provided in ARTICLE FIFTH, above, and even if the result is a reduction in the amount to be exempt from the GST under ARTICLE FIFTH. Disclaimers shall not be considered in making the calculations under this Article.

B. My Trustees shall hold, manage and invest and the amounts held in this trust. My Trustees shall collect and receive any income, and shall pay it to the extent and at such times as the Trustees, in their absolute discretion shall determine, to or for the benefit of such one or more members of a class consisting of my spouse, my children, and other descendants living from time to time (collectively, the "Recipients"), as the Trustees, in their absolute discretion, shall deem necessary or advisable for the health, support and maintenance of the Recipients, in each of their respective accustomed manners of living. Any net income not so paid over or applied for the benefit of the persons named in this ARTICLE SIXTH, shall be accumulated and added to the principal of the trust, at least annually, and thereafter shall be held, administered and disposed of as a part of the trust.

C. My Trustees are also authorized to pay to, or apply for the benefit of, one or more members of a class consisting of the Recipients, as the Trustees, in their absolute discretion, shall determine, such parts of the principal of the trust as my Trustees in their absolute discretion shall deem necessary or advisable for the health, support and maintenance of the Recipients, in each of their respective accustomed manners of living. These payments and applications may be made irrespective of the fact that such payments may exhaust the principal of the trust being held for the benefit of any persons.

D. The determinations of my Trustees as to the amount of principal payments or applications under this ARTICLE SIXTH shall be final and conclusive on all persons with any interest in this trust. Upon the making of any payments or applications under this ARTICLE SIXTH my Trustees shall be fully released and discharged from any further liability or accountability.

E. I recognize that no sum may be disposed of by this ARTICLE SIXTH and that the sum so disposed of, if any, may be affected by the action of my Executor in exercising certain tax elections.

F. My Executor shall divide the portion of my estate governed by this ARTICLE SIXTH into Two (2) separate parts.

1. For the first such part, my Executor shall set apart a fractional share of the portion of my estate governed by this ARTICLE SIXTH (the "Unified Credit Shelter GST-Exempt Sprinkle Trust") which shall be determined with reference to the amount (if any) of my remaining GST exemption (within the meaning of Code Section 2631) that has not been allocated by me or my Executor to any other property during my lifetime or after my death (however, for purposes of the application of this provision, my GST exemption shall first be allocated to property passing under this ARTICLE SIXTH, prior to making any allocation of my GST exemption to property passing under ARTICLE FIFTH, above). I direct that the Unified Credit Shelter GST Exempt Sprinkle Trust portion shall be the largest fractional share of the property governed by this ARTICLE SIXTH that, given the amount of my GST exemption so allocated under this ARTICLE SIXTH, will result in an applicable fraction of One (1) and an inclusion rate of Zero (-0-) (within the meaning of Code Section 2642) for all property comprised in the Unified Credit Shelter GST Exempt Sprinkle Trust. No descendant of mine who is an executor shall participate in the allocation of my GST exemption.

2. The remainder of my estate governed by this ARTICLE SIXTH, if any, shall be allocated to a second part (the "Non-GST-Exempt Unified Credit Shelter Sprinkle Trust"). The Non-GST Exempt Unified Credit Shelter Sprinkle Trust shall be the balance of the property governed by this ARTICLE SIXTH after deducting therefrom the amount allocated to the Unified Credit Shelter GST Exempt Sprinkle Trust portion under Paragraph 1. of this ARTICLE SIXTH.

3. Both the Unified Credit Shelter GST-Exempt Sprinkle Trust and the Non-GST Exempt Unified Credit Shelter Sprinkle Trust shall be held, IN TRUST, NEVERTHELESS, and administered as provided in this ARTICLE SIXTH. However, in making distributions of income or principal to the Recipients, my Trustee is directed to first make distributions from the Non-GST-Exempt Unified Credit Shelter Sprinkle Trust, until such part is exhausted, prior to making any distributions to the Recipients from the Unified Credit Shelter GST Exempt Sprinkle Trust. The intent of this provision is to favor distributions from the Non-GST-Exempt Unified Credit Shelter Sprinkle Trust first so as to preserve the Unified Credit Shelter GST-Exempt Sprinkle Trust, to the extent not distributed to the Recipients as provided in this ARTICLE SIXTH. The intent of this provision is not, however, to prevent or otherwise limit distributions to the Recipients which my Trustee deems necessary or appropriate.

4. In no event shall any property be allocated to the trust, or part of any trust, which the above provisions state is intended to be exempt from the GST tax, if such property interest cannot qualify for the GST exemption pursuant to Code Section 2631 (a) or any successor statute of like import.

5. I recognize, and direct, that no property may be transferred to the Non-GST-Exempt Unified Credit Shelter Sprinkle Trust where my remaining GST exemption at least equals the amount allocated to my Unified Credit Shelter GST Exempt Sprinkle Trust.

G. On the death of my spouse, the property in the Non-GST Exempt Unified Credit Shelter Sprinkle Trust and the Unified Credit Shelter GST-Exempt Sprinkle Trust shall be distributed in accordance with the provisions of ARTICLE SEVENTH.

IF SPOUSE PREDECEASES

1. If my spouse predeceases me, my Executor shall divide my residuary estate into Two (2) separate parts. For the first such part, my Executor shall set apart a fractional share of my residuary estate (the "GST-Exempt Residuary") which shall be determined with reference to the amount (if any) of my remaining GST exemption (within the meaning of Code Section 2631) that has not been allocated by me or my Executor to any other property during my lifetime or after my death. I direct that the GST-Exempt Portion shall be the largest fractional share of my residuary estate that, given the amount of my GST exemption so allocated, will result in an applicable fraction of One (1) and an inclusion rate of Zero (-0-) (within the meaning of Code Section 2642) for all property comprised in the GST-Exempt Residuary. No descendant of mine who is an executor shall participate in the allocation of my GST exemption.

2. The remainder of my residuary estate, if any, shall be allocated to a second part (the "Non-GST-Exempt Residuary"). The Non-GST-Exempt Residuary shall be the balance of the rest, residue and remainder of my estate after deducting therefrom the amount allocated to the GST-Exempt Residuary under Paragraph 1. of this ARTICLE SEVENTH.

3. Both the GST-Exempt Residuary and the Non-GST-Exempt Residuary shall be held, IN TRUST, NEVERTHELESS, and administered as provided in this ARTICLE SEVENTH. However, in

making distributions of income or principal to my Children, my Trustee is directed to first make distributions from the Non-GST-Exempt Residuary, until such part is exhausted, prior to making any distributions to my Children from the GST-Exempt Residuary. The intent of this provision is to favor distributions from the Non-GST-Exempt Residuary first so as to preserve the GST-Exempt Residuary, to the extent not distributed to my Children in my Trustee's discretion, for the benefit of my Grandchildren. The intent of this provision is not, however, to prevent or otherwise limit distributions to my Children which my Trustee deems necessary or appropriate.

4. In no event shall any property be allocated to the any trust, or part of any trust, which the above provisions state is intended to be exempt from the GST tax, if such property interest cannot qualify for the GST exemption pursuant to Code Section 2631 (a) or any successor statute of like import.

SPECIAL TRUSTEE POWERS FOR THE GENERATION-SKIPPING TRANSFER TAX (GSTT)

With respect to the tax on generation-skipping transfers set forth in Chapter 13, the Generation-Skipping Transfer Tax (the "GSTT") of the Code, the Grantor grants the following powers to the Trustee:

a. The power to allocate any portion of the Grantor's GSTT exemption, as set forth in Code Section 2631(a), as amended, or any successor statute, not allocated during the Grantor's lifetime, or by Grantor's executor, to any property with respect to which the Grantor is treated as the transferor for purposes of Chapter 13 of the Code, including, but not limited to, any property transferred by the Grantor during the Grantor's lifetime, at such time and in such manner as set forth in Code Section 2632 or any successor statute and the regulations promulgated thereunder.

b. The power to divide property in any Trust or part thereof being held under this Trust Agreement with an inclusion ratio, as defined in Code Section 2642(a)(1), of neither One (1) nor Zero (0) into Two (2) or more separate Trusts representing fractional shares of the property being divided, with One (1) or more of said shares having an inclusion ratio of Zero (0) and the other share or shares having an inclusion ratio of One (1).

c. With respect to all, or any part, of the principal of any such Trust or part thereof being held under any trust formed under this Trust Agreement which may be subject to the GSTT, by an instrument filed with the Trust records:

(1) The power to create in a beneficiary, other than Grantor's spouse, a general power of appointment within the meaning of Code Section 2041, as amended, that may dispose of the property upon the death of that beneficiary. However, the exercise of such power shall require the consent of the Trustee, other than the beneficiary, if such consent requirement shall not prevent the power from being treated as a general power of appointment as defined in Code Section 2041.

(2) The power to eliminate such a general power of appointment for all or any part of the principal as to which such power was previously created.

(3) The power to irrevocably release the right to create or eliminate such power.

(4) The power to divide the Trust Estate into Two (2) fractional shares based upon the then portion of the Trust Estate that would be included in the gross estate of the beneficiary holding such power if he or she died immediately before such division (in which case the power shall be over the entire principal of One (1) share and over no part of the other share) and each such share shall be administered as a separate trust. However, the Trustee, other than any beneficiary, shall in their sole discretion have the right to thereafter combine such separate trusts into a single trust. In authorizing such action, the Grantor's expresses hope, but does not require, that a general power will be kept in effect when the Trustee, other than any beneficiary, believe the inclusion of the property affected by such general power of appointment in the beneficiary's gross estate, may achieve a significant savings in transfer taxes by having an estate tax rather than a GSTT imposed on the property subject to the general power of appointment, which may also permit a greater use of the GSTT exemption under Code Section 2631(a) of any beneficiary, or spouse of any beneficiary.

Part Three

TRUSTS FOR YOURSELF
AND OTHERS

10 THE LIVING TRUST

What is a revocable living trust? A revocable *inter vivos* trust (the technical name for a "living trust" or a "loving trust") is one of the most talked-about of estate planning techniques. It's a trust for yourself, established during your life primarily to plan for your older age or disability, and its essential features are these:

- You retain complete control over the assets in the trust while you are alive and able to manage your affairs.
- For tax purposes the trust is generally ignored, and all income and deductions are reported on your own tax return (see Chapter 4).
- If you become disabled or infirm, an alternate trustee takes over the management of your assets.
- On your death, provisions that serve the same purpose as a will apply to govern the disposition of your assets. This means your estate will be able to avoid the probate process that is required with a will. Probate is the process of having a will admitted to court and demonstrating its validity.

The following schematic illustrates the use of a revocable living trust and how it works with your durable power of attorney, pour-over will, and tax planning. These concepts are explained in detail in this chapter and other parts of this book.

This chapter will explore in detail both the drawbacks and the benefits of using a living trust. The "For Your Notebook" section following this chapter contains an entire sample living trust, replete with comments, notes, and planning tips.

IS A LIVING TRUST REALLY BETTER THAN PROBATE?

The most important reason usually given for using a living trust is to avoid probate. Another reason is that a living trust can enable you to avoid having your assets disclosed to the public, a result that will not be achieved by a will. In both cases, reality can be quite different. Probate is not necessarily the evil and excessively expensive process many people fear. Although it sometimes can be. A living trust is not necessarily the simple and inexpensive document many people expect. The truth, as is often the

For Your Notebook:

SCHEMATIC OF LIVING TRUST

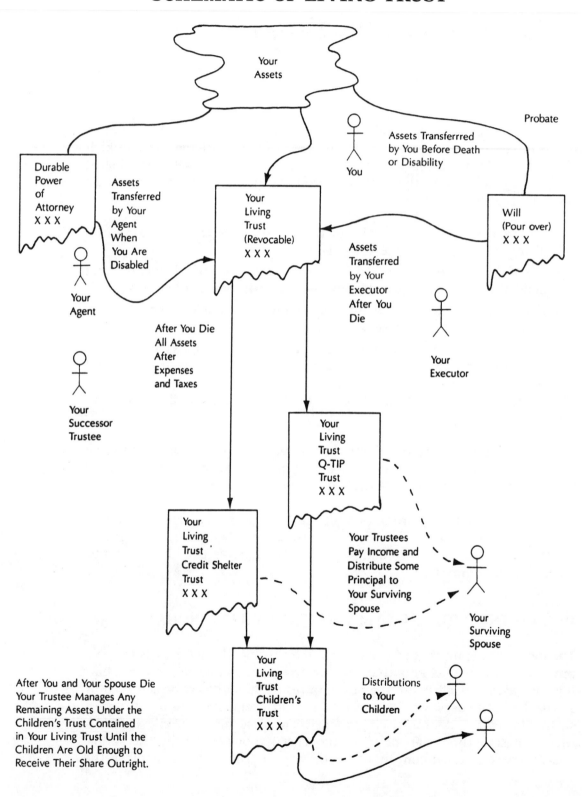

case, lies somewhere in between. The answer is that in the appropriate circumstances a living trust is an outstanding planning tool. In other situations, a living trust can be at best an unnecessary expenditure of time and money, and at worst a nuisance and a mistake.

In deciding whether to use a living trust, the proper approach is to evaluate the costs and benefits of establishing this trust in the context of your overall financial, personal, and tax objectives. To complete this analysis, you need a complete picture. To help you, we'll first present the potential problems in setting up a living trust. Later, we'll look at the other side. We'll also offer an opinion.

THE DOWNSIDE OF ESTABLISHING AND USING A LIVING TRUST

1. *Cost.* To properly establish a living trust, you must retain a lawyer to prepare a trust document, which is no small matter. And the trust document is only step one. You then must arrange to transfer assets to the trust.

    For real estate, you will need to execute a deed and, depending on where you live, complete various tax and other forms. If the property has a mortgage, you will have to review the mortgage for a due-on-sale clause and most likely notify your bank. You should ask the title insurance company whether a new policy in the name of the trust is required. If there are insurance policies on real estate and art, you will have to change these from your name to the name of the trust. Personal property will require a bill of sale to be transferred. New bank accounts may have to be opened. A separate tax identification number may have to be obtained and tax and other filings may be required. These steps can be time-consuming, can require the assistance of an attorney, and can create additional fees and charges, none of which would have to be incurred if you didn't set up the living trust.

2. *Operating Your Living Trust.* Even with all the above steps properly completed, you still must be careful to conduct any business or investment activities for the trust under the trust name, and to keep trust transactions and assets separated from non-trust activities that are conducted under your name. It's a hassle.

3. *Living Trust Costs Are Incurred Now, Probate Costs Are Incurred in the Future.* If all of the above is actually cheaper than probate costs, it still doesn't mean that setting up a living trust is the best option. Remember, the costs of setting up your living trust will be incurred now, whereas probate costs that go with a will may not be incurred for 10, 20, or more years in the future. There is a time value to money. The money you spend today won't be available to earn interest as it would if you had not set up the living trust. If you invested the money, the value at the date of your death could exceed

the cost of probate. Thus, while the actual dollar cost of setting up a living trust and having your trustees transfer assets after your death under the trust may be less than the cost of a probate (assuming that with a living trust you avoid probate completely), on a present-value basis, the cost of probate may easily be less.

4. *A Will Is Needed Whether or Not You Have a Living Trust.* A living trust is not a substitute for a will. You should always have a will, because there is no guarantee that every asset of yours will be owned by the trust at your death. There could have been an improper or incomplete transfer of assets; there may be assets that could not be assigned; and you may not be aware of all assets. Your will can be relatively simple, for example, providing that all assets under the will are simply to be transferred (poured over) to your living trust, but it still should be made. Therefore, by using a living trust you won't eliminate the cost of a will; in fact, you'll increase your legal costs by needing two documents when one may have sufficed.

In unusual instances it may be possible for a person to sign a will but not a living trust. A trust is a type of contract so that in order to have a valid trust, the person establishing the trust must have the comprehension, understanding, and state of mind required to create a binding legal contract. The standard that has been accepted by some courts for a person to sign a will has been lower, only requiring the person signing to be aware of his or her descendants (called "bounty"), and the extent of his or her assets. Thus, when a disabled or infirm person is incapable of signing a contract, but does have sufficient capacity to sign a will, this latter approach should be used.

5. *A Living Trust Does Not Guarantee Confidentiality.* The confidentiality you hope to obtain through the use of a living trust may not be realized. If your will contains a pour-over provision, it will be probated, and the probate process may pull your living trust into the public record. If there are any legal disputes between beneficiaries or other persons claiming an interest in your assets, or if your living trust is contested, these events might easily wind up in court records, which are open to the public.

NOTE: You can include in your legal documents a provision that anyone who challenges his or her distribution will lose any rights to be your beneficiary. This type of clause is called a "no-contest" or *in terrorem* clause. But this won't guarantee against a challenge or insure confidentiality.

If your successor trustee is not certain about the proper interpretation of a provision in your living trust, the trustee may petition the court to interpret your trust agreement and advise him or her of the appropriate action to take. This will obviously defeat any confidentiality your living trust may have provided.

If real estate is transferred to your living trust, your title company (the company that insures your ownership of the property, as distinguished from a casualty insurer, who insures against fire, and so forth) may require that the trust, or at least a summary (called a memorandum), be shown in the public records. Some probate courts require the filing of a copy of your estate tax return. If this is done, all of the assets of your living trust (since they will all be included in your estate) will be part of the public records of the probate court.

The result of all these contingencies is that there may be little additional secrecy offered by the use of a living trust. On the other hand, unless you're a well-known public figure, it is unlikely that the media will have any interest in your will even if it is probated and made available to the public records.

6. *Legal Fees Will Be Incurred on Death Whether a Will or Living Trust Is Used.* When a person with a living trust dies, the assets in that trust still must be transferred to the designated beneficiaries. Thus, whether assets pass through probate or under a living trust, steps still will have to be taken to transfer those assets. When the property is real estate, stocks or other property, the paperwork may not be that different.

Also, the legal fees in probating an estate may be lower than many popular books and articles in financial publications indicate. A number like 5 percent of total assets is often given as the typical legal fee. In many instances, it could be much lower. The size of the estate often has little to do with the work necessary. The nature of the assets, cooperation of family members, and organization of necessary financial and personal records are important factors in determining the legal work involved.

Also, the particular probate court that will handle the estate can have a significant effect on the overall cost of a probate. Some probate courts are extremely efficient, helpful, and professional, which can drastically reduce the cost and time delays involved.

EXAMPLE: In Bergen County, New Jersey, the surrogate's court is so well organized, and the clerks so helpful and efficient, that many matters can be handled quickly and with a minimum of legal involvement. Unlike surrogate courts in other jurisdictions, the court clerks prepare many of the papers necessary, respond quickly to telephone inquiries, and make the entire process far less onerous than most heirs anticipate.

---

7. *Court Costs Are Not Always Significantly Less With a Living Trust.* Even with a living trust, it may not be possible to avoid probate completely. Many of the forms and court filing fees are about the same even if your probate estate (your assets that go through probate in the event of your death) is somewhat reduced through the use of a living trust.

8. *Simple and Inexpensive Steps Can Be Taken to Reduce Probate Expenses.* A significant cost in administering many estates is the time and effort necessary to ascertain exactly what assets and liabilities

the decedent has. Maintaining accurate and complete records during your lifetime can provide substantial savings in professional fees later. This is a simple step, but it is ignored by the majority of people. However, if you are in the position of overseeing a probate, insist on detailed bills from your lawyer and accountant itemizing all steps taken. Obtain estimates in advance and request regular billing and quick notification if actual costs may exceed any budgeted costs. Don't be shy about questioning a bill, retainer agreement, or budget that doesn't make sense.

NOTE: If the decedent prepared a proper will, if all of the heirs are amicable and work together, and if all of the decedent's financial records are well organized, significant savings in time and expense can be realized. A living trust will only help with these matters to the extent that it serves as a catalyst for the decedent to have organized records and resolved potential family disputes prior to death.

---

9. *Executor and Trustee Commissions.* State law provides for a maximum amount that can be charged by persons serving as executors under your will and trustees under your trusts. In some instances, however, additional fees and administrative costs may be permitted. On the other hand, in many situations, close family or friends serve as executor or guardian for no additional fee. Does this mean that fiduciary (executor and trustee) fees will be lower through the use of a living trust than through a will and the probate process? It depends.

10. *Other Probate-Avoidance Techniques Are Available.* If avoiding (minimizing is a more realistic goal) probate is an important goal, the use of a living trust is not the only approach that can accomplish your objective. For example, if you own property as a joint tenant with the right of survivorship (often abbreviated as JTWROS), this form of ownership will pass the asset to the surviving co-owner without probate. This simplistic approach does not permit much of the estate, legal, and other planning discussed in this book to be implemented, but it can be appropriate for younger people.

EXAMPLE: A young couple owns a starter house with a large mortgage, a checking account, and a money market fund worth about $10,000. The simplest approach may be to simply own all assets jointly. On the death of either party, the survivor will obtain ownership of all of the assets.

---

11. *Durable Powers of Attorney May Be a Lower-Cost Solution.* In some instances, particularly if you're young and healthy, the cost of a living trust to provide for disability may be excessive when compared with the use of a durable power of attorney, which is simple and very inexpensive to complete. The preparation of a living trust to avoid probate, even if warranted based on an analysis of the other considerations listed here, would be a premature expenditure for young people.

12. *A Value of Probate Is That Creditor Rights May Be Terminated.* When a will is probated and the necessary filings and publication of notices are made, the rights of creditors against the estate will be cut off in a specified time period. A living trust will not accomplish this, and creditors may retain certain rights for years.

TIP: Leave some assets in your probate estate to be transferred under your will. Also, publish the notice that informs creditors of an estate. There can be no assurance that these steps will prevent the creditors from attacking the assets of the trust, but they may help. Be certain to consult an attorney, because the results are not clear.

NOTE: If you're getting on in years and your primary concern is preventing the loss of all of your assets to cover medical costs that would otherwise be covered by Medicaid, a living trust is not the first step to take. You will have to make outright gifts, or use an irrevocable Medicaid qualifying trust to attempt to keep assets safe. A revocable trust may avoid probate, but you may not have any assets left to probate. The Medicaid-qualifying trust is discussed in Chapter 17.

---

13. *Trustee Actions May Be Subject to Less Scrutiny Than Executor Actions.* The successor trustee under your living trust probably will not operate under any court supervision. There may be no reporting requirements. As long as you fully trust your trustee, this should not be a problem. However, there are situations when having the trustee report to a court could be useful.

14. *A Living Trust Does Not Avoid Estate Taxes.* The use of a living trust itself does not provide any tax benefit. An estate tax benefit can only be derived when the other planning techniques and trusts discussed in this book are incorporated into a living trust.

EXAMPLE: Suppose you establish a living trust that allows you to avoid probate entirely on your $1 million estate. On your death, your living trust provides that your $1 million estate passes outright to your children. Although you've avoided probate, your living trust will do nothing to save estate taxes.

Now change the scenario and suppose that your living trust provides that the first $600,000 of your assets will be transferred to a bypass, or credit shelter trust; the remaining assets are transferred to a Q-TIP trust for the benefit of your spouse (see Chapter 11). (A revocable trust can be used to create a Q-TIP trust, providing an income interest to a surviving spouse.) Your living will, with these provisions, may have enabled you to entirely avoid any estate tax.

---

15. *A Living Trust Can Create Additional Tax.* One of the most basic estate planning techniques is to make gifts of $10,000 or less per year to as many heirs as possible. Gifts not in excess of this amount do not reduce your once-in-a-lifetime $600,000 unified credit and do not create a gift tax cost. However, when the gifts are made through your living trust, the interplay of some complex tax rules could result in the reversion of these gifts to your estate. When a trustee of your revocable living trust makes gifts, giving the property away could be characterized as you (the grantor) relinquishing the right to revoke the living trust to the extent of the property given away (a partial release). If you die within three years of a partial release of such a power, the value of the release could be included in your gross estate and be subject to estate tax. This situation can be avoided: If you make the gifts yourself, directly, instead of through your living trust, you will not have this problem.

TIP: Have the trustee of your living trust make distributions solely to you as grantor, and then you can make the gifts yourself. This will eliminate the potential tax problem. If you are disabled, the trustee can make the distributions to you, and your agent under your durable power of attorney can make the gifts on your behalf. It is important that your durable power of attorney have a specific clause enabling your agent to make gifts.

---

16. *Outright Gifts or Irrevocable Trusts May Be Better Options Than Either a Living Trust or a Will for Certain Assets.* Probate and a will, or a living trust and avoiding probate, are not the only two choices. Again, a thorough review of all estate, financial, insurance, and other goals and status is essential. If your estate is large enough, it may be better to give away certain assets as gifts to your adult children to remove them from your estate than to transfer them into a living trust, which won't remove them from your estate.

EXAMPLE: Suppose your estate is valued at over $2 million, of which $600,000 is stock in a closely held business. If the value of the stock exceeds 35 percent of your adjusted gross estate, your estate will qualify for favorable estate tax deferral provisions. These provisions permit your estate to pay out any estate tax on an installment basis over a period of about 14 years. This can be a tremendous benefit and perhaps minimize the need for expensive insurance coverage. At this moment, your $600,000 worth of stock doesn't meet the 35 percent test. What can you do?

If you transfer your assets to a living trust, or retain your assets in your estate (to pass under your will), this valuable estate tax deferral will not be available. Alternatively, if you give away to your adult children, or transfer to trusts for the benefit of your minor children and grandchildren, $285,715 [$2 million − ($600,000/35%)] of assets other than the stock in the business, your estate will qualify for this favorable tax benefit. If you have five married children, each with four children of their own, you and your spouse can give away $300,000 in a single year using your $10,000 annual gift exclusions. If your family is smaller, the same gifts can be completed on a tax-free basis over a several-year period. In this situation, limiting your decision either to probate or living trust will cause you to miss an important benefit.

THE UPSIDE OF USING A LIVING TRUST

With all the above caveats, is there any reason left to use a revocable living trust? Absolutely. It remains a vitally important and useful estate planning technique.

EXAMPLE: You're a widower age 78 and have few family members other than your children and minor grandchildren, and they all live several hundred miles away. Considering the remoteness of those who can help in a financial emergency, the use of a living trust may be ideal to provide protection against disability.

EXAMPLE: You're in your mid-70s and have an estate worth $17 million. Other than your house and some bank accounts, this estate is comprised of a diversified securities portfolio located in three major brokerage firms. Considering the size of your estate, a living trust to avoid probate and to provide for disability is almost certain to be the appropriate decision. The assets are easy to transfer to the trust's name—simply advise your brokers of what is necessary.

The following is a listing of the uses to which a living trust can be put:

1. *A Living Trust Is the Best Vehicle to Plan for Disability.*

- A power of attorney is a simple approach to enable someone to act in your behalf in the event of your disability. However, a living trust can provide far more detailed provisions and contingency plans for dealing with disability. Under some state laws, the validity of a durable power of attorney can be less certain than that of a successor trustee under a living trust. The successor trustee (the trustee that takes over as trustee when you become disabled) has legal ownership (title) to the assets in the trust, so the line of authority is clearer. Banks and other financial institutions may more readily accept the authority of your trustee than your agent.

NOTE: The two documents, a living trust and durable power of attorney are not mutually exclusive. A durable power of attorney should always be signed as part of any estate plan, even if a living trust is also being used. There are no exceptions. Your durable power of attorney should give your agent the right to make gifts (this addresses the gift tax issue discussed above) and, most importantly, have an express provision giving your agent the authority to transfer assets to your living trust.

Rarely do people transfer every asset they own to their living trusts when they set them up. A checking account, gifts received after the trust was formed, personal property acquired after the trust was formed, and assets that are costly or difficult to transfer (perhaps a car) are often not included in your trust. If you become disabled, the only mechanism to get these assets into your trust is for your agent, acting under a durable power of attorney, to transfer them.

- A living trust is likely to have more detailed provisions for accountability and court review for your successor trustee than a power of attorney.
- For the elderly or others able to handle some but not all of their financial matters, a living trust can be established with a co-trustee assuming primary responsibility for the management of assets. The trust document can include detailed criteria for how the assets should be managed. Since the trust is revocable, you can change and

fine-tune these provisions before you're disabled. This will help you prepare for the best management of the trust when you are disabled, or for its distribution to your heirs after your death.

• As in the example at the head of this section, a living trust is an excellent vehicle for a single person who can't rely on immediate family to handle financial matters in the event of disability.

• A comparison should also be made to another option for providing for financial management of a disabled or incompetent person. This is where a court appoints a guardian, conservator, or committee. The definitions and functions of each differ under each state's laws. The key point, however, is that the same disadvantages arise as with wills. A court will have to become involved, numerous filings and petitions made, hearings attended, and so forth.

2. *A Living Trust Avoids Probate, and Probate Can Be Time-Consuming.* Unless your family has sufficient assets to sustain it during the probate process (or at least until interim distributions can be made), a living trust can prove a simpler and quicker method for getting needed cash and other assets to your heirs. On your disability or death, a properly planned living trust can ensure that investments will continue generating income available to your family, with little, if any, interruption.

3. *A Living Trust Can Help Collect Financial Records for Your Assets.* To properly transfer assets to your living trust, the various legal documents discussed in Chapter 3 have to be completed. Also, a schedule is usually attached to your trust listing each asset transferred. Going through this process forces the collection and organization of all pertinent facts relating to your assets.

4. *A Living Trust Avoids Publicity.* Subject to the many caveats discussed above, a living trust can minimize the publicity and public availability of information concerning your assets and bequests.

NOTE: If you are part of a nonmarital relationship, of which your family members do not approve, the use of a living trust may be helpful in minimizing scrutiny, interference, and potential challenge. (See Chapter 12.)

---

5. *A Living Trust Provides Professional or Organized Management.* You can use a living trust to establish a range of procedures to govern the management of your assets. Here is an ideal tool to test your procedures before death. If you're not satisfied with how things are working, you can always modify the provisions governing management.

6. *A Living Trust Governs Disposition of Pension, Insurance, and Other Assets.* Many assets, for example your IRA account at a local bank, require a beneficiary to be named in the event of your death. Typically, people will name their spouse and their children as alternates. If you name your living trust, you can provide for much more

complex distribution arrangements to best meet your goals. However, this could result in the loss of valuable tax benefits (e.g., spousal IRA rollover options), so consult your tax adviser first.

7. *A Living Trust Minimizes Attack on Your Assets.* A living trust established years before your disability or death may have more credibility than a will created or changed shortly before your death, and provide less chance of a challenge based on fraud or duress. But, as noted above, courts may require a greater level of competence to establish a trust than to execute a will. If a legal challenge is a serious concern, name another person as co-trustee with you, or name a sole independent trustee (without your serving). The acceptance of the trust by an independent trustee can give additional credibility to the trust, and to the fact of your competence to establish a trust at the time it was formed. A trust may also provide the advantage over a will that the challenger may not know the terms of the document when making his or her challenge.

TIP: If either avoiding a challenge or maintaining confidentiality of certain assets is a big concern, don't use a pour-over will. Such a delicate situation could occur when one child is favored over another, when the children of one marriage are favored over the children of another marriage, or when bequests are made to a lover outside of marriage. Instead, leave sufficient assets in your probate estate so that no one will suspect that you had set up a living trust to transfer other assets. However, be sure to discuss these ideas with an attorney.

---

8. *The Administrative Difficulties and Costs of a Living Trust Are Often Overstated.* In many cases, the perceived administrative difficulties and the costs of establishing and setting up a living trust are overstated. When no special tax return needs to be filed, the administrative burdens of having a living trust should not be any greater than the burdens of properly managing assets that you own yourself. Also, the common fears people have over dealing with a long or complex legal document are often unwarranted with a living trust if the document is properly explained.

FOUR STAGES IN THE LIFE OF YOUR LIVING TRUST

Perhaps the best way to understand how a living trust works is to review its life cycle. The process is roughly as follows:

#1—Formation: After a complete review of your tax, estate, financial, insurance and personal goals and status, a comprehensive plan should be formulated. When a living trust is an appropriate component of this plan, you should retain a lawyer to draft the trust. After careful review and approval, the trust should be signed, witnessed, and notarized. Copies of the trust should be given to your accountant, financial planner, broker, and insurance adviser. These people will assist you in properly transferring assets to your trust, as described in detail in Chapter 3. Your insurance

agent's role will be to assist you in changing the names of beneficiaries of your insurance policies to the trust.

NOTE: There generally will not be any benefit to transferring ownership of your insurance policies to a revocable living trust, since this will not keep the proceeds out of your estate for tax purposes. If this is your objective, an irrevocable life insurance trust rather than a revocable living trust is necessary (see Chapter 13).

Give your accountant a copy of the trust so that he or she can include it in your permanent file of important documents. In the event of your death or disability, your accountant will likely be involved in helping your family, and having a copy of your trust will be necessary. Finally, the easiest way to transfer stocks into the name of your trust is through the services of your broker. If you don't have a broker and own all your securities in your own name, getting a broker to assist with the stock transfers can make setting up your trust a lot easier. The alternative is having to write the transfer agent for every security you own and arrange a transfer of ownership to the name of your trust.

TIP: Having a broker should be a part of the planning for your living trust. Remember, a major benefit of a living trust is to make it easier for designated family or friends to assist you in the event of disability, so the broker is for them and not only for you. Even if you're a skilled stock picker, the people you've selected as successor trustees may not have your abilities. Having a broker in place who understands your investment philosophy will provide important continuity and management.

#2—Management Prior to Your Disability: Once the living trust is established, you will continue to manage the assets in your trusts as if they were your own, with one very important exception—every transaction affecting trust assets must be completed in the trust's name and not yours. You cannot sign checks or buy stock for the trust in your name. People constantly go to the effort and expense of setting up a trust and then don't properly transfer assets to the trust or else sign documents in their own name and not the name of the trust. This carelessness can defeat the best intended plans. Remember, the trust is a separate entity from you and the distinction must be respected.

EXAMPLE: John Doe sets up the John Doe Revocable Living Trust. When John buys assets or signs checks on the trust checking account, this should be done as "John Doe, Trustee, of the John Doe Revocable Living Trust." Signature lines must be signed in the following manner:

JOHN DOE REVOCABLE LIVING TRUST

By: _____
       John Doe, Trustee

You sign on the above line. This formality is important for all trusts. If the document you are signing has only a single signature line, you should write in the necessary information and lines.

The trust, with you acting as sole trustee, will generally continue in this manner until your disability. As discussed in prior chapters, it is preferable to have a co-trustee from inception.

#3—You Become Disabled: When you become disabled, your successor trustees will take over the management of your trust assets. At this time, your agent, acting under your durable power of attorney (as discussed above), should transfer to the trusts any assets you own that were not already transferred to the trust.

NOTE: If you are disabled, a properly implemented and funded living trust can provide for the continued management of your financial affairs with little or no court intervention. But this is only one step in the process. As part of your overall planning for disability, you should also sign a living will and health care proxy, which also appoints someone to serve as your guardian (to mange your person). Planning for disability should also take into account your present financial status, and the financial requirements of you and your family in the event of disability. If your financial resources are inadequate, a disability insurance policy may be as important to your well-being as the appropriate legal documents. Finally, have your financial and key personal records in order; otherwise, whoever takes over as trustee or guardian may have an almost impossible task of locating needed information.

#4—After You Die: Your trust will no longer be revocable once you die. On your death, the provisions of your living trust will be implemented by the successor trustees named in your trust. These provisions might include the outright distribution of property to intended beneficiaries (such as adult children), or the continuation of one or several trusts, as provided in your living trust. Several of the different types of trusts described throughout this book can be incorporated into your living trust.

EXAMPLE: Your living trust can provide that on your death, $600,000 of assets are to be held in a credit shelter trust to assure that your spouse has access to the income, and certain rights to the principal, but that the assets won't be included in your spouse's estate. The remaining assets can be held in a Q-TIP trust, which gives the income to your surviving spouse, but on your spouse's death, provides that the assets will go to your children. Further, in the event that your spouse dies while your children are minors, the assets of the trust will be held in a further trust and only distributed as your children reach certain ages. Thus, your living trust contains three additional trusts, which become effective on your death.

EXAMPLE: If your surviving spouse is not a citizen of the United States, then your living trust could contain a special trust called a Q-DOT (see Chapter 11).

EXAMPLE: If your estate is extremely large (more than $1 million for an individual, or more than $2 million for a couple) the generation-skipping transfer tax can be an important consideration. In such a case, your living trust can contain several different types of trusts to deal with this potential tax. For example, you could have a credit shelter trust for $600,000 and a $400,000 Q-TIP trust, which are structured to use your once-in-a-lifetime $1 million generation-skipping transfer tax exemption. Assets above the $1 million amount could be in a second Q-TIP trust.

TIP: The only way to know which of the many different types of trusts are appropriate for inclusion in your living trust is to complete a comprehensive analysis of your overall estate, financial, insurance, and personal planning. The diversity of trusts, and combinations of different trusts, is why it can be so dangerous to rely on "self-help" trust books. No single form that purports to be adaptable by all readers of a book could possibly give everyone the optimal combination of trust arrangements to meet all of their unique goals.

At this point, any assets that were not already transferred to your trust (either by you when you formed the trust, by you at a later date or by someone making a gift to you, or by your agent under your durable power of attorney after your disability) can be transferred under what is known as a pour-over will. A sample pour-over will is included in the For Your Notebook section following Chapter 3. The key provision of this will states that any assets that you may own at your death that were not already in your trust, should be transferred to your trust. While this approach is not essential (your will could provide for how your assets which are subject to probate are to be distributed), it usually is the most efficient way to handle matters, since all of your assets will then be dealt with under the same document.

WHAT PROVISIONS SHOULD BE INCLUDED IN A LIVING TRUST?

Many of the provisions applicable to trusts generally also apply to living trusts. Thus, the earlier chapters dealing with the transfer of assets, selection of trustees, and so forth, should all be reviewed. However, when a living trust is intended to serve you during illness or disability, there are some special provisions you should include.

Provisions for Dealing with Your Disability

The trust should contain detailed instructions stating who should take over and how. It should be clear how to determine that you are disabled so that your successor trustees can take over. The safest approach is to have a co-trustee at all times who can take over management without delay or formality. Further, it should be clear how to determine that you are no longer disabled so that you can reassert control over your financial management. Disability frequently can be short-term and not permanent.

An important part of your living trust is a set of detailed instructions regarding how you should be cared for in the event of disability. Many of the "standard" or "form" trusts simply don't provide this type of personalized detail. Do you want to avoid being placed in a nursing home as long as possible? Do you have preferences for the type of health care facility you should be placed in if it becomes absolutely necessary? Are religious or geographic preferences factors to consider? If so, you should specify your wishes in your living trust. You may want to be located in a certain part of the country (perhaps near your family), or you may want the health care facility to be near a church, mosque, or synagogue so that you can attend services, or you may require that the facility meet your religious dietary requirements. Don't assume that your trustees "will know." This degree of detail also can enable your trustees to respond to a challenge by your heirs regarding the appropriateness of the decisions and expenditures which they make on your behalf.

Provisions for the Five Trust Elements

Remember that the five key elements of every trust are the grantor (person transferring assets to the trust), the trustee (person managing the assets and trust), intent of the trust, the property being transferred, and the beneficiaries (those for whose benefit the property is held in trust). A living trust also has all of these elements, but many overlap. With a living trust, you will be the grantor (as well as initial co-trustee and beneficiary). Regarding your status as grantor, in many estate planning situations, if you are married, both spouses will effectively be the transferor.

> **EXAMPLE:** You and your spouse have a combined estate of $1 million. You have never done any estate planning before, and all assets are owned jointly. You determine with your advisers that a living trust is desired to avoid probate, provide for management of your assets in disability, and encourage proper record keeping. To avoid any estate tax, it is decided that the ownership of the marital assets should be divided equally. On the death of the first spouse, all assets will be transferred to a credit shelter trust to be provided for under the living trust. Thus, even though you will transfer assets to your trust and your spouse will transfer assets to his or her trust, you each will be transferring all of the assets in order to eliminate the joint ownership.

The scope of trust property can vary substantially. If avoiding probate is your concern, you will transfer most or all of your assets to the trust. In other instances, the trust will be merely a standby ready to receive assets in the event of your disability (under a durable power of attorney) or in the event of your death (under a pour-over will). In the latter case, the trust may be funded initially with nominal assets (say $100 to set up a bank account). The co-trustee of your living trust is probably going to be yourself. However, you will name alternate trustees. The beneficiary, at least initially, is likely to be only you. However, you will name various beneficiaries for after your death, and a co-trustee.

The powers granted to the trustees must be carefully considered. These are discussed at length in Chapter 6. However, when setting up a living trust, remember that you can change the powers any time before you become disabled or die.

For a comprehensive review of the provisions to include in a living trust, see the "For Your Notebook" section following this chapter.

WHAT IS THE VERDICT ON LIVING TRUSTS?

In the appropriate circumstances, living trusts can be an ideal vehicle to accomplish many essential planning goals. In inappropriate circumstances, they can be an unnecessary waste of time and money, and even create some hassles and complications in managing your affairs. The conclusion, however, is that this downside is not nearly as severe as the downside of establishing other types of trusts that may be inappropriate. This is because you can always change your living trust to correct any problems. This flexibility is not available for irrevocable trusts (such as the children's trusts, life insurance trusts, and other types of trusts discussed in later chapters). Thus, if it's a close call on whether a living trust is appropriate, and you can easily afford the costs involved, why not go for it?

Whatever your final decision is, it should be made with full awareness of all of the benefits and costs of setting up a living trust, as covered above.

CAUTION: The most important point to remember is that no single estate planning step can be relied on to solve all your problems. Whatever the hot item of the day, whether it's a living (loving) trust, a second-to-die insurance policy, a charitable remainder trust, or any other technique, no single approach can possibly address all of your needs. Nothing less than a comprehensive estate, financial, insurance, and tax plan will provide you with the assurance that you have best addressed all of the possible needs of you and your family.

CONCLUSION

Living trusts are an important and flexible estate and financial planning tool. The benefits they provide can be substantial, but you have to decide whether these will be worth the price. The living trust should be completed as part of an overall estate plan, including a durable power of attorney with authority to make gifts and transfer assets to the living trust, a living will with guardian appointment, and a pour-over will.

For Your Notebook:

SAMPLE LIVING TRUST

[DO NOT USE AS A TRUST FORM. THIS IS ONLY FOR
ILLUSTRATION AND DISCUSSION WITH YOUR ATTORNEY]

YOUR NAME REVOCABLE INTER VIVOS TRUST

THIS TRUST dated as of January -0-, 1992, between, YOUR NAME, who resides at 123 Main Street, CITY, STATE NAME (the "Grantor") and YOUR NAME as the original Co-Trustee and TRUSTEE-2 NAME, who resides at 456 West Street, CITY, STATE NAME, as an original Co-Trustee (the "Trustees"), who declares that this Trust is held and administered as follows:

WITNESSETH:

WHEREAS, the Grantor desires to create a trust, the terms of which are hereinafter set forth, and the Trustees have consented to accept and perform said trust in accordance with such terms;

NOTE: Since this is a revocable living trust, you will serve as both the grantor (person setting up the trust and transferring property to it) and the trustee (person managing the trust in accordance with the trust agreement). In a later section you will name successor trustees to take over for you when you are disabled or die.

NOW, THEREFORE, IN CONSIDERATION OF THE PREMISES AND MUTUAL COVENANTS HEREIN:

I. *TRANSFER OF PROPERTY TO TRUST*

In consideration of the premises and covenants set forth below, the Grantor assigns and transfers to the Trustees, and the Trustees, by the execution of this Trust, acknowledge receipt from the Grantor of the property described in Schedule "A". This property, together with any other property acceptable to the Trustees which may, after the date of this Trust, be transferred to the Trustees by: the Grantor, the legal representatives of the Grantor's estate pursuant to the provisions of the Grantor's last will and testament, Grantor's agent under a power-of-attorney executed by Grantor, or any other person, as well as the proceeds from such property, and the securities or other assets in which such proceeds may be invested and reinvested, shall constitute the "Trust Estate".

NOTE: This provision specifically authorizes the trustees to accept assets transferred under your will. As part of the typical living trust estate plan, you will execute a pour-over will, which transfers all of your probate assets to your living trust.

II. *TRUSTEES SHALL HOLD TRUST ESTATE*

The Trustees shall hold the Trust Estate for the following purposes and subject to the terms and conditions of this Trust.

A. *DURING GRANTOR'S LIFETIME—GRANTOR NOT DISABLED*

1. The Trustees shall hold the Trust Estate, in trust, to pay or apply to or for the benefit of any one or more of the following persons: Grantor and Grantor's Spouse, SPOUSE NAME, and [YOU CAN NAME ANY OTHER PERSONS YOUR TRUSTEES CAN SPRINKLE INCOME TO IN THIS SECTION] (the "Life time Beneficiaries"). The net income of the Trust shall be applied in amounts, whether equal or unequal, as the Trustees, in the exercise of absolute discretion, may consider

desirable for the health, education, support or maintenance, to maintain their accustomed manner of living, of any one of the Lifetime Beneficiaries, and in any other manner in which the Trustees, in their absolute discretion may deem appropriate (the "Distribution Standard"). The judgment of the Trustee, as to the propriety and amount of such payment, shall be conclusive. It is the express desire of the Grantor that the Trustees apply income liberally, without concern for the retention of any monies for future or remainder beneficiaries.

2. The Trustees may accumulate any of the net income not paid or applied for the benefit of the Lifetime Beneficiaries, and add it to the principal of this Trust at least annually and thereafter to hold, administer and dispose of it as a part of the Trust Estate.

3. Trustees shall not, during Grantor's lifetime make any gifts directly to any third parties designated by Grantor. Instead, such gift property shall first be deemed to have been distributed to Grantor who shall then be deemed to have consummated such gift, unless Grantor directs otherwise in writing.

NOTE: This paragraph addresses the technical gift tax problem discussed in the chapter. To implement this planning idea and avoid unnecessarily incurring a gift tax, you should also sign a durable power of attorney that specifically authorizes your agent to make gifts.

B. *DURING GRANTOR'S LIFETIME—GRANTOR DISABLED*

1. The Grantor shall be deemed to be disabled when any additional or successor Trustee (as set forth below) receives written certification from Two (2) physicians regularly attending the Grantor, at least One (1) of which physicians is board certified in the specialty most closely associated with the alleged disability, that the Grantor has become physically or mentally incapacitated, regardless of cause and regardless of whether or not there has been an adjudication of incompetence, mental illness, or need for a committee, conservator, guardian or other personal representative. The Grantor shall be deemed to have recovered from any such disability when the then serving Trustees receive written certification from Two (2) physicians regularly attending the Grantor, at least One (1) of which physicians is board certified in the specialty most closely associated with the alleged disability, that the Grantor is no longer physically or mentally incapacitated, and that Grantor is again able to manage his or her own financial affairs. The Trustees shall not be liable to any person, including Grantor, for the removal of the Grantor as a Trustee, if they acted in good faith on the certificates obtained in accordance with this provision.

NOTE: You must have a specific mechanism for determining whether and when you are disabled. If you are suffering from a particular illness, you may wish to modify this language to account for this. The level of confidence you have in your successor beneficiaries may also influence the language you use.

---

2. Where Grantor is disabled, the next person selected from the provision below ADDITIONAL OR SUCCESSOR TRUSTEES shall serve as co-Trustees in place of Grantor.

3. During Grantor's disability the co-Trustees shall administer the Trust Estate for the care of Grantor, and shall expend any amounts of Trust income or principal as the Trustees in their absolute discretion shall deem necessary or advisable in accordance with the Distribution Standard, as defined above.

4. However, in addition to the standards set forth in the preceding paragraph, and in clarification of those standards, Grantor wishes to make known his wishes that he wishes to have the best medical and health care provided, that he wishes every effort reasonable be made to enable him to continue to reside in his personal residence located at 789 Third Street, CITY NAME, STATE NAME for as long as possible, and that every effort be made to accommodate his health care needs in such home rather than having him relocate to a health care facility. Further, in the

event that Grantor must be relocated to any nursing or health care facility, Grantor directs that every effort possible be made that any such facility have DESIRED AMENITY service facilities, and where possible have, or be within reachable distance to a RELIGIOUS INSTITUTION [GEOGRAPHIC PREFERENCE OR OTHER REQUEST].

NOTE: You should feel free to include any reasonable guidelines for your care during disability. Especially note the word "reasonable." You should phrase many details as suggestions or wishes rather than demands so as not to unduly burden your trustees, but the key point is, don't hesitate to state your personal preferences for care. Also, be certain to sign a living will to further provide for your heath care matters.

---

5. In the event that Grantor has executed a living will and/or health care proxy, Grantor directs the Trustees to apply the assets of this Trust in a manner that is supportive of health care and related decisions made by the health care agent acting under such document.

C. *FOLLOWING THE DEATH OF GRANTOR*

1. The Trustees shall collect and add to the Trust Estate: (i) Amounts payable under insurance policies on the life of the Grantor held in this Trust; (ii) Amounts payable under insurance on the life of the Grantor in which the Trustees has been designated beneficiary; (iii) Amounts payable under the Grantor's employee benefit plans in which the Trustees have been designated as beneficiary; (iv) Property payable to the Trustees by the legal representatives of the Grantor's estate pursuant to the provisions of the Grantor's last will; and (v) Property payable by any other person, whether pursuant to the provisions of such person's last will or otherwise. The Trustees shall then deal with and dispose of these additions as part of the Trust Estate as provided in this Trust.

NOTE: This language enables your living trust to serve as the receptacle for all of your assets, thereby centralizing in a single document all of the decisions you've made about their disposal. This provision will be of little effect, however, if you don't complete the process by properly renaming the beneficiaries of your pension and insurance policies.

---

2. To the extent that the Trustees are either requested in writing by the executor or personal representative of the Grantor's estate, or required as a legal obligation of this Trust under federal or STATE NAME law, the Trustees shall pay:

a. Any expenses of Grantor's last illness and funeral, as well as any of Grantor's debts, as soon after Grantor's death as would be advantageous to the administration of Grantor's estate. These debts, however, shall not include: (i) Obligations secured by mortgages on personal use real estate or cooperative apartments, which debts the Trustees shall only pay in their sole and absolute discretion; or (ii) Debts owing insurance companies secured by insurance policies, which debts shall first be satisfied out of the proceeds of the policies securing them. This Section shall not serve to revive any of Grantor's debts barred by the statute of limitations.

b. Any cash bequests and general legacies for which the Grantor's estate lacks sufficient cash and marketable securities; and

---

NOTE: While this is a practical provision to have in your living trust, if you are using your living trust as the central document to control the disposition of all of your assets on death, consider including any specific bequests (for example, $3,000 to Aunt Edna) and keeping your will to a bare-bones-minimum, pour-over document.

---

c. All estate, inheritance, succession, transfer, and other death taxes imposed by any domestic or foreign jurisdiction by reason of Grantor's death upon or in relation to any property included in Grantor's estate for the purposes of any such tax, where such property passes under the provisions of Grantor's Will, this Trust, or by right of survivorship, be charged against, and paid from the property disposed of under this Trust which would not qualify for the unlimited marital deduction in Grantor's estate. To the extent that there is insufficient property meeting such criteria, such payments shall be charged against other assets under this Trust.

Notwithstanding anything herein to the contrary, the following taxes are excluded from this provision: taxes on the qualified terminable interest property included in Grantor's gross estate through the application of Code Section 2044 and taxes on any generation skipping transfer which shall be charged against the property generating such tax as provided in Code Section 2603(b).

Taxes on any other assets included in Grantor's estate, but not passing under Grantor's Will, this Trust, or by right of survivorship, shall be apportioned against the legal owners of such assets and they shall not, unless required by federal or STATE NAME law, be paid out of this Trust.

NOTE: If your estate or the estate of your spouse will incur an estate tax, it is vitally important to have that tax paid out of the appropriate assets and bequests. The failure to do so can unnecessarily increase the tax cost, or unintentionally reduce the bequest to a preferred heir. This is an extremely complex issue, which can be affected by state tax laws as well as federal, and should be reviewed with a knowledgeable estate planning attorney.

---

3. The Trustees shall not be liable to any person for payments made in reliance on the written request of the executor or personal representative of the Grantor's estate, or made in reliance on an opinion of counsel that such taxes are required to be paid as a legal obligation of this Trust under federal or STATE NAME law.

4. Notwithstanding anything herein to the contrary, the Trustees shall not distribute to Grantor's estate, the proceeds of any life insurance policy to pay debts, liens, or other claims, which would not otherwise be subject to such debts, liens or other claims.

The Trustees shall divide the Trust Estate into the number of parts required under the applicable of the following provisions, each such trust to be administered as a separate trust, and to be known by the title of the provision creating it.

NOTE: Many people misunderstand trusts. Any trust, such as this living trust, can provide for several additional trust arrangements to meet various personal, tax, and estate planning goals. It is very common for a living trust to divide into two, three, or even more, different trusts on your death.

D. *CREDIT SHELTER TRUST*

1. If Grantor's spouse, survives Grantor, then the Trustees shall set aside, in trust as provided below, the largest amount of assets which will not result in any federal estate tax payable in Grantor's estate after giving effect to the unified credit to which Grantor's estate is entitled, as well as any other credits applicable to Grantor's estate. In determining the credits applicable, state death tax credit shall only be considered to the extent that it will not result in an overall increase the aggregate (state and federal) death tax liability due as result of Grantor's death. The amount so calculated shall be reduced by the following: (i) The value of property transferred under the provisions of Grantor's will, and property which passes outside of Grantor's Will, which is included in Grantor's gross estate and which does not qualify for the marital deduction (or for which no marital deduction is claimed in Grantor's estate); and (ii) Administration expenses and principal payments on debts that are not allowed as deductions for Grantor's federal estate tax. For the purpose of establishing the amount disposed of by this Section the values finally fixed in the federal estate tax proceeding relating to Grantor's estate shall be used. In making the determinations required under this Section it is Grantor's intent that this unified Credit Shelter Trust be funded so as to

make the maximum use of Grantor's unified credit, even if the result is a reduction in the amount to be included in a Q-TIP Trust, if one is provided below. Disclaimers shall not be considered in making the calculations under this Section.

NOTE: A credit shelter trust is one that protects ("shelters") certain assets from the federal estate tax by using your $600,000 unified credit (hence "credit shelter trust"). (Also see Chapter 11.)

---

2. Any Credit Shelter Trust established under the preceding Section of this Trust shall be administered as follows:

a. The Trustees shall hold, manage and invest and the amounts held in this Credit Shelter Trust as a separate trust, and in accordance with the provisions herein. The Trustees shall collect and receive any income on assets in the Credit Shelter Trust, and shall pay it to the extent and at such times as the Trustees, in their absolute discretion shall determine, to or for the benefit of such one or more members of a class consisting of Grantor's spouse, and Grantor's children, SON'S NAME and DAUGHTER'S NAME, and other descendants living from time to time (collectively, the "Recipients"). Any net income not so paid over or applied for the benefit of the persons named in this Section, shall be accumulated and added to the principal of this Credit Shelter Trust, at least annually, and thereafter shall be held, administered and disposed of as a part of this Credit Shelter Trust.

b. The Trustees are also authorized to pay to, or apply for the benefit of, one or more members of a class consisting of the Recipients such parts of the principal of the trust as the Trustees in their absolute discretion shall deem necessary or advisable for the health, support and maintenance of the Recipients, in each of their respective accustomed manners of living. These payments and applications may be made irrespective of the fact that such payments may exhaust the principal of the trust being held for the benefit of any persons. The determinations of my Trustees as to the amount of principal payments or applications under this Section shall be final and conclusive on all persons with any interest in this trust. Upon the making of any payments or applications under this Section my Trustees shall be fully released and discharged from any further liability or accountability.

c. Grantor's spouse shall have the right to request of the Trustees of this Credit Shelter Trust to pay over to such surviving spouse, upon written request, out of the principal of this Credit Shelter Trust, in each successive calendar year commencing with the calendar year in which Grantor's death occurs, a sum not exceeding the greater of Five Thousand Dollars ($5,000) or Five Percent (5%) of the assets of the principal of this Credit Shelter Trust valued as of the date of the receipt of such request, provided, however, that only one such request may be made in any such calendar year, and such right to withdraw sums of principal shall not be cumulative from year to year.

3. Following the death of Grantor's spouse, the principal and any undistributed income not then added to principal of this Credit Shelter Trust, shall be disposed of in the manner provided in the Section below DISPOSITIONS AFTER DEATH OF GRANTOR AND GRANTOR'S SPOUSE.

4. This Credit Shelter Trust shall be irrevocable.

E. *Q-TIP TRUST*

All the rest, residue and remainder of Grantor's property, wherever situated, and all property, whether real, personal, tangible or intangible, of any kind and wheresoever situated, of which Grantor died seized or possessed, or which Grantor was entitled to dispose of at death after deduction for debts, funeral expenses and expenses of the administration of Grantor's estate ("residuary estate") shall be disposed of as follows:

1. Provision for the payment of any death or similar taxes, if required under this Trust shall be made.

2. Q-TIP Trust: If Grantor's spouse, SPOUSE NAME, survives Grantor, then Grantor's residuary estate shall be given, devised, and bequeathed to the Trustees, in trust, to hold, manage, and invest such property. The Trustees shall collect the income from the property included in this Q-TIP Trust, and to pay over the net income to Grantor's surviving spouse, or to apply such

income for the benefit of such surviving spouse, in convenient installments but at least quarter-annually, during the lifetime of the surviving spouse. This Section is intended to qualify as a qualified terminable interest property trust under Code Section 2056(b)(7) and shall be interpreted to so qualify. Grantor's executor or personal administrator shall give consideration to minimizing the federal estate tax due on Grantor's death, as well as minimizing the federal estate tax likely to be payable by the estate of Grantor's spouse. Any decisions by Grantor's executor or personal representative as to whether to elect under Code Section 2056(b)(7) to qualify this Q-TIP Trust, or any part of this Q-TIP Trust, for the federal estate tax marital deduction shall be made in the absolute discretion of Grantor's executor or personal administrator and shall be final and conclusive.

3. This Q-TIP Trust shall be irrevocable.

NOTE: A Q-TIP trust provides all income to your surviving spouse. On the death of your surviving spouse the assets in the trust will then go to persons you name, such as your children, rather than to your surviving spouse's new partner or children.

F. *DISPOSITIONS AFTER DEATH OF GRANTOR AND GRANTOR'S SPOUSE*

1. Upon the death of Grantor's spouse, if Grantor's spouse survived the Grantor, the principal and any undistributed income not then added to principal of the Q-TIP Trust; or if Grantor's spouse did not survive Grantor, upon the death of Grantor, Grantor's residuary estate, shall be disposed of as follows:

a. If any child of Grantor has previously died, the share, if any, set aside for his or her then living descendants shall be transferred to such descendants, in equal shares per stirpes. These transfers shall be either in trust, or free from trust, in accordance with the principles set forth in the following Sections.

b. If any child of Grantor shall have then reached the age of Thirty-Five (35) years, the share set aside for such child shall be transferred to such child.

c. If any child of Grantor shall not then have reached the age of thirty-five (35) years, the share set aside for such child shall be held in trust by the Trustees, for the following uses and purposes (the "Distribution by Age"):

(1) To manage and invest the assets of each trust, to collect the income from the trust, and if the child is under the age of Thirty-Five (35) years at the time his or her share is set aside, to apply the net income, and so much of the principal as determined by the Trustee in his sole discretion, for such child's care, support, maintenance, education, or general welfare until he or she reaches the age of Thirty-Five (35) years, to such extent and at such time and in such manner as the Trustees, in their absolute discretion, shall determine, without court order and without regard to the duty of any person to support such child. Any net income not so applied shall be added to the principal of the trust and thereafter shall be held, administered, and disposed of as a part thereof.

(2) When such child reaches the age of Thirty Five (35) years the Trustee shall transfer, convey, and pay over to such child One-Third (1/3) of the principal of the trust, as it shall then be constituted. When such child reaches the age of Forty (40) years, the Trustee shall transfer, convey, and pay over to such child One-Half (1/2) of the principal balance of the trust, as it shall then be constituted. When such child reaches the age of Forty-Five (45), the Trustee shall transfer, convey, and pay over to such child the entire remaining balance of the trust, as it shall then be constituted. Upon the death of such child before reaching the age of Forty-Five (45) years, the Trustee shall transfer the principal of the trust to such persons other than the child, his or her estate, his or her creditors, or the creditors of his or her estate, to such extent, in such amounts or proportions, and in such lawful interests or estates, whether absolute or in trust, as such child may by his or her Last Will and Testament appoint by a specific reference to this power.

(3) If the power of appointment is for any reason not validly exercised in whole or in part by such child, the principal of the trust, to the extent not validly appointed by such child, shall, upon his or her death, be transferred to such child's then living descendants, in equal shares

per stirpes, or, if no such descendant is then living, then the principal of the trust, shall upon his or her death, be transferred to such child's then living spouse. If there is no living spouse, then upon his or her death, the principal of the trust shall be divided into a sufficient number of equal shares so that there shall be set aside one such share for each child of Grantor then living, or for the issue of any deceased child of Grantor, per stirpes, such shares to be disposed of as provided for in this Section. Any beneficiary of such amounts under the age of Thirty-Five (35) shall have such amounts held in trust as provided above, unless the application of the Section concerning the Rule of Perpetuities would require otherwise.

d. If at any time during the life of any child or any one or more of his or her issue, any financial emergency arises as a result of accident, illness, or other unusual circumstances, the Trustees are authorized, in their discretion, to pay to such child, or to any one or more of his or her issue, or to apply to his, her or their benefit, from the capital of the trust estate, the amount or amounts as the Trustees may deem advisable in the circumstances.

NOTE: See the discussion of children's trusts in Chapter 13.

---

2. If any of the Trust Estate is not completely distributed under the above provisions, than such portion of the Trust Estate shall be divided into Two (2) equal portions with one such portion being contributed to the NAME OF FAVORITE CHARITY NO. 1, and the second such portion being distributed to NAME OF FAVORITE CHARITY NO. 2. In the event that either of such organizations does not then exist, the Trustees shall name an organization which succeeds such named organization, or whose charitable purpose most closely follows the purpose such organizations had.

NOTE: It is always best to provide for contingent beneficiaries in case unforeseen events prevent your primary beneficiaries from receiving your assets.

---

3. Grantor's children include SON'S NAME and DAUGHTER'S NAME.

G. *INSURANCE TRUST*

NOTE: See discussion and sample provisions in Chapter 18.

H. *SPECIAL PROVISIONS FOR S CORPORATION STOCK*

NOTE: See discussion and sample provisions in Chapter 19.

III. *STANDARD FOR PAYMENT OF PRINCIPAL; SUPPORT, MAINTENANCE AND RELATED PROVISIONS*

Except as specifically directed otherwise in this Trust, following the death of Grantor:

A. The Trustees of any trust created under this Trust is authorized, at any time, with respect to any person than eligible to receive the net income from such trust, to pay to, or apply for the benefit of, such person as much, or all, of the principal of such trust, as the Trustees, in the exercise of absolute discretion, may consider desirable, necessary or advisable for the health, support and maintenance of such person, in accordance with such persons accustomed manners of living. However, for purposes of the Grantor a broader standard shall apply so that the Trustees are hereby authorized to, and shall endeavor to, pay to, or apply for the benefit of, the grantor, as much, or all of the principal of this Trust as necessary for the comfort and welfare of Grantor, in addition to Grantor's health, support and maintenance.

B. Except for distributions to Grantor, notwithstanding anything herein to the contrary: (i) where a Trustee is a beneficiary under this Trust, the Trustees may make distributions which the Trustees in their absolute discretion shall deem necessary or advisable for the health, support and maintenance of the beneficiaries in accordance with their respective accustomed manners of living; (ii) where any person eligible to receive any property or income distribution from this Trust is then acting as a co-fiduciary such person shall not participate in the exercise of any discretionary power granted hereunder with respect to the distribution of any property, principal or income of this Trust, or any trust formed hereunder.

C. If the Trustees of this Trust, or any trust hereunder, deems the net income payable from such trust not sufficient to support any beneficiary entitled to receive such income, then the Trustees may, as often as they deem necessary, pay to or apply for the use and benefit of such beneficiary such part of the principal of such Trust, up to and including the whole thereof, as the Trustees in their discretion believes necessary in accordance with the standard set forth above.

D. In exercising its discretion hereunder, the Trustees shall take into consideration the income, earning capacity, resources and other sources of funds of any beneficiary (except Grantor), together with any other factor which the Trustees may deem pertinent, including the accustomed manner of living of such Beneficiary, but need not require the exhaustion of personal resources as a condition for making disbursements under the authority of this Trust. The judgement of the Trustees as to the propriety and amount of all such payments shall be conclusive.

E. The Trustees may, in their discretion, require as a condition precedent to the distribution of any Trust assets for support or advancement, that the beneficiary (except Grantor) furnish evidence of his or her financial condition, income, earning capacity and assets, in form and content satisfactory to the Trustees. The Trustees shall be entitled to rely upon the written certification of any beneficiary, or the guardian, committee or conservator of such beneficiary, as to the nature and extent of such beneficiary's needs for support, and the inadequacy of such beneficiary's resources apart from the Trust. The Trustees shall not be required to make further inquiry as to the authenticity of the facts so certified.

IV. *RESIDENCE OF GRANTOR*

A. This provision shall only apply to the extent that interests in Grantor's residence are not included in the Credit Shelter Trust set forth above.

B. The Trustees shall allow the Grantor's spouse to occupy and use until her death, the residence (or any interest therein) used by Grantor as a principal residence at the time of Grantor's death. The Trustees shall, at the discretion of Grantor's surviving spouse, sell such residence and, if Grantor's surviving spouse so directs, purchase or build another comparable residence to be used as a home for the surviving spouse. Grantor's surviving spouse shall not be required to pay any rent for the use of any such home.

C. To the extent not inconsistent with the Q-TIP trust or other dispositions provided for above, on the death of Grantor's surviving spouse, in the discretion of the Trustees, the residence (or any interest therein) may be retained by the Trustees for use as a residence by the minor children of Grantor, if any. The provisions of this Section shall apply notwithstanding that an interest in such home may be held by a trust for the benefit of a beneficiary not residing in such residence and notwithstanding the fact that a child having such residency is not a beneficiary of a then existing trust. Subject to the above occupancies, such residence, any interest therein held by the Trustee, or the proceeds from its sale, shall be part of the principal of this Trust (or the applicable trusts established hereunder). All taxes, insurance, repairs, and assessments concerning such residence may, in the discretion of the Trustee, be paid out of the portion of the Trust Estate (or the principal of any trust established hereunder) containing such residence.

NOTE: This is simply illustrative of the types of provisions you can add to your living trust to meet specific goals or desires. A living trust should be tailored to meet your wishes. Don't rely on standard forms from books unless your goals and wishes are also "standard."

V. *SPENDTHRIFT PROVISION*

With the exception of the Grantor, or as specifically provided to the contrary in this Trust, no transfer disposition, charge or encumbrance on the income or principal of any trust, by any beneficiary under this provisions of any trust established under this Trust, by way of anticipation shall be valid or in any way binding upon the Trustees. The right of any beneficiary, except the Grantor, to any payment of income or principal is subject to any charge or deduction which the Trustees make against it under the authority granted to them by any statute, law or by any provision of this Trust. No beneficiary, except Grantor, shall have the right to transfer, dispose of, assign, or encumber such income or principal until the assets shall be paid to that beneficiary by the Trustees. No income or principal shall be liable to any claim of any creditor of any such beneficiary.

NOTE: The purposes of a spendthrift provision are discussed in Chapter 16. This illustrative trust is assumed to have been formed by you. You have reserved the right to revoke the trust. Based on these characteristics, this trust is not intended to, and will be unlikely to, provide protection against creditors or Medicaid-related claims. The primary use of this spendthrift provision is to protect, to the extent possible, the assets of the various trusts set up after your death from the creditors of the beneficiaries of those trusts.

VI. *ADMINISTRATION OF TRUST; TERMINATION OF TRUST*

For the Trustees's convenience in administering the trusts created under this Trust, the Trustees, in the exercise of absolute discretion, may administer as a unified account the assets of any trust created under this Trust and any property held under the provisions concerning donee property held for a person under a disability. However, the Trustees shall keep a separate record of all transactions.

Notwithstanding anything to the contrary contained in this Trust, if the Trustees shall determine that the aggregate value or the character of the assets of any trust created under this Trust, or the aggregate value or the character of the assets being held for donees under disability, makes it inadvisable, inconvenient or uneconomical to continue the administration of such trust, trusts or assets, then the Trustees, in the exercise of absolute discretion, may transfer the Trust Estate or property, equally or unequally, to or among one or more persons then eligible to receive the net income thereof.

VII. *DISTRIBUTIONS TO A PERSON UNDER A DISABILITY*

A. Whenever pursuant to the provisions of this Trust, any property is to be distributed to a person under a disability ("donee property"), title to that property shall vest in that person under a disability, but the payment or transfer of the property may be deferred until the disability ceases. If the transfer of property is deferred under this Section, that donee property shall be held by the Trustees, who shall apply the principal and income thereof, or so much of such principal and income as the Trustees, in the exercise of absolute discretion, may determine, for the comfort and welfare of the person under a disability. This determination by the Trustees shall be made without regard to the income or other resources of the person under a disability, or of his or her parents or spouse.

B. When the disability ceases, the Trustees shall transfer to the person formerly under a disability the remaining donee property, and any accumulations of income or principal ("Remaining Property"). If the person under a disability should die, the Trustees shall deliver the Remaining Property to the legal representatives of the estate of that person. Notwithstanding the foregoing provisions the Trustees may, at any time, in the exercise of absolute discretion, deliver all or a portion of the donee property which shall then remain, together with any accumulations, of income, to a parent, guardian, custodian under the Uniform Gifts (Transfers) to Minors Act of the State, committee, conservator of the property, or an individual with whom such person under a disability resides, and the receipt by such person or entity shall constitute a full discharge of the Trustees for such payment or delivery. The powers granted to the Trustees shall be applicable to any donee property dealt with in this Section and shall continue until the actual distribution of the donee property.

VIII. *TRUSTEES' COMPENSATION*

Each Trustee acting hereunder, except for Grantor and Grantor's spouse shall be entitled to withdraw from the Trust Estate, without obtaining court or other approval, the compensation which is allowed to a trustee under the laws of the State which govern compensation to the trustee of an inter-vivos, or testamentary trust, as appropriate, computed in the manner and at the rates in effect at the time the compensation is payable.

IX. *TRUSTEES' DETERMINATIONS FINAL*

The exercise by the Trustees of the discretionary powers herein granted with respect to the payment, distribution or application of principal or income of any trust created under this Trust is final and conclusive upon all persons and shall not be subject to any review whatsoever. Grantor intends that the Trustees shall have the greatest latitude in exercising such discretionary powers, and that the persons entitled to receive the principal of any trust created under this Trust shall upon the termination of such trust be entitled only to such principal as may remain after the last exercise of the Trustees's continuing discretionary powers. However, under no circumstances shall any person who may be acting as a Trustees participate in the exercise of any power granted under this Trust with respect to the discretionary payment, distribution or application to him or her of principal or income of any trust.

X. *INVESTMENT STANDARDS*

Grantor wishes to state his non-binding preference that at no time should securities and other investments held in this Trust be used as an active trading account. Grantor wishes that investment decisions be made, to the extent feasible, with a long term time horizon, with the objective of earning income or capital appreciation, and not for the purposes of generating short term trading profits.

NOTE: It is generally unwise to set too detailed an investment standard since it is impossible for you to anticipate the investment climate a few years or decades into the future. However, if you strongly believe that you must state some preference for consideration by your trustees, the above approach could be used. The problem you create by setting standards is that you may unintentionally bind or create liability exposure for your trustees for not adhering to the standard you indicate. Think carefully about any such restrictions.

XI. *POWERS OF THE TRUSTEES*

The Trustees shall have in addition to, and not in limitation of, the powers granted elsewhere in this Trust, or the powers allowed by law, the following powers:

A. To invest and reinvest any assets comprising the Trust Estate in any securities or other property, whether real or personal, of any class, kind or nature (including an undivided interest in any one or more common trust funds), as the Trustees may deem advisable without regard to any restrictions of law on a trustee's investments.

B. To exercise voting rights in person or by proxy, rights of conversion or of exchange, or rights to purchase or subscribe for stocks, bonds or other securities or obligations which may be offered to the holders of any asset, and to accept and retain any property which may be acquired by the exercise of any such right with respect to any stocks, bonds or other securities or obligation included in the Trust Estate, in the Trustees's absolute discretion.

C. To employ or retain accountants, custodians, agents, legal counsel, investment advisers, and other experts as the Trustees shall deem advisable. To rely on the information and advice furnished by such persons. To fix the compensation of such persons, and in the case of legal counsel, who may also be acting as a Trustees hereunder, to take payments on account of legal fees in advance of the settlement of the Trustees's account without applying to or procuring the authority of any court.

D. To the extent permitted by the laws of the State, the Trustees may hold securities in the name of a nominee without indicating the trust character of such holdings, and may hold unregistered securities, or securities in a form that will pass by delivery.

E. To retain and continue for any period deemed appropriate by the Trustees, in exercise of absolute discretion, any asset, whether real or personal, tangible or intangible, included in the Trust Estate, constituting the Trust Estate.

F. To sell at public or private sale and to exchange or otherwise dispose of any stocks, bonds, securities, personal property, or other asset constituting the Trust Estate at the time, price, and terms as the Trustees deems advisable.

G. To grant options for the sale or exchange of any asset comprising the Trust Estate, at times, prices and terms which the Trustees deems advisable, without applying to or procuring the authority of any court.

H. To sell, exchange, partition, convey and mortgage, and to modify, extend, renew or replace any mortgage which may be a lien on all, or any part, of any interest in real property included in the Trust Estate.

I. To lease any real or personal property, whether or not for a term beyond the period of time fixed by statute for leases by a trustee, and whether or not, extending beyond the termination of any Trust, and upon such terms as the Trustees deems advisable, without obtaining the approval of any court.

J. To foreclose mortgages and bid in property under foreclosure and to take title by deed in lieu of foreclosure or otherwise.

K. To extend the time of payment of any bond, note or other obligation or mortgage included in the Trust Estate, or of any installment of principal thereof, or of any interest due thereon. To hold such instrument after maturity, as a past due bond, note or other obligation or mortgage, either with or without renewal or extension. To consent to the modification, alteration and amendment of any terms or conditions of such instrument, including those regarding the rate of interest, and to waive any defaults in the performance of the terms and conditions of such instrument.

L. To compromise, adjust, settle or submit to arbitration upon terms the Trustees deems advisable, in absolute discretion, any claim in favor of or against the Trust Estate. To release with, or without, consideration any claim in favor of the Trust Estate.

M. To participate in any refunding, readjustment of stocks, bonds or other securities or obligations, enforcement of obligations or securities by foreclosure or otherwise, corporate consolidation by merger or otherwise or reorganization which shall affect any stock, bond or other security or obligation included in the Trust Estate. To participate in any plan or proceeding for protection of the interests of the holders of such instruments. To deposit any property under any plan or proceeding with any protective or reorganization committee and to delegate to such a committee the discretionary power with respect thereto. To pay a proportionate part of the expenses of a committee. To pay any assessments levied under such a plan, and to accept and retain any property which may be received pursuant to any such plan.

N. To borrow money for the purpose of raising funds to pay taxes or for any other purpose deemed by the Trustees, in absolute discretion, beneficial to the Trust Estate, and upon such terms as the Trustees may determine. To pledge as security for the repayment of any loan any assets included in the Trust Estate.

O. To make any distribution under any Trust, in cash or in property, or in any combination of cash and property. To make non-pro rata distributions of cash and property then included in the Trust Estate.

P. To exercise for the benefit of the Trust Estate, and for any property included in the Trust Estate, all rights, powers and privileges of every nature, which might or could be exercised by any person owning similar property absolutely and in his own right. In connection with the exercise of any or all of such rights, powers and privileges, even where such right, power or privilege may not have been specifically mentioned in this Trust. To negotiate, draft, enter into, re-negotiate, or otherwise modify any contracts or other written instruments which the Trustees deems advisable, and to include in them the covenants, terms and conditions as the Trustees deems proper, in the exercise of absolute discretion.

Q. To combine the assets of this Trust with the assets of any other trust following Grantor's death where the beneficiary or beneficiaries, and the distribution scheme of this Trust and such other trust or trusts are nearly identical, and such combination would result in economies of administration.

NOTE: See the discussion of trustee powers in Chapter 6.

XII. *TRUSTEES' EXERCISE OF AUTHORITY*

Any authority, discretion or power granted to or conferred upon the Trustees by this Trust may be (a) exercised by such of them as shall be, or the one of them who shall be, acting hereunder from time to time, and (b) by such one of them who shall be so designated by an instrument in writing delivered to such one Trustees by the Trustees. Where there are more than Two (2) Trustees the decision of the majority shall control. Where there is Two (2) Trustees, except where only one is permitted to act as a result of the application of other provisions hereunder, the decision of the Trustee whose name appears first in this Trust Agreement shall control. If neither of such Trustees names appear in this Trust Agreement then the decision of the first of such Trustees appointed hereunder shall control.

XIII. *THIRD-PARTY RELIANCE*

No bank or trust company, corporation, partnership, association, firm, or other person dealing with the Trustees, or keeping any assets, whether funds, securities or other property of the Trust Estate, shall be required to investigate the authority of the Trustees for entering into any transaction involving assets of the Trust Estate. Nor shall such person be required to see to the application of the proceeds of any transaction with the Trustees, or to inquire into the appropriateness, validity, expediency or propriety thereof, or be under any obligation or liability whatsoever, except to the Trustees; and any such person, bank or trust company, corporation, partnership, association or firm shall be fully protected in making disposition of any assets of the Trust Estate in accordance with the directions of the Trustees.

XIV. *TRUSTEES' LIABILITY*

A. The Trustees shall not be individually liable for any loss to or depreciation in the value of the Trust Estate occurring by reason of (i) the exercise or non-exercise of the powers granted to the Trustees under this Trust; or (ii) a mistake in, or error of, judgment in the purchase or sale of any investment or the retention of any investment, so long as the Trustees shall have been acting in good faith.

B. Every act done, power exercised or obligation assumed by the Trustees, pursuant to the provisions of this Trust, shall be held to be done, exercised or assumed, as the case may be, by the Trustees acting in the Trustees's fiduciary capacity and not otherwise, and every person, firm or corporation contracting or otherwise dealing with the Trustees shall look only to the funds and property of the Trust Estate for payment under such contract or payment of any money that may become due or payable under any obligation arising under this Trust, in whole or in part, and the Trustees shall not be individually liable therefor even though the Trustees did not exempt itself from individual liability when entering into any contract, obligation or transaction in connection with or growing out of the Trust Estate.

XV. *TRUSTEE'S CONSULTATION WITH COUNSEL*

The Trustees may consult with legal counsel (who may counsel to the Grantor) concerning any question which may arise with reference to the Trustees's duties or obligations under this Trust, and the opinion of such counsel shall be full and complete authorization and protection in respect of any action taken or suffered by the Trustees in good faith and in accordance with the opinion of such counsel.

XVI. *RESIGNATION OF TRUSTEES*

A. Any Trustees hereunder may resign at any time without obtaining prior judicial approval. Such resignation shall be deemed complete upon the delivery of an instrument in writing declaring such resignation to the Grantor, or if the Grantor should then be deceased, to the remaining

Trustees hereunder, or should there be no remaining Trustees, to the successor Trustees hereunder. Such resigning Trustees shall promptly deliver the assets of the Trust Estate to the remaining or successor Trustees hereunder.

B. The resigning Trustees shall, at the request of the remaining or successor Trustees hereunder, promptly deliver such assignments, transfers and other instruments as may be reasonably required for fully vesting in such remaining or successor Trustees all right, title and interest in the Trust Estate.

C. Each Trustees acting hereunder shall be entitled to withdraw from the Trust Estate, without obtaining judicial authorization, the compensation which is allowed to a trustee under the laws of the State governing compensation to the trustee of a testamentary trust, computed in the manner and at the rates in effect at the time such compensation shall be payable.

XVII. *ADDITIONAL OR SUCCESSOR TRUSTEES*

A. If Grantor becomes disabled (as defined herein) or dies, or designates in a written instrument, the Grantor's spouse shall serve as Trustee. If either Grantor's spouse or TRUSTEE-2 NAME is unable or unwilling to serve as Trustee, or for any reason shall fail to qualify or cease to act as Trustee, then ALTERNATE TRUSTEE, who resides at 111 Hill Street, CITY NAME, STATE NAME, shall serve as Trustee. If she is unable or unwilling to serve as Trustee, then ALTERNATE TRUSTEE, who resides at 555 State Street, CITY NAME, STATE NAME, shall serve as Trustee. If ALTERNATE TRUSTEE is unable or unwilling to serve as Trustee, then SON'S NAME and DAUGHTER'S NAME, jointly, who reside at 123 Main Street, CITY, STATE NAME and 456 Main Avenue, CITY NAME, STATE NAME, respectfully, shall serve as co-Trustees. If SON'S NAME and DAUGHTER'S NAME, jointly are unable or unwilling to serve as co-Trustees, then the remaining of them shall alone serve as co-Trustee. If any person named herein is unable to serve, than the remaining person named herein shall serve alone as trustee.

NOTE: Name as many successor trustees as possible. Don't be concerned if one or more of the trustees is also elderly and may not be available to serve when the time comes. By stating several options, you'll increase the likelihood of having a person designated by you, rather than a person designated by a court, serve as trustee. Also, you can require certain trustees to serve together as co-trustees, while allowing others to serve individually.

B. The Trustees may appoint an additional or successor Trustees which may be an individual (other than the Grantor), or a bank or trust company. This appointment shall be by an instrument in writing delivered to the Trustees. It shall become effective on the date or condition specified in the instrument. Prior to the specified date or condition, however, the appointment may be withdrawn by an instrument in writing delivered to the Trustees. In the event that there should be no Trustees acting hereunder for a period of Thirty (30) days, the Grantor appoints as a successor Trustees the individual (other than the Grantor) or the bank or trust company to be designated by an instrument in writing signed by the law firm of Martin M. Shenkman, Attorney-at-Law, or any successor firm, and delivered to the Grantor and Trustees, or if the Grantor should then be deceased, to the legal representatives of the estate of the Grantor.

C. The acceptance of trusteeship by any Trustees not a party to this trust shall be evidenced by an instrument in writing delivered to the remaining Trustees hereunder. Should there be no remaining Trustees, to the Grantor, or if she should then be deceased, to the legal representatives of the estate of the Grantor, or to such person as designated by a court of competent jurisdiction.

NOTE: These last provisions ensure that if the trustees you name can no longer serve, successor trustees will be available to carry out your wishes as expressed in your trust agreement.

XVIII. *ACCOUNTING*

A. No Trustees acting under this Trust is under a duty to render a judicial accounting upon resignation or otherwise. Notwithstanding anything herein contained to the contrary, the Trustees, in the exercise of absolute discretion, may submit any account to a court for approval and settlement.

B. The Trustees may render an accounting upon the termination of any trust created under this Trust, and at any other times which the Trustees, in the exercise of absolute discretion, may deem necessary or advisable. The written approval of all persons, who are not subject to a legal disability, and who are entitled to receive the net income of any trust created under this Trust, and all persons not subject to a legal disability then presumptively entitled to the principal of any trust, as to all matters and transactions shown in the account, shall be final, binding and conclusive upon all such persons all persons who may then be, or thereafter become, entitled to any income or principal of any trust. The written approval or assent of the persons mentioned in this Section shall have the same force and effect in discharging the Trustees as a decree by a court of competent jurisdiction. However, any such written approval shall not enlarge or shift the beneficial interest of any beneficiary of any trust created under this Trust.

C. If the Trustees is accounting to another fiduciary, then the written approval of the other fiduciary shall be final, binding and conclusive upon all persons beneficially interested in the estate or trust estate represented by such other fiduciary.

NOTE: See the discussion of trust accounting in Chapter 22.

XIX. *NO BOND REQUIRED*

No bond or security of any kind shall be required of any Trustees acting hereunder.

XX. *TRANSACTIONS WITH GRANTOR'S ESTATE*

The Trustees is authorized and empowered, at any time and from time to time, (i) to purchase at fair market value from the legal representatives of the Grantor's estate any property constituting a part, or all, of the Grantor's estate, and (ii) to loan for adequate consideration to the legal representatives of the Grantor's estate such part, or all, of the Trust Estate, upon such terms and conditions as the Trustees, in the exercise of absolute discretion deems advisable.

XXI. *VIRTUAL REPRESENTATION CLAUSE*

In any proceeding involving the Trust Estate created under this Trust, it shall not be necessary to serve process upon, or to make a party to any such proceeding, any person under a disability where another party to the proceeding who is not under a disability has the same interest as the person under a disability.

XXII. *SIMULTANEOUS DEATH*

A. If Grantor's spouse shall die simultaneously with Grantor or in such circumstances as to render it difficult to determine who died first, then Grantor's spouse shall be deemed not to have survived Grantor and that the provisions of this Trust shall be construed upon such assumption.

B. If any beneficiary under this Trust, or any trust created hereunder, other than Grantor's spouse, shall die simultaneously with another beneficiary, or in such circumstances as to render it difficult to determine who predeceased the other, and if the rights of one of them depend upon his or her having survived the other, then the beneficiary whose rights depend upon such survivorship shall be deemed to have predeceased the other beneficiary and that the provisions of this Trust, and any trust created hereunder, shall be construed upon such assumption.

C. If any beneficiary under this Trust, or any trust created hereunder, other than Grantor's spouse, shall die within Thirty (30) days after Grantor's death, such beneficiary shall be deemed to have predeceased Grantor.

XXIII. *ADDITIONAL ASSETS*

The Grantor, or any other person, may assign or transfer to the Trustees securities or other property, whether real or personal, tangible or intangible, reasonably acceptable to the Trustees ("Addition"). All Additions shall be added to the Trust Estate and the Trustees shall hold and dispose of any Addition as part of the Trust Estate subject to the terms and provisions of this Trust.

XXIV. *INTENT OF GRANTOR CONCERNING CERTAIN DISTRIBUTIONS*

Grantor hereby declares that Grantor has carefully thought about the distributions set forth in this Trust and acknowledges that Grantor has taken into consideration all individuals, including both relatives and non-relatives that have been named beneficiaries or who Grantor has determined not to name beneficiaries. In the event any beneficiary or non-beneficiary shall contest any aspect of this Trust, or endeavor to have it declared invalid, or to otherwise change the distributions provided for in this Trust, then the Grantor directs that the rights of such person shall be determined as if such person predeceased the execution of this Trust without living issue.

Specifically, Grantor states that Grantor has considered their daughter, DAUGHTER #2 NAME, and has determined that she has sufficient resources for her care and that Grantor has determined not to make any bequests or other distributions to her.

NOTE: This type of provision is called an *in terrorem* clause. It is intended to prevent a challenge of the distributions to your intended beneficiaries by making it clear that you have considered the particular person and intentionally have not provided any bequest to him or her.

XXV. *REVOCABLE TRUST*

A. The Grantor has been advised with respect to the difference between revocable and irrevocable trusts and hereby declares that this Trust and the Trust Estate created hereby are revocable. The Grantor has retained the power to alter, amend, revoke or terminate any Trust provision or interest, whether under this Trust, or any rule of law. Grantor has all reversionary interests in this Trust or the Trust Estate. The Trustees shall have the power to use any of the Trust Estate for the benefit of Grantor's estate, as such term is defined in Regulation Section 20.2042-1(b).

B. The Grantor, during Grantor's lifetime may, at any time and upon successive occasions, revoke this Trust in whole or in part, or may alter or amend any of its provisions and any amendment may be similarly canceled or amended; provided, however, that the duties and responsibilities of the Trustees shall not be substantially changed without the Trustees' written consent. If the Grantor is incompetent, such power to revoke or amend the Trust may be exercised by the Grantor's guardian or conservator at the direction of a court of competent jurisdiction. Further, during Grantor's lifetime, Grantor's power to revoke or amend all or any part of this Trust shall be exercisable by the Grantor's legally authorized attorney-in-fact or agent, in the same manner and under the same conditions as the Grantor could have exercised them. However, the Trustee's duties, powers, or liabilities cannot be changed without the Trustees' prior written consent.

NOTE: This is a key element of any revocable living trust. It specifically states your intent to reserve the right to change the trust in any manner you want. However, the trust becomes irrevocable on your death.

XXVI. *DEFINITIONS*

The following terms when used in this Trust are defined as follows:

A. "Child" is an issue in the first degree, unless specifically provided otherwise.

B. Grantor's children are SON'S NAME and DAUGHTER'S NAME.

C. Grantor's spouse is SPOUSE NAME.

D. "Addition" means any cash or other assets transferred to the Trust to be held as part of the Trust Estate. The amount of any contribution is its federal gift tax value, as determined by the Trustees at the time of the transfer.

E. "Issue" is a descendant in any degree, whether natural or adopted.

F. "Per stirpes" is a disposition of property whereby issue take a portion thereof in representation of their deceased parent, with division to be made into such number of equal shares at each succeeding degree of relationship from the common ancestor that there shall be one share for each person of such degree living at the time of such division and one share for the issue collectively then living of each person of such degree who is then deceased; such division to be made although there may not then be any person living within such degree.

G. "Trustees" is the Grantor, and after either: (i) Grantor's designation of a co-trustee or a replacement trustee or trustees; (ii) Grantor's disability; or (iii) Grantor's death, the persons named as additional Trustees in this Trust, or those persons appointed by a court, and any and all successors to any of such persons, are referred to as Trustees. The term "Trustees" shall be read as required in the appropriate context and may be masculine, feminine or neuter and singular or plural, as the sense requires.

H. "Donee Property" is any net income of any trust created hereunder or all or any part of the Trust Estate distributable to a person under a disability to be held by the donee of a power to manage during disability.

I. A "person under a disability" is either a person who has not attained the age of Thirty-Five (35) years or a person who, for such period as the Trustees shall determine, is deemed by the Trustees, in the exercise of absolute discretion, to be physically or mentally incapable of managing his or her affairs although a judicial declaration may not have been made with respect to such disability.

NOTE: This provision, and certain related provisions enable your trustees to hold property in trust for longer than you have provided when the beneficiary you named is unable to properly manage the assets due to disability, drug addiction, incarceration, minority, and so forth.

J. "In Trust" is to manage, invest and reinvest the principal of a trust and to collect the income thereof.

K. "Trust Estate" is the then remaining principal of any trust, as then constituted, and upon the termination of such trust any accrued and undistributed income.

L. "Income", "Principal" are defined as follows. All cash dividends, other than those described hereafter, shall be income. All corporate distributions in shares of stock (whether denominated as dividends, stock splits or otherwise, and cash proceeds representing fractions thereof) of any class of any corporation (whether the corporation declaring or authorizing such distributions or otherwise) shall be principal. Dividends on investment company shares attributed to capital gains shall be principal whether declared payable at the option of the shareholders in cash or in shares or otherwise. Liquidating dividends, rights to subscribe to stock and the proceeds of the sale thereof, and the proceeds of unproductive or under-productive property shall be principal. There shall be no apportionment of the proceeds of the sale of any asset of the Trust Estate (whether real or personal, tangible or intangible) between principal and income because such asset may be or may have been wholly or partially unproductive of income during any period of time.

M. "State" means STATE NAME.

XXVII. *CONSTRUCTION*

A. The validity, construction and effect of the provisions of this Trust shall be governed by the laws of the state of STATE NAME. This Trust may be executed in more than one counterpart, each of which is an original, but all taken together shall be deemed one and the same instrument. Headings have been inserted for convenience only and shall not serve to limit or broaden the terms of any provision.

B. Any provision of this Trust to the contrary notwithstanding, this Trust, and any other trusts created under this document shall be interpreted so as not to violate the rule against perpetuities. Notwithstanding anything herein to the contrary this Trust shall terminate upon the expiration of twenty-one (21) years after the death of the grantee, and if any trust created hereunder has not sooner terminated, the Trustees shall at said time pay over, convey and deliver the trust fund or funds then in their possession to the persons then entitled to receive the income therefrom in the same shares or portions in which such income is then being paid or payable to them.

NOTE: This technical provision embodies an old legal concept called the rule against perpetuities. The objective is to prevent people from tying assets up in trust for an inordinately long period of time.

XXVIII. *BINDING AGREEMENT*

This Trust shall extend to and be binding upon the executors, administrators, heirs, successors and assigns of the Grantor and the Trustees.

IN WITNESS WHEREOF, the undersigned Grantor and Trustee have executed this Trust as of the date first-above written.

Witness:

_____ _____ (L.S.)

YOUR NAME, Grantor

_____ _____ (L.S.)

YOUR NAME, Trustee

11 TRUSTS FOR YOUR SPOUSE

The estate and gift tax laws generally tax any transfer unless a specific exemption applies. The three most common exemptions are:

1. The annual $10,000 per donee gift tax exclusion.
2. The once-in-a-lifetime $600,000 unified credit.
3. The unlimited marital deduction for transfers to your spouse.

When your estate makes a transfer that qualifies for the marital deduction, the amount transferred to your spouse, or to certain trusts for the benefit of your spouse, is deducted from the value of your gross estate, thereby reducing any estate tax due. Similarly, this amount is not subject to the gift tax. These rules mean that an unlimited amount can be transferred to your spouse. The marital deduction is the backbone of common estate planning, and when the combined estate of both spouses is less than $1.2 million, this approach can be effective. For a larger estate, this simplistic approach can be quite costly, as will be discussed in the chapter.

HOW THE MARITAL DEDUCTION AFFECTS TRANSFERS TO YOUR TRUSTS

A number of requirements must be met for a transfer to qualify for the estate tax marital deduction. The property must pass from you to your surviving spouse. The rights and property transferred to your spouse cannot be what is called a terminable interest. "Terminable interest" means the interest will end or fail as the result of (1) the passing of time, (2) the occurrence of an event or contingency, or (3) the failure of an event or contingency to occur. There are a number of exceptions from the terminable-interest rule, and these are critical to the use of trusts for transfers to your spouse.

Here is such an exception: If your surviving spouse is given a life estate coupled with a power of appointment in the property, this will qualify for the marital deduction. The criteria involved are that your surviving spouse be given the right to all of the income for life, payable at least annually, and that he or she has the power, exercisable by the spouse alone, to appoint the entire interest in the property as he or she chooses.

The Q-TIP Trust

The name "qualified terminable interest property trust" (Q-TIP for short) says it all. This trust is the most important exception to the rule denying a marital deduction for property interests that may terminate. The advantage of the Q-TIP technique is that your estate can qualify for the estate tax marital deduction without your having to give complete control over the ultimate disposition of your assets to your spouse. The rules are as follows:

- Your spouse is given a life estate in particular property.
- Your spouse has the right to all of the income from that property payable at least annually.
- The property must pass from you.
- No person has a power to appoint any part of the property to any person other than the surviving spouse.
- The necessary election is made by your executor to have the property qualify.

On the death of the surviving spouse, the entire value of the Q-TIP property is included in his or her gross estate. These assets will be taxed at his or her top marginal tax brackets. If this is not a first marriage, the use of a Q-TIP technique to provide for your current spouse will help ensure that your children from your previous marriage will be able to inherit assets. However, discuss the effects that state law concerning a "spousal right of election" may have with your attorney.

Using the Credit Shelter Trust for "Zero Tax"

There is no requirement to claim the maximum marital deduction to which your estate is entitled. It is often not the best approach to do so. Simply having each spouse leave everything to the other can be a costly mistake when the combined estate of the last spouse to die will or might exceed the $600,000 unified credit.

For large estates, it's advantageous to utilize the $600,000 unified credit in both spouses' estates. The proper use of the unified credit in the estate of the first spouse to die will keep those assets free of estate tax and ensure that they do not enter the surviving spouse's estate. It is not advisable to use a marital deduction to the extent that it results in decreaseing the unified credit used.

The classic zero-tax approach is to establish a "credit shelter" trust (so called because the assets are sheltered from the estate tax by the unified credit), or "bypass" trust (so called because it bypasses the surviving spouse's estate). Up to $600,000 of assets are placed in this trust, and the trustee is given the right to pay income to the surviving spouse, and perhaps to the children or certain other beneficiaries. In addition, the surviving spouse may be given certain limited invasion rights of the trust principal. The remainder of the estate can be given outright or in a Q-TIP trust to the surviving spouse, and no tax will be due on the estate of the first spouse to die. The purpose of the credit shelter trust is generally to provide as much control as possible over the trust assets by your surviving spouse but stop just short of the degree that would result in having the assets taxed in your spouse's estate. For a sample credit shelter trust provision, see the "For Your Notebook" section following this chapter.

TAX RULES AFFECT PLANNING FOR A NONCITIZEN SPOUSE

If your spouse is not a United States citizen, the unlimited estate tax marital deduction will not be available. Thus, the use of a Q-TIP trust as described above will not prevent the imposition of a gift or estate tax.

Credit Provision

There is a credit provision that can mitigate this result to some extent, which works as follows: If you bequeath property to your spouse who is a noncitizen, the property transfer is subjected to the estate tax. However, in recognition of the fact that it would not have been taxed had your surviving spouse been a citizen, a credit will be available to the noncitizen spouse's estate on his or her death (for the amount of tax paid by *your* estate on the earlier transfer).

Special Gift Tax Rule

The gift tax rules also present traps to your estate planning when your spouse is not a citizen, stating that the unlimited marital deduction will not be available for a gift to a noncitizen spouse. However, there is a mechanism that allows the annual per donee gift tax exclusion to be increased from $10,000 to $100,000 without incurring tax. To qualify, the gift must be one of a present interest (see Chapter 8). This provision is quite valuable in that substantial assets can be transferred to the noncitizen spouse during your life, if necessary, to complete any estate planning objectives.

The Q-DOT Trust

Short of having your spouse become a U.S. citizen, the most important strategy in planning for a noncitizen spouse is to use a qualified domestic trust (Q-DOT), which can take advantage of the marital deduction without limit. To qualify, a Q-DOT, must meet the following requirements:

1. *Trustees*. At least one of your trustees must be either a United States citizen or corporation. This requirement must be included in the trust documents. Provisions should be made for alternate trustees to ensure compliance with this requirement. For example, a final alternate could be a United States bank or trust company.

2. *Income*. Either the surviving spouse must be entitled to all of the income from the trust, payable at least annually, or the trust must meet the requirements to qualify for the marital deduction.

3. *Regulations*. The trust must meet additional requirements prescribed by IRS regulations. One is that your executor must make an irrevocable election on the United States estate tax return with respect to the trust. However, your executor is not required to make the election. The executor's right to make or not make the election should appear in your will or in the Q-DOT trust.

Estate tax will be levied on distributions of principal (corpus) from the Q-DOT other than annual income distributions, and calculated as if the amount distributed had been included in the estate of the first-to-die, citizen spouse. This calculation adds all prior distributions from the Q-DOT to your taxable estate in order to push the tax on the Q-DOT distributions into the highest federal estate tax brackets. An exception is provided for certain hardship distributions. In addition, a tax will be assessed on the property remaining in the Q-DOT upon the death of the second spouse, and is calculated in the same manner.

When a trust does not meet the requirements of a Q-DOT, the IRS may provide the flexibility of reforming the trust so that it does qualify.

CONCLUSION

For married couples, the use of the gift and estate tax marital deduction can be the most important planning technique to minimize the overall gift and estate tax burden on transfers to living trusts or trusts that become effective on your death. However, simply claiming the maximum marital deduction (all your property to your spouse on your death, and vice versa) is never the optimal approach if you and your spouse have assets in excess of $600,000. Planning is also imperative to avoid what could be a substantial estate tax when one spouse is not a United States citizen. Either the spouse can become a citizen or you can use a special trust, called a Q-DOT, to defer the estate tax.

For Your Notebook:

SAMPLE CREDIT SHELTER PROVISION

[DO NOT USE IN A TRUST WITHOUT CONSULTING AN ATTORNEY]

UNIFIED CREDIT SHELTER SPRINKLE TRUST FOR SPOUSE AND CHILDREN

1. If my spouse survives me, I give to my Trustees, in trust, the largest amount which will not result in any federal estate tax payable after giving effect to the unified credit to which I am entitled, as well as any other credits applicable to my estate. In determining the credits applicable, state death tax credit shall only be considered to the extent that it will not increase the state death tax liability. The amount so calculated shall be reduced by the following: (i) The value of property transferred under my Last Will which do not qualify for the marital deduction; (ii) Property passing outside of my Last Will which are included in my gross estate and which do not qualify for the marital deduction (or for which no marital deduction is claimed); and (iii) Administration expenses and principal payments on debts that are not allowed as deductions for my federal estate tax. For the purpose of establishing the amount disposed of by this Section the values finally fixed in the federal estate tax proceeding relating to my estate shall be used. In making the determinations required under this Section it is my intent that this Unified Credit Shelter Sprinkle Trust be funded so as to make the maximum use of my unified credit.

2. My Trustees shall hold, manage, and invest the amounts held in this trust. My Trustees shall collect and receive any income, and shall pay it to the extent and at such times as the Trustees, in their absolute discretion, shall determine, to or for the benefit of such one or more members of a class consisting of my spouse and my children, as the Trustees, in their absolute discretion, shall determine. Any net income not so paid over or applied for the benefit of the persons named in this Section, shall be accumulated and added to the principal of the trust, at least annually, and thereafter shall be held, administered, and disposed of as a part of the trust.

3. My Trustees are also authorized to pay to, or apply for the benefit of, one or more members of a class consisting of my spouse and children, as the Trustees, in their absolute discretion, shall determine, such parts of the principal of the trust as my Trustees, in their absolute discretion, shall deem necessary or advisable for the health, support, and maintenance of the Recipients, in each of their respective accustomed manners of living. These payments and applications may be made irrespective of the fact that such payments may exhaust the principal of the trust being held for the benefit of any persons. The determinations of my Trustees as to the amount of principal payments or applications under this Section shall be final and conclusive on all persons with any interest in this trust. Upon the making of any payments or applications under this Section my Trustees shall be fully released and discharged from any further liability or accountability.

NOTE: The nature of the assets should also be considered. If the assets already in your surviving spouse's estate are likely to appreciate rapidly, it may prove costly to add more assets to the second estate; at current values the $600,000 unified credit in the second estate will suffice to eliminate the estate tax cost, but perhaps not in the future.

For Your Notebook:

EXAMPLES OF THE BENEFITS OF USING A CREDIT SHELTER TRUST

The tax benefits of using a credit shelter trust can be significant. The first illustration shows estate that did not use a credit shelter trust and incurred a tax cost of $235,000. In the seco example, by using the credit shelter trust, the federal estate tax is eliminated.

UNPLANNED $1.2 MILLION ESTATE OF SURVIVING SPOUSE

COMPUTES ESTATE OR GIFT TAX

Year of Death (or Gift)	1992
Taxable Estate	$1,200,000
Tentative Tax Base or Taxable Gift	$1,200,000
Unified Credit Remaining	$ 192,800

If Transfer at Death		*If Lifetime Gift*	
Federal Estate Tax:	$427,800	Federal Gift Tax:	$427,800
Unified Credit:	$192,800	Unified Credit:	$192,800
State Tax Credit:	$ 45,200		
Net Federal Estate Tax:	$189,800	Net Federal Gift Tax:	$235,000
Assumed State Death Tax:	$ 45,200		
Total Tax Payable:	$235,000		
Net Estate Remaining:	$965,000	Net Estate Remaining:	$965,000
% of Estate Lost:	19.6%	% Cost of Gift:	19.6%

Chart prepared using *Estate Planning Tools* software copyright Commerce Clearing House, Inc., Chicago, IL.

PLANNED $1.2 MILLION ESTATE WITH CREDIT SHELTER TRUST FOR SURVIVING SPOUSE

COMPUTES ESTATE OR GIFT TAX

Year of Death (or Gift)	1992
Taxable Estate	$600,000
Tentative Tax Base or Taxable Gift	$600,000
Unified Credit Remaining	$192,800

If Transfer at Death		*If Lifetime Gift*	
Federal Estate Tax:	$192,800	Federal Gift Tax:	$192,800
Unified Credit:	$192,800	Unified Credit:	$192,800
State Tax Credit:	$ 14,000		
Net Federal Estate Tax:	$ 0	Net Federal Gift Tax:	$ 0
Assumed State Death Tax:	$ 14,000		
Total Tax Payable:	$ 14,000		
Net Estate Remaining:	$586,000	Net Estate Remaining:	$600,000
% of Estate Lost:	2.3%	% Cost of Gift:	0.0%

Chart prepared using *Estate Planning Tools* software copyright Commerce Clearing House, Inc., Chicago, IL.

For Your Notebook:

SAMPLE PROVISIONS
FOR YOUR NONCITIZEN SPOUSE

[DO NOT USE THESE ILLUSTRATIVE PROVISIONS IN A TRUST UNTIL REVIEWING THEM WITH YOUR ATTORNEY]

QUALIFIED DOMESTIC TRUST (Q-DOT) WHEN GRANTOR'S SPOUSE IS NOT A CITIZEN OF THE UNITED STATES

Grantor gives and transfers to the Trustee, in trust, to hold, manage invest and reinvest the same, to collect the income therefrom and to pay over the net income to Grantor's spouse, SPOUSE NAME, or to apply the same for the benefit of Grantor's spouse, in convenient installments, but at least annually, during the life of Grantor's spouse and to apply to the benefit of Grantor's spouse such account of trust principal, or all thereof, at such times and in such manner as the Trustee may decide is appropriate or necessary for the health, support and maintenance of Grantor's spouse.

a. To ensure that the trust under this Subsection is a qualified domestic trust under Code Sec. 2056(d)(2)(A), Code Sec. 2056A(a), and the regulations thereunder, and that the Trustee may elect to qualify the assets transferred under this Subsection for the marital deduction, then notwithstanding anything herein to the contrary:

b. At all times, at least one trustee shall be either an individual citizens of the United States or a domestic corporation, and where no Trustee meets this requirement any remaining Trustee shall immediately appoint an additional Trustee who does meet this requirement.

c. No distribution, other than a distribution of income, may be made from this trust unless at least one Trustee has the right to withhold from such distribution the tax imposed by Code Section 2056A, if any is so required.

d. The Trustee shall follow any requirements prescribed for qualified domestic trusts (including but not limited to requirements as to location of assets), and any provision of this Trust that conflicts with any such requirement shall be reformed so as not to violate these provisions.

e. Any provisions required by statute, regulation or ruling trust shall be treated as incorporated by reference as part of this Subsection.

f. The Trustee may amend the terms of this trust to add to it any administrative provisions required to make it a qualified domestic trust and the amendment shall be retroactive to the date of this Trust.

g. If this trust shall cease to qualify as a qualified domestic trust under Code Sec. 2056(d)(2)(A), Code Sec. 2056A(a), and the regulations thereunder, the Trustee shall pay the tax required under Code Section 2056A(b)(4), if required.

Upon the death of Grantor's spouse the principal and any undistributed income not then added to principal of the Trust created under this Subsection shall be disposed of as provided in the Section entitled.

12 TRUSTS FOR NONMARITAL PARTNERS

Nonmarried couples face several difficulties in planning for their estates that married couples do not. These additional problems stem from the bias that the tax and property laws have in favor of married couples, with the result that trusts become even more important when couples are not married.

The goals of committed unmarried partners are similar to those of married pairs. They want to ensure the availability of the personal residence and other specified property to the survivor of the couple. They want protection for each in the event of illness or disability. They want privacy for their arrangements; and, to the extent possible, they want to minimize estate and gift taxes. Trusts can be used for all of these purposes.

TAX PROBLEMS AFFECTING NONMARRIED PARTNERS

The federal tax laws, and many state laws, are extremely biased against couples who live together outside of marriage. The result is that there are several significant restrictions that complicate planning for trusts. The following are some important differences from the marital situation.

- Laws of intestacy provide that on the death of one spouse, the survivor, by operation of law in the absence of a will, shall inherit a portion of the decedent's property. This right is not accorded to the surviving partner of an unmarried couple. Therefore, it is essential that the title to property be structured, and alternative arrangements such as trusts be implemented, to protect the survivor. If these steps are not taken, the property will pass to the decedent's family members rather than the surviving partner, which can have devastating financial consequences for the surviving partner.

- Under the laws of most states, a surviving spouse has the right to make an election against the will of a deceased spouse. This can permit the surviving spouse to obtain a statutory minimum amount of property even if the deceased spouse changed his or her will to disinherit the surviving spouse. This right is not available to a surviving partner when a state-recognized spouse relationship did not exist. Therefore, specific steps must be taken to ensure such protections.

One way this concern can be addressed is by having property owned as joint tenants with the right of survivorship. With the title thus structured, the surviving partner will inherit the deceased partner's interest by operation of law and without regard to the provisions under the deceased partner's will, which may have been changed without the survivor's knowledge or desire. Another approach is to transfer the property to an irrevocable trust.

- Another difference from a marital situation is that a person can make unlimited transfers of property to his or her spouse during life as gifts, and after death through intestacy or under a will, without having these transfers incur federal or state gift and estate taxes. Nonmarried partners, however, face substantial and costly problems in making such transfers. This one point requires a thorough discussion.

ESTATE AND GIFT TAX DIFFERENCES FROM THE MARITAL SITUATION

As described in the previous chapter, the classic zero-tax estate plan for married people is this: Some assets (often in an amount equal to the $600,000 unified credit) are transferred to a credit shelter or bypass trust. The surviving spouse is given all of the income generated by this trust and certain limited rights to the principal of the trust (the limitations are designed to keep the assets from being taxable in the *surviving* spouse's estate). The remainder of the estate of the first spouse to die is given outright or in a trust qualifying for the marital deduction (Q-TIP trust) to the surviving spouse. The effect of this planning is to avoid any tax on the estate of the first spouse to die—that is, the surviving spouse can benefit from the assets of the first spouse to die *unreduced* by estate tax costs.

Zero-Tax Planning Is Not Possible

What happens if we adapt this zero-tax strategy to the nonmarried situation? A trust similar to a bypass or credit shelter trust can be a useful tool when both partners have significant estates and each wishes to benefit different people when the last of the couple dies. Such a trust provides a similar benefit as for married couples of keeping assets from being bunched into the taxable estate of the surviving partner. That is, the surviving unmarried partner will have substantial access to the funds in the trust without having those funds added to his or her own taxable estate. When the second of the nonmarried partners dies the assets will be distributed to beneficiaries designated by the first partner. This could provide a substantial estate tax savings.

The problem comes with the second step of the estate plan, which cannot be utilized. The transfer of any assets above $600,000 to the surviving nonmarried partner will not qualify for the marital, or any other, estate tax deduction.

One suggestion to address this potentially costly problem of a significant estate tax on the death of the first partner to die (as compared with no tax on the first death for married couples) is for the partner with the most significant assets to purchase life insurance to cover the estate tax. The insurance could be owned in an irrevocable life insurance trust in order to remove the proceeds from the reach of creditors, and to keep the proceeds out of the taxable estate of the first nonmarried partner. Another approach is a gift program while both partners are alive.

Other Gift and Estate Issues

Married spouses are permitted to make unlimited transfers to each other without triggering any gift tax. For persons other than a husband and wife, the maximum amount that can be transferred in any year to one donee (recipient) is $10,000. Any transfers above this amount will first be applied to reduce the $600,000 unified credit, and thereafter a tax will be triggered. When one of the nonmarried partners has an estate that is substantially larger than the other partner's, it is wise to begin an annual gift program to transfer assets to an irrevocable trust. The less wealthy partner can be named as current income beneficiary. Rights to income and principal similar to those available with a credit shelter trust can be given to the partner. On the death of the second partner, the trust could revert back to family members of the partner setting up the trust (or to any other beneficiaries he or she chose).

When spouses own property jointly, only one-half of the value of the property is included in the estate of the first spouse to die. With nonmarried couples, the entire value of the property is included in the estate of the first to die unless the survivor can demonstrate contribution toward the acquisition of the property. This means that considerable care should be taken to document the contribution of each partner toward the purchase of any property (for example, a personal residence shared by the partners, as well as any other valuable property).

Other difficulties arise if personal property (jewelry, art, and so forth) owned by either partner has substantial value. It is often difficult, if not impossible, to demonstrate ownership of such assets, particularly when they may have been acquired long ago, or as a gift. One possible solution is to have the title to the assets transferred into a revocable living trust. This can be done at a modest cost and can serve to demonstrate which partner has the ownership of such assets.

WHICH TRUST STRUCTURE IS BEST FOR NONMARRIED PARTNERS' ASSETS?

It was noted above that a nonmarried couple's property can be owned as joint tenants with the right of survivorship; on the death of the first partner, title will automatically transfer to the survivor. If the estate is substantial, however, a trust is the better approach. Under joint ownership, for federal estate tax purposes, the full value of the property will be included in the estate of the first to die, unless the survivor can demonstrate that he or she has made a contribution to the acquisition or improvement of the property—that is, with an estate exceeding $600,000, there will be a federal estate tax.

Revocable Trust

A trust agreement has several advantages over joint ownership. The trust is far more flexible and can address other issues either of the partners deems important. If a revocable trust is chosen, there are no immediate gift tax consequences (because the transfer is not complete). Unlike a joint-tenant arrangement, a trust can also provide for the management and treatment of the property in the event that either or both of the partners are disabled.

Irrevocable Trust

Alternatively, the arrangement could be structured as an irrevocable trust. The partner transferring assets to the trust could retain a general power of appointment so that the transfer still would not be complete for federal gift tax purposes, thus avoiding any current tax cost for the transfer. However, under this approach, the entire balance of the trust would be included in the estate of the partner who transfers the assets to the trust.

Another point in favor of an irrevocable trust is that, even though it is ineffective as a transfer for federal gift and estate tax purposes, it may be effective for purposes of local law. If so, this legal status could help insulate the assets of the trust from creditors, potential malpractice claimants, and, perhaps most importantly, from the claims of Medicaid and other health care providers (see Chapter 17).

Confidentiality

Whether a revocable or irrevocable trust is used, the trust can provide the benefit of confidentiality to the extent that it keeps those assets out of probate. If the family of either partner is against the relationship, this secrecy could prove to be a critical protection.

CONCLUSION

Because of the bias built into state and tax laws favoring married couples, estate and financial planning for partners who are not married is far more difficult than in the more common, married situation. Nevertheless, a number of valuable steps involving the use of trusts can facilitate the current and long-term goals of nonmarried partners.

13 TRUSTS FOR CHILDREN

When you think of trusts, you also think of children. It's natural because children have important financial needs but cannot manage their funds, and an essential characteristic of trusts is that they provide for the separation of ownership of an asset (in the trustee) and its beneficial enjoyment of that asset (the beneficiaries). The need to protect children from themselves, from a potential divorce, or from creditors makes trusts the ideal approach to providing for the future welfare of your children.

TAX PLANNING AFFECTS THE CHOICE AND STRUCTURE OF YOUR CHILDREN'S TRUST

The high gift, estate, and generation-skipping transfer tax rates can provide a strong impetus to make gifts that take the maximum advantage of the annual $10,000 gift tax exclusion. As explained in Chapter 8, however, it is more difficult to qualify for the $10,000 per year exclusion in using a trust than in making a direct gift because the gift must be characterized as having a present interest. This can be done through the use of a Crummey power, or through a special trust known by the IRS Code Section creating it, a 2503(c) (both described in this chapter). If the trust is not properly structured, you risk having the property given to the trust pulled back into your estate and taxed when you die.

To avoid estate tax, you, the parent (or other person making the gift), must limit your control over the trust assets. You also should not use the trust to meet your legal obligation as a parent to support your child. When trust income or assets are used for education, medical, or other obligations that the law requires a parent to meet, the income earned by the trust may be taxed to the parent.

NOTE: Alternative approaches to structuring gifts to your children are presented in *The Estate Planning Guide* (John Wiley & Sons, Inc., 1991).

GIFTS MADE UNDER THE UNIFORM GIFTS (TRANSFERS) TO MINORS ACT (A NONTRUST APPROACH)

One of the most commonly used arrangements for transferring assets to a child and removing them from your estate is not a formal trust but is a gift made under the Uniform Gift (or Transfers) to Minors Act. The Uniform Transfers to Minors Act differs from the Uniform Gifts to Minors Act; the former may be more recently enacted and broader in scope, permitting investments in real estate and other assets. This general method is referred to by the acronym UGMA or UTMA.

There are two major advantages of the UGMA approach: It costs nothing, and it's easy to use. Simply tell your broker or bank teller that you want to open an account under the Uniform Gifts (or Transfers) to Minors Act with your name as guardian. You then can administer the account for the child's benefit. When the child reaches the age of majority (the age at which state law considers the child to be an adult in financial matters), the assets will belong to the child.

The Uniform Gift to Minors Act has a number of drawbacks that should be carefully considered. The effect of making a gift under this act is to irrevocably transfer the property to the child and indefeasibly vest legal title in the child. This can be contrasted with trust arrangement, where the trustees own legal title to the property transferred. The powers you can have as custodian for the UGMA account include collecting, holding, managing, investing, and reinvesting the custodial property; you also can pay to your children, or expend for their benefit, the amount reasonably required for their support, maintenance, education, and benefit.

As part of the UGMA structure, it is possible for a minor, upon reaching age 14, to petition the court to have a statement of the money, stock, or other assets in the account. Also upon reaching age 14, the minor can petition the court to require the custodian to make payments for his or her support, maintenance, or education. When a trust is used, by contrast, it is within your control as the grantor to decide what rights to assign to the beneficiaries and trustees. The UGMA or UTMA laws differ in each state so be certain to review the details with your lawyer.

In order to designate a successor trustee under a UGMA account, a custodian must execute and date a written designation and have the document witnessed. When a trust arrangement is used, alternate trustees are almost always named in case the initial trustees can no longer serve.

For all these reasons, if the assets you're putting into your child's name are likely to become large enough to justify the cost of setting up a trust and the filing of tax returns each year, the use of a trust should definitely be considered.

GIFTS MADE TO MINOR CHILDREN THROUGH A TRUST—WHAT ARE THE OPTIONS?

All of the factors and choices already mentioned in designing a trust to meet your objectives need to be considered, plus a few more.

- Who will be the trustees? Should you choose the same persons who are named as guardians under your will? On the plus side, this kind of control avoids any conflict between the guardian's need for money for your children and a trustee's opinion of what is appropriate to spend. Nevertheless, many parents prefer to separate these functions so that some checks and balances are built into the arrangement. Further, serving as a guardian requires personal skills. Serving as a trustee requires financial skills. Having different people for these functions could produce better performances for each.

- A trust can contain a spendthrift provision to limit the rights of creditors of your children to the assets of the trust.

- The trustee can be authorized to distribute income of the trust among your children (a sprinkle power) based on their individual need rather than on a predetermined basis, such as equally.

- A right for the trustee to spend the principal (not just income) can be provided in the event of emergencies.

- You must decide at what ages your children should be given the assets from the trust. A common approach is one-third at ages 25, 30, and 35. The idea is to accustom the child to receiving money gradually so that if the child is irresponsible at the first distribution, there will be two more opportunities to learn responsibility. Some parents prefer earlier distribution, others later. The key is to consider the child's maturity and nature. You must determine whether you should have one trust for all of your children, or separate trusts for each child.

Besides considering all of those factors, there are a number of different structural arrangements, each with somewhat different tax consequences, that can be used in providing for children. An important factor in all of these trusts is being able to qualify for the annual $10,000 gift tax exclusion, and not use up any of your once-in-a-lifetime $600,000 exclusion. Remember that you can join with your spouse in each giving $10,000 a year, for a total of $20,000 per year to unlimited persons. To be sure the assets given to trusts stay out of your estate for estate tax purposes, all of the trusts must be irrevocable (you can't change them after you've set them up) and your powers must be limited.

Income-Only Trust (Section 2503(b) Trust)

Under this trust, the income must be distributed annually to your child or other beneficiary. This will permit you to qualify for the annual gift tax exclusion. The child then will be taxed on all of the income earned by the trust. If the child is under 14, the "kiddie tax" will apply. The Kiddie Tax will generally result in the income of a child under age 14 being taxed at the highest tax rate of the parent. See *The Estate Planning Guide* (John Wiley & Sons, Inc., 1991) for details. However, the income can be distributed to a Uniform Gift to Minors Act trust without disqualifying you from the benefits of the annual exclusion. The assets in the trust will have to be income producing for the IRS to respect the arrangement (for example, raw land that isn't leased—and doesn't produce income—won't work).

This trust offers additional flexibility over the 2503(c) special minor's trust described below in that the remainder beneficiary (the person who gets the trust property after the trust ends) doesn't have to be the same person who gets the trust income while the trust is in existence. When different beneficiaries are named, great care must be taken in how the trust agreement is worded. If the child-beneficiary receiving certain income during the existence of the trust has an emergency, should the trustee be permitted to dip into trust principal? This action will reduce the amount available to the person receiving the assets when the trust terminates. Clear rules advising the trustee what to do are important.

Right to Withdraw Under a Crummey Power

With the exception of the Section 2503(c) trust discussed below, if a trust can accumulate income, you will not qualify for the annual $10,000 tax exclusion on gifts to the trust. The exception is the degree to which the gift qualifies as being of a present interest. It qualifies up to the amount that the child can withdraw each year from the trust. This right to withdraw is called a Crummey demand power.

The Crummey power is named after a famous tax case in which the court sustained the taxpayer's argument that when the beneficiary had an opportunity to withdraw the funds currently but did not elect to do so, the transfer to the trust qualified as a gift of a present interest, and hence was eligible for the annual gift tax exclusion. Exercising a Crummey power means that the child beneficiary has the absolute right to presently enjoy the gift made by the parent, even if the child doesn't exercise this right and the money remains in the trust. The existence of this right enables the parent to avoid any gift tax. A host of complications in using this approach mandate careful review with your attorney, and the following discussion is intended only to highlight some of the concerns. (Also see Chapter 5 for sample demand power provisions.)

To establish a Crummey power, the trust must give the beneficiary a reasonable opportunity to withdraw the money. This is accomplished by having the trustee give written notice to the child stating that the withdrawal right for monies contributed exists and that the child has some period of time, say 30 to 60 days, to send in a written request demanding that the money be distributed. This period should expire by the year end. Also, it's best to send the notice by certified mail so that you can prove that this action was carried out.

Care must be taken that the right of the child beneficiary to withdraw funds doesn't create a problem called a secondary gift-over. This can be illustrated by an example with a typical trust.

EXAMPLE: You set up a trust for the benefit of your son and daughter. Any monies not paid out or withdrawn are to be accumulated until the youngest child reaches age 35, at which time the monies are to be distributed equally to each child. A Crummey power is provided so that each child has the right to withdraw one-half of the amount contributed each year, up to a maximum of the $10,000 annual exclusion. The demand power that the son has is also considered a power to appoint the amount not withdrawn to your daughter.

When the son fails to exercise this power, he is deemed to make a gift to the trust. If the total gift you made to the trust for the year was $20,000, the son will be deemed to have made a gift back to your daughter of the $10,000 he does not elect to withdraw from the trust under his power. This is a taxable gift for your son (and similarly, for your daughter).

One solution to the gift-over problem is to limit the annual gifts to the lesser of 5 percent of the trust principal or $5,000. A special rule provides that the end (lapse) of a power that is limited to the lesser of 5 percent or $5,000 will not create any gift tax implications. When the beneficiary's right to withdraw exceeds this amount, a technique called a hanging power is used. A hanging power permits the child's power to withdraw to lapse only when it won't create a gift under the 5 percent or $5,000 rule. Under this approach, the beneficiaries' unexercised right to withdraw $10,000 of trust property each year (the amount you contribute and on which you claim an annual gift tax exclusion) will lapse at the rate of $5,000 per year. The name "hanging power" is a result of the fact that the child's withdrawal right may continue to "hang" until future years and lapse at the rate of $5,000 per year long after you've stopped making contributions to the trust.

Another solution is to have separate trusts for each child. When this approach is used, the failure of the child to exercise his or her right to withdraw money will be a gift to the trust and not to a sibling.

This issue of Crummey and hanging powers is important to consider when establishing many types of trusts, when planning for gift taxes (Chapter 8), and when planning for life insurance trusts (Chapter 18).

Special Trust for Children Under Age 21 (Section 2503(c) Trust)

The law provides a special rule that permits you to transfer $10,000 per year to a trust and even if trust accumulates income, you can qualify for the annual gift tax exclusion. The rule includes the following criteria:

- The trust must be set up to benefit a minor child.
- The trustee must have the ability to use the income for the benefit of the minor child without restriction.
- The trust assets must be invested in income-producing assets (stocks, bonds, and CDs, but not raw land).
- When the child reaches age 21, the trust must be distributed to the child. The child can be given the right to require that the assets of the trust be distributed when he or she reaches age 21, but voluntarily choose not to take the money. Giving the child the right to take the money may increase the risk of the child's obtaining the assets of the

trust earlier than with a trust using a Crummey power, but it is a safer approach to claiming the benefits of the annual exclusion.

- If the child dies prior to age 21, the trust assets must be distributed to the child's estate, or in a manner that the child appoints.

This type of trust is commonly used in planning for minor children. A sample trust provision, with explanations and planning suggestions, appears in the "For Your Notebook" section following this chapter. For income tax purposes, the trust will pay tax on income it keeps, and the child will pay tax on income distributed to him or her.

MAKING GIFTS IN TRUST TO YOUR GRANDCHILDREN

When you can afford to make gifts to your grandchildren as well as your children, you will face rules similar to those described above. However, there is another potentially important tax benefit of using a regular gift program for grandchildren, rather than setting aside a lump sum. Gifts that qualify for the annual $10,000 gift tax exclusion can also escape the clutches of the extremely expensive generation-skipping transfer tax (see Chapter 9).

The use of a trust is even more complex when the beneficiaries are grandchildren instead of children. For example, if a single trust is established for both a child and a grandchild, and the child dies, the grandchild's status as a "skip person," and as the sole remaining beneficiary, may trigger the GST tax. As a general rule, you will do best in establishing a separate trust for each if large transfers are involved. When planning gifts for grandchildren, the GST rules should be considered in addition to the ones in this chapter.

TRUSTS FOR THE SPECIAL CHILD

When a child has special needs as a result of a handicap or illness, a well-planned trust agreement can provide for his or her care long into the future, after you are no longer able to assist. Such a trust can raise several unique issues.

CAUTION: When planning for the special child, establishing a trust is only one step. It is very important to sign a durable power of attorney so that in the event of your disability, someone else can disburse funds for the child's benefit. Your durable power of attorney can even include a provision authorizing expenditures.

Also, pay careful attention to the provisions of your will. Select guardians who are willing and able to assist your child. Be certain that enough guardians are selected so that care will be provided throughout life, not merely through age 18 or 21. This long time horizon is an important difference in planning for the special child. A guardianship designation with several alternates, including a state agency as a final selection, may be essential.

The Sensitive Issue of Allocating Resources

A basic planning goal for many families is to preserve as much of the family's wealth as possible for later generations. This can be very difficult when a special child is involved because the youngster's medical needs can severely deplete the family's resources.

NOTE: One of the most difficult issues for many families is how to apply limited resources. One extreme choice would be to apply all of the family's resources to the special child, to the exclusion of the others. At the other extreme would be to allocate no resources to the special child and let the various government programs provide for care. Where on this spectrum your decision will fall depends on several factors, including personal feelings, the extent of family resources, the needs of all of your children and other family members, the nature and extent of government programs, and so forth.

EXAMPLE: If you are extremely wealthy, you may be able to plan for all of your children, including ensuring the maximum care and attention for your special child. You want the best and will pay for it, and the loss of government resources that could otherwise be available to your child are not a concern. On the other hand, if your financial resources are extremely limited, you may be forced to disinherit your special child, not out of lack of love, but rather out of the necessity to rely on government programs. The disinheritance can also be intentional if another child can be fully trusted to provide for the special child. The estates for which planning is most difficult are those in between the two extremes. With the moderate estate, there is a desire to preserve some resources for the family unit but also to provide for the special child.

When planning any trust for a special child, each of the available government or charitable programs must be considered, along with their requirements and qualifications. Medicare and Social Security are two important federal programs. Social Security can provide benefits if the special child is totally disabled. Medicare provides for limited basic medical coverage.

Supplemental Security Income (SSI) Medicaid, welfare, and other programs may be available as well. To qualify for these need-based programs, the income and assets of the recipient must be quite limited. Qualifying for these programs is a cornerstone of planning. The trust arrangement you set up must not result in the child's being considered to have more income or assets than the requirements permit, or the benefits will be lost. Various states have additional programs, such as the cost-of-care type, that may also be available.

Attempting to preserve wealth for the family unit as a whole without undue depletion to meet the special needs of one child, while maximizing the use of public and other program resources available to the special child, is not a simple goal. The requirements can often be contradictory. The laws and various entitlement programs are not only complex, but they also change frequently. Any trusts you establish are subject to all of the concerns of avoiding creditors mentioned earlier and discussed further in Chapters 16 and 17. (Every trust for a special child will include a spendthrift provision. Although a spendthrift provision is never fool-proof, it can provide valuable protection.)

The Life Insurance Trust

One of the most effective and important tools for a family with a special child and with limited resources is the irrevocable life insurance trust, discussed in Chapter 18. The purchase of life insurance can be an important safety net to ensure a minimum level of support for the special child. The trust format allows you to provide for all of the contingencies needed for continuing care. By using an irrevocable trust arrangement you can keep the insurance proceeds out of your estate.

A trust also can be set up to hold assets for the benefit of the special child, and to provide for distributions. The trust can be set up during your lifetime or created under your will after your death. The critical provisions of any trust are those that determine when distributions can be made. When a trust requires that all of the income (or any other mandatory amount) be distributed to the special child, or for his or her benefit, these amounts undoubtedly will be taken into account when income tests are made to determine eligibility for government benefits. When the trustee has the discretion to apply trust income and principal for the support or maintenance of the special child, the income and assets of the trust similarly will be taken into account and disqualify the child from many government benefits that otherwise may have been available.

Trustee Powers and Provisions

When the trustee has discretion to apply income in any manner to several different beneficiaries, it will be more difficult for any state or government agency to argue that the income or assets of the trust are available to the special child. But even if the special child is the only beneficiary, there are some steps that can help. For example, you can include a provision indicating that the trust's income and assets cannot be distributed to or for the benefit of the special child when the distributions or expenditures would jeopardize qualification for government benefits or distributions from charitable organizations. In other words, your trust can clearly state that the trustee is not to make distributions that can be met from other government or charitable sources. Distributions should only be made to fill in the gaps in those programs, and to provide additional items for personal comfort.

A more extreme provision can be included that will terminate the trust and require the distribution of all assets to children other than the special child in the event that a state or other government agency can reach the trust assets. The objective of such a provision is to dissuade government agencies from suing the trust for reimbursements for medical care.

There is no need to limit the trust to the formal language and provisions only. You also can state your personal preferences for the care of your child and instruct your trustees in informal language.

Whenever drafting a trust for a special child, your choice of trustees must consider the caveats raised above concerning the selection of guardians. Planning for the special child is often for life, not merely until age 30 or 35 as with many other children's trusts. Thus, several alternate trustees should be named, and a corporate trust department should be named as a final trustee.

CONCLUSION

Planning for the welfare of your minor children is often the most important estate planning objective. The various approaches that can be used should be analyzed in light of the tax, financial, and emotional aspects of your family, and in light of any special needs of a particular child.

For Your Notebook:

SAMPLE 2503(c) MINOR'S TRUST PROVISIONS

[DO NOT USE IN A TRUST
UNLESS REVIEWED FIRST WITH YOUR ATTORNEY]

CODE SECTION 2053(C) TRUST PROVISIONS

a. *Accumulated Income Paid at Age 21*

Upon the beneficiary of the trust having attained the age of Twenty-One (21) years such beneficiary shall have the sole and absolute power and discretion and right to compel immediate distribution to such beneficiary of the entire corpus of the trust with the entire accumulated income and all accrued income absolutely and free of any trust. Such election shall be exercised by a written notice demanding such distribution, executed by the beneficiary and delivered to and received by the Trustee within Sixty (60) days after the beneficiary shall attain the age of Twenty One (21) years. Upon receiving such notice the Trustee shall distribute to the beneficiary the entire corpus of the trust including any accumulated or accrued income.

b. *Notice Given of Right to Distribution at Age 21*

The Trustee shall give written notice to the beneficiary, via certified or registered mail, of the beneficiaries right to exercise the election set forth in this Section.

c. *Disposition of Trust Estate on Beneficiary's Death Before Age 21*

Upon the death of the beneficiary before reaching the age of Twenty-One (21) years, the principal of the Trust Estate, and any net income then remaining in the hands of the Trustee shall be transferred, conveyed and paid over to or for the benefit of such person or persons or corporation or corporations or the estate of the beneficiary, to such extent, in such amounts and proportions, and in such lawful interests or estates, whether absolute or in trust, as the beneficiary may in such beneficiary's Last Will appoint by a specific reference to this power. If the power of appointment is for any reason not validly exercised in whole or in part by the beneficiary, the principal of the Trust Estate and any such net income, to the extent not validly appointed by such beneficiary, shall, upon death of such beneficiary, be distributed to the siblings of such beneficiary, or the issue, per stirpes, of any deceased sibling.

d. *Application of Trust Estate Where Beneficiary Elects Not to Receive Trust Estate upon Attaining Age 21*

(1) If the Beneficiary does not make the election to have this Trust corpus, including accumulated and accrued income, distributed as provided above, then this trust shall continue beyond the date of the beneficiary's Twenty-First (21st) birthday as provided herein. This provision shall be limited so as not to violate any of the provisions of Code Section 2035(c), or the regulations or cases thereunder.

(2) The Trustee shall hold for the beneficiary in trust, to pay or apply the net income to or for the benefit of the beneficiary, in annual or more frequent installments and to distribute the principal of such trust in accordance with the Distribution By Age procedures.

(3) Should the Beneficiary die prior to the distribution of the entire trust estate as provided herein, the trustee shall transfer and pay over the trust estate as provided above.

14 TRUSTS FOR CHARITIES

CHARITABLE REMAINDER TRUSTS

If your estate is quite large, and the needs of your family and other heirs are sufficiently provided for, you may consider providing for certain charitable causes. Whether or not making a large charitable bequest has been a major goal of yours, the tax and other benefits can be so significant that potential donors may decide to increase their donations through trust arrangements.

One of the most important arrangements is a charitable remainder trust. If you have some charitable intent but don't want to part with a property or its benefits (that is, the income the property generates) at this time, a deferred-giving program may be instituted, in which you create a remainder interest in the property in favor of a charitable organization.

Under a charitable remainder trust, you donate property (real estate, stock, and so forth) to a charity and receive a charitable-contribution income tax deduction in the year of the donation, but the charity will not receive the full benefit of the property until some future time. Under this structure, you can reserve an income interest in the charitable remainder trust. Thus, the income generated from the sale of the donated property will be paid to you for your life and thereafter to your spouse for his or her life. After the death of both of you, the charity will obtain full use and benefit of the donated property. The amount of the charitable deduction you take is equal to the fair market value of the property at the time of the donation, less the present value of the income interest retained by you and your spouse.

In addition to the current income tax deduction, you also may receive a valuable estate tax benefit. If you're one of the income beneficiaries of the charitable trust, the value of the trust will be included in your gross estate when you die. However, since the interest will pass to the charity, there will be an offsetting estate tax charitable contribution deduction. Thus, the value of the property donated effectively will be removed from your estate. Taking into account the savings in federal estate tax, state inheritance tax, and probate and administrative costs, you can transfer substantial assets to a deserving charity at very little actual cost.

There are several types of charitable remainder trusts, including (1) an annuity trust, in which a fixed annuity is provided to the income beneficiaries; and (2) a unitrust, in which the income return is variable and based on the fair market value of the property each year. With the exception of gifts of a remainder interest in a personal residence or farm property, you will only qualify for an income, gift, and estate tax deduction if the charitable donation is in a trust that qualifies either as an annuity trust or a unitrust.

- *Annuity Trust.* An annuity trust will provide a fixed annuity to the people you designate in the trust agreement as the income beneficiaries. The minimum rate of return cannot be less than 5 percent, and it must be a fixed or determinable amount. This income is calculated from the fair market value of the property transferred to the trust. Once the trust is established, no further contributions can be made to it. When the trust income is insufficient to meet the required annual return, principal must be invaded.

- *Unitrust.* A unitrust provides a variable annuity to its income beneficiaries. The minimum rate of return, as with the annuity trust, must be 5 percent. This rate is calculated from the fair market value of the property, determined on an annual basis. If the annual income earned by the trust property is insufficient to meet the required distribution to the income beneficiaries, principal may, but doesn't have to, be invaded. If principal is not required to be invaded, then the trust must provide that the deficit will be made up in later years. Once a unitrust is established, additional contributions may be made in later years under certain conditions.

   The valuation of the remainder interest of the unitrust is determined under methods provided for in the Treasury regulations and considers the value of the property transferred to the trust, the age of the income beneficiary, and the payout rate.

   The drawback of the unitrust is that it requires an annual appraisal. Many kinds of property are difficult to value (for example, closely held business interests and real estate), and the cost of annual appraisals could be a prohibitive. For this reason, an annuity trust is likely to be the more practical choice when such assets are to be contributed.

Using Insurance in Planning for a Charitable Remainder Transaction

The basic goal in combining insurance products with a charitable remainder plan is to preserve intact the value of the estate passing to your heirs. The concept is quite simple: You establish an irrevocable life insurance trust for the benefit of your heirs. The trustee (or the heir, when direct gifts are made) purchases insurance on your life in an amount that is sufficient to replace the value of the assets you transferred to the charitable remainder trust. It's a classic textbook plan, and if all goes well, the following goals can be achieved:

- You provide for a favorite cause or organization.
- Your income tax savings provide cash flow to make continuing gifts to the trust, or to the heir directly.

- On your death, the insurance proceeds from insurance owned by your life insurance trust are not taxable in your estate, and your heirs receive an amount approximating the value of the assets you had transferred to the charitable remainder trust.

EXAMPLE: A donor owns real estate worth $1 million, with an adjusted cost basis of $200,000. Transferring the property to a charitable remainder trust could generate a $400,000 contribution deduction. This could provide an income tax savings of approximately $140,000. In addition, the donor will avoid an approximate $220,000 capital gain on the sale of the property. The trustee may be able to pay the donor an annual income of $60,000. The donor and his wife can make a joint annual gift to their son and daughter-in-law totaling $40,000 under the gift tax exclusion (a $10,000 gift to each recipient by each spouse). This amount can be used by the son to purchase life insurance on the donor's life of $1 million, sufficient to replace the $1 million worth of real estate transferred to the charitable remainder trust.

The son will inherit the same $1 million on the parents' death that he would have received had the planning not been undertaken. However, without this planning, the $1 million real estate asset could have been reduced by a 55 percent marginal estate tax. Thus, the planning potentially doubles the actual inheritance.

The charitable remainder trust technique assumes that an income stream will be paid to a life beneficiary (the donor) for some period of time. If the sole life beneficiary should die prematurely, the family unit will be denied the benefit of the expected income stream. To avoid this result, in the appropriate circumstances, the charitable remainder planning can be combined with a life insurance policy that supplements the family's income stream when the life beneficiary dies prematurely. This can be done, for example, with a life insurance trust for the benefit of the children or spouse of the named life beneficiary. The life insurance trust should be structured to ensure that the proceeds will not be included in the estate of the life beneficiary. When the cost of the insurance is a factor and the family decides to protect only against the risk of the loss of the expected income stream, an insurance arrangement can be used providing for decreasing coverage (to approximate the decline in the loss of expected income as the life beneficiary lives through the intended term of the trust).

Income-Only Unitrust Option of a Charitable Remainder Trust

A modified form of charitable remainder unitrust can be used when there is an income-only arrangement. Under this type of unitrust, the beneficiary only receives trust income up to (or below) the fixed percentage yield, but this arrangement can be structured to include a make-up provision: When the net income of the trust exceeds the specified percentage of trust assets, the excess can be paid to the income beneficiary to the extent of the aggregate shortfall in prior years. The shortfall is based on the difference between the amounts paid in prior years and the amounts calculated under the specified percentage method. This concept is best illustrated with an example:

EXAMPLE: Donald Donor has a substantial income, is getting on in years, and wants to provide for his favorite charity. Donald expects to retire in five years, and upon retirement, he expects his income to drop to a lower tax bracket. Donald Donor establishes an income-only charitable remainder unitrust with a make-up provision. This trust is funded with a $1 million initial contribution, which is invested in low-dividend growth stocks. The unitrust percentage is set at the lowest permissible amount, which is 5 percent. The dividends on the stock portfolio produce a mere .75 percent return, or $7,500, which is paid to the donor.

After year five, Donald Donor retires. The stock portfolio, which has appreciated to $1.5 million, is liquidated and invested in high-yielding bond instruments. These bonds produce a return of 8 percent, or $120,000. Ordinarily, Donald would receive only 5 percent of the $1.5 million asset value, or $75,000. But as a result of the make-up provision, he can be paid additional amounts in each of the remaining years of the trust to make up for the earlier shortfall years. If the shortfall totals $212,500 [(5 years × $50,000) − (5 years × $7,500)], Donald Donor will be entitled to all of the income from the income-only unitrust for a number of years to come.

CAUTION: A flaw in the approach taken above is the assumption of lower tax rates upon retirement. The client who would engage in such a sophisticated transaction is likely to have a substantial income even after retirement, so that the maximum tax rate could apply both pre- and postretirement. Further, many tax practitioners anticipate increases in future tax rates, not decreases.

What to Include in Your Trust Agreement

- *Choice of Trustee.* While you, as the grantor, may be named as co-trustee, be careful when the assets of the trust don't have an objective or reasonably determinable market value (for example, interests in a closely held business).
- *Restrictions on Investments.* A trust can be disqualified as being a charitable remainder trust if the trust document restricts the trustee from investing in a manner that could result in the realization of reasonable income or gain.

EXAMPLE: A trustee was required to retain certain antiques for the life of the donor beneficiary. Since the antiques obviously could not produce any income, it was impossible to pay the required annual amounts to the beneficiaries, and the trust was disqualified.

While selective investment in real estate and growth securities may not jeopardize the trust status, caution should be exercised. Within reason, and with proper drafting, the trustee of a charitable remainder trust can use the investment-selection process to control the income when the donor beneficiary is in a high tax bracket, or not in need of funds.

If properly structured, a charitable remainder trust can be funded with tax-exempt securities. The donor then could receive a substantial tax deduction, as well as tax-free annual payments, and realize an advantageous economic return on the transaction.

- *Designating the Charitable Remainder Beneficiary.* The remainder of the trust must be paid over to a charity (as described in Internal Revenue Code Sections 2055, 2522, and 170). Multiple charities can be used as long as it is made clear what each charity should receive upon termination of the trust. It is advisable to name a fall-back beneficiary in the trust agreement in the event that the named charity goes out of existence, or remains in existence but no longer qualifies. A private foundation can be named as the charitable remainder beneficiary, but a host of restrictions may apply.

TAXATION ISSUES OF CHARITABLE REMAINDER GIVING

Effect on Estate and Gift Taxes

Properly structured, large charitable gifts can significantly reduce potential estate and gift taxes. This reduction can help avert potential estate liquidity problems, increasing flexibility to retain relatively nonliquid business or real estate interests. The estate tax charitable deduction rules, except for the noticeable absence of percentage limitations, are generally similar to the rules applicable for income tax purposes.

A deduction for charitable contributions is permitted for gift tax purposes on qualifying gifts to charities. A contribution after your death, such as under the provisions of a living trust you established during your life, to a qualified charitable organization can provide an estate tax deduction. The amount of the charitable deduction is limited by the amount or value that actually becomes available to the charitable organization. For example, when the charitable bequest is reduced as a result of an allocation for administrative expenses, or by estate tax (as a possible result of an improperly drafted tax allocation clause), the charitable contribution deduction will be reduced accordingly. In that case, each dollar of tax deduction could reduce the amount of the charitable bequest and thus increase the tax due. Calculating the net tax cost requires solving a simultaneous equation.

When the estate includes closely held active business interests on which the estate tax is deferred for the approximately 14-year period prescribed under Code Section 6166, the IRS has held that the estimated amount of the interest expense to be paid on the deferred tax may have to be applied to reduce the amount of a charitable bequest made from the residuary.

How Are Beneficiaries and Trusts Taxed on Their Income?

The amounts paid to a trust beneficiary under a charitable remainder trust retain the character they had in the trust. Regular trusts characterize payments according to the trust's income and other activities during the particular year. A charitable remainder trust characterizes payments over the entire history of the trust.

Thus, the income paid to the donor beneficiary of a charitable remainder unitrust or annuity trust is taxed as ordinary income to the extent of the trust's current and prior undistributed income.

After all ordinary income is exhausted, amounts will be taxed as follows:

1. As a short-term capital gain to the extent of current and past undistributed short-term capital gains.
2. As a long-term capital gain to the extent of current and past undistributed long-term capital gains.
3. As other income, such as tax-exempt income, to the extent of the trust's current and past undistributed income of such character.
4. As tax-free distributions of principal.

The trust generally will be exempt from tax. However, when the trust generates unrelated business taxable income, it can be subject to tax.

Generation-Skipping Transfer Tax

While the generation-skipping transfer tax (GST tax) will not apply to charitable gifts, GST tax considerations could be important if the donor's grandchild (or another skip person) is made the income beneficiary of the charitable remainder trust. The complex generation-skipping transfer tax was discussed in Chapter 9. When such a situation occurs, the donor must carefully plan the allocation to the trust of any remaining GST lifetime $1 million exemption.

EXAMPLE: Assume that Donald Donor transferred $500,000 into a charitable remainder unitrust. The value of the remainder interest is $275,000. Assume further that Donor has $450,000 of his GST tax exemption still available. He could allocate $225,000 [$500,000 total value − $275,000 charitable remainder value] of his remaining GST tax exemption to the trust. The trust will have an inclusion ratio of zero, and no GST tax will be due (see Chapter 9).

Tax Effect of Gifts to Benefit Both Your Spouse and a Charity

Special rules apply when a donor wants to transfer property to both a spouse and a charity. These rules permit the donor to take advantage of both the charitable contribution deduction and the marital deduction, and thus can provide valuable planning benefits. For example, assume that you transfer property to a charitable remainder trust and you and your spouse are the sole income beneficiaries; the only other beneficiary is a charity. On your death, your estate will qualify for both a charitable contribution deduction and an estate tax marital deduction.

An alternative approach is simply to establish a qualified terminable interest property (Q-TIP) trust for your spouse, with the remainder interest to go to a specified charity on your spouse's death. Q-TIP trusts permit your spouse to receive all of the income from the trust during life; on his or her death, the trust assets go to the persons—in this case the charity—that you designate. (See Chapter 11.) While this approach is simpler, there can be no income tax deduction, as would be available if a charitable remainder trust were used, with you and your spouse named as an income beneficiary.

There is more flexibility in planning the payment of income under a charitable remainder trust than by using a Q-TIP with a charitable remainder beneficiary. This is because the charitable remainder trust doesn't have to be required to pay income at least annually, as does the Q-TIP.

What Tax Deduction Can You Get?

The donor of property to a charitable remainder trust is entitled to a deduction for income, estate, and gift tax purposes. The deduction is based on the present value of the charitable remainder interest. For income tax purposes, the gift of a remainder interest to a charity is treated as a gift to the remainderman. If the remainderman charity is a public charity, the maximum deduction is allowed, up to either 30 percent or 50 percent of the donor's adjusted gross income.

CHARITABLE LEAD TRUST

A charitable lead trust is the exact opposite of a charitable remainder trust. When a charitable lead trust is used, the charity receives the income from a property for a specified period of years and then the property is transferred to designated beneficiaries, such as your children. Obviously, the estate tax benefits are minor since only the income accumulation from the years of the trust is removed from the estate.

The following two examples show the tax results of setting up a charitable lead trust under two different scenarios.

EXAMPLE: You transfer $450,000 to a charitable lead trust that will pay an annuity for 10 years. The result of this arrangement is that the charity will receive $40,000 per year for each of 10 years, payable in equal quarterly amounts, while you will qualify for a current income tax charitable deduction of $280,992.07.

EXAMPLE: You transfer $450,000 to a charitable lead trust based on life expectancy, instead of for a fixed 10-year period. Payments will continue for the rest of the lives of you and your spouse, who are presently 58 and 56. You will get a charitable contribution deduction of $434,637.26. The remainder interest will only be worth $15,362.74.

NOTE: Your charitable contribution deductions are subject to various limitations. See Shenkman, *The Estate Planning Guide* (John Wiley & Sons, Inc., 1991), for a discussion of these.

EXAMPLE:

CHARITABLE LEAD ANNUITY TRUST FOR A TERM OF 10 YEARS

Inputs for Charitable Lead Annuity Trust—Term of Years

Transfer Date:	02/1992
Table Rate:	7.60%
FMV of Trust:	$450,000
Dollar Payout:	$10,000
Payment Period:	4
Pay at Beginning or End of Period:	End
Payment Years:	10

CHARITABLE LEAD ANNUITY TRUST FOR TWO LIVES

Charitable Lead Annuity Trust—Two Lives Calculation

Transfer Date	1/1992
Table Rate	8.2%
Fair Market Value of Trust	$450,000
Stated Dollar Amount Payout	$10,000
Payment Periods in Year	4
Payments Made at Beginning or End of Period	End
Ages of Persons Whose Lives Determine the Term of the Trust	58 and 56
Annual Payout to Charity	$40,000
Annual Percentage Payout	8.889%
Two-Life Annuity Factor	10.5474
Payout Frequency Factor	1.0302
Present Value of Annuity	$434,637
Remainder = FMV of Trust Less PV of Annuity	$15,363
Charitable Deduction for Income Interest	$434,637

Chart prepared using *Estate Planning Tools* software copyright Commerce Clearing House, Inc., Chicago, IL

POOLED-INCOME FUND

Under a pooled-income arrangement, you contribute property to the charitable trust and in exchange have the right to participate in an investment pool managed by the charity. The trust pays each donor (there can be many) a share of the income from the pooled trust. On your death, the remainder interest in the trust must go to the charity.

CONCLUSION

Charitable giving with trusts can present valuable planning opportunities if you are charitably inclined and have the available resources. The benefits can be far greater than expected. However, always obtain competent legal, tax, and insurance advice since charitable trusts are some of the most complicated to work with.

> **NOTE:** Before incurring significant fees on your own, contact the charities to which you are considering donating. Many of the larger charities have qualified advisers on staff who can help you plan your charitable trusts.

On the other hand, always review the reasons for using a charitable trust. If you really just want to be generous, an outright gift to the charity is far simpler.

For Your Notebook:

SAMPLE CHARITABLE REMAINDER UNITRUST

[DO NOT USE AS A TRUST AGREEMENT
WITHOUT DISCUSSING WITH YOUR LAWYER]

TRUST AGREEMENT made this -0-th day of January 1992, between GRANTOR'S NAME, as Grantor, and TRUSTEE-1 and TRUSTEE-2, as Trustees, to establish a charitable remainder unitrust, within the meaning of Revenue Procedure 89-20 and section 664(d)(2) of the Internal Revenue Code of 1986 as amended (the "Code"), called the GRANTOR NAME 1992 Charitable Remainder Unitrust.

I. *Funding of Trust*

The Grantor transfers to the Trustees the property described in Schedule A, and the Trustees accept such property and agree to hold, invest, manage and distribute such property as the Trust Estate under the terms set forth in this Trust Agreement.

II. *Payment of Unitrust Amount*

A. The Trustees shall pay to the Beneficiaries described below, in each tax year of the Trust until the termination of the Trust, a unitrust amount equal to INTEREST RATE percent (___%) of the net fair market value of the assets of the Trust (the Trust Estate) valued as of December 31 of each tax year of the Trust (the "Valuation Date").

B. ALLOCATION% of the unitrust amount shall be paid to each of BENEFICIARY-1 ("BENEFICIARY-1") and BENEFICIARY-2 ("BENEFICIARY-2"). If BENEFICIARY-2 is not living on any date as of which any part of the unitrust amount is payable to such beneficiary, such part shall be paid to BENEFICIARY-1. If BENEFICIARY-1 is not living on any date at which any portion of the unitrust amount is payable to such beneficiary, such part shall be paid to ALTERNATE BENEFICIARY NO. 1 if he is then living, or, if he is not then living, in equal shares to such of BENEFICIARY-1's children, then living, or, if neither of them is then living, to BENEFICIARY-2, if she is then living.

C. Any person to whom any part or all of the unitrust amount is payable pursuant to the terms of this Trust Agreement are referred to herein as a "Beneficiary" or "Beneficiaries."

D. The unitrust amount shall be paid annually on the last day of each tax year of the Trust or within a reasonable time thereafter, for a period of TERM IN YEARS (___) years from the date this Trust Agreement was executed, from income and, to the extent that income is not sufficient, from principal. Any income of the Trust for a tax year in excess of the unitrust amount shall be added to principal of the Trust Estate. If the net fair market value of the Trust assets (Trust Estate) is incorrectly determined, then within a reasonable period of time after the value is finally determined for Federal tax purposes, the Trustee shall pay to the Beneficiaries (if an undervaluation) or receive from the Beneficiaries (if an overvaluation) an amount equal to the difference between the unitrust amount properly payable, and the unitrust amount which was actually paid to the Beneficiaries.

III. *Proration of the Unitrust Amount*

In determining the unitrust amount, the Trustees shall prorate the amount on a daily basis for a short tax year and for the tax year in which the Trust terminates.

IV. *Distribution to Charity*

The Trust shall terminate TERM IN YEARS (___) years from the date this Trust Agreement is signed and the Trustees shall then distribute all of the then principal and income of the Trust (other than any amount due) any Beneficiary or his or her estate under the preceding Sections (i.e., the remaining Trust Estate), to the NAME OF CHARITABLE FOUNDATION (the "Charitable Organization"). If the Charitable Organization is not an organization described in, and qualified under, Code Sections 170(c), 2055(a), and 2522(a) at the time when any principal or income of the Trust is to be distributed to it, then the Trustees shall distribute the principal or income to such one or more organizations described in the foregoing Code Sections, as the Trustees shall select in their absolute discretion.

V. *Additional Contributions*

If any additional contributions are made to the Trust Estate after the initial contribution, the unitrust amount for the year in which the additional contribution is made shall be INTEREST RATE percent (____%) of the sum of:

A. The net fair market value of the Trust assets as of the valuation date (excluding the assets added and any income from, or appreciation on, the assets); and

B. That proportion of the value of the assets so added that was excluded under (a) that the number of days in the period that begins with the date of contribution and ends with the earlier of the last day of the tax year or the date on which this Trust terminates bears to the number of days in the period that begins on the first day of such tax year and ends with the earlier of (i) the last day in such tax year; or (ii) the date on which this Trust terminates. In the case where there is no valuation date after the time of contribution, the assets so added to the Trust Estate shall be valued at the time of contribution.

VI. *Valuation of Trust Assets for a Short Tax Year*

A. In the case of the first tax year of the Trust, the Trust assets (Trust Estate) shall be valued as of December 31, 1992 and the unitrust amount shall be paid within a reasonable time after that date.

B. In the case of the taxable year in which the Trust terminates, because the valuation date will not occur before the termination date, the Trust assets shall be valued as of the date on which the Trust terminates.

VII. *Prohibited Transactions*

The income of the Trust for each taxable year shall be distributed at a time, and in a manner, so that it will not be subject to the Trust to tax under Code Section 4942. Except for the payment of the unitrust amount to the Beneficiaries, the Trustees shall not engage in any act of self-dealing, as defined in Code Section 4941(d), and shall not make any taxable expenditures, as defined in Code Section 4945(d). The Trustees shall not make any investments that jeopardize the charitable purpose of the Trust, within the meaning of Code Section 4944, or retain any excess business holdings, within the meaning of Code Section 4943.

VIII. *Powers and Rights of the Trustees*

A. Each Trustee designated in this Trust Agreement shall qualify as a Trustee by mailing or delivering a signed and acknowledged instrument of consent to act as such Trustee to the firm that made such designation.

B. If at any time there is no Trustee, TRUSTEE-3 shall become Trustee, or, if she fails or ceases to act as Trustee, TRUSTEE-4 shall become Trustee, or, if he fails or ceases to act as Trustee, TRUSTEE-5 shall become Trustee, or, if she fails or ceases to act, the individual or trust company designated from time to time by the firm of LAWYER NAME, now doing business at LAWYER'S ADDRESS, or by any successor firm, shall become Trustee. Any designation hereunder shall be made by a signed and acknowledged instrument mailed or delivered to the Trustee so designated. At any time before any designation becomes effective, it may be revoked in similar manner. Any such designation shall be effective at the time specified in the instrument of designation but not before the delivery of an instrument of qualification pursuant to the terms of this Trust Agreement.

NOTE: It's always advisable to name as many successor trustees as possible to avoid the possibility of not having a named trustee to serve. A common safety procedure is to say that if none of the named trustees can serve, your lawyer can name a trustee, or, alternatively, a specified corporate trustee (such as the trust department of a bank) can serve.

C. The Trustees may designate any individual or a bank or trust company to execute and deliver on behalf of the trust any and all papers which may be required to effect the sale, transfer or delivery of any asset of the Trust Estate, or the purchase or other acquisition of assets by the Trust, and to sign, alone, checks, drafts or other orders for the payment or withdrawal of funds from any bank account for the trust. Where such a designation is made, it shall be in writing signed by the Trustees and may be revoked or changed at any time. No person or corporation acting in reliance on any such designation shall be charged with notice of any revocation or change of such designation unless he shall have received actual notice.

D. Each of the Trustees acting from time to time shall be entitled to commissions or compensation for acting as Trustee as shall be allowed from time to time under the applicable laws of the State of STATE NAME.

NOTE: Part of the benefit of using a charitable trust can include the commissions earned by the trustees. For example, if you have a child who is skilled in investment matters, the child could serve as trustee and earn commissions for the work. When properly done and supported by the facts, this can provide a valuable method of transferring additional income to your heirs without the imposition of substantial estate taxes.

E. No Trustee, whether named in this Trust Agreement or designated as provided above, shall be required to give any bond or other security, in any jurisdiction, for the faithful performance of the duties of Trustee.

F. In any judicial proceeding relating to this Trust Agreement, where a party to the proceeding has the same interest as a person under a disability, it shall not be necessary to serve the person under a disability.

IX. *Investment of Trust Assets*

Nothing in this Trust Agreement shall be construed to restrict the Trustees from investing the Trust assets in a manner that could result in the annual realization of a reasonable amount of income or gain from the sale or disposition of Trust assets.

X. *Definition of Trustees*

A. Wherever used in this Trust Agreement, the word "Trustees" and all references to the Trustees shall mean the Trustees named in this Trust Agreement, and any successor Trustee, named herein or designated as provided above, or appointed by a court of competent jurisdiction, qualified and acting hereunder from time to time. In addition to, and in amplification of, all the powers conferred on trustees by law, the Trustees are hereby authorized and empowered, subject to the provisions contained in this Trust Agreement, in their sole and absolute discretion:

1. To grant options for the sale of property or to lease property, for periods of any duration, even periods which extend beyond the term of this Trust Agreement.

2. To invest and reinvest any of the principal of the Trust Estate in any property, real or personal, as they may determine (including, without limitation, mutual funds, common trust funds or investment trusts), and retain any property transferred or added to the principal in the same form in which it was received.

3. To employ any investment advisers or counsel, agents, corporate custodians, brokers, accountants and attorneys which they may select, and pay the fees and charges thereof out of income or principal or partly from them. The trustees are authorized to delegate discretionary trading authority to the investment advisers without any liability for investment losses resulting from the decisions made by any investment counsel. Any Trustee, and any partnership or corporation in which any Trustee may be interested or by which the Trustee may be employed, can be retained in any such capacity, and in such event, the fees and charges which shall be payable to

the Trustee, or to any such partnership or corporation, is in addition to commissions or compensation which would otherwise be allowable to the Trustee, subject to the provisions of this Agreement. No Trustees shall be liable for any loss or damage to the trust or any part of the Trust Estate arising out of or resulting from any act or omission to act on the part of the Trustees taken or based upon the opinion or recommendation of, or arising out of or resulting from the act or omission to act of, any such investment adviser, custodian, broker, agent, accountant or attorney employed by the Trustees in good faith.

4. To pay fiduciary commissions to any Trustee, subject to the provisions of this Trust Agreement, at any time or times during the administration of this Trust, without prior judicial approval, without bond, and in advance of the settlement of the account of such Trustees.

5. To pay the fees and charges of any investment advisers, corporate custodian, broker, agent, accountant or attorney. These fees may be paid whether or not any Trustee is, or is interested in, the investment adviser, custodian, broker, agent, accountant or attorney.

B. With respect to any Beneficiary:

1. If any Beneficiary shall, in the reasonable opinion of the Trustees, become incapacitated as a result of illness or for any other cause, in lieu of paying net income or principal to that Beneficiary, the Trustees may in their discretion, choose to dispose of the income or principal in one or more of the following ways:

a. By making payment to a legally appointed guardian, committee or conservator of such Beneficiary;

b. By making payment, on behalf of such Beneficiary, to a trustee under any revocable inter vivos trust established by such Beneficiary prior to his disability where such trustee has been delegated the right to handle the Beneficiary's financial affairs in the event of disability, to such Beneficiary's attorney-in-fact under a durable power of attorney, to any person with whom the Beneficiary resides or who has charge of his care; or

c. By application of the amounts directly for the use or for the benefit of the Beneficiary.

d. By making any payment or application described in paragraph (A) hereof without requiring any bond or other security for the payment or application made of the funds. A receipt for the amount of the payment or application shall be absolute protection to the Trustees and shall constitute a complete release and discharge from all further accountability, responsibility and liability and as to the disposition of the funds or property by the person or corporation to whom such payment was made.

e. At any time, without prior court approval but subject to applicable legal limits, to remove all or any part of the assets comprising the Trust Estate, or the situs of administration of the Trust to another jurisdiction and, in connection with the move, to elect that the laws of such other jurisdiction shall thereafter govern to such extent as may be necessary and appropriate, and upon such election the courts of the other jurisdiction shall have the power to carry out the purposes of this Trust Agreement. The Trustees may exercise absolute discretion in regard to the above matters for any reason, including the convenience of the Trustees or of the Beneficiaries of the trust.

2. Exercise all power and discretion granted in this Trust Agreement after the termination of this Trust and until all the assets are fully applied or distributed.

XI. *Miscellaneous Provisions*

A. *Irrevocable Trust.* The Grantor understands the meaning of an irrevocable trust and hereby declares that this Trust is irrevocable.

B. *Applicable Law.* The operation of the Trust shall be governed by the laws of the State of New York. However, the Trustees are prohibited from exercising any power or discretion granted under said laws that would be inconsistent with the qualification of the Trust under Code Section 664(d)(2) and the regulations thereunder.

C. *Savings Provision.* The Trustees have the power to amend this Trust Agreement in any manner required for the sole purpose of ensuring that this Trust qualifies and continues to qualify as a charitable remainder unitrust within the meaning of Code Section 664(d)(2).

D. *Tax Year.* The taxable year of the Trust shall be the calendar year.

IN WITNESS WHEREOF the parties hereto do hereby execute this Trust Agreement as of the date set forth above.

WITNESSES:

_____

GRANTOR NAME, Grantor

_____

_____

TRUSTEE-1, Trustee

_____

_____

TRUSTEE-2, Trustee

_____

SCHEDULE A [Property Transferred to Trust—Omitted]

[NOTARY FORMS OMITTED]

15 GRATS, GRUTS, AND EVEN PRITS

If your estate is quite large, and you're able to transfer substantial assets to an heir, you may be interested in setting up one of the grantor-retained income trusts described in this chapter.

GIFT TAX CONSEQUENCES

The primary purpose of a grantor-retained annuity trust (GRAT) and a grantor-retained unitrust (GRUT) is to minimize the gift tax cost when someone with a large estate makes a substantial gift. This goal is achieved by giving a remainder interest. A remainder interest is a future interest; you retain the right to own and benefit from property some number of years into the future. The point of the planning is that the gift will be worth less than if it had been effective immediately, and that will make for a lower gift tax.

EXAMPLE: You transfer a $25,000 10-year CD to a trust. You are to receive all of the income for seven years, at which time the entire trust will become the property of your son. Your son is said to receive the remainder interest in your trust. It is obvious that the value of your son's interest is significantly less than if you had given him the CD immediately. The amount of the reduction in the value is based on the fact that your son will not be receiving any use of the CD (that is, the interest it generates) during the seven-year period.

NOTE: Remember that a requirement for a gift to qualify for the $10,000 annual gift tax exclusion is that the gift must be of a present interest (see Chapters 8 and 13). Thus, gifts made to a GRAT or GRUT will not qualify for the $10,000 gift tax exclusion.

The tax laws have stringent valuation rules when you, as the grantor, retain an interest in assets transferred to a trust set up for the benefit of your family. The greater the value that can be attached to the interest you keep, the smaller the value of the interest given to the trust, and hence the lower the gift tax. These valuation rules, however, state that the interest you keep must be valued at zero unless certain requirements are met. The effect is that the entire value of the asset will be considered given away, and your gift tax could reflect this value.

What interests meet the requirements so that you can reduce the gift tax you will owe on the transfer? One kind is a payment that is a fixed annuity, required to be paid at least once per year. A GRAT, in which you retain an income stream based on a fixed annual payment for a set number of years, meets these requirements. A GRUT, in which a set percentage of the value of the trust assets is paid at least annually, also meets these requirements. The larger the GRAT or GRUT payment you will receive, the lower the value of the gift. Thus, you could structure the gift, and the GRAT or GRUT payment, so that the value of the gift equals a specific figure, such as the amount remaining of your $600,000 unified credit. This way, you could make the biggest gift possible without triggering any current gift tax cost.

ESTATE TAX CONSEQUENCES

Another purpose of a GRAT or GRUT is to remove assets (and their appreciation) from your taxable estate. To accomplish this goal, you (as the grantor) transfer assets to a trust for some number of years. The period can be either a fixed number of years or for your life (or the life of another designated person), or the shorter of the two. Limited other options are permitted. During that period, the trust will pay you an amount of income each year as calculated in some prescribed manner. The annual payment must be irrevocable. When the number of years is up, your income interest in the trust will end, and the assets will go to the persons you designated in the trust agreement to receive it (called remaindermen). The remaindermen can receive the assets of the trust outright, or the assets can be held in another trust arrangement for their benefit.

NOTE: Removing the future appreciation in the property from your estate can be the most significant benefit of using one of these techniques.

Essentially, you must outlive the trust in order to obtain real benefit from the planning. If you outlive the trust, all of the trust assets will be given to the persons you named to receive them, and none of those assets should be taxable in your estate. If you don't outlive the trust, all of the trust assets will be included in your estate, which means that the planning will have been unsuccessful.

NOTE: How, then, do you determine if this type of planning is appropriate? Consider your general health and life expectancy. If your health is failing, it may not warrant the difficulties and expense. One approach is to ladder your trusts. Have a GRAT due in five years, a GRAT due in seven years, and a GRAT due in 10 years. If you live just over seven years, at least the planning benefits of two of your trusts will be achieved. The longer you live, the more of your trust transactions will be effective to remove assets from your estate. Is this partial success worthwhile? When a substantial estate is involved, the only real downside is the cost of setting up the trust.

You can provide that if you die during the term of the trust, the trust will become a Q-TIP trust for your spouse. Then, even though the assets of the trust will be included in your estate, they will not create a tax cost because of the marital deduction. Be sure your attorney has addressed this alternative in drafting the tax-allocation provisions of your will.

If your grandchildren are named as remainder beneficiaries of your GRAT or GRUT, you'll have to review the generation-skipping transfer tax rules with your tax adviser (see Chapter 9).

HOW THE GRAT OR GRUT OPERATES

What happens if the assets in the trust fail to generate sufficient income to make the required annual payments to you? Some portion of the principal (assets) of the trust will have to be distributed back to you. Thus, there can be some "leakage" of assets from such a trust back into your estate. On the other hand, if the trust assets earn more income than is required to pay the annual income amount to you, this additional income can be accumulated in the trust for the benefit of the remainder beneficiaries.

The higher the interest rate that is used to calculate your annual payment (whether in the form of an annuity if you use a GRAT, or a varying amount if you use a GRUT), the lower the value of the assets considered to be given away for gift tax purposes. However, the higher the payment, the more difficult it will be for the trust to make the required payments. Either high-yielding assets will have to be transferred to the trust, or some of the payments will have to be made out of the principal of the trust. If the return earned on the assets transferred to your trust is considerably less than the rate required to be paid, there may be little principal left in the trust when it terminates.

These effects are somewhat different for a GRAT and a GRUT because of the different ways in which the annual payments are calculated. For a GRAT you receive an annual payment that is either a fixed amount or a percentage of the value of the assets transferred to the trust. For a GRUT, the annual payment is based on a percentage of the annual value of the trust's assets. So with a GRUT, if you get a payment that exceeds the trust's income, it reduces the trust's assets and the next year's payments will be lower (since they will be calculated based on a lower principal amount).

If the property transferred to the trust, whether GRAT or GRUT, is not valued properly, the annul payment will be incorrect. Therefore, the trust must require that a transfer must be made (for example, an extra payment to the beneficiary) to correct any errors in the payments.

PERSONAL RESIDENCE TRUST

Another technique, called a personal residence trust (PRIT), sometimes can be used to remove a large personal asset from your taxable estate with only a moderate gift tax cost. This approach involves the transfer of personal-use property, your home, to a trust that is similar to those described above. You retain the right to use the asset (analogous to the right to an annual income payment made with a GRAT or GRUT) for a set number of years, after which the asset goes to the persons you designated in the trust agreement (remainder beneficiaries). A PRIT set up for a personal residence has the same potential problem of a GRAT or GRUT: If you don't survive the term of the trust, the transferred assets will be included in your estate. One particular difficulty with a residence PRIT is that it can't hold any assets besides your house, and a limited amount of cash. This limitation is strict. The trust agreement must specifically prohibit the trustees from holding more cash than is needed for making mortgage payments and meeting other permitted trust expenses.

If you outlive the term of a PRIT ownership of the house is transferred to the trust beneficiaries, your children. If you want to continue living in the house you will have to rent it from them.

CONCLUSION

GRATs, GRUTs, and PRITs are complex tax-advantaged trust arrangements. The amount of assets involved when setting up these trusts is usually considerable. Further, the tax laws are currently changing, with new regulations being issued. The investment decisions you make can be as important to the success of some of these trusts as the tax and legal matters. Therefore, you should carry out this type of planning with competent tax, legal, and investment advisers.

For Your Notebook:

EXAMPLES OF THE BENEFITS OF USING A GRAT

The tax benefits of using a GRAT containing a $150,000 gift over five years are illustrated in the three following examples, showing annuity payments at a 5 percent, 6 percent, and 7 percent rate.

EXAMPLE:

GRANTOR-RETAINED ANNUITY TRUST FOR $150,000 GIFT AT 5 PERCENT

Grantor-Retained Annuity Trust—Term

Transfer Date	2/1992
Table Rate	7.6%
Term of Trust	5
Principal	$150,000
Rate of Annuity	5.000%
Payment Period	12
Payments Made at Beginning or End of Period	End
Annuity Factor	4.0352
Payout Frequency Factor	1.0344
Amount of Payment Per Period	$625
Total Annual Payments	$7,500
Value of Annuity Interest Retained by Grantor	$31,305
Taxable Gift (PV of Remainder Interest)	$118,695

Chart prepared using *Estate Planning Tools* software copyright Commerce Clearing House, Inc., Chicago, IL.

EXAMPLE:

GRANTOR-RETAINED ANNUITY TRUST FOR $150,000 GIFT AT 6 PERCENT

Grantor-Retained Annuity Trust—Term

Transfer Date	2/1992
Table Rate	7.6%
Term of Trust	5
Principal	$150,000
Rate of Annuity	6.000%
Payment Period	12
Payments Made at Beginning or End of Period	End
Annuity Factor	4.0352
Payout Frequency Factor	1.0344
Amount of Payment Per Period	$750
Total Annual Payments	$9,000
Value of Annuity Interest Retained by Grantor	$37,566
Taxable Gift (PV of Remainder Interest)	$112,434

Chart prepared using *Estate Planning Tools* software copyright Commerce Clearing House, Inc., Chicago, IL.

EXAMPLE:

GRANTOR-RETAINED ANNUITY TRUST FOR $150,000 GIFT AT 7 PERCENT

Grantor-Retained Annuity Trust—Term

Transfer Date	2/1992
Table Rate	7.6%
Term of Trust	5
Principal	$150,000
Rate of Annuity	7.000%
Payment Period	12
Payments Made at Beginning or End of Period	End
Annuity Factor	4.0352
Payout Frequency Factor	1.0344
Amount of Payment Per Period	$875
Total Annual Payments	$10,500
Value of Annuity Interest Retained by Grantor	$43,827
Taxable Gift (PV of Remainder Interest)	$106,173

Chart prepared using *Estate Planning Tools* software copyright Commerce Clearing House, Inc., Chicago, IL.

Part Four

TRUSTS FOR ASSETS

16 USING TRUSTS TO PROTECT ASSETS FROM CREDITORS

For many people, a primary reason to set up a trust is to insulate assets from the reach of creditors. If you're a professional, your concern may be to avoid potential malpractice claimants.

EXAMPLE: You're a doctor. If you're sued and your malpractice insurance is insufficient, or if an exception to the policy denies coverage for a particular event, you will be personally liable. Insulating some of your assets to preserve them in the event of a successful malpractice challenge could be your most important estate and financial planning step.

Unfortunately, the concept of transferring your assets to a trust to avoid creditors and other claimants is far more difficult to achieve in practical terms than many people are led to believe. This chapter will explore the issues involved in using trusts to protect assets, and explain some of the steps to consider when attempting this type of planning.

GENERAL (NONTRUST) CONSIDERATIONS WHEN PLANNING FOR ASSET PROTECTION

Asset protection is an extremely complex task, in part because it touches on so many different legal disciplines. Laws governing property ownership, taxation, estate planning, debtor/creditor relationships, bankruptcy, corporations, and possibly more all can be important. For example, operating as a professional corporation (a "P.C.") is no guarantee of insulation from liability. Even as a shareholder of a professional corporation, you generally will remain liable for acts of malpractice committed by you or persons working under your supervision, although a P.C. can help limit liability.

EXAMPLE: You own several real estate properties as investments. You own one property individually and have a 50 percent interest in two other properties through a general partnership format. If a tenant is injured on one of the rental properties and successfully sues for more than the amount of your insurance, you will be personally liable. In this situation, transferring assets to a trust to avoid the reach of

---

creditors is not the best alternative. A better approach would be to change the structure of your real estate properties to S corporations or limited partnerships, each of which can provide you with limited liability (that is, your liability will be limited to the value of your equity in the particular property).

Trust arrangements to avoid creditors may be more expensive and may be subject to attack more easily than certain alternative arrangements. As mentioned above, when the activity giving rise to the risk is incorporated, or structured as a limited partnership from inception, this type of structure can provide substantial protection from liabilities. Also, using a corporation or limited partnership arrangement for each separate business or substantial investment asset can prevent a domino effect in the event that one asset becomes subject to a lawsuit. These approaches have the benefit of considerable certainty and have endured the test of time.

NOTE: The present discussion can be considered only an indication of the problems that may be encountered, and competent legal assistance should always be obtained.

Debtor/Creditor Laws

With debtor/creditor relationships, your attorney will have to consider any applicable state laws, as well as federal bankruptcy laws. Many states have adopted some version of the Uniform Fraudulent Transfers Act. The rules are often applied very strictly to protect *creditors*. When you transfer property with the intent to defraud your creditors, the transfer will not be successful. A transfer of assets to hinder or delay your creditors from collecting can be voided. Further, if you find yourself in bankruptcy, your prior attempts to hinder creditors could have substantial adverse consequences. The bankruptcy judge may not allow you to discharge certain debts. Thus, you may end up making your situation worse than if you had done nothing at all. Before attempting any transactions that could move assets out of the reach of your creditors, carefully consider these substantial risks, which not only will cause the attempt to be ineffective but may also cause harm.

Almost any transfer for which you don't receive a fair price (consideration) will be suspect. Further, even when transfers are made for a fair price, if they occur within certain time periods before a declaration of bankruptcy or insolvency (a legal statement that liabilities are greater than assets), they could be subject to question. A court could characterize these transfers as "preferences" and set them aside.

Several factors (called "badges of fraud") can indicate a possible intent to defraud creditors:

- Transfer of assets immediately before or after incurring a significant debt.

- Transfer of substantially all of your assets at the same time.
- Transfer of assets outside the United States.
- Transfer of assets when you are nearly insolvent.
- Transfer of assets to a close relative or business associate.
- Transfer of assets for a price less than the value of the assets transferred.

These rules are very complex and vary by state, so always consult with an attorney before making any transfer.

Transferring Assets to a Spouse

Many asset-protection plans are founded on the outright gift, or transfer of assets to your spouse's control. While your creditors generally may not be able to reach assets of your spouse, there are several exceptions. For example, if your spouse co-owns the business involved or cosigned a note that is being sued upon, the creditors may also be able to reach your spouse's assets.

When a husband and wife own assets as tenants by the entirety, there are special privileges. This type of ownership can provide some measure of protection from creditors, depending on state law, if the creditor has a claim against only one of the spouses. Even this protection, however, is not foolproof. When one spouse dies, the creditors of the surviving spouse will be able to reach the entire asset. When the property is held by spouses as tenants in common, it is unlikely that any particular protection will be afforded.

Barring the applicability of a fraudulent conveyance statute (described above), giving away an asset is probably the best way to protect it from your creditors. However, there are also many complications and drawbacks to the gift approach.

EXAMPLE: Giving away all of your assets to your spouse can have significant tax drawbacks, even if it is successful from a creditor-protection perspective. A basic estate tax plan for a couple with combined assets over $600,000 is to divide the ownership of assets, at least to the point at which each spouse owns $600,000. Then the zero-tax approach described in Chapter 11 is used. A credit shelter trust protects the first spouse's estate from tax, and on the death of the second spouse, that spouse's unified credit shelters $600,000 of assets from tax. *p. 145*

Credit protection planning, however, may dictate that one spouse transfer all assets to another spouse. This could waste the $600,000 unified credit of the spouse concerned about creditors.

The above example highlights an important limitation on planning for asset protection—potential transfer tax costs. Of course, over the long term, substantial assets can be transferred using the annual $10,000 gift tax exclusion. If you have to work in a short period of time, however, this annual per donee exclusion may be insufficient. Thus, direct transfers could trigger a gift tax (or use up a portion of your once-in-a-lifetime unified credit), and, when the transfers are to grandchildren, they could trigger a generation-skipping transfer tax as well.

NOTE: You should not need the income or value of an asset when making a gift. Any gift that has strings attached may be completely ineffective in removing assets from the reach of creditors.

Transferring assets to your spouse to avoid creditors has another potential risk—divorce. Although many states have equitable-distributions laws, they will not guarantee that no negative consequences will result from the transfer. Equitable-distribution laws seek to divide assets fairly, without regard to who has title to the assets. Even if the end result will be the same whether you keep your assets or transfer them to your spouse to avoid your potential creditors, the transfer still could have an important effect on the dynamics of the divorce process. If your spouse has title to all of the assets, it may be easier for him or her to raise money for legal and other fees to argue the divorce. Further, it could take months, or even years, before you see your equitable share of assets returned.

Liability Insurance

Finally, never overlook the benefits of having adequate insurance protection.

TIP: Many people who are concerned about estate planning and asset protection overlook one of the least expensive and most important planning steps—buying umbrella liability insurance. This won't provide protection against professional malpractice, but if you're in a car accident, or someone is injured on your property, an umbrella liability insurance policy can provide substantial coverage above the limits contained in your homeowners and auto insurance policies. A policy providing as much as $5 million in coverage may cost under $500. This is not much to pay for the additional protection. Prices vary by area, risk, etc.

THE TRUST APPROACH TO PROTECTING ASSETS

Once you've exhausted the other approaches to asset protection, consider using a trust arrangement.

Spendthrift Provision

When an objective is to insulate the trust assets from the creditors of the beneficiaries, the trust should include a spendthrift provision.

NOTE: A spendthrift provision can be effective when you set up a trust for your children or your parents, or when another person sets up a trust for you, but it is unlikely to be effective when you set up a trust for your own benefit.

A spendthrift provision states that the trust is intended to provide for the health, education, maintenance, and support of the beneficiary. The standard should not be broad and unlimited. Thus, language to the effect that the trust assets can be used for the comfort and welfare of the beneficiary would be inappropriate. The key statement, however, prevents the beneficiary from assigning (promising) any part of his or her interest in the trust.

SAMPLE TRUST CLAUSE:

Spendthrift Clause.

Except as may be otherwise provided in this Trust Agreement, no transfer disposition, charge, or encumbrance on the income or principal of any trust created under this Trust Agreement, by any beneficiary by way of anticipation, shall be valid or in any way binding upon the Trustee. The right of any beneficiary to any payment of income or principal is subject to any charge or deduction which the Trustee makes against it under the authority granted to them by any statute, law, or by any provision of this Trust Agreement. No beneficiary shall have the right to transfer, dispose of, assign, or encumber such income or principal until the assets shall be paid to that beneficiary by the Trustee. No income or principal shall be liable to any claim of any creditor of any such beneficiary.

Including this type of provision in a trust can provide important protection against creditors of the beneficiaries, but the barrier is not impenetrable. When creditors provide necessary items, such as food, clothing, medical care, and shelter, some state laws permit these creditors to force the trustee to reimburse them from trust assets by exercising available discretionary powers. The IRS, as might be expected, can pierce a trust's spendthrift provision in order to claim back taxes.

NOTE: The laws concerning spendthrift provisions vary from state to state. If creditor protection for your beneficiaries is an important concern, be certain to review the matter with a local attorney. Further, all distribution provisions of your trust should be carefully reviewed, because once assets are distributed and in the hands of the beneficiary, no protection from creditors is available.

Remember that the other distribution provisions of your trust can help support the protections sought through a spendthrift provision. You can limit the discretionary authority of the trustees to distribute income or principal for the beneficiaries (see below). But you have to evaluate the likely consequences, too, lest your caution create later hardship by denying a needy beneficiary access to funds intended for his or her welfare. See the discussion in Chapter 7.

Trustee and Grantor Rights

When planning the use of trusts to shield assets, carefully evaluate the powers and rights given to the trustees and the grantor. If you are the grantor and you seek to protect your assets from creditors, you should not have any right to the trust's assets. If you can reach the trust assets for your own benefit, it is likely that your creditors will be able to reach them also. Even if another person sets up a trust for your benefit, the degree of discretion that the trustees have to distribute trust income or assets to you can be important in determining the level of protection from creditors that will be afforded.

The rule of thumb here is that the more difficult it is for any monies to be distributed to you, the more likely it is that some protection from creditors will be achieved. As stated previously, the rules are broadly interpreted to protect creditors. Thus, even if you cannot receive any money from the trust but you *can* use trust assets to discharge your legal obligation to support your children, a court would probably view this right as being for your benefit, with the result that the assets of the trust could be reachable by your creditors. On the other hand, if a trustee can only distribute money for your health and maintenance, and in order to do so the trustee must first obtain the approval of a beneficiary whose interests are adverse to yours (that is, a distribution to you will reduce the future distributions to that beneficiary), such a trust may avoid attack by your creditors.

What Trusts Can You Use?

Several trusts that may be able to insulate assets from creditors are the following:

- *Irrevocable Children's Trust.* You transfer assets to one trust for the benefit of all of your children, or use multiple trusts and have one for each of your children. Your spouse (if not subject to the risk of malpractice claimants or creditors) and another family member serve as co-trustees. The trust assets could achieve some measure of protection from your creditors.

- *Revocable Living Trust for Your Spouse.* Transfer all assets that are not likely to generate malpractice or creditor claims to a revocable living trust of which your spouse is the sole beneficiary. Name your spouse and another person as co-trustees. When you and your spouse are obviously a single economic unit, the courts may look less favorably on this type of trust as an impediment to creditors. See the caveats discussed above concerning transfers to your spouse.

- *GRUTs and GRATs.* Grantor-Retained Unitrusts and Grantor-Retained Annuity Trusts are used primarily for tax savings when making large gifts (see Chapter 15). However, these trusts may also provide a measure of asset protection. The reason is that you, as grantor, do not have the unilateral right to transfer the asset—this is because the remainder beneficiary has a significant right and your current interest is clearly limited to specified income payments. These income payments, however, may be at risk.

- *Charitable Remainder Trust.* Transfer assets to a charitable remainder trust in which your spouse receives income for life from the charity, and on his or her death, the charity receives all of the assets remaining in the trust (see Chapter 14).

- *Irrevocable Life Insurance Trust.* You transfer cash or other assets to an irrevocable trust that names your family as heirs and your friends or other family members as trustees. The monies are used to buy insurance on your life. The monies so transferred and the insurance purchased could be unreachable by your creditors (see Chapter 18).

TIPS TO CONSIDER WHEN PLANNING TO PROTECT ASSETS

With so many caveats, is it worth trying to transfer assets to a trust to avoid future credit risks? Certainly, but several precautions should be exercised:

1. Transfer assets earlier rather than later. The longer a transfer is made before an event occurs that gives rise to a malpractice or creditor's claim, the greater the likelihood that the transfer will be respected. A transfer made after creditors are hot on your trail and law suits are pending is unlikely to provide any protection. In fact it may destroy any credibility you had.

CAUTION: This rule is often construed in the manner most favorable to the creditors or malpractice claimants. Thus, if an event (cause of action) that gives rise to a lawsuit has occurred, even though the matter has not yet been brought to trial, it may be too late to make the transfer. Some courts have held that liabilities that were at best contingent at the date assets were transferred should be protected against the results of those transfers.

Your professional advisers will be cautious about the timing of any transactions they assist you with because they won't want to risk being involved in a fraud. The biggest problem with advance planning in this area is the same as in all areas—procrastination. Until the risk is all too real, many people will be too busy to take the necessary precautions.

2. Carefully document as many reasons as possible for the transactions *other than* avoiding creditors or potential malpractice claimants.

EXAMPLE: A doctor is concerned about protecting her assets from malpractice claims. She also seeks to minimize a substantial potential estate tax. The doctor retains an estate planner, who drafts a detailed memorandum analyzing the various steps that can be taken to minimize future estate taxes. Some of these steps have the ancillary benefit of possibly removing certain assets from the reach of creditors, although this point is not mentioned in the tax memorandum. With this memorandum, the doctor can demonstrate that business purposes existed for the transactions.

3. Exert as little control over the trust as possible. For example, the transfer of assets to a trust whose only current beneficiary is you is less likely to be successful in insulating assets than a trust whose current beneficiary is a class consisting of your spouse, your children, and your spouse's parents. When the trust cannot be revoked or modified by you, it is more likely to withstand an attack by creditors than if you have the right to revoke or modify the trust, or to change the beneficiaries. The trust should preclude any distributions to family members that would satisfy your support obligations under local law.

4. Don't retain possession of any of the assets transferred to the trust.

5. Plan with your family members. If your parents have listed you in their will for an outright bequest, see if they will revise their wills to leave the money to you in a trust, with a spendthrift provision and an independent trustee, or to a trust for the benefit of your spouse or children. Assets given to you outright generally will be reached by your creditors with little problem.

6. Make the trustees as independent of you as possible. Ideally, they should not be relatives, business associates, or anyone who arguably could be controlled by you.

7. Review the beneficiary designations of all assets such as insurance, IRA plans, pension arrangements, and so forth. If your estate is named, change the beneficiary to your spouse, living trust, or another person (watch the tax consequences).

8. Make the transfers while you have significant net worth, not when you're teetering on the brink of bankruptcy.

TIP: If you're contemplating a large transfer, have your accountant prepare a personal financial statement that demonstrates your net worth. While you may be confident that your net worth is substantial, at some future time, a court may view your situation as being less rosy.

---

9. Avoid using a grantor trust. This will make it more difficult for your creditors to learn of the trust's existence. For example, with a revocable living trust, all of the trust's income will appear on your tax return, which is likely to be a key disclosure item in a court proceeding. However, if the trust is irrevocable, so that no item of the trust is reflected on your personal tax return, it may not be discovered—particularly if another person is the grantor. However, this should be an incidental benefit to establishing any trust. If a court

finds that you intentionally concealed assets, it may be less inclined to respect the transfer.

10. Always consult a lawyer. The legal pitfalls that can jeopardize your planning are substantial. Also, there are other techniques, such as the limited partnership or S corporation mentioned above, that may be useful.

CONCLUSION

Several types of trusts can prove useful in protecting your assets from prospective malpractice claimants and creditors. However, this planning must be coordinated with your estate planning (since you may lose the benefit of your unified credit), your business planning (the legal structure of your various business and investment interests is important), and your insurance planning (insurance can provide important protections for all of your assets).

17 THE MEDICAID-QUALIFYING TRUST

If you're older, and perhaps becoming infirm, a major concern may be to avoid losing assets to pay for medical expenses. For many people, paying for long-term nursing-home care poses the greatest threat to their financial independence through the potential destruction of any savings or inheritance they had hoped to pass to their children.

HEALTH CARE OPTIONS AND QUALIFYING FOR MEDICAID

There are three basic options in paying for extended health care: private funding, private insurance, or governmental programs. Private funding is not feasible for most senior citizens; only the well-to-do can afford to pay the tremendous costs of long-term health care and still retain assets for personal luxuries *and* leave an inheritance for their children. Private insurance is often inadequate or unaffordable, and medigap insurance is of limited assistance. The remaining option is to rely on state and federal programs such as Medicaid.

Medicaid is not the only governmental aid program to be considered in your planning, although it is the primary long-term nursing-home-care program. Many senior citizens may qualify for the Supplemental Social Security Income program (SSI). States often provide supplements in addition to the monthly SSI benefit. Medicare is a federally funded program to provide money for hospital and medical costs.

Requirements

There are several general criteria for receiving Medicaid. (Since the states have discretion to apply more or less restrictive requirements, it is also important to consider individual state laws.) In general, you must (1) be a citizen or resident of the United States, and possibly a permanent resident of the state in which you are applying for coverage; (2) be over 65 or disabled;

(3) meet a resource test to show that your financial resources (assets) do not exceed a certain amount; and (4) have income below a certain level.

These rules mean that to qualify for Medicaid, you will have to divest yourself of all but a limited amount of assets that state law permits you to retain. This is often tantamount to voluntary impoverishment. Some assets can be set outside the tests for determining Medicaid eligibility, however, and trusts can play a key role in accomplishing this aim.

The Principle of "Spending Down"

The key to planning with Medicaid-qualifying trusts is understanding the definitions of assets and income. To qualify for Medicaid you must "spend down," or divest yourself of income and assets to get to the permitted levels.

Only a modest amount of income can be retained, with the balance going to fund your medical care. Income that is counted in determining whether you meet the Medicaid requirements is called "available income," and it can include certain income of your spouse as well as your own. It is defined as income that can be used to meet your basic needs.

Assets that are counted can include all property owned either in your name or your spouse's name, certain property in joint name, and certain property transferred for less than a fair price within a certain number of months (often 30) before you seek Medicaid. Transfers of exempt assets (also called inaccessible resources), such as the transfer of your home to your spouse or a disabled child, among others, should not be counted. A few other properties are also considered exempt assets under many state laws and, therefore, are not counted in determining whether you qualify for Medicaid. These permissible assets may include, in addition to your home, a car of limited value, some personal effects, a burial plot, a wedding band, and a few other nominal assets. They don't amount to much.

Obviously, a critical factor for planning is determining what assets won't be counted. Transfers that you can prove were intended to be carried out for fair consideration, or that were made exclusively for purposes other than trying to qualify for Medicaid, will not be counted. These exceptions vary from state to state and should be carefully reviewed. Whether other assets will be counted for the financial resource test is more difficult to ascertain. For example, what about assets owned by a trust for your benefit? The answer, which is the basis for planning with a Medicaid-qualifying trust, is presented below.

WHY USE A TRUST, AND
WHAT DILEMMA DOES IT RAISE?

There are several approaches you can use to protect your limited resources:

- Use nonexempt assets to invest in assets that *are* considered exempt (that is, assets like your home, which do not have to be applied toward medical bills).

- Make gifts to children.
- Transfer assets to a Medicaid-qualifying trust.

Like the asset-protection trusts described in the preceding chapter, a Medicaid-qualifying trust is intended to shield assets from claimants; in this case, the claims relate to medical care and health care facilities. The use of a trust offers important advantages over gifts. When you make a gift, you lose complete control over the assets given away. Further, the assets still could be subject to creditors, or be lost through a divorce of the recipient. When you transfer the assets to a trust, the trust instrument provides some control over the authorized uses of the assets, and it may be able to insulate the assets from the creditors or divorce of an individual recipient.

Here is the dilemma: If it is not properly structured, a Medicaid-qualifying trust might be reachable by creditors to pay for medical care. But if it *is* properly structured, you will lose substantial control over almost everything you own. Neither alternative is ideal. The second choice is preferable, however, if there are family members and others in whom you have confidence to serve as trustees; the use of a Medicaid-qualifying trust is preferable to losing your assets completely.

THE DRAWBACKS: RISKS AND UNCERTAINTIES ABOUND

This trust is subject to the same uncertainties and risks as asset-protection trusts, as well as several problems peculiar to Medicaid planning. In fact, a Medicaid trust is even more difficult to plan for than other asset-protection trusts because the assets of both spouses can be considered in the calculations of Medicaid eligibility.

The entire planning process is complicated by the interplay of confusing federal, state, and other rules. Further, these rules are changing at a rather rapid pace. Therefore, before completing any attempt at a Medicaid-qualifying trust, be sure to consult with an attorney who is an expert in elder law. A specialist in estate planning isn't enough; you need someone who is regularly active in elder law and who is familiar with Medicaid and other applicable rules. In many situations, familiarity with local authorities can be as important as familiarity with applicable laws. Experience is important. Here are some of the drawbacks:

- Divesting yourself of most of your assets can be a dangerous game because once you've divested yourself, you have no ability to reclaim control or use of those assets. Situations change. The beneficiaries of your largesse may decide to be less generous with you than you expected, or even less generous than they promised. These risks are real, and asset divesture should not be undertaken without very careful consideration.

- Even if everything is done by the book, it's still possible that the transfer of assets to a trust intended to be a Medicaid-qualifying trust will not be successful. The state still may attempt to assert a lien against the trust assets for unpaid medical bills. Or creditors may argue that the application of your state's fraudulent conveyances act should enable them to reach the trust's assets. The risks are compounded when the laws include what are called third-party recovery provisions, which direct state Medicaid agencies to take all reasonable actions to ascertain the liability of third parties to pay for medical care and services. Various court cases have found that the Medicaid recipient's estate, the spouse of the Medicaid recipient, and even other relatives could be held accountable in the appropriate circumstances.

• The issue of reaching assets transferred to a Medicaid-qualifying trust is largely one of public policy. How much respect should be given to the intent of the grantor versus the interest of taxpayers bearing the costs of funding the Medicaid program. Congress has acted once and may act again. Prior to 1986, you could have set up a discretionary trust and successfully avoided Medicaid restrictions. In 1986, Congress changed the laws: When a trustee has the power to appoint income to you, the grantor, it will be assumed that the trustee has exercised the greatest possible discretion in your favor. These restrictions also apply when a trust is established by your spouse.

CASE STUDY EXAMPLE: A psychiatric patient inherited $300,000 from his parents. At the time of his inheritance he already owed the state for more than one year of care. He transferred the assets to a trust. The trustees were given discretionary power to pay income to the patient or invade principal for his benefit. His creditors sued, and the court decided that if the trustee could invade principal of the trust for the patient's benefit, the entire amount of the trust should be available to cover medical bills. The rationale for the decision was that no person should be allowed to set up his or her own trust and use it to protect assets from creditors. This case also highlights the importance of coordinating planning at the family level. If the patient's parents had set up the trust under their wills rather than bequeathing the property directly to their son, the entire estate might have remained intact to provide for him.

HOW TO STRUCTURE A MEDICAID-QUALIFYING TRUST

One approach to a Medicaid-qualifying trust is to have a relative establish an irrevocable trust for your benefit that can provide only for luxuries and not for necessities. It is hoped that this type of restriction will prevent the attachment of trust assets to pay for necessities, which Medicare otherwise would cover. Another approach is to have a third party set up a sprinkle trust. This is an arrangement in which the trustee has the authority to sprinkle income to any of the named beneficiaries (only one of whom will be you) in the trustee's sole discretion. When the distribution of any money is within the absolute control of an *independent* trustee, the state should not be able to attach trust assets to pay for your medical and nursing-home care. Further, language is often included directing the trustee to refuse demands by governmental agencies for funds and even to terminate the trust distributing the assets to other beneficiaries if challenged. The trustee can be prohibited from using trust income or principal for any expenditure for which the state would otherwise provide coverage.

What Provisions Should You Include in Your Medicaid-Qualifying Trust?

A Medicaid trust is usually intended to provide generous distributions during your lifetime. Thus, principal and income are both permitted as distributions. When one spouse is institutionalized, principal should be distributed to beneficiaries *other than* you and your spouse or those obligated to support either of you. Selecting these people, the alternate or contingent beneficiaries, is one of the most difficult aspects of Medicaid planning. These beneficiaries must be trusted to use some of the money they receive to provide certain assistance and care to you, but they can't have any legal obligation to do so or the planning won't be effective.

When a single individual is involved rather than a couple, the planning may differ. In such situations, there is no noninstitutionalized partner to worry about, and you may want to ignore the Medicaid planning and simply use your funds for your own needs. However, if you still want to use a Medicaid-qualifying trust, when you are institutionalized the income from the trust will be distributed only to persons other than yourself and those whom the law makes obligated to support you.

Additional provisions are as follows:

- The trust obviously should contain a spendthrift clause.
- It is important to grant the trustee wide discretion and power in making distributions so that the trustee really will be independent. The drawback to this is that you will have no way of compelling any distribution from the trust other than by demonstrating that the trustee has abused his or her discretion.
- You should have·no right to demand any income or principal distributions from the trust.
- Since any income distributed to you in excess of the Medicaid eligibility limit may be considered as available income for medical care, your trust can include language restricting the amount of income that can be paid to you to the maximum amount for Medicaid eligibility. Additional language can provide that income from the trust can only be used to supplement public assistance benefits.
- Remainder beneficiaries should be named for the trust. These beneficiaries often will receive income or assets of the trust only after you and your spouse have died. The existence of remainder beneficiaries will encourage the courts to protect the interests of these beneficiaries from creditors seeking reimbursement for nursing-home or other claims.

What Assets Should Be Transferred?

Your house, except where state law treats it as exempt, may be an ideal asset to transfer to the trust. This approach can preserve cash assets that may be necessary to meet health care expenses for the period of time before Medicaid payments begin (30 months in many instances).

TAX CONSIDERATIONS OF USING MEDICAID-QUALIFYING TRUSTS

Several important and tricky tax issues can arise in planning a Medicaid-qualifying trust. If the trust is irrevocable, and you have no control or interest in the trust whatsoever, the likelihood of the trust's withstanding a demand by medical creditors, assuming all other requirements are met, will be greater than if you used a revocable trust or a trust over which you have some control or interest. However, there are potentially adverse tax consequences to using an irrevocable trust with no interest or control.

A transfer to an irrevocable trust will be considered a completed transfer and could trigger a gift tax. Further, the complete transfer of a home to the trust will defeat any possibility of a later sale that qualifies for the once-in-a-lifetime $125,000 exclusion (because it is no longer your home). Also, any assets transferred to such a trust will not qualify for a step-up in tax basis on your death. A "step-up" means that the tax basis in the asset will be increased at death to equal the fair value of the asset at that date, thus eliminating any income tax cost your heirs would incur on an immediate sale of the asset.

There is an approach to disposing of assets so that they don't count in the tests to determine Medicaid qualification, while still retaining the favorable tax benefits. This approach is to have the transfer of assets be complete for the purposes of local law and, therefore, sufficient to meet Medicaid rules. However, you will retain a limited power of appointment over the trust's assets, so that for federal tax purposes the transfer will not be considered complete.

CAUTION: Pay attention to any new developments in the law. The government has strong financial incentives to try to limit this type of planning, and may develop stricter regulations.

When you retain this element of control over the trust, it may be taxed as a grantor trust. This means that the income still could be reported on your income tax return.

CONCLUSION

Setting up a Medicaid-qualifying trust can provide numerous advantages. However, great care must be exercised in preparing the trust document to meet your specific objectives if you are to succeed in obtaining protection from the state on account of Medicaid payments. Also, laws are rapidly changing as various states and government agencies seek to limit the ability to avoid paying for your own care. Finally, you must always consider who's pushing this type of planning since parents and children will have opposite objectives. The parents want to assure their care. The children want to preserve their inheritance.

For Your Notebook:

SAMPLE MEDICAID TRUST PROVISIONS

[DO NOT ADD THESE PROVISIONS TO ANY TRUST AGREEMENT WITHOUT REVIEWING WITH A LAWYER]

1. Until the earlier to occur of the death of YOUR NAME or her becoming a resident of a regular nursing home or a skilled nursing or health related facility, the Trustees shall pay over to or for the benefit of YOUR NAME all of the net income of the trust estate. Said net income shall be paid in monthly installments as nearly equal as may be practicable. At the earlier to occur of the death of YOUR NAME or her becoming a resident of a regular nursing home or a skilled nursing or health related facility, the payment of income to YOUR NAME under this Trust Agreement shall cease. If payment of income to YOUR NAME hereunder shall cease for any reason and at the time that payment of such income to her hereunder shall cease SPOUSE NAME shall not be a resident of either a regular nursing home or a skilled nursing facility or health related facility, the Trustees shall have the discretion to pay over to or for the benefit of SPOUSE NAME all or any part of the trust income as the Trustees shall determine to be advisable for his support, maintenance and comfort until the earlier to occur of said SPOUSE NAME death or his entry into either a regular nursing home or a skilled nursing facility or health related facility, at which time the Trustees' discretion to distribute income to said SPOUSE NAME shall cease.

2. The Trustees shall have no right to invade the principal of the Trust for the Grantors, and the Grantors shall have no right to demand any part of the trust principal.

3. At any time during the term of this Trust the Trustees shall have the authority to make a distribution of principal from this Trust to a class consisting of the following persons: a child of the Grantors, a sibling of the Trustee, issue of the Grantors, and any next of kin of either of the Grantors; provided, however, that no such distribution shall be made to a person then serving as a Trustee; and provided further that in no event shall the aggregate distributions of principal hereunder in any calendar year (including the calendar year 1992), exceed the sum of DOLLAR AMOUNT ($_____.00) Dollars.

4. The last to die of the Grantors shall have the right, by a specific provision in his or her Last Will and Testament duly admitted to probate and referring to this provision, to appoint such part or parts, or all, of the principal of the Trust estate remaining after the death of the second to die of the Grantors, to or among such persons composed of the following class: children of the Grantors and grandchildren of the Grantors. Any such appointment shall supercede the provisions hereinabove set forth in this Trust Agreement with respect to the distribution of the Trust estate after the death of the second to die of the Grantors.

NOTE: These provisions are illustrative of the types that would be included in the appropriate locations in a Medicaid-qualifying trust. Because of the rapid changes in the law and the differences from state to state, the use of any Medicaid-qualifying trust should be carefully reviewed with an attorney specializing in elder law.

These provisions were supplied by Sanford I. Ruden, partner in the New York City and Freehold, New Jersey, law firm of Ruden & Cramer.

18 THE LIFE INSURANCE TRUST

Insurance is one of the most valuable and flexible assets a person can own. Insurance can be used to establish funds for your children's education, to provide living expenses for your spouse and children in the event of your untimely death, to create an estate, and to meet substantial estate tax costs. The main benefit insurance offers, however, can also create its most significant problem. Insurance matures on death into money—perhaps a substantial amount. This sudden wealth can create large tax costs, while attracting creditors, malpractice claimants, and others who see potential resources to tap.

One of the best solutions to these problems is to use a life insurance trust to own your policies and to retain and manage the proceeds of those policies after death.

INSURANCE AND TRUSTS

When an insurance trust is properly planned, the insurance proceeds not only can avoid taxation in your estate, but they also can avoid taxation in the estate of your surviving spouse, even though he or she benefits from the insurance monies held in trust. (Your surviving spouse cannot hold a general power of appointment over the insurance proceeds if they are to be excluded from his or her estate.) The surviving spouse can receive some or all of the annual income from the insurance trust, distributions of the principal in the trust, and even a right to demand up to $5,000 or 5 percent of the trust principal in any year. Another important benefit of using a trust is to provide children, and perhaps your surviving spouse, with more formal or professional management of what is likely to be a substantial sum of money.

A measure of protection from creditors and from divorce implications also may be obtained, depending on state law. Liquidity for estate needs can be provided when the trustee is authorized to purchase assets from your estate. For those concerned about publicity, the insurance proceeds included in the trust are not included in your probate estate. This chapter will show how life insurance trusts can be used to achieve all of these goals.

WHAT IS A LIFE INSURANCE TRUST?
WHAT IS SECOND-TO-DIE INSURANCE?

A life insurance trust is really a misnomer. Almost any trust can own a life insurance policy, or receive the proceeds of a policy for which the trust is named beneficiary. Many of the trusts discussed thus far specifically mention insurance (for example, see Chapters 11, 13, 14, and 16). (See the general provisions presented in Chapter 3 suggested for use in defining assets available to a trust. One paragraph used language that is broad enough to include insurance, and the second paragraph specifically discussed proceeds from insurance policies.)

Although almost any trust can receive insurance proceeds, what is generally thought of as a life insurance trust is one that is formed in order to own life insurance policies on your life, or even the life of another person, such as your spouse.

EXAMPLE: Your estate is worth $2 million, and your estate taxes and expenses are estimated at $800,000. You purchase an $800,000 life insurance policy to cover the cost. The policy, however, is included in your estate since you own it at death. Now your estate has been increased to $2.8 million, and your taxes and expenses have increased to $1.2 million. Thus, one-half of the insurance you spent hard-earned dollars to purchase will go to Uncle Sam.

As an alternative, you can set up an irrevocable life insurance trust to own the policy, and the proceeds will not be included in your estate. Your estate still will be valued at $2 million and your taxes and costs at $800,000, but your trustee now will have a pool of $800,000, which can be used to purchase nonliquid assets from your estate and provide it with cash to meet its tax and expense obligations. The value of the assets then held in the trust can be used to provide for the needs of your loved ones.

While the above example can apply to anyone, insurance, particularly second-to-die insurance, is tailor-made for use by a married couple wanting to provide for estate tax and children. "Second-to-die insurance" is a policy that only pays when the second of you and your spouse dies. It's less likely for two people to suffer an unexpected and premature death than one person, so the insurance is cheaper to purchase than conventional insurance because the insurance company has reduced its risk.

Use of the Marital Deduction

The estate tax laws provide for an unlimited marital deduction. Any assets that you leave outright to your spouse, or in a special Q-TIP trust, are not subject to tax on your death, no matter how large your estate. Thus, your estate can avoid tax entirely simply by leaving everything you own to your surviving spouse. When your surviving spouse dies, the second-to-die insurance benefit is triggered, and cash is made available to pay estate taxes, meet expenses, and provide for heirs. When the marital deduction and second-to-die insurance are combined with the benefits of an irrevocable life insurance trust to (1) keep the proceeds out of the taxable estate of both you and your spouse, (2) minimize the ability of creditors to attack the funds, (3) avoid probate, (4) permit confidentiality, and (5) provide for management of the proceeds after death, you have one of the best and simplest estate planning techniques.

Compound Interest

The good news doesn't stop there. This approach can be made even more interesting for those who can afford it by taking advantage of the benefits of compound interest. If you pay for your second-to-die policy in one lump sum, or make several large payments over a relatively short period of time, the amount you pay will appear quite modest, depending on your age and health, compared with the ultimate proceeds your estate will receive. This is the principle behind the barrage of advertisements in financial journals touting, "Pay Your Estate Tax at 10 cents on the Dollar." Assuming a young healthy couple, reasonable returns on investment, and so forth, this can happen.

EXAMPLE: You and your spouse estimate that you will need $2 million in insurance proceeds to cover estate tax costs and provide for your children. You're both young and in good health. You set up an irrevocable insurance trust and purchase a single-premium second-to-die insurance policy for $200,000. Your estate problems are just about solved.

Although most things that sound too good to be true *aren't* true, the insurance-funded estate plan is as close as you can get. On the other hand, no one technique is either perfect or enough. Setting up this type of insurance arrangement does nothing to address your other estate planning needs, so don't ever stop here. You still need properly drafted wills, powers of attorney, living wills, and, possibly, other trusts. And it's possible that in your particular case, an insurance trust, or even the insurance coverage itself, won't be needed.

BEFORE GOING FOR A LIFE INSURANCE TRUST, CONSIDER ALL THE ALTERNATIVES

If the combined estate of you and your spouse is safely under $1.2 million, you won't have any federal estate tax costs. Therefore, you should only be buying insurance for meeting family needs; don't buy insurance to place in trust to pay for an estate tax you won't face. If your combined estate is above $1.2 million, carefully review the following advice before making any purchase of an insurance product.

Think Comprehensively

Never purchase any large insurance policy without first undertaking all of the basic estate planning steps to reduce your estate taxes. To the extent that these other steps can reduce estate taxes, you may be able to reduce (or even eliminate) the amount of insurance you buy, sometimes substantially. At the minimum, the following basic estate planning steps should be considered:

1. Make maximum use of the $600,000 unified credit for both you and your spouse. This typically will be accomplished by making sure that each of you has sufficient assets in your individual name (joint property won't work) and that the first spouse to die has left up to $600,000 in a credit shelter or bypass trust. This will provide income to the surviving spouse but avoid taxation in the estate of the surviving spouse. The use of both unified credits can eliminate estate tax on the first $1.2 million of assets (these credits are phased out for estates over $10 million).

2. Use an annual gift program, if appropriate. Each person can give away up to $10,000 per year. You and your spouse together can give away $20,000 per year to as many people as you want. If you have four children, each of whom is married and has two children, you can make 16 gifts of $20,000 per year. This can remove $320,000 a year from your estate.

3. Examine alternative sources to pay for the estate tax, which may include selling assets, mortgaging property, or using cash or other liquid assets. Such steps should be carefully evaluated in light of the needs of your heirs and the nature of your assets.

4. Consider other common techniques to reduce or defer tax costs. For example, interests in closely-held businesses can qualify for a benefit in which the estate tax due on their value may be paid over approximately a 14-year period. Uncle Sam is effectively lending you the money. Also, interests in real estate used in a family business or farm can qualify for favorable valuation provisions that can reduce tax costs.

A Case in Which Insurance Is Not the Best Approach

Individual circumstances vary enormously, and planning must vary accordingly.

EXAMPLE: A couple in their sixties has an estate worth approximately $8 million dollars. The estate is comprised of $2.5 million of cash and marketable securities, and $5.5 million of real estate. The real estate consists of eight individual residential rental properties. There are no mortgages on any of the properties. The couple purchases an expensive (because of their age) second-to-die insurance policy in the names of their children as owners and beneficiaries.

This plan is defective for several reasons. First, the insurance policies become assets of their children, subject to risk of the children's creditors or malpractice claimants. If either of their children divorces, the policies are marital assets that could be subject to equitable distribution. There is no control over how the children will use the money. While the children may be mature and reasonable, no one can foresee what the future will bring, or what $4 million in cash in each child's hands will do. The money should be available to provide liquidity to the estate if necessary by purchasing properties, but will it? The premiums on the insurance policies are so large that they could exceed the annual gift tax exclusions and thus use up some of the couple's unified credit. If the parents have retained any incidents of ownership in the policies, the insurance proceeds may be included in their estates.

In the above example, the couple hasn't made any attempt at even basic estate planning to reduce their estate tax costs. This couple arguably has no need for insurance for liquidity or estate tax purposes. Without proper wills, including a credit shelter trust, the $600,000 unified credit of the first spouse to die will be wasted. The availability of the second unified credit has been ignored. Thus, $1.2 million of their estate should not even be subject to taxation.

Further, the couple has no aggressive ongoing gift program. Trusts could be set up for each child and grandchild and annual $20,000 gifts of favorably valued minority interests in real estate assets could be made. This technique could substantially reduce the size of the estate over the life expectancy of the couple (ironically, it is this same life expectancy that enters into the insurance company's calculations of premiums). A GRAT (Chapter 15) could be combined with a family partnerhsip to gift substantial interests at modest or no current tax cost.

The third important point is that the estate is very liquid. The substantial cash and marketable securities easily could be used to fund any remaining estate tax cost. In addition, with eight individual real estate properties, some could be sold to raise cash. The concern of being pushed into a sale when the market is bad is not as significant when there are eight assets involved. The properties have strong cash flow and no debt. It also would be a relatively simple task to mortgage any of the properties to raise cash.

Finally, as an active real estate business (management, maintenance, leasing), most of the estate will qualify for estate tax deferral rules, so that the tax could be paid over nearly a 14-year period.

The moral of this story is quite simple: Nothing can substitute for a comprehensive estate plan. No single approach can safely eliminate the need to carefully review your goals, assets, needs, and so forth, with several professional advisers. Further, there is no shortage of astute and well-qualified insurance sellers, estate planners, and financial advisers who can help you properly assess your insurance needs in the context of your overall estate plan. Get the right help so that you can protect your family at the right cost. This means, evaluate your advisers even before you evaluate their advice. Find out their qualifications and credentials. Ask specifically how they are compensated.

TIP: If an insurance salesman is pushing a large second-to-die policy on you without having addressed the four basic estate planning steps outlined above (either directly or with your estate planner), run for the hills. When you get there, take a quarter and call the National Association of Personal Financial Planners (NAPFA) at (800) 366-2732 for a list of fee-only financial planners in your area. NAPFA financial planners can evaluate your needs without the conflict of interest of a potentially huge commission for selling you an insurance product.

REVOCABLE OR IRREVOCABLE—HOW DOES IT AFFECT CHOOSING A TRUSTEE?

Irrevocable

Most life insurance trusts are carefully structured to be irrevocable in order to ensure that the proceeds will not be included in your estate (or your spouse's estate if second-to-die insurance is involved).

CAUTION: When a second-to-die insurance policy is to be placed in an irrevocable insurance trust, neither spouse should be a trustee or beneficiary.

If the trust is irrevocable, it is preferable that you not be a trustee. This is true even though you can serve as a trustee in certain very limited circumstances (when your powers over the trust are solely as a fiduciary and cannot be exercised for your benefit, and when your becoming a trustee was not part of a prearranged plan). When a second-to-die policy is used, your spouse also should not be a trustee. A statement should be added to the trust document prohibiting either you or your spouse from being appointed a successor trustee. The grantor of the trust should not be given the right to change the trustee.

Therefore, the usual answer to the question, revocable or irrevocable, is the latter. In some instances, however, insurance will be placed in a revocable trust. Be certain that you have carefully reviewed the consequences of using a revocable trust with your tax adviser before using this approach.

Revocable

Why use a revocable trust? When a revocable trust is used, there is no gift tax cost on the transfer of money or policies to the trust. This is because the gift to a revocable trust is considered incomplete for gift tax purposes. No tax costs can be triggered until you relinquish control over the trust assets. A revocable trust also can help you achieve any of the benefits that the living trust described in Chapter 10 can provide: management, avoiding probate, confidentiality, and so forth.

What about the objection that a revocable trust cannot provide estate tax savings? If the insurance involved is only on your life, and the proceeds will be payable to your spouse, there will be no estate tax cost on your death as a result of the unlimited marital deduction. Further, if your spouse is young, or if you have young children, the insurance proceeds may be spent before his or her death, so that there would be no estate tax cost at that time either.

If the proceeds remain and your estate is less than $600,000, there will not be any additional cost. In fact, this can be an affirmative tax planning technique to use your lifetime exclusion. In that case, however, the trust should not qualify for the marital deduction.

The important benefit that a revocable insurance trust can offer in situations where tax costs aren't a concern is that it can be changed when circumstances change. If you divorce, you can change beneficiaries, and you can't do this with an irrevocable life insurance trust.

WHAT STEPS ARE NECESSARY TO SET UP YOUR LIFE INSURANCE TRUST?

STEP #1. Evaluate your insurance, estate tax, and living-expense needs with your financial planner, accountant, and insurance agent.

STEP #2. Determine whether the trust should be revocable or irrevocable and what provisions should be included, and have your lawyer prepare the trust document. Sign it.

STEP #3. Complete all applications and forms from your insurance agent using the name of the trust as the purchaser and take any required medical examinations to qualify for the insurance desired. There is no point in incurring legal and other fees if your health or other problems prevent you from qualifying for insurance. If you already have existing insurance policies that will be transferred to your insurance trust, skip this step.

STEP #4. If you are planning to transfer existing insurance policies to your life insurance trust, contact your insurance agent and request that he or she provide you with a written estimate of the value of the insurance policies being transferred, the balance of any loans outstanding, and the amount of the policy that can be borrowed against.

The value of the policies is important to know because if it is too great (which could occur with large-dollar whole life or similar policies), there could be a gift tax cost on making a transfer. This doesn't mean that you shouldn't transfer such a policy to your insurance trust, but it does mean that the tax consequences should be planned for (see page 214). Since you will lose all rights to borrow against the policy, it is best to give policies with little or no cash value. This will also minimize any gift tax implications. If there are loans outstanding, there can be tax problems from the transfer. Finally, the amount you can borrow against the policies should be considered because you will be losing this right when the policies are transferred.

STEP #5. Have your accountant obtain a federal tax identification number by filing Form SS-4 with the IRS. Your lawyer should make sure that your accountant has a copy of the insurance trust so that the correct name is used. Your lawyer should also provide your insurance agent with a copy of the insurance trust so that your agent will have the correct name of the trust and trustee for use in the applications for the insurance. Its always best to have everything filled out correctly from the beginning rather than correct it later.

STEP #6. Your trustee should take a signed copy of your trust agreement and your tax identification number to a bank and open a bank account. Deposit a nominal amount to get the account started, or a larger amount in the event that your trustee will have to pay an insurance premium.

STEP #7. Your trustee can pay for the insurance premium and accept the policy. If existing policies are being transferred, the necessary steps discussed in the following section should be addressed. Considerable care should be taken in structuring the payment of premiums. It is essential that the trust, and not you, the insured, pay the premiums to the insurance company. Further, if money is transferred each year to the insurance trust to pay for the insurance premiums, the transfers should not be exactly equal to the insurance premiums.

STEP #8. You should probably include an annual demand or Crummey power when you transfer your policies to a trust (or set up a new insurance trust). When the insurance is given to a trust, the $10,000 annual gift tax exclusion will not be available unless the insurance (and later cash contributions to pay premiums) to the trust can qualify as a gift of a present interest. For the transfer to qualify, the trust essentially must give the beneficiary a right to withdraw up to the $10,000 value of the insurance policy in the year the gift to the trust is made. The use of this arrangement, called a Crummey Power, is discussed at length in Chapter 13. Be sure to send the required notice.

If the value exceeds the $10,000 exclusion ($20,000 if you and your spouse make a joint gift), a gift tax cost may be triggered for that year or a portion of your lifetime $600,000 exclusion may be used.

STEP #9. Your accountant will prepare the necessary annual tax returns which will be signed and filed by your trustee.

HOW ARE EXISTING INSURANCE POLICIES TRANSFERRED TO YOUR TRUST?

When existing insurance policies are owned in your name, there can be substantial advantage in transferring those policies to another owner—

perhaps a trust. To successfully accomplish this goal, the policy, including all incidents of ownership in the policy, must be given away. Further, this gift must be accomplished at least three years prior to your death, or else the proceeds will be included in your estate and will be taxable.

You Can't Have Any Incidents of Ownership

Estate tax won't be due on insurance proceeds that are paid to a beneficiary other than your estate (or the executor of the estate) if you (the insured) had no incidents of ownership in the insurance policy at the time of your death and for three prior years. This incidents-of-ownership test is vitally important and, unfortunately, broad and complex.

EXAMPLE: You transferred an insurance policy to your spouse five years before death. However, you retained the right to borrow against the policy in the event of a business emergency. This single right (incident of ownership) could result in the inclusion of the entire policy proceeds in your estate. Further, if you make a commitment to make the premium payments in the policy application and then die before three years, the IRS may argue that the proceeds should be included in your estate. The courts, however, have held that the mere payment of premiums should not result in the inclusion of the policy proceeds in your estate.

An "incident of ownership" means the right to do any of the following: borrow the cash value, change the name of the beneficiary, assign the policy to another person, borrow against the policy, and so forth. To eliminate all incidents of ownership and remove the proceeds of an insurance policy from your estate, you must assign the policy to a new owner and irrevocably surrender every power over the policy and all of the benefits the policy can provide. When you transfer insurance to a trust, you should not have a reversionary interest equal to more than 5 percent of the value of the policy. That is, there cannot be more than a 5 percent possibility that the insurance policy or the proceeds of the policy will return to you.

WHAT TO INCLUDE IN YOUR LIFE INSURANCE TRUST

Your life insurance trust agreement should address several matters to properly serve your needs.

- Your trust should specifically permit the trustee to accept insurance policies and proceeds of insurance policies as assets contributed or paid to the trust.
- The annual Crummey power often should be included to minimize the tax consequences of contributing money to the trust.
- The provisions that address how the insurance proceeds should be distributed are quite important. When minor children are involved

consider all of the discussions in Chapter 13. Since the proceeds may not be paid until many years into the future and anticipating what circumstances your family or loved ones may face is so difficult, it's often best to give more, rather than less, flexibility and discretion to your trustee to allocate income and principal of the trust to the beneficiaries, such as a special child, most in need.

- The trustee can be given authority to invest in any assets, including real estate and closely-held business interests, your estate will own. This means your trustee could purchase assets from your estate and provide cash needed to pay estate taxes. If your estate includes expensive equipment or valuable property, the trust also could use insurance proceeds to purchase these nonliquid assets. When the trustee is granted this right, it is generally advisable to have the trust document give the trustee broad powers for the management, lease, improvement, and so forth, of the property.

- To realize the estate tax benefits of removing life insurance proceeds from your estate, the trust must be irrevocable. This means you cannot reserve any rights to receive the assets transferred to the trust, or to change the provisions of the trust. When the trust terms meet this requirement, no additional steps are necessary. However, it has become customary to add a clause to the trust stating that you specifically intend that the trust is irrevocable.

- If you are married, your life insurance trust can provide that if the insurance should be included in your estate as a result of your dying within three years of making the transfer, the proceeds will be transferred into a trust that qualifies for the marital deduction. This typically will be a qualified terminal interest property trust, more commonly called a Q-TIP. There are a number of requirements, including a right of your spouse to receive all of the income from the trust, at least annually, for life.

- The trustee should be authorized (but not required) to purchase insurance and take any steps necessary to maintain the desired insurance in force. This should include the use of income or principal to pay for premiums and the right to purchase additional policies. However, the trustee should not be required to pay any debt or expense of your estate.

CONCLUSION

Substantial tax savings can be achieved by properly planning the ownership of your life insurance policies. However, care must be taken to give up all incidents of ownership to ensure that the insurance will be removed from your estate. If a trust is used, attention must be given to the trust terms to meet your personal objectives. An insurance trust can be combined with many of the other trusts discussed in this book, and the relevant chapters should be reviewed.

For Your Notebook:

SAMPLE LIFE INSURANCE TRUST PROVISIONS

[THESE PROVISIONS SHOULD NOT BE INCLUDED IN ANY TRUST AGREEMENT WITHOUT FIRST CONSULTING A LAWYER]

NOTE: The following paragraphs are selected provisions that relate to insurance. To complete your insurance trust, all of the provisions common to trusts (see Chapters 2 through 7) will be necessary. Also any provisions similar to those illustrated in the chapter that permit the trust to hold insurance proceeds obviously would be included.

I. *Insurance Trust Provisions*

A. *Insurance Provisions Generally*

1. The Trustee shall accept and hold all policies of insurance upon the life of the Grantor which shall be assigned by the Grantor, or any other person, to the Trustee. The Grantor intends to assign all right, title and interest, and every incident of ownership, in the policies of insurance listed in Schedule A (the "Policies"). On signing this Trust Agreement, Grantor shall deliver to the Trustee all the Policies.

NOTE: It is important to transfer all interests you have in the insurance policies to the trust in order to avoid having the proceeds taxed in your estate. While reciting this intent in the trust agreement is helpful, it isn't enough. Be certain to carefully review this matter with your insurance agent to be sure all necessary papers have been completed to transfer the policies.

---

2. During the life of the Grantor, the Trustee shall take any action concerning the Policies which the Trustee considers appropriate for the benefit of the Trust Estate, and which are not inconsistent with the terms of this Trust. These actions can include, but are not limited to, the: (i) Modification, exchange or surrender of any Policies or other insurance policies; (ii) Receipt and collection, at maturity or otherwise, of amounts payable under an insurance policy, or in settlement of, or upon the surrender of, any insurance policy; (iii) Receipt and collection of dividends or other increments on any insurance policy, and (iv) The distribution of any insurance policies and dividends or other increments.

NOTE: For the insurance trust to be successful, control over the insurance policies must rest in the hands of the trustee. If you begin to specify in great detail everything the trustee can and cannot do, you may defeat the purpose of setting up the insurance trust. The following paragraphs continue this theme by making certain that the trustee has the sole authority to make decisions concerning the insurance.

---

3. The Trustee shall not be under any obligation to make payments of any premiums, dues, assessments or other charges which may become due and payable on any insurance policy held under any trust created under this Trust Agreement, or for which the Trustee is designated beneficiaries. The Trustee is not obligated to see that the above payments are made or to notify the

insured or any other person that such payments are or will become due. The Trustee shall not have any liability if the above payments are not made, or are not made on a timely basis.

4. Notwithstanding anything in this Trust Agreement to the contrary, any form executed by Grantor to assign any insurance policy to the Trustee or any trust formed under this Trust Agreement, or any form designating the Trustee as a beneficiary under any insurance policy on Grantor's life, the Grantor shall not be deemed to have entered into any covenant or agreement with the Trustee requiring that the Trustee maintains the Policies, or any other insurance policies, in full force.

5. The Trustee shall take appropriate action to collect amounts payable under, or in settlement of, any insurance policy, whether at maturity or otherwise, to which the Trustee is or may become entitled. The Trustee is not responsible for their inability to enforce the collection of any proceeds or amounts payable under any insurance policies.

NOTE: This last sentence is important to provide some comfort to your trustee. As explained in Chapter 6, every trust agreement makes provisions to indemnify your trustee. While you certainly expect your trustee to act reasonably, you do not want your trustee to be held responsible by your heirs for problems or events beyond his or her control.

6. The Trustee, may, but is not required to, engage in any litigation to enforce the payment of any insurance policy until the Trustee shall have been indemnified against all expenses and liabilities which the Trustee may believe could relate to such litigation. The Trustee may utilize any property comprising the Trust Estate to meet expenses reasonably incurred in connection with enforcing the payment of any insurance policies.

NOTE: This gives the trustee the necessary authority to pursue claims for unpaid insurance. This can be quite important when the insurance companies are protesting the claims.

7. When the net proceeds of any insurance policies, or other net amounts receivable under any trust formed under this Trust Agreement, shall be collected by the Trustee, the Trustee shall deal with and dispose of the same as set forth in this Trust Agreement. The terms "net proceeds" or "net amount" mean the proceeds, or the amounts of any policies, after reduction for any loans, advances, interest, or other indebtedness relating to such policies.

8. With respect to any policies of insurance held under this Trust, the Trustee may make payment of the premiums thereon out of income or principal of this trust and may exercise any and all options, rights and privileges in such policies including, without limitation, the right to obtain and receive from the insurance companies issuing such policies advances and loans on such policies, to direct the disposition of dividends or surplus, to convert such policies or to surrender them and receive the proceeds.

NOTE: This provision, similar to those above, is intended to give the trustee broad authority to deal with the insurance policies and make any changes necessary. If you're young, the likelihood of unforeseen events makes this flexibility important to grant.

B. *Grantor Shall Assist Trustee in Obtaining Insurance*

Grantor agrees to execute any documents reasonably necessary for the Trustee to implement such Trustee's duties under this Trust Agreement, including but not limited to completing and executing any forms necessary to the purchase of insurance, where such acts will not result in the inclusion in Grantor's estate of any such insurance.

NOTE: The best approach to getting an insurance policy into your insurance trust is to have the trust buy the insurance initially. This is far preferable to your purchasing insurance and transferring it to the trust. While it may sound unnecessary since you may be the grantor setting up the trust, remember that the insurance trust is a separate legal entity from you.

C. *Trustee Application for Insurance on Grantor's Life*

Should the Trustee apply for any insurance policy on the Grantor's life, the Grantor agrees to submit to reasonable medical examinations upon reasonable notice.

D. *Indemnification of Insurance Companies*

The Grantor hereby relieves the insurance companies which issued the policies of insurance described in the annexed Schedule A, and any other insurance company which may issue any policies of life insurance which may be deposited with the Trustee hereafter or which become subject to the terms of any trust created under this Trust Agreement, from any responsibility to see to the execution and performance of the terms and conditions of this Trust Agreement. Further, to the extent required by any insurance company issuing any insurance policies, the Trustee is authorized to take any reasonable steps necessary to:

1. Discharge that insurance company from any and all liability for any amounts paid to the Trustee, or to third parties in accordance with directions of the Trustee;

2. Confirm that no such insurance company shall have any obligation whatsoever to see to the application of any amounts paid by such insurance company to the Trustee; and

3. Assure that any such insurance company shall be fully protected in taking or permitting any action in reliance on any instrument or document executed by the Trustee in their capacity as such Trustee and that such insurance company shall not incur any liability for so doing.

NOTE: These provisions are intended to encourage the insurance companies to deal with your trustee. If your trustee has the authority to relieve the insurance company of the concerns listed above, this may facilitate the cooperation necessary to best implement your plan.

E. *Alternate Disposition for Insurance Proceeds Included in Grantor's Estate*

1. Notwithstanding anything herein to the contrary, if the amounts payable under insurance policies on the life of the Grantor held in this Trust or the amounts payable under insurance on the life of the Grantor for which the Trustee has been designated beneficiary (collectively, the "Proceeds") are included in the Grantor's gross estate for the federal estate tax, and Grantor's spouse is then living, then the Trustee shall hold such proceeds, in trust, and shall manage, invest, and reinvest the same, to collect the income thereof, and to pay over the net income to Grantor's spouse, or to apply the same for the benefit of such spouse, in convenient installments, but at least annually, and so much of the principal as may be necessary or appropriate in accordance with the Standard For Payment, during such spouse's life.

2. Upon the death of Grantor's spouse, the principal of the trust, as it shall then be constituted, shall be transferred to Grantor's living descendants as provided in the Section Distribution To Children's Trust(s), [insert cross-reference to children's trust, or other distribution provisions elsewhere in your trust agreement].

3. Where included in Grantor's estate, and where Grantor's spouse survives Grantor's death, this Section is intended to qualify the Proceeds as a qualified terminable interest property

(Q-TIP) trust under Code Section 2056(b)(7), and this Section shall be interpreted in such manner.

NOTE: This provision is intended as a tax savings clause in the event that your plans don't work as intended and the proceeds from insurance on your life are included in your estate. This could occur, for example, when you transfer policies you presently own to a trust and don't survive three years, or when you retain an incident of ownership that is flagged. This paragraph seeks to rectify that problem through use of the unlimited estate tax marital deduction. In the appropriate circumstances, this could salvage what otherwise may have been a disastrous result for your family.

The following illustrative provision is merely one paragraph from the general limitations on trust powers discussed in Chapter 6 since it can be important to trusts intended to hold insurance policies:

II. *Limitations on Trustee Discretionary Authority*

A. If Grantor's spouse, SPOUSE NAME, serves as a Trustee under this Trust, SPOUSE NAME shall have no incidents of ownership, rights, powers, privileges of any nature with respect to the life insurance policies purchased or acquired by the Trustee on the life of either Grantor or Grantor's spouse.

In addition to all of the above provisions, where insurance is transferred to your trust, the details concerning the policies should be stated in the schedule of assets transferred to the trust (See Chapter 3):

SCHEDULE A
PROPERTY TRANSFERRED TO TRUST

1. Cash in the amount of $_____.00.

2. Life Insurance policy insuring the life of GRANTOR'S NAME, with the NAME OF INSURANCE COMPANY. Policy Number: POLICY NUMBER issued DATE POLICY ISSUED.

19 THE VOTING TRUST, THE QUALIFIED SUBCHAPTER S TRUST, AND THE MASSACHUSETTS REALTY TRUST

As explained in Chapter 1, trust property is one of the five key elements of any trust. Without property, there is no funded trust. A trust which is not funded is of limited use until it is funded. Chapter 3 discussed some of the many kinds of property that can be transferred to a trust and issues involved in making the transfers. Many of the other chapters addressed the concept of trust property as part of the discussion of planning for the estate and gift tax, providing for adequate management of assets and their eventual distribution to beneficiaries, and, most recently, protecting assets from creditors and Medicaid agencies.

The previous chapter was devoted to the issues involved in transferring one specific asset, life insurance, to a trust. Now this chapter is concerned with trusts for three more specific types of assets: stock in a corporation (transferred for voting purposes only), ownership of stock in a subchapter S corporation, and real estate property owned in Massachusetts.

THE VOTING TRUST FOR CORPORATE STOCK

A voting trust is a legal arrangement in which shareholders join together to have their stock voted by a designated person who is the trustee. The trustee has an irrevocable right to vote stock in a corporation for a designated period of time, often 10 years. If the trustee had the right to sell the stock, or receive its dividends, this would not be a voting trust but one of the other types discussed in this book. The only purpose of a voting trust is to vote stock; depending on the laws in your state, it may be illegal for it to do more.

The reasons for using a voting trust can be as varied as the relationships in a family business. Voting trusts are not restricted to closely held businesses; they can be used with corporations of any size. Large and even publicly traded corporations use voting trusts for holding stock of subsidiary or parent corporations. However, the focus here is on the use of voting trusts by small and closely held businesses.

When Should You Consider Using a Voting Trust?

Certain shareholders may prefer not to be actively involved in business matters, and thus use the voting trust as a convenience. Several shareholders in a closely held business may be geographically distant from the corporate headquarters and view a voting trust as a way to address this problem. Shareholders may want to vote their shares as a block in order to exert more influence. For example, investors who enter into a joint venture, organized as a corporation, with a developer may want to pool their votes in order to protect their interests vis-a-vis the developer. But the most common use of a voting trust arrangement is probably in the context of a parent who makes gifts of stock to children and grandchildren.

EXAMPLE: Father owns 55 percent of an S corporation that is involved in the manufacture of computer parts. An S corporation can only have a single class of stock. Therefore, when Father wants to make gifts of stock to his children to reduce his potential estate tax, he must give the same common shares that he owns. If Father transfers 10 percent of the shares to each of his two children, he will have reduced his voting control of the corporation to 35 percent. Since this is less than the 45 percent interest that his partner owns, his voting control of the corporation will depend entirely on the willingness of both of his children to vote their shares exactly as he wants them to. Father is unwilling to risk losing control over his corporation and his livelihood. One solution is to have the children transfer their shares of stock to a voting trust. Father then can give away the stock interests without sacrificing any of his voting control over the corporation. A simpler alternative in some cases is to issue the children non-voting stock.

Another situation in which a voting trust is useful is divorce. The voting trust arrangement permits the ex-spouse who is active in a business to continue to control its affairs, while the other ex-spouse can protect his or her interest under the divorce settlement by actually owning stock.

EXAMPLE: Ex-Wife owns 60 percent of a design business. Ex-Husband is awarded 25 percent of the value of the business as part of the equitable-distribution divorce settlement. Ex-Wife has resigned herself to giving up the amount necessary to resolve the divorce; however, if she actually transfers 25 percent of the stock to Ex-Husband she will lose control of the business. Worse yet, she will have put a sizable portion of the stock into the hands of someone who may be adverse to the business and other shareholders. A solution is to give Ex-Husband the 25 percent of the stock but require that his shares be transferred to a voting trust controlled by Ex-Wife. Ex-Husband should protect his interests at this point and negotiate a shareholders' agreement that has reasonable restrictions on how much Ex-Wife and other shareholders can withdraw as salary or benefits. Without this additional protection, there may be no money left in the corporation for distribution as dividends on the stock.

In one case a court refused to permit an ex-spouse to revoke a voting trust agreement. The court reasoned that since the use of the voting trust arrangement for a closely held business was bargained for at arm's length and was an integral part of the divorce settlement agreement, the ex-spouse should not be able to change it.

Don't overlook simpler approaches. Instead of having a voting trust, shareholders could sign a proxy giving a designated person a right to vote their shares. Alternatively, a shareholders' agreement could provide rules for governing the corporation's operations. For example, it could require that certain decisions be made by more than a 50 percent, or a 75 percent, vote of the shareholders. However, the voting trust can be a more fluid arrangement, giving the trustee greater latitude to respond to unforeseen situations.

How Does a Voting Trust Work?

When a voting trust is going to be used, several steps are necessary:

STEP #1. The shareholders who will participate in the arrangement must retain a lawyer to prepare a voting trust agreement.

STEP #2. The corporation must approve the voting trust agreement. This could require an action of the shareholders or board of directors, depending on the terms in the other legal documentation of the corporation. The simplest approach for a closely held business, if acceptable under your state's laws, is to use a single document called a "Unanimous Written Consent of All Shareholders and All Directors." When there are only a handful of shareholders and directors, having them all sign, whether or not it is required by law, is a simple process and ensures that everyone is in agreement. Be certain to attach a copy of the voting trust agreement to the official minutes and place it in the corporate kit (typically, a ring binder embossed with the corporate name that contains all official corporate documents).

NOTE: Some courts have held that a voting trust agreement is not valid unless a copy is filed with the corporation. Be certain that this is done in the exact manner required by state law.

STEP #3. When all of the participants agree on the terms of the agreement and a trustee is selected, the agreement should be signed by each shareholder, the trustee, and the corporation. You should even consider having the successor trustees sign the agreement now (although they could sign at a later date, if and when they are needed to replace the initial trustee). The record of agreement in the corporate minutes described in Step #2 is a prerequisite for an officer of the corporation's being able to sign the trust.

STEP #4. Each shareholder in the voting trust arrangement then transfers his or her stock certificates to the corporation, which then transfers the stock to the trustee of the voting trust.

CAUTION: If the stock certificates are merely handed to the trustee and not transferred officially on the corporation's books, the shareholders may not be prevented from voting their shares of stock.

Your rights as a holder of a voting trust certificate are governed by the provisions of the voting trust agreement and any applicable local laws. You generally will be required to follow any actions taken by the voting trustee.

STEP #5. The trustee issues voting trust certificates (see the sample in the "For Your Notebook" section of this chapter) to each shareholder.

What Should Be Included in Your Voting Trust Agreement?

The agreement, as illustrated in the "For Your Notebook" section of this chapter, is quite simple and straightforward (be sure to have your lawyer review applicable state law and the corporation shareholders' agreement for any regulations or restrictions that could affect the voting trust agreement):

- The names of the trustee and the shareholders who are participating should be listed, and the length of time the voting trust will last should be specified.

- It should be clearly stated that all income will be distributed by the corporation directly to the shareholders and not retained by the trustee.

- The responsibilities, duties, powers, and rights of the trustee must be specified in the trust agreement.

- Be certain that the voting trust agreement gives you the right, at any reasonable time, to obtain a copy of the names and addresses of all participating shareholders and to inspect the records and books of the corporation.

- The agreement should say whether the participating shareholders have the right to change or revoke the voting trust. In the case where a parent is giving stock to a child, for example, the voting trust agreement will probably be made irrevocable.

- If the trustee is to be compensated, the exact arrangements should be spelled out in the agreement.

How Does a Voting Trust Affect Other Trust Planning?

You should be able to have your will, or perhaps even a revocable living trust, transfer your voting trust certificates (which effectively transfers the stock) to a testamentary trust on your death. Check the shareholders' agreement for other restrictions, however.

THE QUALIFIED SUBCHAPTER S TRUST FOR STOCK IN AN S CORPORATION

Your estate plan may call for the annual giving of S corporation stock to your children or other beneficiaries in order to accomplish the general estate planning objective of removing assets from your estate. You or your fellow shareholders may be concerned about the transfer of voting rights to children. One technique that can be used is to set up a voting trust arrangement as discussed in the previous section. Another approach, which is the focus of this section, is to transfer the stock to a special trust, with a trustee who you feel will vote the stock in a mature and professional manner. When this approach is used, care must be exercised because S corporation stock is an asset that involves a number of special tax requirements when transferring to a trust.

What Is an S Corporation?

An S corporation is a corporation under your state's laws that allows shareholders to limit their liability. This means that in the event of a lawsuit, the corporation will be held liable, but only the amount you've invested will be at risk; your personal assets hopefully won't be at risk. Although limited liability is far from a fail-safe protection (you may have signed personal guarantees or accidentally transacted business in your name, and so forth), it's almost always worth striving for. This structure, then, provides another approach to protecting assets (see Chapter 16).

The "S" designation in an S corporation is because of the special federal (and sometimes state) tax treatment such corporations enjoy. S corporations are taxed like partnerships. The income and deductions flow through to you and are listed on your personal tax return. Unlike the case with income earned from regular corporations, you pay tax only once. A regular corporation pays tax on its income, and then if it distributes a dividend to you, you pay a second tax on this same income. This single-tax advantage of the S corporation has made it a common ownership form for many, if not most, small, family, and closely held businesses.

The requirements that must be met in order for a corporation to obtain the benefits of S corporation status are as follows:

- Only one class of stock is allowed. This means that every share of stock must confer identical rights regarding corporate profits and assets if the corporation should be liquidated. The shares are allowed to differ with respect to voting rights, as well as transfer, repurchase, and redemption rights.

- The maximum number of shareholders is 35. A husband and wife are treated as one shareholder for this limitation.

- Only United States residents (not corporations) can be shareholders. However, certain trusts and estates are allowed to be shareholders.

- A timely and proper S corporation election must be made.

- An S corporation may not own 80 percent or more of another corporation.

- The S corporation must be a domestic corporation (organized under the laws of one of the states).

Using the QSST

The special trust for holding S corporation stock, called a QSST, can be a very useful estate planning technique.

EXAMPLE: Grandfather has a retail business operated as an S corporation. His estate is quite large, and his children are reasonably well off. Grandfather wants to transfer stock to reduce potential estate taxes and create an income flow for the grandchildren. He sets up a qualified S corporation trust for each of his minor grandchildren. (He can't use a single trust to sprinkle income among the various grandchildren since this type of trust will violate the S corporation rules, and his retail corporation will lose its tax-favored status.) He then makes gifts of $20,000 (jointly with his spouse) of stock each year to each grandchild's trust. As an additional benefit, the stock is insulated from the creditors, malpractice claimants, and divorce claims of both the grandfather and each of the grandchildren.

To obtain the benefits in the above example, the trust must meet a number of strict requirements. An S corporation can only have qualified shareholders, and the same goes for S corporation trusts. The beneficiary must be treated as the owner of the portion of the trust that consists of S corporation stock.

NOTE: You can have a trust with S corporation stock as an asset, as well as other assets. In effect, such a trust will be treated as two separate trusts: (1) a qualified S corporation trust (QSST) that meets all the requirements outlined here; and (2) a regular trust that can accumulate or sprinkle income in any manner. Your trust agreement should include the flexibility to deal with both types of assets. What we are concerned with in this discussion is the portion of your trust that contains S corporation stock.

CAUTION: Carefully consider the types of assets that could be transferred to your trust. If it seems at all possible that stock in an S corporation could find its way into any irrevocable trust you set up, the trust should include the necessary S corporation provisions.

This portion of your trust will qualify as a QSST if it meets the following conditions:

1. There can be only one current income beneficiary, and this beneficiary must be a citizen or resident of the United States. This requirement helps ensure that the beneficiary will be taxed by the United States.

2. All of the trust's income must be distributed, or at least must be required to be distributed, currently, and during the life of the current income beneficiary, only this one person can receive income from the trust.

3. If any principal of the trust is distributed while the current income beneficiary is alive, the money must be distributed to this one beneficiary.

4. The interest of the current income beneficiary in the trust must end on the earlier of the death of that beneficiary, or the termination of the trust. If the trust ends during the life of the current income beneficiary, the trust assets all must be distributed to this one person.

Consider the implications of these rules: The trustee cannot have the power to sprinkle trust income, or to make discretionary distributions of principal to different beneficiaries, or to accumulate income that is not distributed (because all income must be distributed currently, and all to one person). These requirements can significantly infringe on your planning. Consider that typical children's trusts, where several children are beneficiaries of a single trust, will not qualify. A charitable remainder trust also cannot qualify.

A Grantor trust qualifies since all income is taxed to one person, the grantor. A trust over which a person other than the grantor has complete control qualifies. (This may be a trust in which the current beneficiary has a power exercisable solely by himself or herself to vest the corpus or the income in himself or herself.) An example of a trust in which the income is fully taxable to you is the revocable living (loving) trust described in Chapter 10. The typical credit shelter or bypass trust used in many estate plans can create serious problems if the decedent owned shares in an S corporation (see Chapter 11).

One further requirement states that a trust to which S corporation stock is transferred pursuant to the terms of a will can only be an S corporation shareholder for 60 days, after which the S corporation status will be lost. These requirements are illustrated in the sample S corporation trust provisions in the "For Your Notebook" section following this chapter.

CAUTION: S corporation shareholders must review their estate plans to avoid future problems. Representations should probably be obtained in the shareholders' agreement that estate plans will be reviewed and changed if necessary.

Special Election Required for Trust to Qualify as a QSST

It's not enough for your lawyer merely to include the necessary provisions in your trust agreement for it to qualify to hold S corporation stock. There are several important filing requirements to be made with the IRS for your trust to qualify as a QSST.

- This election must be made separately by the current income beneficiary for each S corporation stock held by a trust. For example, in an earlier example, a grandfather made gifts of S corporation stock to trusts for each of his grandchildren. Now each grandchild, as the current income beneficiary of each trust, must make the required election.

- The election should be filed with the IRS office where the S corporation files its income tax returns (*not* in the IRS office where the beneficiary lives or works, unless they happen to be the same IRS office).

- The election must clearly indicate that it is an election under Internal Revenue Code of 1986 § 1361(d)(2). The election should demonstrate that the beneficiary, or other person, is, in fact, entitled to make the election.

- The election must be made within two and a half months of the date on which the trust first becomes a shareholder. Also, the election must be filed before the QSST election is effective.

NOTE: While every effort should be made to making a timely and proper election, the IRS has shown compassion to some of those missing the deadline. This doesn't mean miss the deadline. It means, if you inadvertently do, try letting your tax adviser pursue the IRS's gratitude with a request for a waiver of the particular provision (whether its the election or something else). You might just have some luck.

- If there are successive income beneficiaries, there is no need to make a new election.

NOTE: Carefully review with your tax adviser whether the election should be made. Once the election is made, you cannot change it.

The beneficiary of a QSST should be given the necessary information for tax filing. This becomes somewhat confusing because of the various legal entities involved, and because the guidance from the IRS is a bit sparse. The S corporation should distribute income to the trust and provide the trust with a Form 1120-S, Schedule K-1, reflecting all income or loss to the trust from the S corporation for the year. The trust then could attach a copy of this form to the Form 1041, Schedule K-1, which the trust gives the beneficiary.

THE MASSACHUSETTS REALTY TRUST

Throughout this book great effort has been made to illustrate how diverse and flexible a planning tool trusts can be. Although the Massachusetts realty trust has limited applicability, only affecting those who purchase or already own land in Massachusetts, it does further demonstrate why it is wise to consult with a lawyer to learn of the many options that may be available to you. The simple trusts that are discussed most often in trade books and financial literature do little justice to this complex and valuable topic.

What Is a Massachusetts Trust?

When structuring the ownership of real estate purchased in Massachusetts, a common approach is to use a Massachusetts land or realty trust as the named owner. The Massachusetts realty trust is an arrangement whereby the trust holds nominal (name-only) title to the real estate for the beneficial owners (you and other investors). Secrecy is an important benefit if you want it. If you purchase real estate directly, your name will appear in the public records. However, with a Massachusetts realty trust, your name won't appear on the deed, and you don't have to file a schedule of the trust beneficiaries with the county registry of deeds. Any third-party buyer, lender, or other person can rely on a certificate of the trustees that they have the requisite authority to act for the trust and its beneficiaries (the real property owners).

Using a Massachusetts realty trust has economic advantages as well. When this type of trust owns real estate, you can avoid the payment of deed stamps on transferring the property. This is done merely by transferring beneficial interests in the trust (using assignment forms similar to those illustrated in Chapter 3) to the new owners. This can provide a substantial savings.

Finally, the Massachusetts realty trust can be a convenient mechanism when the owners anticipate frequent transfers of property, since it is much easier to assign trust interests than to change the deed to the property. If a partnership with a non-Massachusetts corporate general partner wanted to transfer Massachusetts real property and didn't have the property in a trust name, it would have to prove that it had proper authority to conduct business in Massachusetts and that the necessary corporate actions had been completed. By using a Massachusetts realty trust as a nominal title holder, these complications would be eliminated.

Problems with Using a Massachusetts Land Trust

There are four important problems with operating a Massachusetts realty trust. First, some investors mistakenly believe either that the mere use of a trust or the anonymity provided by the Massachusetts realty trust limits their liability. It doesn't. With a nominee trust, the beneficiary and not the trustee is probably going to be liable.

A second important shortcoming involves taxation. It is standard to be taxed and be subject to probate in the state where you reside (in legalese, your domicile). Many states will also subject you to tax and probate if you own real estate within their borders. One of the advantages of many of the trusts described in this book is that they allow you to avoid probate (called ancillary probate) in states other than your state of residence. The way it works is that when you own an interest in a trust, you will own intangible property (trust interest, partnership interest, or stock in the corporation) and not real estate (the real estate is owned by the trust).

With a Massachusetts realty trust, unfortunately, this is not the case. The estates of non-Massachusetts domiciliary will probably be taxable on their interests in the Massachusetts real estate owned through a Massachusetts realty trust. On the other hand, they would not be taxable on interests in a partnership owning Massachusetts real estate because the partnership interest is likely to be considered personal property, not subject to tax. Having the land owned by a Massachusetts realty trust will not convert it from a real to personal property interest. Therefore, if you own an interest in a Massachusetts realty trust, you won't avoid probate and estate tax.

Third, even the confidentiality benefit may not be as strong as you would wish. A bank lending mortgage money for the building may insist on seeing the deed and schedule of beneficiaries, even though they can rely on the trustee's representations concerning the owners.

A fourth potential problem relates to the income tax status of the Massachusetts realty trust. It is not absolutely certain that the trust will avoid being taxed. However, several steps may help you avoid tax problems:

- The trustees should not have any powers other than those specifically granted to them by the beneficiaries. (It's okay for a trustee also to be a beneficiary.)
- Don't open bank accounts in the trust's name.
- The trust agreement should not give the trustee power to use the funds from the property.
- Disbursements and receipts should not be handled by the trustees.
- The trust should not engage in any activity other than the mere holding of legal title to the property, and the trust agreement should include this limitation. If there is any activity conducted to manage the real estate, consider having an independent management company perform it.

- Finally, the financial and tax records should be maintained in the name of the beneficiaries and not in the name of either the trust or the trustees.

What Paper Work Is Necessary?

The trust agreement is recorded with the registry of deeds for the county where the property is located. It should include the names of the trustees but should not include the schedule of beneficiaries. The trustees should maintain a signed schedule of beneficiaries, which is updated to reflect changes. It's best to have at least two trustees. When one trustee is to resign and a replacement is to be appointed, the remaining trustee can authorize the necessary acts so that the names of the beneficiaries won't have to be disclosed. The trustees should be certain that the Schedule of Beneficial Interests executed by the beneficiaries contains a hold-harmless clause to protect the trustees from claims.

The trust agreement should explicitly authorize third parties (for example, banks, management companies, and insurance companies) to deal directly with the trustees in order to protect the anonymity of the beneficiaries.

Ancillary Considerations: Tax Filings, Other Entities

Many advisers file 'inactive' Massachusetts and federal trust tax returns. Since a land trust is a mere nominee, providing no insulation from liability, it is common for the ultimate owners to organize as a limited partnership or occasionally an S corporation (but that creates its own unique tax problems for real estate) which in turn owns the trust interests. This decision can best be reached with your tax and legal advisers who assist you in setting up the trust.

CONCLUSION

Voting trusts, qualified subchapter S trusts, and the Massachusetts realty trust present an array of options for managing, holding and protecting specific assets, whether from the risk of creditors, liability, or loss of control, and from gift and estate taxes. It is important to pay close attention to the laws affecting each of these trusts—for example, S corporation trusts must hold qualified S corporation stock. The time period for which a voting trust may exist could be limited by state law. The Massachusetts realty trust has limited applicability, but in the appropriate situations, it can provide important financial benefits and confidentiality.

These specialized trusts serve to illustrate the tremendous flexibility and unique benefits available from proper trust planning.

For Your Notebook:

SAMPLE CORPORATE RESOLUTION AUTHORIZING PARTICIPATION IN THE VOTING TRUST

[USE ONLY FOR DISCUSSION WITH YOUR LAWYER]

XYZ CORPORATION, INC. UNANIMOUS CONSENT OF ALL SHAREHOLDERS AND ALL DIRECTORS

The Undersigned, being all the shareholders and all of the Directors of the Corporation hereby take the following actions:

RESOLVED, that the Corporation agree to and execute the XYZ CORPORATION, INC. VOTING TRUST AGREEMENT, substantially in the form attached hereto.

RESOLVED, that the following persons shall transfer their shares of common stock on the books and records of the Corporation to the trustee of XYZ CORPORATION, INC. VOTING TRUST AGREEMENT:

> John Doe
> Jane Doe
> Baby Doe

RESOLVED, that the officers of the Corporation are hereby authorized and directed to take any actions reasonably necessary to implement the above resolutions, including but not limited to directing the transfer of the above shares to the name of the trustee of the XYZ CORPORATION, INC. VOTING TRUST AGREEMENT on the Corporation's books.

Dated: January -0-, 1992

_____
Father Doe, Shareholder and Director

_____
John Doe, Shareholder

_____
Jane Doe, Shareholder

_____
Jane Doe, as Custodian under the Uniform Transfers to
Minors Act, for Baby Doe, Shareholder

_____
OTHER SHAREHOLDER #1, Shareholder and Director

_____
OTHER SHAREHOLDER #2, Shareholder and Director

For Your Notebook:

SAMPLE VOTING TRUST AGREEMENT

[FOR DISCUSSION WITH YOUR LAWYER]

XYZ CORPORATION, INC., VOTING TRUST AGREEMENT

VOTING TRUST AGREEMENT dated the 1st day of January, 1992, between and among XYZ CORPORATION, INC., a STATE NAME corporation doing business at CORPORATION'S ADDRESS (the "Corporation"); FATHER'S NAME, who resides at 123 West Street, CITY NAME, STATE NAME ("Father"); CHILD-1 NAME, who resides at CHILD-1 ADDRESS ("CHILD-1 NAME"); and CHILD-2 NAME, who resides at CHILD-2 ADDRESS ("CHILD-2 NAME") (collectively CHILD-1 NAME and CHILD-2 NAME are referred to as the "Shareholders"); and TRUSTEE NAME, who resides at TRUSTEE ADDRESS, and his successors in the trust (the "Trustees").

WHEREAS, in order to secure continuity and stability of policy and management of the Corporation, the certain Shareholders deem it advisable to deposit all of their shares of the Corporation's capital stock ("Shares") with the Trustee; and

WHEREAS, the Trustee has consented to act under this Agreement for the purposes herein provided;

IT IS, THEREFORE, AGREED:

I. *Agreement*

Copies of this Agreement shall be filed in the office of the Corporation and shall be open to the inspection of the Shareholders during business hours. All Voting Trust Certificates issued as hereinafter provided shall be issued and held subject to the terms of this Agreement. Every Shareholder entitled to receive Voting Trust Certificates representing shares of capital stock, their transferees and assigns, upon accepting the Voting Trust Certificates issued hereunder, shall be bound by the provisions of this Agreement for a period of ten (10) years from the date of this Agreement.

NOTE: While 10 years is a common duration for a voting trust arrangement, shorter periods can be used. Be sure to ask the lawyer drafting the document whether your state has any restrictions on the term of a voting trust.

II. *Transfer of Stock*

The Shareholders, simultaneously with the execution of this Agreement, shall assign and deliver all of their Shares of capital stock to the Trustees, to be held by the Trustees subject to the terms of this Agreement. At the execution of this Agreement, the following Shares shall be so transferred:

Shareholder	Number of Shares	Outstanding Stock
CHILD-1 NAME	125.0	10%
CHILD-2 NAME	125.0	10%

NOTE: The more children and other recipients there are of a gift of stock, the more useful a voting trust will become as a method of securely controlling the voting interests in a corporation.

The Trustee shall immediately cause the stock to be transferred to himself, as Trustee, on the books of the corporation, and shall endorse all certificates held by them hereunder with the following legend:

"This certificate is held subject to a Voting Trust Agreement dated the 1st day of ——————, a copy of which is in the possession of —————————— as Trustee, and in the office of the Corporation."

NOTE: A "legend" is simply an inscription that is typed or stamped on the face of a stock certificate. The purpose is to alert any potential buyer of the stock to the restrictions involved. This is similar to the step that is almost always taken in a closely held business of stamping a legend on each stock certificate stating that the transfer of the shares is subject to restriction under a particular shareholders' agreement.

III. *Voting Trust Certificates*

Upon receipt by the Trustee of the certificates for shares of capital stock and the transfer of the same into the names of the Trustee, the Trustee shall issue and deliver to the Shareholders Voting Trust Certificates for the shares so deposited. The Voting Trust Certificates shall be in the following form:

No. ——————   —————— Shares

XYZ CORPORATION, INC.
A STATE NAME Corporation

VOTING TRUST CERTIFICATE FOR S CORPORATION STOCK

This certifies that —————————— is entitled to all the benefits arising from the deposit with the Trustee under the Voting Trust Agreement dated ——————, of certificates for —————— (——) shares of the capital stock of XYZ CORPORATION, INC., a STATE NAME corporation, in such Trust Agreement and subject to the terms thereof.

Stock certificates for the number of shares of capital stock represented by this certificate, or the net proceeds in cash or property of such shares, shall be due and deliverable hereunder upon the termination of such Trust Agreement as provided therein.

This certificate shall not be valid for any purpose until duly signed by the Trustee.

IN WITNESS WHEREOF, the Trustee has signed this certificate on January 1, ——.

By: ————————————————
     TRUSTEE NAME, Trustee

IV. *Dividends; Distributions; Tax Attributes*

A. Each Shareholder shall be entitled to receive, and shall receive, payments from the Trustee of all cash dividends or other distributions made by the Corporation with respect to the stock of the Corporation held by the Trustee hereunder.

B. Any and all tax benefits each Shareholder shall recognize shall be the same benefits which would be recognized had that Shareholder held said Shares directly.

NOTE: These requirements must be met to protect the tax status of the corporation as an S corporation. When the stock is of a C corporation (that is, a non-S corporation), these requirements will not have to be adhered to unless some requirement exists under state law.

V. *Voting*

At all meetings of Shareholders of the Corporation, and in all proceedings affecting the Corporation, the Trustee shall vote the shares transferred to him hereunder in such manner as he may determine, in his sole and absolute discretion.

VI. *Liability of the Trustee*

The Trustee shall not be liable for the consequence of any vote cast in good faith by him.

VII. *Dissolution of the Corporation*

In the event of the dissolution or total or partial liquidation of the Corporation, whether voluntary or involuntary, the Trustee shall receive the monies, securities, rights or property to which the holders of the capital stock of the corporation deposited hereunder are entitled, and shall distribute the same among the registered holders of Voting Trust Certificates in proportion to their interests, as shown by the books of the Trustee, or the Trustee may, in his discretion, deposit such monies, securities, rights or property with any bank or title and trust company doing business in the state of STATE NAME, with the authority and instructions to distribute the same as provided above, and upon such deposit all further obligations and liabilities of the Trustee in respect to such monies, securities, rights or property so deposited shall cease.

VIII. *Trustee*

A. The Trustee shall have the right at any time hereafter to designate a successor Trustee to act upon the death or resignation of a Trustee. Such designated successor Trustee shall not be required at the time of his succession to be a Shareholder of the corporation, and no such succession shall give any such successor Trustee any rights to require shares in the Corporation. Such designation may be made by filing in the principal office of the Corporation, an appointment in writing of such successor Trustee duly executed and acknowledged. Any such designation of a successor Trustee may be revoked in whole or in part by the Trustee at any time, without notice to any person, by filing a notice of revocation in the same form as the appointment hereinabove provided for and in the same place. Upon the death or resignation of the Trustee, the designated successor Trustee shall become successor Trustee hereunder; and upon the death or resignation of a Trustee without having appointed a successor Trustee, a successor Trustee shall be designated by a majority of the Shareholders party to this Agreement at a meeting called for that purpose. The rights, powers and privileges of the Trustee named hereunder shall be possessed by the successor Trustee with the same effect as though such successor had originally been a party to this Agreement. The word "Trustee" as used in this Agreement means the Trustee or any successor Trustee acting hereunder.

B. In the event of the unwillingness or inability of TRUSTEE NAME to serve as Trustee, then SUCCESSOR TRUSTEE #1 shall serve as successor Trustee ("Successor Trustee").

C. In the event of the death, disability, inability or unwillingness of both the Trustee and Successor Trustee to act hereunder, without the Trustee or Successor Trustee having appointed a further successor Trustee, then SUCCESSOR TRUSTEE NO. 2, shall serve as Trustee.

IX. *Term*

A. This Agreement shall continue in full force and effect until the earlier of the following events:

1. The 10th anniversary date of this Agreement.

2. The execution and acknowledgment by the Trustee hereunder of a document of termination duly filed in the office of the Corporation.

3. 90-days following the final distribution from the Corporation of its remaining assets in dissolution or complete liquidation of the Corporation.

4. As required under the laws of the State of STATE NAME.

B. Upon termination of this Agreement, the title and possession of each Share of stock of the Corporation which was delivered to this Trust shall be delivered back to its beneficial owners.

X. *Compensation of Trustees*

Where TRUSTEE NAME shall serve as Trustee hereunder he shall serve as Trustee without compensation for such services. Any successor Trustee shall be permitted to charge the customary fees for hourly services, or for similar services, in the State of STATE NAME for rendering the services hereunder as Trustee. Any Trustee shall have the right to incur and pay reasonable expenses and charges as may be necessary for carrying this Agreement into effect. Any such fees, charges or expenses shall be reimbursed to the Trustee by the Shareholders who are party hereto shall be jointly and severally liable to reimburse same. In no event may any expense be charged against this Trust.

XI. *Notice*

Any notice to or communication with any party to this Agreement shall be deemed sufficiently given or made if mailed by registered or certified mail addressed to the holder of Voting Trust Certificate, or to the Trustee, at the address appearing above, unless Notice in accordance with this Section is given of a new address. For any Notice to be effective, a copy of such Notice must also be given to the Corporation, and to: CORPORATION'S LAWYER'S NAME, who does business at CORPORATION'S LAWYER'S ADDRESS.

XII. *Modification*

The Trustee is authorized, and is hereby granted by each Shareholder and the Corporation an irrevocable power of attorney, to make any modification to this Agreement necessary to assure the continued compliance of this Agreement with any requirements necessary to maintain the Corporation's status as an S Corporation and to assure that all requirements of Internal Revenue Code of 1986 Section 1361(c)(2)(A)(iv), as amended, and Treasury Regulation Section 1.1361-1A(h)(3)(ii), as amended, shall be complied with.

NOTE: These references are to various laws governing requirements to be shareholders of an S corporation. The purpose is to prevent an inadvertent violation of the tax requirements for proper characterization as an S corporation.

XIII. *Benefit*

This Agreement shall inure to the benefit of and be binding upon the Corporation, the Shareholders, their successors and assigns, and upon the Trustees and their successors.

XIV. *Counterparts*

This Agreement may be executed in counterparts.

IN WITNESS WHEREOF, the parties have hereto duly executed the Agreement as of the date set forth herein.

XYZ CORPORATION, INC.

By _____
      NAME OF PRESIDENT, President

SHAREHOLDERS JOINING VOTING TRUST: TRUSTEE:

_____   _____
CHILD-1 NAME   TRUSTEE NAME

_____
CHILD-2 NAME

[Notary forms and witness lines omitted].

For Your Notebook:

SAMPLE QUALIFIED SUBCHAPTER S
TRUST PROVISIONS

[FOR DISCUSSION WITH YOUR LAWYER ONLY—DO NOT
USE AS A TRUST]

NOTE: The following is an excerpting of some of the key provisions to be included in a QSST. For a complete trust agreement, you must assemble the provisions relating to grantor, beneficiaries, and so forth, in this book and in Shenkman, *The Estate Planning Guide* (John Wiley & Sons. Inc., 1991).

I. *S Corporations and Qualified S Corporation Trust (QSST)*

   a. With respect to any part of the Trust Estate which is stock in a corporation electing under the provisions of Section 1362 of the Code of 1986 to be taxed as an S corporation ("S corporation Assets"), this Trust Agreement is intended to be a Qualified Subchapter S Trust, as such term is defined under Section 1361(d) of the Code. Notwithstanding any provision to the contrary in this Trust Agreement the Trustees shall, with respect to such stock, operate such part of any such trust in a manner consistent with such requirements. All provisions of this Trust Agreement which affect such part of any such trust shall be construed consistently with the requirements of a Qualified Subchapter S Trust.

NOTE: This provision implicitly acknowledges that you can have more than one portion (that is, a portion without S corporation stock) in a single trust.

---

   b. Notwithstanding anything herein to the contrary, as to the S corporation Assets, the Trustees shall:

   (1) During the life of the beneficiary of such part of such trust there shall be only one (1) current income beneficiary of any such part of such trust formed under this Trust Agreement. In the event that more than one person could be a current income beneficiary under any such part of such trust under this Trust Agreement which could hold stock in an S Corporation, the Trustees are authorized to divide such trust into as many individual trusts as necessary in order to comply with the applicable provisions of the Code, if the Trustees deem appropriate in their absolute discretion.

   (2) All of the income, as defined in Code Section 643(b), of the S corporation Assets shall be distributed currently to the current income beneficiary.

   (3) Any corpus distributed during the life of such current income beneficiary, pursuant to the provisions elsewhere in this Trust, may be distributed only to such beneficiary.

   (4) The income interest of the current income beneficiary in this Trust shall terminate on the earlier of such beneficiary's death or the termination of this Trust.

   (5) If this Trust terminates during the life of the current income beneficiary, the Trustees shall distribute all S corporation Assets to such beneficiary.

   (6) If upon the death of the beneficiary of such trust would not meet the requirements of a Qualified Subchapter S Trust, then the Trustees shall distribute the S corporation Assets to the person or persons then constituting income beneficiaries of such part of such trust, if and only if, such distribution would enable the S corporation Assets to continue to meet the requirements of an S corporation in their hands. Any such distribution shall be made within the time periods required by the Code to prevent disqualification of the S corporation elections of the S corporation Assets.

(7) The Trustees are authorized to make any minor technical corrections necessary to the terms of this Trust Agreement to assure that, with respect to the S corporation Assets, such part of such trust shall continue to meet the requirements of a Qualified Subchapter S Trust.

NOTE: There is no guarantee that this type of savings clause will work, but it is an attempt to give the trustee the power to correct any minor problem in the trust that could otherwise disqualify the trust as a QSST.

---

(8) The Trustees may pay to the current income beneficiary, in addition to all other payments provided under this Trust, an amount approximately equal to the federal, state and local income taxes imposed on the current income beneficiary with respect to the S corporation Assets, on account of any income or gain allocated to trust principal, according to applicable accounting principles.

II *Trustees Shall Hold Trust Estate*

A. The Trustees shall hold the Trust Estate for the following purposes and subject to the terms and conditions hereof.

B. During the life of the Grantor:

1. The Trustees shall hold the Trust Estate with respect stock in S corporations included in the Trust Estate, in trust: To pay or apply to or for the benefit of the Grantee all of the net income thereof; or

2. The Trustee shall hold the Trust Estate with respect to assest other than stock in S corporations to accumulate any other amounts not paid or applied in [cross reference omitted] above, and add the same to the principal of this Trust at least annually and thereafter to hold, administer and dispose of same as a part of the Trust Estate.

NOTE: A qualified subchapter S trust may also have assets other than S corporation stock. The above provisions permit the trustee to exercise discretion as to whether to pay out, or accumulate, this non-S corporation income. However, income from the S corporation stock must be paid out currently in order for the trust to continue to qualify.

III. *Definitions*

The following terms when used in this Trust are defined as follows:

A. "Income," "Principal" are defined as follows. All cash dividends, other than those described hereafter, shall be income. All corporate distributions in shares of stock (whether denominated as dividends, stock splits or otherwise, and cash proceeds representing fractions thereof) of any class of any corporation (whether the corporation declaring or authorizing such distributions or otherwise) shall be principal. Dividends on investment company shares attributed to capital gains shall be principal whether declared payable at the option of the shareholders in cash or in shares or otherwise. Liquidating dividends, rights to subscribe to stock and the proceeds of the sale thereof, and the proceeds of unproductive or under-productive property shall be principal. There shall be no apportionment of the proceeds of the sale of any asset of the Trust Estate (whether real or personal, tangible or intangible) between principal and income because such asset may be or may have been wholly or partially unproductive of income during any period of time.

Notwithstanding anything in this definition to the contrary, all income attributable to S corporation stock shall be distributed as required for the trust to retain its status as a qualified S corporation trust.

For Your Notebook:

SAMPLE QSST ELECTION

[DO NOT USE WITHOUT CONSULTING YOUR LAWYER]

CERTIFIED MAIL RETURN RECEIPT
Internal Revenue Service
Holtsville, New York 00501

   Re: XYZ COMPANY, INC.
      E.I.N.—12-3456789

QUALIFIED SUBCHAPTER S TRUST ELECTION BY BENEFICIARY

This is an election to treat a qualified Subchapter S trust as a grantor or IRC Sec. 678 trust under IRC Sec. 1361(d)(2). This election is to become effective as of _____. XYZ Company, Inc., a New York corporation, in which the Qualified Subchapter S Trust ("QSST") holds stock, has already filed its S corporation election under IRC Sec. 1362(a).

As required by Temp. Reg. Sec. 18.1361-1(a), the following information is provided:

   1. S Corporation: XYZ Company, Inc., 123 Main Street, City Name, New Jersey 12345. E.I.N. 12-3456789.

   2. Trust: XYZ Qualified Subchapter S Trust, Trustee Main Avenue, New York, New York 00000. E.I.N. 98-7654312.

   3. Current Income Beneficiary: NAMES AND ADDRESSES, and Social Security No.: _____.

   4. The trust is a shareholder of XYZ Company, Inc.

   5. All of the trust's income is required to be distributed currently to the Current Income Beneficiary.

   6. The Current Income Beneficiary is a United States citizen or resident.

   7. The trust agreement provides that the Beneficiary shall be the only current income beneficiary during the Beneficiary's life.

   8. The trust agreement provides that any principal distributed during the life of the Current Income Beneficiary will only be distributed to the Current Income Beneficiary.

   9. The Current Income Beneficiary's income interest will terminate on the earlier of the Beneficiary's death or the termination of the trust.

   10. If the trust terminates during the lifetime of the Current Income Beneficiary all trust assets will be distributed to the Current Income Beneficiary.

_____   Date: _____

Part Five

TRUST TAXATION
AND ACCOUNTING

20 HOW TRUSTS AND BENEFICIARIES ARE TAXED

Trust tax rules are some of the most complex in the tax law. For the brave reader, this chapter highlights several of the important principles of trust taxation. To properly plan and understand the uses of trusts, it is essential to have at least a general understanding of how trusts are taxed. While many of the self-help books on trusts may perform a service in alerting you to the benefits of using trusts, these books are far too simplistic to help you do the job right. Whatever your level of enthusiasm for tackling tax matters, this and the following chapters should demonstrate how important it is to have proper tax, accounting, and legal advice when planning, setting up, administering, and eventually terminating any trust.

THE ISSUE OF REVOCABILITY

The threshold issue in determining how your trust will be taxed is whether the trust income is reported on your personal return or on a separate tax return for the trust. When you create a trust in which you have the right to take the assets back (a revocable grantor trust), there is no new tax entity; the trust is disregarded for income tax purposes. The substantial control that you exert over the trust results in your having to report all of the trust's income and deductions on your own income tax return. A common example is the living trust frequently used to avoid probate and provide for the management of your assets in the event that you are disabled (see Chapter 10).

While there are a number of important tax issues connected with grantor trusts, these have been discussed in some detail in Chapter 4. In this chapter, the central discussion of taxation refers to trusts that are treated as separate tax entities and file separate tax returns. The majority of trusts described in this book fall into such a category. An irrevocable trust will generally be treated as a separate tax entity as long as the grantor does not retain any impermissible powers.

OVERVIEW OF TRUST TAXATION

Generally, when a trust is a separate tax entity, filing a separate tax return, it will be taxed in a manner that is somewhat similar to the way an individual is taxed. The starting point for determining a trust's tax liability is calculating income, as would be done for an individual. Then several modifications are made. One of the differences between individual and trust taxation is that the trust will pay tax only on income that it accumulates. When the trust distributes its income to its beneficiaries, the trust will be treated as a conduit. The income and deductions will be taxed to the beneficiaries to the extent that the income is passed out of the trust to them. A trust, however, is not a perfect conduit. For example, losses generally do not pass through the trust to the beneficiaries until the year in which the trust terminates. Thus, when a trust has a capital loss (say, from selling stock) and no capital gain, the loss is not passed to the beneficiaries. (However, capital losses can be used to offset capital gains of the trust.)

General Income Issues

Like any taxpayer, a trust must use a method of accounting that clearly reflects its income. The gross income of a trust is generally determined in the same manner as gross income of an individual. Thus, trust income received by the trust during the tax year includes (1) income accumulated in the trust, (2) income that is to be distributed currently by the trustee to the beneficiaries, and (3) income that, in the trustee's discretion, either can be distributed to the beneficiaries or accumulated. The IRS has held that when a trustee waives or refunds trustee fees and commissions, this amount also should be treated as income to the trust. A trust is generally required to report its income and deductions using a calendar year. When a trust distributes income in the year it was earned to the trust's beneficiaries, as noted above, the trust is generally treated as a conduit, and the tax cost is passed to the beneficiary. The trust reports the income but then it takes a tax deduction for the amount distributed (or required to be distributed) to the beneficiary.

Determining who bears the actual tax liability on any income—the trust or the beneficiary—depends on a complex calculation called "distributable net income," or "DNI." DNI is explained in some detail below.

When the income of the trust is reported in part by the trust and in part by the beneficiary, there may be some benefit gained from taking advantage of the lower tax bracket of each. In the past, this had been an important consideration in establishing a trust. However, changes in the tax law have limited, but not eliminated, this benefit. For 1991, for example, the first $3,450 of taxable trust income was taxed at the lowest (15 percent) income tax rates. Therefore, if the beneficiary were in a 31 percent (or higher) tax bracket, there could be a tax savings by having the trust accumulate, and not distribute, $3,450 of income.

CAUTION: Carrying this strategy to its logical conclusion, it would seem that if you set up enough trusts, you could have all income taxed at the lowest tax bracket. Unfortunately, there are restrictions to prevent this abuse. When there are multiple trusts, special rules may apply to deny this benefit of repeated use of lower tax brackets and other trust-splitting techniques (see below.)

Another planning strategy used in past years also has been curtailed. Trusts formerly chose to use tax years ending on January 31 of each year in order to defer the amount of income to be reported by the beneficiaries. With the exception of certain charitable trusts, this is no longer possible.

Rules for Multiple Trusts

There are many different types of trusts available, and taxpayers may wish to operate several different trusts. Because each trust does have some income taxable at the lowest tax rates, and has its own exemption amount, there can be a tax advantage to having several trusts. To prevent abuse of the tax benefits of using multiple trusts, the tax laws provide that in certain situations, multiple trusts will be treated as a single trust. This will occur when the trusts have substantially the same grantors and beneficiaries, and when a principle purpose of the trust is to avoid tax. A husband and wife are treated as the same person for purposes of determining whether the grantors are the same.

Trust Tax-Return Filing Requirements

The trustee must file a federal income tax return, Form 1041, when the trust has gross income of $600 or more. When income is required to be distributed currently, or is properly distributed to a beneficiary, the trust is regarded as a conduit with respect to that income, and the trust is allowed a deduction against its gross income.

Many trusts are also required to file estimated tax returns, similar to those filed by individual taxpayers. An important exception is provided for certain trusts that are primarily responsible for paying the debts, taxes, and expenses of a decedent; these trusts are exempt for two years from the requirement to pay estimated taxes.

When a trust does make estimated tax payments, if the payments exceed the tax liability, the trustee can elect to give the benefit of these excess tax payments to the beneficiaries. To do this, the trustee should attach Form 1041-T, Transmittal of Estimated Taxes Credited to Beneficiaries, to the trust's tax return.

Special rules can apply for grantor trusts. Generally, grantor trusts must obtain a tax identification number and file trust tax returns even though all of the income and deductions are reported on the individual grantor's personal tax return. When you are the sole grantor and trustee, and you retain the right to revoke the trust, the requirements to obtain a tax identification number and file a trust tax return do not apply. Certain additional combinations of grantor and trustee are also permitted.

DEDUCTIONS AND LOSSES AVAILABLE TO TRUSTS

Trusts are entitled to certain tax deductions in calculating their income. Generally trusts are allowed the same tax deductions and credits as individual taxpayers, with the important difference that trusts are not permitted to claim the standard deduction that individual taxpayers may claim. The 2 percent floor on miscellaneous itemized deductions applicable to individuals is similarly applicable to trusts. A number of trust expenses may be subject to this limitation, including tax-return-preparation fees, safe-deposit box rentals, legal and accounting fees, investment counsel fees, and so forth. A trust must make special calculations to determine its adjusted gross income. For example, the expenses paid or incurred to administer the trust are deductible in arriving at adjusted gross income.

EXAMPLE: A trust has $10,000 of adjusted gross income. It incurs $1,000 of expenses, which are chargeable against income and which are subject to the 2 percent floor rule. This means that the first $200 of these expenses are not deductible [$10,000 × 2 percent]. Trust income after deductions is, therefore, $9,200 [$10,000 − ($1,000 − $200)].

The special reduction of itemized deductions that individual taxpayers are required to make does not apply to trusts.

A trust is permitted to deduct expenses that are ordinary and necessary business expenses incurred in its business, such as expenses incurred in the production of income and expenses to determine its tax liability. When a trust owns a house occupied personally by a beneficiary, the trust may not be able to deduct maintenance and similar costs. Instead, these personal expenses may be treated as a distribution to that particular beneficiary. Reasonable amounts incurred for trustee fees are deductible. The deductions, however, are only allowed for items that are obligations of the trust. For example, when a beneficiary, rather than the trust, pays a trustee fee, no deduction is allowed to either the beneficiary or the trust.

No deductions are allowed for the expenses allocable to tax-exempt income.

EXAMPLE: A trust earns the following income:

Ordinary stock dividends	$12,400
Tax-exempt bond interest	$ 4,500
Total income	$16,900

The trust incurs the following expenses:

Office expenses	$ 1,000
Account fee—paid to brokerage firm holding tax-exempt bonds	$ 250

The expenses allocable to the tax-exempt income are comprised of two components. The $250 account fee relates solely to the tax-exempt bonds and is not deductible in its entirety. The office expense fee, it is assumed, was incurred in earning all income and in managing all assets. So this amount can be allocated ratably between the ordinary stock dividends and the tax-exempt bond interest, as follows:

$$\frac{\$4,500 \text{ tax-exempt interest}}{\$16,900 \text{ total income}} \times \$1,000 \text{ expenses} = \$266$$

Thus, $266 of the office expenses are not deductible. The total expenses that relate to the tax-exempt income and that are not deductible are $516 [$250 + $26].

Depreciation deductions are allowed, but these may have to be allocated between the beneficiaries and the trust based on the allocation of trust income. Bad debt deductions, net operating losses, and casualty losses are also permitted, but they may not all pass through to the beneficiary in each tax year. Charitable contribution deductions are permitted for amounts paid to recognized charitable organizations under the terms of the trust. The charitable-contribution rules are more generous for trusts than for individuals. Individual taxpayers are permitted deductions only for contributions up to a certain percentage of their income; these rules do not apply to trusts. The contributions, however, must be made pursuant to the terms of the trust agreement and must be paid out of trust income (not principal).

Like individual and certain other taxpayers, trusts are subject to the complicated passive loss rules, which limit the ability to deduct losses from rental real estate and other passive investments. The passive loss limitations are applied to beneficiaries on the passive income or deductions distributed to them; they are applied to the trust on the passive income or deductions that it does not distribute.

Special Deductions: Simple and Complex Trusts

There are several special deductions to which trusts are entitled, but the rules vary depending on whether the trust is characterized as simple or complex. A simple trust is one that is required by the trust agreement to distribute all of its income currently; it makes no distributions other than of current income, and it has no provision for charitable contributions. Even if the trustee does not distribute all of the income as required, this will not affect the characterization. The fact that capital gains must be allocated to principal rather than income, under applicable state law or the trust provisions, also will not affect the characterization. Any trust not characterized as a simple trust is characterized as a complex trust. One special deduction is an exemption amount allowed for trusts. Simple trusts are entitled to an exemption of $300; complex trusts, $100.

Distributable Net Income (DNI) Deduction for Trusts

The most important deduction available to a trust is the deduction for distributions to beneficiaries. In the simplest terms, DNI is roughly equivalent to the trust's taxable income (rather than its income determined under accounting concepts), although there are modifications and adjustments. The rules for DNI are different for simple and complex trusts. The trust's deduction for distributions is limited to its DNI. DNI also limits the amount taxable to the beneficiary. (Distributions to a beneficiary in excess of DNI are generally subject to income tax.) Also, the DNI concept preserves the character of income distributed out of the trust. The concept behind a deduction for the trust's distributable net income is for the purpose of distributing current income to its beneficiaries, a trust is treated as a conduit, passing tax consequences to those beneficiaries. The calculations of exactly how this occurs require the use of a confusing tax concept called DNI.

To recapitulate, DNI accomplishes three purposes:

1. It determines the maximum amount on which a beneficiary will be taxed in any year.
2. It determines the maximum amount that can be deducted by a trust for distributions made to beneficiaries in any year.
3. It provides for the character (tax-exempt income or non-tax-exempt) of the income that the trust passes to a beneficiary.

For a domestic trust, DNI is calculated based on modifications of the trust's taxable income. The modifications include the following:

- Any deduction claimed for distributions to beneficiaries is added back.
- The personal exemption is added back.
- Tax-exempt interest, less deductions allocated to it, is added back.
- Capital gains that are allocated to the principal of the trust and that are not paid or required to be distributed to a beneficiary are subtracted.
- Capital losses that aren't used to offset capital gains are subtracted.

The rules for DNI are different for simple and complex trusts. For a simple trust, a deduction is available equal to the amount that the trustee is required to distribute currently, even if the actual distribution is made after the close of the tax year.

EXAMPLE: You're the only beneficiary of a simple trust that is required to distribute all of its income each year. Therefore, the trust will be entitled to a $300 exemption amount.

The trust had the following income and expenses:

Dividends and interest (ordinary income)	$13,556
Expenses relating to ordinary income	$ 2,350
Capital gain (allocable to principal)	$ 4,500
Expenses relating to capital gain income	$ 1,250

You would receive a current distribution of $11,206 [$13,556 of ordinary income − $2,350 of expenses relating to ordinary income].

The trust's DNI is $9,956 [$13,556 ordinary income − $2,350 expenses relating to ordinary income − $1,250 expenses relating to capital gain income]. Note that capital gains are not included in the calculation of DNI since it is assumed that the trust document requires that they be allocated to the principal of the trust and that they not be treated as income.

The amount that you, as beneficiary, would have to report on your tax return for the year is limited to the $9,956 of the trust's DNI.

The trust would receive a tax deduction for the amount actually distributed to you. Thus, the trust's taxable income would be:

Dividends and interest (ordinary income)	$ 13,556
Capital gain (allocable to principal)	+ 4,500
Total trust income	$ 18,056
Expenses relating to ordinary income	− 2,350
Expenses relating to capital gain income	− 1,250
Exemption amount (simple trust)	− 300
Deduction for distribution to beneficiary	− 11,206
Trust's taxable income	$ 2,950

NOTE: The capital gain in the above example will be taxed to the trust at its tax rates. However, when the trust realizes a taxable gain on property within two years of receiving that property, special rules may apply.

Taxation of Complex Trusts

While it must appear that the tax rules even for "simple" trusts are quite complex, the rules for complex trusts are still more difficult. The reason is that while simple trusts pay out all income currently, complex trusts may accumulate income. If income can be accumulated, some portion of the distributions in any year also can be made from principal amounts. The principal can consist of original assets given to the trust, or accumulations in prior years.

NOTE: Many of the trusts described in this book are complex trusts. In order to provide your trustee with the most flexibility, and to give the beneficiaries the most rights, many of the sample trust provisions empower the trustee to accumulate income or make distributions out of principal if an emergency arises.

With complex trusts, two different categories of distributions must be considered: (1) current income that is required to be distributed to the beneficiaries in that year (this is similar to the concepts discussed above for simple trusts—the beneficiaries are taxed on this first category of income to the extent of DNI); and (2) all other amounts that are paid, credited, or required to be distributed by the trust to its beneficiaries (beneficiaries will only be taxed on this amount if the distributions in the first category do not use up all of the trust's DNI for that year).

A complex trust may deduct the amount of income that is required to be distributed during that year. This can include both income and principal required to be distributed, to the extent that the amount was actually paid. When different types of income are distributed, the deduction available to the trust for the distribution is allocated in the same proportion that each type of income bears to the total DNI, unless state law or the trust instrument provides for a different allocation. Rules for allocating the different deductions and classes of income to the amounts received by the beneficiary are also provided.

For a complex trust, the trustee can elect on an annual basis to treat as if made in the prior year any distribution to a beneficiary within the first 65 days after the year end.

TAXATION OF TRUST BENEFICIARIES

A beneficiary of a simple trust is taxed on the income required to be distributed, whether or not it actually is distributed during the tax year. The income, however, cannot exceed distributable net income. If it does, then each class of income is allocated so that only a proportionate amount is included. Each item of income retains the same character as it did to the trust, unless applicable state law or the trust instrument provides for a different allocation.

A beneficiary of a complex trust must include in income his or her allocable share of trust income required to be distributed, whether or not such income actually is distributed. The beneficiary must also include in income any amounts that are properly paid or credited during the year. When the trustee makes the election to include the amount paid within 65 days following the close of the tax year, the beneficiary must include income in the earlier year in conformity with the trustee's election. When the amount of income required to be distributed exceeds the allocable share of distributable net income, the beneficiary includes in income a proportionate amount. Ordering rules are provided for making these allocations.

When a trust has more than one beneficiary, and each beneficiary receives a distinct share, such separate share treatment is required to be followed for purposes of calculating distributable net income.

Trusts must also calculate alternative minimum tax and the amount allocable to each beneficiary. This is referred to as "distributable-net, alternative-minimum taxable income."

Different Types of Trust Income Are Allocated to the Beneficiaries

As noted earlier, trusts are generally treated like a conduit—passing taxable income and deductions to their beneficiaries.

EXAMPLE: A simple trust distributes all of its interest income currently in equal amounts to Jane and Tom. The trust earns a total of $6,000 during the year, with no expenses. Therefore, each receives $3,000. However, the analysis cannot stop here. Of the $6,000 earned by the trust, $2,000 was interest on tax-exempt bonds, and $4,000 was interest on CDs. Jane and Tom each should be allocated $1,000 of tax-exempt income and $2,000 of ordinary income to comprise their $3,000 shares.

There is yet another important concept involved in basic trust taxation, however: there can be advantages in allocating different types of income to different beneficiaries. For example, if one beneficiary is in a low tax bracket, and another beneficiary is in a high tax bracket, it would save money to allocate taxable income to the low-bracket beneficiary, and tax-exempt income to the high-bracket beneficiary. The kiddie tax (see Chapter 11) could make it advantageous to allocate tax-exempt income to a beneficiary under age 14, while older children who are beneficiaries would receive allocations of taxable income.

There are inevitable restrictions on obtaining any tax advantage. In this case, the trust document must specifically make the desired allocation. This means you would have to have anticipated events when you first signed the trust—not a simple task. Further, there must be an economic effect independent of the income tax benefits of the allocation for the IRS to recognize it.

EXAMPLE: Assume that Jane from the above example was allocated the entire $2,000 of tax-exempt income. Jane's share would then consist of $2,000 of tax-exempt income and $1,000 of taxable income. Tom would receive $3,000 of taxable ordinary income. First of all, the trust agreement must provide for this. But what if the trust agreement provides that when the tax-exempt and non-tax-exempt bonds are sold, the gain will be divided equally between Jane and Tom. This will make it appear that the only concern in allocating tax-exempt income to Jane was the income tax benefit. The IRS probably would not accept such an allocation. If, however, any gain or loss on the tax-exempt bonds were allocated to Jane, and she were allocated only one-third of the gain or loss on the other bonds, then Jane would bear the economic risks and rewards of the tax-exempt income allocated to her, and the allocation might be accepted.

How Is a Beneficiary Taxed on Receipt of Income Accumulated by a Trust?

Trusts may accumulate, rather than currently pay out, income. One reason for doing so could be that the trust is in a lower tax bracket than the beneficiary. The phase-out for the low tax brackets that trusts have, however, will often limit this benefit. For tax years beginning in 1992, income of $3,600 and below is taxed in the 15 percent bracket; income over $3,600, in the 28 percent bracket; and income over $10,900, in the 31 percent bracket. There are important nontax reasons to accumulate income. When the current beneficiary doesn't need the money, and the remainder beneficiary will likely need the money, the trustee can choose to hold income rather than distribute it, assuming that the trust agreement gives him or her the power to do so.

EXAMPLE: You set up a trust for the benefit of your spouse. On your spouse's death, the income and, eventually, the principal of the trust will go to your child. Your spouse is the current beneficiary. Your child is the remainder beneficiary. Since your spouse has substantial income, the trust agreement authorizes your trustee to distribute income to your spouse if necessary; you don't require distribution. This could be a credit shelter trust as described in Chapter 9 rather than a Q-TIP marital trust. Your spouse does exceptionally well in the stock market and has no need for any income from the trust. Rather than expose the income to your spouse's creditors, your trustee saves the money for future distribution to your child.

Although the tax laws that affect income accumulated by trusts are quite complex, the economic and personal benefits of having a trust that can accumulate income outweigh the difficulties of dealing with the tax rules.

How and when should income that is accumulated by the trustee in one year, and distributed in a later year, be taxed? The answer is found in another confusing bit of regulation, called "throwback rules." The idea is to tax the trust's income as if it had been paid to the beneficiary in the year it was earned, rather than being held by the trust. In theory, this result is achieved by "throwing back" the income to the beneficiary's tax return for the year in which the income was earned and could have been distributed.

This is the result "in theory" because there are several modifications and assumptions that distort this process in order to make the required calculations easier. The tax laws provide what is called a "shortcut method" for making the throwback calculation. The approach is to average the amount of income involved over the years during which the income was earned by the trust. The average income earned by the trust is added to the beneficiary's income for a five-year period, with the lowest and highest years being dropped from the calculation. Thus, three year's worth of the beneficiary's income (as reported on the beneficiary's personal tax return) is used in the calculation of the additional tax on the accumulation distribution. The average tax for this three-year shortcut period is then multiplied by the number of years during which the trust accumulated income. This is the preliminary tax that can be reduced by any tax credits. What follows is a more detailed explanation of the throwback rules.

The Throwback Rules

To properly understand taxation of an accumulation distribution, which is a feature of many of the trusts you will want to work with, and many of the trusts presented in this book, a formal definition of terms must be reviewed. Here is the technical definition of a throwback calculation:

A throwback calculation is only required when (1) there is an accumulation distribution, and (2) in at least one preceding tax year there was trust income that was not distributed (called undistributed net income or UNI).

Each of the technical terms included above also needs to be defined:

- *Accumulation Distribution.* This term refers to the excess of the non-required distributions from the trust over the trust's DNI. In figuring the accumulation distribution, the trust's DNI is reduced by the required distributions made to the trust's beneficiaries in that year. It is not uncommon for an accumulation distribution to occur in the final year of a trust.

- *Preceding Tax Year.* This is limited to the five tax years prior to the year in which the accumulation distribution is made.
- *Undistributed Net Income.* This income occurs when the trust's DNI for the year is greater than the amounts distributed to the beneficiaries and any "tax imposed on the trust" on the income not distributed.
- *Tax Imposed on the Trust.* This term refers to taxes that are allocable under the IRS rules to the undistributed portion of the trust's DNI.

EXAMPLE: A trust has DNI of $25,000. The trust makes distributions to its beneficiaries of $15,000, leaving $10,000 of undistributed income. The trust pays income taxes of $1,750 on this amount. The trust's undistributed net income is $8,250 [$25,000 − ($15,000 + $1,750)].

With this background, an example of how the amount of an accumulation distribution is calculated can be presented:

EXAMPLE: Years ago, you set up a trust for the benefit of your children. A friend is the trustee. In 1992, the trust has total income of $22,500. Administrative expenses are $1,750. Thus, the distributable net income, or DNI, of the trust is $20,750 [$22,500 − $1,750]. The trust agreement requires the trustee to distribute $15,000 to the beneficiaries. The trust agreement also gives the trustee the discretion to distribute principal for certain purposes. The trustee exercises this right and distributes an additional $15,500 to one of the beneficiaries to use as a down payment on the purchase of a new home. The accumulation distribution is calculated as follows:

Amounts other than required distributions distributed to the beneficiaries		$ 15,500
DNI	$ 20,750	
Distributions required to be made currently to beneficiaries	− 15,000	
Taxes paid by trust on undistributed DNI	− 1,200	
Undistributed net income		− 4,550
Accumulation distribution for the year		$ 10,950

Once it has been established that an accumulation distribution has occurred, and the amount has been determined, the next general step is to calculate the throwback tax that is due. This step requires a few intermediate steps.

When an accumulation distribution occurs, the amount of the accumulation distribution is allocated to each prior tax year of the trust that had undistributed net income.

EXAMPLE: In 1992, a trust has an accumulation distribution of $10,950, as calculated in the previous example. Undistributed net income for the trust for the prior five years is as follows:

Year	Undistributed Net Income
1986	$3,401
1987	$1,540
1988	-0-
1989	$2,909
1990	$2,875
1991	$1,331

The $10,950 is allocated to each of the prior years up to the amount of the undistributed net income in each of those prior years:

Year	Undistributed Net Income	Accumulation Distribution Allocation
1986	$3,401	$ 3,401
1987	1,540	1,540
1988	-0-	-0-
1989	2,909	2,909
1990	2,875	2,875
1991	1,331	225
		$10,950

Only $225 was allocated against the 1991 undistributed net income since that was all that was necessary in order to allocate the entire $10,950 of the accumulation distribution. The remaining 1991 UNI of $1,106 [$1,331 − $225] would remain for allocations of future year accumulation distributions.

If the accumulation distribution exceeds the amount of undistributed net income of the trust's prior years, then the excess is treated as a tax-free return of the investment made in the trust.

The next step is to calculate the taxes that were attributable to the undistributed net income of the trust in each of the prior years. The idea behind this step is quite reasonable. The trust reported certain income on its tax return and paid a tax on that income. One of the underlying concepts of trust taxation is that the trust is a mere conduit that should pass income and deductions to the beneficiaries, who should pay the tax on that income. Since the trust had accumulated income, it originally had to pay the tax. Now that the income has been distributed, to get back (roughly) to the intended scenario of the beneficiary's bearing the tax burden, a calculation is made as to what tax cost the beneficiary should pay. However, since the trust has already paid some tax, the beneficiary should get some credit for the tax paid. If this were not done, the IRS would be taxing the same income twice.

Before finding the tax that was attributable to the undistributed net income of the trust in each of the prior years to which the accumulation distribution is allocated, another intermediate step must be taken. The goal is a result that is equivalent to what would have occurred had the beneficiary paid the tax originally. If the trust had not paid a tax, the trust would have had more income to distribute. So the tax paid by the trust and attributable to the undistributed net income (UNI) in each prior year is added to the undistributed net income to arrive at a figure of what the beneficiary could have received as a distribution. This is called the "total deemed distribution." This step is needed because, as illustrated in one of the prior examples, the tax paid by the trust was subtracted from DNI in calculating the undistributed net income of the trust.

EXAMPLE:

Year	UNI	Tax Attributable to UNI	Total Deemed Distribution
1986	$ 3,401	$1,023	$ 4,424
1987	1,540	352	1,892
1988	-0-	-0-	-0-
1989	2,909	544	3,453
1990	2,875	512	3,387
1991	225	92	317
	$10,950	$2,523	$13,473

The next step is to calculate the tax that the beneficiary must pay on the total deemed distributions, as calculated in the above example. This calculation also requires a series of steps:

STEP #1.   Determine to which of the trust's prior tax years the accumulation distribution is to be allocated.

STEP #2.   Deduct from the accumulation distribution amounts that would not have to be included in the beneficiary's income if it had been distributed (for example, tax-exempt income).

STEP #3.   Divide the result in Step #2 (the accumulation distribution less tax-exempt income) by the number of years identified in Step #1. This is an "average accumulation distribution amount."

STEP #4.   For the five tax years immediately preceding the year of the accumulation distribution, take the beneficiary's income, and eliminate the highest and lowest years.

STEP #5.   Add to the beneficiary's taxable income for the three years remaining after Step #4 the average accumulation distribution amount calculated in Step #3.

STEP #6.   Calculate the amount of income tax that the beneficiary would have paid in each of the three years involved, with the addition of the average accumulation distribution amount to each of those years.

STEP #7.   Subtract from the recalculated tax the actual tax paid by the beneficiary in each of those years. The net result is the additional tax that would have to be paid in each of those years.

STEP #8.   Average the additional taxes due for each of the three years.

STEP #9.   Multiply the average tax increase by the number of years in Step #1.

STEP #10. Subtract from the total tax calculated in Step #9 the total taxes deemed distributed to the beneficiary. The net amount is the additional tax that the beneficiary must pay on receipt of an accumulation distribution.

Although it may be hard to believe, this method of calculating the beneficiary's tax is referred to as the "shortcut" method.

An important exception to these complicated throwback rules exists. When income was accumulated before the beneficiary became 21, this tax will not apply. Several more complicated exceptions and special rules can affect a throwback calculation. These can apply when a foreign trust is involved, or there are multiple trusts, or the trustee's records are inadequate. In all cases where an accumulation distribution is involved, seek qualified professional help.

CONCLUSION

The tax rules for how a trust and beneficiary are taxed are extremely complicated. However, the benefits of using trusts to properly protect you, your family, your privacy, and your assets should not be deterred by this complexity since the benefits of using trusts will often outweigh the costs of complying with the trust tax rules. This complexity, however, makes it almost essential to retain specialized professional accountants or tax advisers.

21 HOW A TRUST IS TAXED ON THE SALE OR DISTRIBUTION OF PROPERTY

Many of the trusts illustrated in this book terminate at a specified time, or on the happening of a specified event, such as a child reaching age 35. In many instances, property may be sold prior to the termination, or the property may be distributed to the beneficiary on the termination of the trust. There are several possible tax and legal consequences of these major trust transactions. While the income tax consequences described in the preceding chapter tend to apply each year, the sale or distribution of assets tends to be less frequent. The amounts involved, however, make these sale and distribution transactions quite important. The gain or loss to be realized by the trust, or a beneficiary who receives property distributed from a trust, depends on the determination of the investment in the property, called the "tax basis."

DETERMINING THE TRUST'S INVESTMENT (TAX BASIS) IN PROPERTY

The calculation of the gain or loss realized upon the sale of property acquired by a trust or beneficiary is made under special rules for determining the investment in the property. This, in turn, is dependent on the method by which the property was acquired and the nature of the property sold. When your trustee acquires property by way of a gift, the trustee uses the grantor's adjusted tax basis for calculating any gain.

EXAMPLE: Grandparent gives stock that cost $70,000 and is worth $95,000 to a trust for the benefit of Grandchild. The trust's tax basis in the stock, assuming no gift tax is paid, is $70,000.

The calculation of adjusted tax basis becomes somewhat more complicated when the donor incurs a gift tax as a result of making the gift. In this case, the adjusted tax basis in the property is increased by the amount of gift tax paid.

EXAMPLE: If Grandparent pays $20,000 of gift tax to make the gift of stock from the above example, the trust's tax basis in the stock is increased to $90,000 [$70,000 + $20,000].

The amount by which the adjusted tax basis in the property can be increased as a result of the gift tax paid by the donor/grantor is subject to a cap. The gift tax can only be used to increase basis to the extent that it is attributable to the appreciation in the property given to the trust. This is the excess of the fair market value of the property as of the date of the gift over the grantor's adjusted tax basis in the property.

EXAMPLE: Still using the first example, assume that Grandparent incurs a gift tax at a 50 percent rate. The gift tax will be $35,000 [.50 × $70,000]. If the full gift tax were added to the donor's tax basis, the trust's tax basis would be $105,000 [$70,000 + $35,000]. This amount, however, would exceed the fair value of the property, so the basis for the trust is limited to the $95,000 fair market value of the property.

TIP: The general rule for capital gains is that they are allocated to the principal of the trust and are not considered part of current income. Thus, they will be taxable to the trust at the trust's tax rates. It can be advantageous in some situations to include a provision in the trust document permitting the trustee to allocate certain capital gains to income, rather than principal. This could enable the trustee to distribute the capital gains to beneficiaries who may be taxed at a lower tax rate than the trust. This is because the lowest tax rates for trusts are phased out at amounts of income much lower than those at which the low tax brackets for individuals are phased out.

When a loss is realized by the trust on the later sale of property, the trust's adjusted tax basis (investment) is the lower of (1) the donor/grantor's adjusted tax basis in the property; or (2) the fair market value of the property at the time of the gift to the trust.

EXAMPLE: Assume that the trustee of Grandchild's trust sold the stock (the same one given by Grandparent) four years later for $50,000. The amount of tax loss for the trust is $20,000 [$50,000 − $70,000]. The loss is figured by the lower of (1) the $70,000 tax basis of Grandparent; or (2) the $95,000 fair market value of the property at the date of the transfer.

When property is received by a trust from an estate (that is, under a will), the trust's tax basis is the fair market value of the property in the estate on the date of death, or at a date six months after the date of death if the estate elects to value all assets at that date (the alternate valuation date).

Where do you find the information for the above calculations? Hopefully, the trustee has maintained the proper records. If the records are not readily available, consider the following resources:

- If a gift tax return was filed by the grantor or other person giving property to the trust (donor), a copy of this return should provide the necessary information. If neither the trustee, the donor, nor the accountants for the trust and donor have copies, the IRS may be able to provide one upon request. It is also important to determine whether a gift tax was paid when the gifts were made to the trust. For example, if the gifts qualified for the unlimited marital deduction (there's no gift tax on transfers to your spouse), or if the amount given to your trust was within the remaining $600,000 unified credit of the donor, then no gift tax cost may have been paid on the transaction of setting up your trust.

   If no gift tax return was filed when the initial transfers were made, however, it is not possible to correctly determine any adjustment that may be required in order to calculate the appropriate tax basis for the property, inclusive of adjustments for gift tax purposes.

- If the property was transferred to the trust under someone's will, the adjusted tax basis of the assets transferred from the estate to the trust generally will be the fair market value of the assets as of the date of death. The best approach is to obtain a copy of the tax return. If this can't be done, estimating the market value of the asset at the date of death from reasonable sources, like newspapers if the property is stock, may be the only approach available.

TAX CONSEQUENCES OF A DISTRIBUTION TO A BENEFICIARY

Generally, no gain or loss results from a transfer of property from a trust to a beneficiary under the terms of the trust instrument. There are several exceptions. When appreciated property is distributed in satisfaction of the beneficiary's right to receive a specific dollar amount, or when property other than the required property is distributed, gain may be recognized.

EXAMPLE: Grandparent transfers various assets to a trust for the benefit of several grandchildren. When each grandchild reaches age 35, he or she is to receive $35,000. When the first grandchild reaches age 35, the trustee transfers stock with a tax basis of $24,000 and a fair market value of $35,000. The trust must report a gain of $11,000 [$35,000 − $24,000].

Thus, a trust must recognize taxable gain or loss when a cash bequest is satisfied by distribution of other property.

When a stated percentage of the principal of a trust is distributed to a beneficiary before the termination of a trust, it is not considered to be a satisfaction of the trust's obligation for a definite amount of cash or equivalent value in property. The transaction is simply treated as a partial distribution of a share of the trust principal. Therefore, no sale or exchange is deemed to have occurred, and no gain or loss can be recognized.

The beneficiary's tax basis will be the same as the tax basis of the trust. Any gain or loss is deferred until the beneficiary disposes of the property involved.

EXAMPLE: A beneficiary receives a distribution from a trust of stock worth $35,400. The trust's tax basis in the stock was $23,000. Assuming that the trustee does not make an election under Code Section 643(e) to recognize gain or loss on the distribution, the beneficiary's tax basis in the stock will be $23,000. The distribution will also be considered to carry out to the beneficiary DNI to the extent of the lesser of the adjusted basis in the property or the fair value of the property. In this case, DNI of $23,000 would be considered to be distributed (see Chapter 20).

Distributions of property, such as stocks, bonds, or other trust assets (in tax jargon, "distributions in kind"), are also included. The amount of income to be recognized by the beneficiary depends on whether the trustee makes an election under Internal Revenue Code Section 643(e) to recognize income on the distribution of property. The result of this election is as if the property had been sold for its fair market value at the date it was distributed. This election is to be made on the tax return for the year in which the distribution occurs. The election must apply to all distributions made by the trust during the entire tax year. The trustee can't choose to make the election for some property, but not for other property.

If this election is made, the beneficiary's basis in the distributed property is the trust's adjusted tax basis prior to the distribution, increased (decreased) by the gain (loss) recognized by the trust. Thus the tax basis of the beneficiary becomes the fair market value of the property on the distribution.

EXAMPLE: Years ago, your trust purchased stock in XYZ, Inc., for $1,000. The stock is now worth $5,000. If the trust distributes the stock to you, your tax basis in the stock is $1,000, the same as the trust's. Therefore, if you sell the stock, you will realize the gain. Your tax basis will be stepped up, or increased, to the $5,000 fair value of the stock only if the trustee makes a special election to recognize the $4,000 of gain in the trust. When the trustee makes this election, the trust will receive a deduction for a distribution to you of the $5,000 value. When should a trustee consider making an election to pay a tax? When the tax cost to the trust of reporting the gain on the property distributed would be less than the tax cost to the beneficiary. This could occur, for example, when the trust had capital losses from other stock sales that could offset the gain.

SPECIAL RULE WHEN TRUST SELLS PROPERTY QUICKLY

A special tax is imposed on a trust that sells or exchanges property within two years after the property was transferred to the trust, and before the grantor's death. Under this special rule, the trust is taxed at the grantor's tax rate. The idea behind this rule is to prevent anyone from gaining a tax advantage by transferring property to a trust, only in order to have the trust sell it. The amount of gain that the trust has to recognize is the lesser of the actual gain the trust recognized on its sale of the property and the excess of the fair market value of the property over the trust's tax basis immediately after the transfer of the property to the trust.

In other words, this special rule treats the transaction as if the grantor had sold the property and then transferred the proceeds, net of the applicable tax cost, to the trust. There are several situations that are exempted from this special rule—namely, when the trust is formed on death, or is a charitable remainder trust. Special rules apply in several other circumstances, such as when the kiddie tax (Chapter 12) applies, when there is an installment sale, and when there are net operating losses.

CONCLUSION

One of the most important concepts in taxation of the distribution or sale of property by a trust is finding the tax basis of the property. You will need to know whether any gift tax was paid on the original donation to the trust to properly determine this figure. Distributions to a beneficiary generally are not subject to tax on gain or loss, unless the appreciation is an aspect of the required distribution, or a distribution is made apart from the required assets. As usual, there are exceptions and variations on these general principles, and it is important to consult with a professional.

22 TERMINATING A TRUST

No trust can continue forever. At some point, every trust must end, whether as a result of the provisions of the trust agreement, actions of the trustee, or the requirements of law. It is important to understand how, when, and why a trust can or should be terminated. These considerations affect how your trust agreement should be written. Whether you are a trustee or beneficiary, there are also important tax and legal considerations to be considered. You need to know your rights in order to properly protect your interests and fulfill your responsibilities.

WHEN AND HOW CAN A TRUST BE MODIFIED OR TERMINATED?

The most common situation for a termination is when the trust has achieved its purposes so that its life naturally closes.

EXAMPLE: You establish a trust for your children. Your objective is to provide for management of monies that you've set aside for your children's benefit, and to ensure, to the extent possible, that the monies remain insulated from your creditors. In order to provide flexibility for your trustees, you've set up a single trust for all three children. Your trust provides that when the youngest child reaches age 25, the trust should terminate and the trustee should distribute all remaining income and principal equally among your children. Thus, on your youngest child's 25th birthday, the trustee begins making final distributions and starts to wind up the trust. Your trust will terminate soon thereafter.

In the above situation, the trust ends when its prescribed function has been completed. But there are circumstances in which a trust can be modified or terminated by special action or as part of the terms of the trust.

Revocable Trust

You, as the grantor of the trust, may have reserved the right to terminate (revoke) when you set up your trust. You could have included such a provision in your trust, or, in some instances, you could have relied on the law. Remember that this type of right makes the trust taxable as a grantor trust, and all income from the trust must be reported on your personal income tax return rather than on a separate trust tax return. A sample revocability clause is presented in Chapter 4.

Irrevocable Trust

If the trust is not specifically revocable by you, it is probably improper for you to terminate the trust by unilateral action, and you should adhere to the rules for an irrevocable trust. An irrevocable trust can only be terminated when all of the beneficiaries consent and no material purpose of the trust is defeated. For example, if a trust has a spendthrift provision (prevents creditors from attacking the trust assets and prohibits beneficiaries from assigning their trust interests), the termination of the trust by agreement of the beneficiaries may defeat a material purpose. However, if the grantor also consents in such a situation, the trust still may qualify for termination.

CAUTION: Be certain that everyone with any interest in the trust agrees. It's best to have everyone, no matter how contingent their interest, sign a release (discussed below) based on a full accounting. Then nobody can later claim that they agreed to the termination of the trust based on misleading information. However, in many family situations these formalities are often ignored. Be particularly careful to have an attorney review the trust document to identify such parties.

Determining who has an interest in the trust and must therefore consent to an early termination (or other modification) of the trust is not a simple task. Not only must the provisions of the trust be analyzed carefully, but applicable state laws (both statutes and cases) should be consulted.

EXAMPLE: You set up a trust with the income going to your spouse for life. On your spouse's death, the income and then principal go to your children, or if one of your children is deceased, to that child's issue (your grandchildren). What if there are no grandchildren alive at the time you wish to terminate the trust? Must the grandchildren not yet born be included? At least one court has said that it is not necessary to include such contingent beneficiaries.

EXAMPLE: Here is a different scenario: You set up a trust with the income going to your spouse for life. On your spouse's death the income and then the principal go to your grandchildren. The grandchildren in the previous example were contingent beneficiaries. They would only obtain an interest in the trust if your children died before your spouse. In this example, any grandchild born will receive an interest in the trust at some point in the future. Thus, the grandchildren here are remainder beneficiaries. They will receive the remainder of the trust after the current beneficiary, your spouse, dies. In this situation, therefore, your grandchildren, even those not born at the time you seek to modify or revoke the trust, may have to consent.

What if the beneficiaries are minor children, or are disabled and unable to make legal decisions for themselves? Clearly, the consent of these beneficiaries is required, but they themselves cannot provide the consent. If a court will accept the decision of a guardian of these individuals, the trust can be revoked or amended. Otherwise, it cannot. The court's decision whether to accept the guardian's signature may depend on whether the changes or termination of the trust would be in the best interests of those minor or disabled beneficiaries.

What happens if the grantor of the trust has died? It may be impossible to amend the trust. This is why it is so important to understand all of the provisions of your trust, to try to anticipate as many different circumstances as possible, and to leave as much flexibility as is reasonable with the trustee to deal with unforeseen circumstances.

CAUTION: What if every possible party cannot agree in writing to amend or revoke a trust? Lawyers may try to resolve this issue by having everyone available and competent sign an agreement to terminate the trust and having each person agree to indemnify everyone else in the event of a problem. However, when any of the persons with interests in the trust do not participate, or are minors, there is always a risk that some time in the future the actions could be challenged. When the amounts of money involved are large, exercise considerable caution because the indemnifications may be useless.

Other situations in which an irrevocable trust can be terminated are the following:

- Your trust can be rescinded or reformed if there was fraud, duress, undue influence, or a mistake when the trust was set up. These situations are unusual.

- Subsequent impracticability, impossibility, or illegality of the trust can result in the termination of the trust, when such conditions did not exist when your trust was formed.

- A trust can terminate upon merger. This is a legal doctrine stating that when the trustee and the beneficiary are the same person, there can be no trust.

- A trust can be terminated or modified by operation of law. Most states, for example, have a law (known as the rule against perpetuities) requiring that a trust not continue beyond some specified time. A typical rule-against-perpetuities statute requires that the trust be terminated within 21 years of the death of the last person (beneficiary) living when the trust was formed. Every trust, therefore, should contain a provision stating that if the trust has not already terminated, it will terminate at the date prior to violating the rule against perpetuities. A sample provision is included in Chapter 7.

Terms Within a Trust Allowing for Termination

A trust can be terminated in accordance with the terms of the trust agreement. This can be accomplished by a provision that establishes a specified period for the trust, or when the trust agreement grants the power to another to terminate the trust.

EXAMPLE: The language in a typical trust may provide that the trustee may distribute ". . . so much or all of the principal as the trustee, in his or her sole and absolute discretion, shall at any time and from time to time deem necessary or advisable for Grantor's said wife's health, maintenance, support, or education."

Under this broad provision, the trustee may choose to distribute all of the income and assets in the trust at his or her discretion.

There are other situations in which your trust can terminate, unproblematically, if you have provided the appropriate flexibility in your trust agreement.

EXAMPLE: You establish a trust for the benefit of your only daughter. The trust is to terminate when she reaches age 35, and all income and principal are to be distributed. However, as a result of large distributions to help your child acquire her first home, and a few years later to start her own business, the trust only has $12,565 when your daughter is age 31. It is uneconomical to continue the trust, given the amount of the trustee fees, accounting fees, and administrative costs. What are your options?

If you provided your trustee with the right to terminate the trust when its operations became uneconomical, then your trustee could choose this earlier date for termination and distribute the proceeds to your daughter. The following trust clause could be used:

SAMPLE TRUST CLAUSE:

Distribution of Trust Estate When Amount Is Less Than Specified Sum.

In the event that the principal remaining in the trust for any beneficiary shall be less than Twenty Thousand ($20,000.00) Dollars, the Trustee may, in the Trustee's sole and absolute discretion, immediately distribute such remaining principal to such beneficiary.

TIP: Always look at the provisions of your trust governing when beneficiaries are to receive distributions of income and principal when trying to ascertain when the trust should terminate.

When a disabled beneficiary is involved, the trustee usually is given the power to defer termination of the trust and distribution of the assets. The following are illustrative provisions in a trust agreement that permit the trustee to defer payment and hence defer termination of a trust:

SAMPLE TRUST CLAUSES:

Whenever any property is to be distributed to a person under a disability, the payment or transfer of the property may be deferred until the disability ceases. If the transfer of property is deferred under this Section, the property shall be held by the Trustee, who shall apply so much of the principal and income as the trustee deems necessary for the benefit of the person under a disability.

A "person under a disability" is a person who, for such period as the Trustee shall determine, is deemed to be physically or mentally incapable of managing such person's affairs. It is not required that a judicial declaration have been made with respect to such disability.

The Windup Period

When a trust has terminated under any of the situations described above, the trust itself may continue to exist for an additional period, during which the trustee is allowed to wind up the affairs of the trust. For example, a trust set to end when a child reaches 21 does not automatically terminate on the child's 21st birthday. During this additional period, the trust will continue to exist as a separate taxable entity (assuming it was previously a taxable entity distinct from the grantor).

A trust continues to be recognized as a taxable entity until all trust property has been distributed to successors and a reasonable time after this event has elapsed for the trustee to complete the administration of the trust. A reasonable amount of assets can be set aside in good faith to pay unascertained or contingent liabilities and expenses (other than a claim by a beneficiary). However, when the final distribution of the trust principal is unreasonably delayed, the trust may be considered to have terminated at an earlier date.

Once all trust assets have been distributed, the windup phase should include the preparation of a final accounting by the trustee. This accounting should then be submitted to all of the beneficiaries for their approval. Generally, the trustee will require the beneficiaries to approve the accounting in writing and sign a release to the trustee absolving the trustee of any further liability. A sample trust release is included in the "For Your Notebook" section following this chapter. Once the trustee has received the release, all remaining assets will be distributed to the beneficiary. A final tax return then will be filed.

TAX CONSEQUENCES OF TERMINATING A TRUST

When a trust is considered terminated for tax purposes, the gross income, credits, and deductions of the trust subsequent to termination become the responsibilities of the beneficiaries who succeed to the property.

Although trusts are entitled to an exemption ($300 for complex trusts, $100 for simple trusts), if a final distribution of assets is completed during the tax year, all income of the trust must be reported as distributed to the beneficiaries, without reduction for the exemption amount. One final point is that a trust cannot be characterized as simple in its final year because no trust will be considered simple when it distributes principal.

Other special rules apply in the final year of a trust. When a net operating loss, deductions in excess of gross income, or a capital loss carryover occur, these tax events become available to the beneficiary succeeding to the property. This is an exception to all other years, when tax losses generally are not passed through to the trust's beneficiaries. Thus, in the final tax year of the trust, any losses the trust realized in prior years on the sale of capital assets, which could include stock, bonds, real estate, and other assets, that did not offset capital gains in those years will be passed through to the beneficiaries.

All capital gains realized in the year a trust terminates are included in the trust's calculation of distributable net income (DNI). If the distribution is postponed until the year following the sale, the gain still may be taxable to the trust.

After a trust terminates, questions can arise concerning what income is required to be paid out currently. When income earned before the terminating event was required to be paid out currently, that income should be treated in the same manner even though it was actually paid out to the beneficiaries after the terminating event. Income and capital gains earned after the termination will be required to be distributed currently if the trust agreement or state law specifies this treatment. This income then will be taxed to the beneficiaries and not the trust. In many situations, the trustee will not be able to distribute income currently because of the need to determine expenses or the exact amount distributable to each beneficiary. This temporary withholding of funds by the trustee should not affect the tax treatment of this money as being taxable to the beneficiaries and not the trust.

TRUST ACCOUNTING PROCEDURES

It is important to understand the difference between trust accounting and tax accounting. The tax accounting rules, as detailed in Chapter 20, are used to determine the tax costs to the trust and the beneficiary. Accounting rules used by the trustee (called "fiduciary accounting") are used in determining the calculations of income and principal distributed to the various beneficiaries. These fiduciary accounting rules will be reflected in the accounting rendered to the beneficiaries by the trustee.

What Is Fiduciary Accounting?

A trustee may provide some type of accounting when the trust terminates. This may be done as part of the trustee's request for the beneficiaries to sign a release to the trustee in advance of the final distribution from the trust. When a new person assumes the responsibility of being a trustee, or an existing trustee resigns, it also can be advisable to have some form of accounting in order to establish the status of the trust at such time.

TIP: If you are an incoming successor or replacement trustee, insist on a detailed accounting to cut off any liability you may have for matters that occurred prior to your become a trustee.

Trusts also may contain general provisions absolving the trustee of any responsibility to provide an accounting unless required by law. When an accounting is provided, the trust agreement may provide that the accounting should be conclusive and binding on the beneficiaries. Unfortunately, there is no fixed standard and common meaning of fiduciary accounting. The accounting principles can be governed by state law, the trust agreement, or local custom.

Examples of the differences between trust accounting and tax reporting rules, include the following:

- The trustee may choose an accounting year based on the date the trust was established. However, most trusts must use the calendar year for tax reporting.
- The trustee may have to distinguish between principal and income deductions. For income tax purposes, the distinction is not as important.

EXAMPLE: A grantor establishes a trust for the benefit of his second wife and the only child of his prior marriage. The income is to be paid to the second wife for life, and on her death, the remaining investment (called principal or corpus) is to be distributed to the child. Deductions incurred by the trust must be categorized as those relating to income and those relating to principal. This is critically important since it will affect the actual amounts to which the wife and child will be entitled.

What a Final Trust Accounting May Include

The cover page of a trust accounting should disclose basic background information, such as the name of the trust, the date the trust was established, the names of the trustees, the date of the accounting, and the period covered by the accounting.

An accounting should include some type of summary that indicates the level of detail the report provides, and separate totals should appear for assets at the beginning of the accounting, transactions during the period, and assets at the end of the accounting period. The summary should be followed by detailed schedules that analyze each of the components of the summary. For example, the balance of the trust at the beginning should show all of the assets originally transferred to the trust when the trust was formed. This can be accomplished quite readily by attaching a listing that either was attached to the original trust agreement or was included in the estate of the person under whose will the trust was created. For assets transferred to the trust under a will, the fair value of the assets at the date of death could be disclosed.

The transactions section could show the total dividends and interest received, in aggregate, on each security owned. A separate section should detail capital gains and losses on the sale of any trust assets. For certain transactions, however, items should be listed individually and not grouped. Items deserving this detailed disclosure could include penalty and interest charges incurred on tax returns and extraordinary appraisal costs. When stock dividends, stock splits, dividend reinvestment, and similar transactions occur, a detailed report will be necessary to analyze the results of the trust.

Trustee commissions and fees must be disclosed. Distributions to the beneficiaries should be disclosed with sufficient detail to identify specific bequests, distributions of income, and distributions of principal. Payment of expenses and, if applicable, payment of creditors and funeral and other administrative expenses should be disclosed. This detail is necessary to determine that income, principal, and deductions have been properly allocated among the beneficiaries.

> **NOTE:** As a guideline, consider what information is necessary to determine trustee commissions and fees. When trustee fees are based on income or asset values, then the appropriate details will have to be disclosed.

The cost of assets purchased by the trustee during the term of the trust should be disclosed. For assets received during the administration of the trust, such as from the grantor, the fair value of the assets on the date of their receipt may be the appropriate figure to disclose. For assets received and sold, it is important to disclose the method of accounting used to determine the gain or loss.

> **EXAMPLE:** A trust was formed with 1,000 shares of XYZ, Corp. common stock, valued at $10 per share on the date the grantor formed the trust and transferred the shares. Years later, the grantor died and under her will an additional 1,000 shares of XYZ, Corp. common stock were transferred to the trust. The value of the shares then was $1,000 per share. Three years later, the trustee sold 500 shares of XYZ, Corp. stock for $1,150 per share. If the trustee calculates the gain on the basis of average cost, the gain will be far different than if it is calculated on the assumption of first-in, first-out ("FIFO").
>
> Under the average-cost method, each share cost $505 [[(1,000 × $10) + (1,000 × $1,000)]/2,000 total shares]. The gain is $645 per share [$1,150 − $505]. On the FIFO method, the cost of each share sold is the $10 initial value of the first shares received. The gain under the FIFO method is $1,140 per share [$1,150 − $10]. If the trustee commissions are based on income, the consequences can be substantial.

Generally, the first value of assets reported should be used consistently throughout the reporting done by the trustee. One exception is when assets received from the grantor's estate are subject to an IRS audit and the values finally determined by the IRS differ from those reported initially. In some states, a new (successor) trustee may disclose an adjustment to the initial asset values in order to disclose the value of the assets at the date the trustee began to serve.

To make any report meaningful, the current fair value of each asset could be disclosed along with the carrying value (determined as described above). The extent of the effort to obtain current values may depend on state law or the use of the asset. For example, marketable securities can readily be listed at their fair value based on published stock listings. But real estate would have to be appraised, and the cost of an appraisal would be uneconomical in many situations. For example, if the real estate is a house being used as a personal residence, with no reasonable expectation of a sale for the foreseeable future, an appraisal obviously is not needed.

If the accounting is to be filed with a court it will be notarized and signed under oath. In addition, any particular requirements of the court will have to be followed. For example, when there is a charitable beneficiary, the filing requirements may be more onerous in order for the state to protect the interests of the charity.

What to Consider When Reviewing a Final Trust Accounting

When you receive a trust accounting, whether as an incoming successor trustee, or as a beneficiary, what should you look for? Consider the following:

- What is the total trustee commissions and fees paid? How were they calculated?
- Is the basis on which the trustee commissions and fees were calculated correct? Does it comply with the provisions of the trust agreement and local law?
- If there is more than one trustee, does state law, or the trust agreement, provide for a maximum fee for all trustees in the aggregate? If so, has it been complied with?
- Verify that the math in the report is accurate and that the numbers on all of the detail schedules agree with the summary.
- Review any losses reported for unusual items. Was the trustee responsible for the losses incurred?
- Review all administrative expenses. Are the amounts and nature of the expenses reasonable?

CONCLUSION

The termination of a trust is as much a part of its function as the distribution of income and principal during its operation. The termination can have important legal and tax implications, and it's important to plan properly for when and how a trust can be concluded. Both the trust agreement and the requirements of local law must always be considered.

For Your Notebook:

SAMPLE GENERAL RELEASE
AND INDEMNIFICATION

[DO NOT USE THIS SAMPLE FORM TO OBTAIN AN ACTUAL RELEASE]

TO ALL TO WHOM THESE PRESENTS SHALL COME OR MAY CONCERN, KNOW THAT on this -0-th day of January, 1992:

BENEFICIARY NO. 1 AND BENEFICIARY NO. 2, individuals, with an address at 123 Main Ave., City Name, State Name, being all the remainder beneficiaries of the Jane Doe Irrevocable Trust, jointly and severally as Releasor, in consideration of One Hundred Twenty Two Thousand Dollars each ($122,000.00), for an aggregate of Two Hundred Forty Four Thousand Dollars ($244,000.00) and other good and valuable consideration received from:

NAME OF TRUSTEE,

an individual with an address at 333 West Street, City Name, State Name, as Releasee, receipt of which is hereby acknowledged, releases and discharges:

NAME OF TRUSTEE, Trustee

(the "Releasee"), and Releasee's heirs, executors, administrators, successors, transferees and assigns, from any and all actions, causes of action, suits, debts, dues, sums of money, accounts, reckonings, bonds, bills, specialities, covenants, contracts, controversies, agreements, promises, variances, trespasses, damages, judgments, extents, executions, claims, and demands whatsoever, in law, admiralty, or equity, which against the Releasee, the Releasor, the Releasor's heirs, executors, administrators, successors, transferees and assigns, ever had, now have or hereafter can, shall or may have, for, upon, or by reason of any matter, cause or thing whatsoever, which relates to the Jane Doe Irrevocable Trust and certain transactions and matters relating thereto, from the beginning of the world to the day of the date of this Release.

Releasor hereby agrees to hold Releasee harmless and indemnify Releasee against any costs or claims, including reasonable attorney fees, arising out of these matters.

Whenever the text hereof requires, the use of singular number shall include the appropriate plural number as the text of the within instrument may require.

This Release and Assignment may not be changed orally.

IN WITNESS WHEREOF, the Releasor has hereunto set Releasor's hand and seal:

WITNESS: RELEASOR:

_____   _____
                                                  BENEFICIARY NO. 1

_____   _____
                                                  BENEFICIARY NO. 2

TRUST RECEIPT AND RELEASE

Re: JANE DOE IRREVOCABLE TRUST

BENEFICIARY NO. 1 and BENEFICIARY NO. 2, the undersigned beneficiaries of the Jane Doe Irrevocable Trust, acknowledge having received the benefit of distributions on her and his behalf in the amount of approximately One Hundred Twenty Two Thousand Dollars ($122,000.00) each, for an aggregate of Two Hundred Forty Four Thousand Dollars ($244,000.00) and do hereby:

1. Accept and approve the attached accounting of receipts and disbursements for the Trust with the same force and effect as if it had been duly filed and audited in the Probate court, in the County of COUNTY NAME, state of STATE NAME, and had been adjudicated and confirmed absolutely.

2. Agree that if any just and proper claim is hereafter presented to the Trustee of the Trust, to be responsible for his pro rata share of the same, up to the amount of his distribution.

3. Release NAME OF TRUSTEE, Trustee of the Jane Doe Irrevocable Trust any Trusts formed thereunder, of and from any and all claims she or he has under the law against the said Trust, or the same NAME OF TRUSTEE in his capacity as Trustee of the Jane Doe Irrevocable Trust and as Trustee of any trusts formed thereunder.

4. Declare that this instrument shall be legally binding upon him and her and upon his or her heirs, assigns, and personal representatives.

IN WITNESS WHEREOF, I have hereunto set my hand and seal this -0-th day of January, 1992.

WITNESS:

_____

_____

_____

BENEFICIARY NO. 1
Social Security #

_____

BENEFICIARY NO. 2
Social Security #

GLOSSARY

Accounting. A detailed analysis of all income, gains, losses, transactions, and assets (at the beginning and ending of the period) presented when a trustee is terminated or resigns, and when a trust is terminated. If a formal accounting is submitted to the probate or surrogate's court, it will have to conform to any rules of the particular court.

Allocation. The process by which items are credited to different accounts. For example, cash receipts from a particular transaction may be allocated between income and principal. This can be important since income may be paid to the current income beneficiary of the trust, while the principal is designated for a remainder beneficiary, such as a charity.

Alternate Valuation Date. The valuation of assets included in an estate six months following the date of death. Assets are usually taxed based on their value as of the date of death. However, an executor may elect instead to have the assets (except those already distributed or disposed of) valued six months later, which can be useful when important assets have declined in value.

Annual Exclusion. An amount up to $10,000 per year that every person is allowed to give to any other person without incurring any gift tax. There is no limit on the number of these gifts you can make to different people in a year. To qualify for this exclusion, a gift must be of a present interest, meaning that the recipient can enjoy the gift immediately. This can present problems when you make gifts to trusts.

Attorney-in-Fact. An agent who is given written authorization by you to take certain actions on your behalf.

Basis. A tax concept used to calculate both depreciation and gain or loss when an asset is sold. The *adjusted basis* is the original purchase price, less depreciation, plus improvements.

Beneficiary. A person who receives the benefits of a trust or of transfers under your will—in legal jargon, sometimes referred to as *cestui que trust.*

Bequest. Any property transferred under your will.

Bypass Trust. See *Credit Shelter Trust.*

Capital. The value of an asset—the principal—rather than the income from the property.

Charitable Remainder Trust. The donation of property or money to a charity when the donor reserves the right to use the property or receive income from it for a specified number of years (or for life, or for the duration of the life of a second person such as a spouse). When the agreed period is over, the property belongs to the charitable organization. The trust can be an annuity trust (pays a fixed amount each year) or a unitrust (pays an amount based on a percentage of asset values held by the charity).

Commission. A fee paid to a trustee. The commission is usually regulated by state law and often is limited to a maximum percentage of assets, income, or distributions.

Credit Shelter Trust. A trust designed not to qualify for the unlimited estate tax marital deduction so that it will use up your lifetime $600,000 exclusion (unified credit). This is often the same as a bypass trust because such a trust bypasses, is not included in, your surviving spouse's estate.

Crummey Power. The right given to a beneficiary to withdraw up to $10,000 per year from a trust when gifts of such amount are made to the trust. This enables the person making the gift to qualify it for the annual $10,000 gift tax exclusion and avoid any gift tax.

Decedent. The person who died.

Descendant. A person who is a relative in a direct line from another person, an issue.

Devise. Real estate transferred under a will.

Donee. A person who receives a gift. Gifts can be made to trusts as well as to individuals.

Donor. A person who makes a gift.

Durable Power of Attorney. A document in which you grant certain people (your attorneys-in-fact) the authority to handle your financial matters, which will remain valid even if you become disabled. A plain (not durable) power of attorney will not necessarily be valid in that event.

Estate Tax. A transfer tax that the federal government assesses on your right to transfer assets on your death. The tax generally applies only to estates worth more than $600,000.

Executor. A person designated to manage your estate upon your death (marshalling assets, paying expenses and taxes, and making distributions to beneficiaries). *Executrix* is the feminine form. Also called a *personal administrator.*

Fiduciary. A person in a position of trust and responsibility, such as your executor or the trustee of a trust.

Generation-Skipping Transfer Tax (GST Tax). A tax assessed on transfers in excess of $1 million to grandchildren, great grandchildren, and anyone at least two generations below the donor. When a trust is used, this

$1 million exclusion must be allocated very carefully if the entire value of a trust is to remain exempt.

Gift. The transfer of property without receiving something of equal value. The federal government will assess a transfer tax when the value of the gift exceeds the annual exclusion and your unified credit is exhausted.

Gift Splitting. A technique by which the annual gift tax exclusion can be doubled from $10,000 to $20,000 per person if you're married and your spouse consents to join in the gift.

Grantor. The person who establishes a trust and transfers assets to it. Also called *trustor, settlor,* and occasionally *donor.*

Grantor Trust. A trust whose income must be reported on your own tax return.

Guardian. The person you designate as responsible for your minor children or other person requiring special care. The term is also used in connection with a person appointed with charge of assets.

Guardianship. The process of having a court appoint a person to be responsible for a disabled person or minor.

Heirs. The persons who receive your assets following your death.

Incidents of Ownership. All rights in an insurance policy. To remove insurance from your taxable estate you must give up all incidents of ownership.

Inheritance Tax. A tax based on the value of property that taxpayers inherit, which is imposed in a number of states.

Insurance Trust. A trust established to own your insurance policies and thereby prevent them from being included in your estate. See *Life Insurance Trust.*

Inter vivos Trust. See *Living Trust.*

Irrevocable. A trust that cannot be changed after you've established it. This is an essential characteristic in order to have assets you give to the trust removed from your estate.

Joint Tenancy. A legal form of ownership in which you and your spouse, or another person, own assets jointly and when one of you dies the property automatically passes to the surviving partner. This approach is too often used as a means of avoiding probate even though it is not necessarily the optimal tax strategy.

Legacy. Property transferred by your will. The person receiving it is called the *legatee.*

Life Insurance Trust. A trust intended primarily to hold life insurance. Almost always an irrevocable trust formed to keep insurance proceeds out of the taxable estate of the insured and the owner of the policy.

Living Trust. A trust organized during your lifetime—in legal jargon, an *inter vivos* trust. One example is a revocable living trust, used to plan for disability, avoid probate, and so forth.

Living Will. A document in which you can specify which life-saving measures you do, and do not, want to be taken on your behalf in the event of extreme illness. This instrument is often used in conjunction with a health care power of attorney, which appoints someone to act as your representative for health care matters.

Marital Deduction. An exemption from the estate tax for an unlimited amount of assets that can be transferred from one spouse to the other. This approach is too often used as the beginning and end of estate planning.

Massachusetts Real Estate Trust. A special trust formed under Massachusetts law for holding the title to real estate in order to provide confidentiality and minimize transfer costs.

Medicaid-Qualifying Trust. A trust intended to shield assets from the reach of health care providers and government agencies and programs that cover nursing-home-care costs.

Minor. A person who is not old enough to be an adult under state law.

Notary. A public officer or clerk who attests or certifies a document. Notarization is usually required for any documents to be filed in public records. Trusts and schedules attached to trusts are often notarized even when it is not strictly required because the notarization provides an independent proof of the date that the trust was established, or that certain property was transferred to the trust. This can be useful when the date of a property transfer is significant for tax purposes.

Per Capita. A distribution made equally to the number of persons at a specific level of relationship (e.g. grandchildren) receiving property. See *Per Stirpes.*

Per Stirpes. A distribution made equally among family lines so that, depending on the number of issue in that family line, the individuals may receive more or less than had the distribution been made per capita.

Pour-Over Will. A provision under a will stating that certain assets, often the remainder, are to be transferred ("poured over") to a trust. The will is said to contain a pour-over clause, and the trust is said to be a pour-over trust. This technique is commonly used when a living trust is formed to hold all assets in an effort to avoid (or at least minimize) the impact of probate.

Power of Appointment. The right and authority to transfer or dispose of property that you do not own. Depending on the terms, this right can cause the value of the asset to be included in your estate. Retaining a power of appointment can be done intentionally when establishing a Medicaid-qualifying trust in order to avoid adverse tax consequences for the transfer. It is also used in planning to avoid the generation-skipping transfer tax.

Present Interest. A requirement of a gift for it to qualify for the annual $10,000 gift tax exclusion. See *Annual Exclusion.* Gifts to trusts will not generally qualify as being of a present interest, and one way to address this is through the use of a Crummey power.

Probate Court. The court that has the power to deal with wills and related matters. Known by different names in different states, such as *surrogate's court* or *orphan's court.*

Qualified Domestic Trust (Q-DOT). A trust to which assets are transferred if your spouse is not a United States citizen, so that your estate will be entitled to the unlimited marital deduction.

Qualified S Corporation Trust (QSST). A trust that contains special provisions through which it can own stock in a corporation that has elected favorable tax treatment as an S corporation.

Qualified Terminable Interest Trust (Q-TIP). A trust that qualifies for the unlimited marital tax exclusion. This means there will be no estate tax on the value of the property transferred to your spouse in a Q-TIP trust on your death. Your spouse must receive all income at least annually. With this trust, your spouse can obtain income and other benefits, your estate can avoid tax, and you can designate who will receive the property remaining in the trust on your spouse's death.

Remainder Beneficiary. The person who will receive the assets of a trust after the interests end of persons who are currently receiving income.

Res. Principal or assets of a trust.

Residuary. The assets remaining in your estate after all specific transfers of property are made and all expenses are paid. When a pour-over will is used, the residuary will be poured into your living trust. In other situations, the residuary could be carved up into several smaller trusts, including a credit shelter or bypass trust to use your $600,000 unified tax credit and a Q-TIP or Q-DOT trust for your surviving spouse. When transfers are made to minor children or any person under a disability, additional trusts are usually provided for.

Reversionary Interest. A possible return of property to you that you have given away. You retain some interest in or control over the property.

Revocable Trust. A trust that you can change, amend, or revoke any time you wish. The most common revocable trust is a living or loving trust.

Rule Against Perpetuities. A law that makes an interest in property void if it won't take affect within a specified period. A common period in many states is the lifetime of a person living when the trust was set up, plus 21 years.

S Corporation. A corporation whose income is taxed to its shareholders, thus avoiding a corporate level tax. When stock in an S corporation is transferred to a trust, special issues are raised that must be addressed to avoid terminating the favorable tax status of the S corporation.

Second-to-Die Insurance. Insurance for a couple that pays a death benefit only on the death of the last spouse to die. This payment method makes the cost less than insurance on just one person's life. Designed for an estate plan in which, on the death of the first spouse, all assets are given tax-free to the surviving spouse using the unlimited marital deduction. On the death of the second spouse, the insurance benefit is paid and provides the cash to pay the estate tax. Also called *survivors insurance.*

Section 2053(c) Trust. A special trust established for minor children that permits gifts to it to qualify for the annual $10,000 gift tax exclusion even though they are not gifts of a present interest. This approach can be used for trusts for children under age 21 instead of a Crummey power which raises certain problems.

Settlor. The person who sets up a trust. See *Grantor.*

Spendthrift Provision. A clause in a trust that prohibits the beneficiary from appointing any interest in the trust in advance of receiving a distribution. The purpose is to limit, to the extent possible, the ability of creditors to reach trust assets.

Sprinkle Power. A trustee's right to distribute income in any proportions to several named beneficiaries, rather than equally. For example, when you set up a trust for your children, you cannot know which child may have greater needs at some distant future time, so the trust gives the trustee discretion to pay more income to the child most in need at the time.

Tenancy by the Entirety. A special type of joint tenancy for a husband and wife that provides limited protection from creditors and malpractice claimants, but has several drawbacks in comparison with a trust.

Testamentary Trust. A trust formed at your death, often under the provisions of your will. Examples include a credit shelter trust, Q-TIP trust, Q-DOT trust, and various trusts for minor beneficiaries.

Trust. An arrangement in which property is held and managed by a person (trustee) for the benefit of another (the beneficiary) under a fiduciary relationship. The terms of the trust are generally governed by a contract that you the grantor have prepared when you establish the trust.

Trustee. The person (fiduciary) who manages and administers a trust you establish.

Trustor. The person who sets up a trust. See *Grantor.*

Unified Credit. An exemption of $600,000 of transfers from the gift or estate tax to which every taxpayer is entitled. The primary purpose of a credit shelter trust is to use the unified credit.

Uniform Gifts (Transfers) to Minors Act (UGMA or UTMA). A method of holding property for the benefit of another person, such as your child, which is similar to a trust, but which is governed by state law. It is simpler and much cheaper to establish and administer, but is far less flexible.

Voting Trust Agreement. An agreement between certain shareholders and a trustee by which stock in a corporation is held in the name of the trustee and voted by the trustee. This type of trust does not affect the economic interests in the corporation, as dividends are paid directly to the shareholders.

Will. A legal document completed in accordance with state law that states how your assets will be distributed on your death. The will also appoints an executor for your estate, may establish trusts for your children and name a trustee for those trusts, names guardians for your children, and so forth.

INDEX

Accountant:
  financial statement preparation, 196
  gift tax return, filing of, 89
  itemized bills from, 116
  life insurance trusts and, 214
  living trusts and, 122
Accounting, *see specific types of accounting*
Addition, defined, 81
Adoption, effect on trusts, 47
Adverse interests:
  taxation issues and, 43
  trustee selection and, 55
Agency relationships, 6–7
Annual gift tax exclusion, *see* Gift tax
    exclusion
Annuity trusts:
  charitable remainder trusts and, 167–168
  grantor-retained, *see* Grantor-Retained
    Annuity Trusts (GRUTs)
Anonymity, advantage of, 7
Art, transfer of, 27
Asset distribution:
  personal considerations regarding, 72
  trustee's powers, 70–72
Asset ownership:
  legal *vs.* beneficial, 4–5
  sample schedule of, 33
Asset protection:
  asset transfer to spouse, 191–192
  debtor/creditor laws, 190–191
  grantor rights, 194
  liability insurance, 192
  planning for, 189–190, 195–197
  spendthrift provisions, 192
  trustee rights, 194
  trusts, types of, 194–195
Asset transfer:
  attached schedule, 23
  as building block, 13
  costs, 24–25, 29
  fair market disclosure, 269
  overall planning for, 23–24
  partial, 33
  process of, 25–28
  recordkeeping, 27
  requirements, 30
  sample clauses, 22
  sample schedule of, 29

  taxation issues, 24–25
  time factors involved, 24–25
  types of assets and, 25–28
Attorney(s):
  asset protection and, 197
  asset transfer process, 25
  creditor's rights, 117
  elder law expertise, 201, 206
  grantor as trustee/co-trustee decision, 45
  itemized bills from, 116
  life insurance trusts and, 214
  living trusts, role in, 121
  real estate transfer, 113
  trust termination, 264–265
  voting trusts and, 223
Attorney-in-fact, defined, 24

Bank account, opening of, 26
Beneficiaries:
  alternates, 48, 51
  charities as, 6, 48
  contingent, 133
  co-trustee as, 49
  defined, 5–6
  designations and rights:
    generally, 14
    tax planning for, 50–51
    withdrawals by, 48–50
  distributions to:
    disclosure of, 270
    taxation of, 259–261
    trust termination and, 266
  grantor as, 44
  grandchildren as, 183
  language regarding:
    generally, 47
    sample, 14
  living trusts and, 125
  Massachusetts Realty trusts, 231
  Medicaid-qualifying trusts, 203
  naming of, 47–48, 51
  powers of, 8
  Qualified S Corporation Trusts, 228
  renaming of, 129
  skip persons as, 51
  spouse as, 48–49
  taxation of:
    calculation of, 254–256

Beneficiaries *(Continued)*
 charitable remainder trusts and, 171
 distributions to, 259–260
 generally, 250
 generation-skipping tax and, 51
 income allocation to, 250–251
 receipt of income, 251–252
 simple trusts and, 250
 tax basis of, 260
 throwback rules, 252–256
 tax bracket of, 251
 as trustee, 48–49, 71
 types of, 8
 voting trusts, 233
 withdrawals by:
 five-and-five power, 49–50
 limitations on, 71
 spouse as beneficiary and trustee, 48–49
Bill of Sale, sample, 31
Broker, living trusts and, 122
Building blocks:
 asset transfer, 13
 beneficiaries designations and rights, 14
 grantor's rights and powers, 13–14
 income distribution, 15–16
 introductory paragraphs, 11–13
 miscellaneous provisions, 16
 principal distribution 15–16
 trustee's rights, obligations and powers,
 14–15
Business interests, transfer of, 27
Buy-out provisions, 27
Bypass trusts, *see* Credit shelter trusts

Capital gains and losses:
 recognition of, 259
 tax basis and, 257–259
 trust termination of, 268
C corporation, voting trusts and, 234–235
Charitable contributions, tax treatment of, 247
Charitable lead trusts:
 generally, 173–174
 income and principal distribution
 provisions, 15
Charitable remainder giving:
 beneficiaries, taxation of, 171–172
 charities, gifts to, 172–173
 estate and gift taxes, effect on, 171
 generation-skipping transfer tax, 172
 spouse, gifts to, 172–173
 tax deductions, 173
 trusts, taxation of, 171–172
Charitable remainder trusts:
 asset protection and, 194
 beneficiaries of, 171
 defined, 167
 establishment of, 7
 funding of, 170–171
 income-only unitrust option, 169–170
 insurance and, 168–169
 special tax rules, 261
 successor trustees, naming of, 177

 tax rates and, 170
 trust agreement, inclusions in, 170–171
 trustee:
 commission, 178
 selection, 170
 types of, 167–168
 unitrusts, sample, 176–180
Charitable trusts, *see specific types of
 charitable trusts*
Charities:
 as beneficiaries, 6, 48
 distributions to, sample provisions, 79
Child, defined, 81
Children:
 defined, 81
 trusts designed for, *see* Children's trusts
Children's trusts:
 asset protection and, 194
 Crummey power and, 157, 160–161
 distributions, sample provisions, 76–78
 educational and medical benefits, 157
 gift of a present interest, 157
 gift tax exclusion and, 157, 159
 grandchildren, gifts to, 162
 hanging power, 161
 income-only trusts (Section 2503(b) Trusts),
 159–160
 living trusts and, 132–133
 minors:
 special trust rules for, 161–162
 tax law requirements and, 69
 options, 159
 sample provisions, 166
 secondary gift-over problem, 160–161
 separate, 76, 161
 special child, *see* Special child trusts
 Uniform Gifts to Minors Act, 158–159
 Uniform Gift (or Transfers) to Minors
 Act, 158
Code, defined, 81
Common living trusts, establishment of, 7
Complex trusts, tax treatment of, 247, 249
Confidentiality:
 living trusts and, 114–115
 Massachusetts Realty Trusts and, 230
 nonmarital partners and, 156
 pour-over wills, 121
Consent of shareholders, sample, 34
Contracts, sample assignment, 36
Corporate stock:
 S corporations and, 225–229
 voting trusts and, 221–225
Co-trustee(s):
 business partner as, 55
 as beneficiary, 49
 defined, 5
 distribution decisions, 50, 55
 grantor as, 44–45, 72
 institution as, 55
 living trusts, role in, 119, 123–124, 139, 194
 multiple, 55
 naming of, 55

Creditors, protection from, 39, 44, 117, 156, 207
Credit shelter trusts:
    benefits, examples of, 150
    estate tax planning and, 91
    income distribution, spouse and, 69
    purpose of, 147
    revocable living trusts and, 40, 130–131
    sample provision, 149
    S corporation shares and, 227
    tax benefits, generally, 48
    zero tax, 146–147
Crummey demand power:
    children's trusts and, 160–161
    gift tax exclusion and, 89–90
    life insurance trusts, 214
"Cy press," function of, 48

Declaration of gift:
    need for, 28, 31–32
    sample, 30
Definitions, placement in trust agreement, 81
Depreciation, tax treatment of, 247
Direct skip transfer, 97–98
Disability planning:
    insurance policies and, 123
    living trusts and, 8, 119, 123–125, 129
    protection during, 39
Disinheritance, special child and, 163
Distributable net income (DNI):
    calculation of, 248
    complex trusts, 248
    defined, 244, 247
    purposes of, 248
    simple trusts, 249
Distribution of income and principal:
    beneficiaries and, 259–261, 266, 270
    building blocks of trust, 15–16
    generation-skipping tax (GST) and, 98
    miscellaneous provisions:
        generally, 72–73
        sample, 80–83
    personal considerations, 72
    sample provisions, 74–79
    tax considerations, 69–70, 253–255
    trustees and, 64, 69–72, 76, 118
    types of:
        accumulated, 252–254
        partial, 259
        total deemed, 254–255
    See also specific types of trusts
Divorce:
    asset protection and, 207
    irrevocable trusts and, 41, 76, 213
    trust self-destruct provision, effect on, 75
    voting trusts and, 222–223
Donee property, defined, 81
Donor, defined, 4
Durable power of attorney:
    asset transfer and, 21
    defined, 6
    vs. living trusts, 116, 119

Estate planning attorney:
    gifts of present interest and, 89
    living trusts and, 130
    trust self-destruct provision, 75
Estate planning, significance of, 125–126, 211
Estate taxes:
    avoidance of, 39, 44
    exclusion, see Estate tax exclusion
    living trusts and, 117
    rates, 90
Estate tax exclusion:
    calculation of, 93
    gross estate:
        fair market value of, 92
        inclusions in, 91–92
    property valuation, 92
Executor, commission, 116
Exhibits, as building block, 16

Fair market value:
    beneficiaries, distribution to, 260
    gross estate and, 92
    tax basis, determination of, 258–259
Fiduciary accounting, defined, 268–269
Filing requirements:
    generally, 245
    gift taxes, 30, 89, 259
    Massachusetts Realty Trusts, 231
Five-and-five power, 49–50
Five key elements of trusts:
    asset transfer and, 13
    defined, 4–6
    introductory paragraphs, inclusion in, 12
    living trusts and, 125
Foreign trusts, throwback rules, 256
Funded trusts, defined, 21
Furniture, transfer of, 27

Generation-skipping tax (GST tax):
    annual gift tax exclusion and, 95, 99
    beneficiaries and, 51
    calculation of, 96, 98–99
    charitable remainder giving and, 172
    deferral of, 98
    direct skip, 97–98
    distributions, taxable, 98
    educational and medical benefits and, 99–100
    effects of, minimization of, 99–100
    inclusion ratio, defined, 100
    marital status and, 102–103
    million-dollar exemption:
        allocation of, 100–101
        utilization of, 100
    minority discounts, 96
    planning approaches, 101–102
    purpose of, 96
    sample trust provisions, 104–107
    termination, taxable, 98–99
    triggering events, 97–99
    trust establishment, 101–102
    wealthy and, 95, 103
Gift splitting, 88

Gift tax:
    exclusion, *see* Gift tax exclusion
    tax basis and, 257–259
    tax return, filing of, 259
Gift tax exclusion:
    benefits of, 87–88
    completion rules, 90
    establishment of trust and, 12
    exceeding, 88–89
    gifts of present interest, 89–90
    gift splitting, 88
    living trusts and, 117–118
    partial transfers and, 33
    See also specific types of trusts
Grandchildren, gifts to, 162, 222. *See also*
    Generation-skipping transfer tax
Grantor(s):
    control by, 8, 14
    defined, 4
    living trusts and, 125
    rights and powers:
        regarding beneficiaries, 44
        generally, 13–14,
        revocability/irrevocability, 39–41
        sprinkle power, 72
        taxation and, 42–44
        termination rights, 263
        trustee selection, 5
    as trustee/co-trustee, 44–45, 72
    trusts, *see specific types of grantor trusts*
Grantor-Retained Annuity Trusts (GRATs):
    asset protection and, 194
    benefits of, examples, 185–186
    estate tax consequences, 182–183
    example of, 12
    gift tax consequences, 181–182
    grandchildren, as beneficiaries, 183
    income stream, 182
    ladder the trusts strategy, 182
    operation of, 183
    purpose of, 181
    valuation rules, 181
Grantor-Retained Unitrusts (GRUTs):
    asset protection and, 194
    estate tax consequences, 182–183
    gift tax consequences, 181–182
    grandchildren, as beneficiaries, 183
    operation of, 183
    purpose of, 181
    valuation rules, 181
Grantor trusts, characterization as, 42–43, 263
Gross estate:
    fair market value of, 92
    inclusions in, 91–92

Hanging power, 161
Health care options, 199
Health care proxy, appointment of, 123

In terrorem provision, 141
In trust, defined, 81
Incident of ownership, defined, 215

Inclusion ratio, defined, 100
Income:
    calculation, 244, 250
    defined, 81
    determination as, 244–245
    distributable net income (DNI), *see*
        Distributable net income (DNI)
    distribution, provisions regarding, 15–16.
        See also Distribution of income and
        principal
    tax-exempt, 246
    undistributed net income, 253
    See also Distribution of income and
        principal
Insurance:
    agent, *see* Insurance agent
    charitable remainder planning and, 169
    coordination with, 9
    disability policy, 123
    probate and, 207
Insurance agent:
    life insurance trusts and, 213, 217
    living trusts and, 121–122
Intent of trust:
    defined, 6
    living trusts and, 125
Inter vivos trusts:
    establishment of, 7
    grantor's rights and powers, 39
    introductory paragraphs, 11
    See also Living trusts
Introductory paragraphs:
    information included in, 12–13
    need for, 11
    sample clauses, 12
Irrevocability:
    asset transfer and, 24
    decision considerations, 40–41
    defined, 8
Irrevocable trusts:
    decision considerations, 40–41
    estate tax and, 91
    grantor as trustee/co-trustee, 44–45
    life insurance, *see* Life insurance trusts,
        irrevocable
    purposes of, 39
    real estate transfers, 26
    sample clause, 40
    termination of, 41, 264–265
IRS forms:
    Form 1041, Schedule K-1, 229
    Form 1120-S, Schedule K-1, 229
    Form SS-4, 13, 17–19, 26, 214
Issue, defined, 81

Jewelry, transfer of, 27
Joint tenant form of ownership (JTWROS),
    benefits of, 116

Kiddie tax:
    application of, 159
    special tax rules, 261

Language:
  beneficiaries and, 14, 47
  living trusts and, 128
  Medicaid-qualifying trusts, 202–203
  trustee distributions, 69
Life insurance trusts:
  alternatives, consideration of, 209–212
  asset protection and, 194
  benefits of, 207
  compound interest, 209
  comprehensive thinking and, 210–211
  Crummey power, 214–215
  defined, 208
  distributions, 215
  example of, 210–211
  existing policies, transfer to, 214–215, 219
  incidents of ownership, 215–216
  inclusions, generally, 215–216
  irrevocable, 122, 164, 209, 216
  marital deduction, use of, 208–209, 213, 220
  provisions, sample, 217–220
  Q-TIP trusts and, 216
  revocable, 212
  setting up process, 213–214
  trustee:
    authority of, 215–218
    cooperation of, 219
    indemnity of, 218
    selection of, 212–213
Limited partnerships:
  partnership interests, transfer of, 27
Living trusts:
  administration of, 121
  assets:
    disposition of, 120–121
    management, 120
    transfer to, 122–123
  confidentiality, 114–115
  costs:
    additional taxes, 117–118, 128
    commissions, executor and trustee, 116
    court costs, 115
    legal fees, 115
    probate, 113–116
    real estate transfers, 113
    wills, 114
  co-trustee role, 119, 123–124, 139
  disability planning and, 8, 119, 123–125, 129
  distribution, 117–118
  durable power of attorney and, 116, 119, 128
  establishment of, 7
  flexibility of, 126
  four stages of, 121–124
  vs. gifts, 118
  investment standards, 136
  vs. irrevocable trusts, 118
  language in, 128
  legal fees, 115
  multiple trusts under, 123–124, 130
  nonmarital relationships and, 120
  operation of, 113

  perpetuities, rule against, 143
  vs. probate, 111, 113, 117, 120
  provisions of:
    disability planning, 124–125
    five trust elements, 125
    in terrorem, 141
  publicity and, 120
  purpose of, 111
  recordkeeping requirements, 120
  sample, 127–143
  schematic of, 112
  successor trustee, 116, 119, 123, 139
  taxation and, 117, 128, 243
  trustees, supervision of, 117
  wills and, 114
Living will, need for, 123
Loving trusts, establishment of, 7. See also
      Living trusts

Malpractice claims, avoidance of, 44, 156
Marital deduction trusts:
  income and principal distribution
      provisions, 15
  purpose of, 8
Marriage, irrevocable trusts and, 41
Massachusetts Realty Trusts:
  beneficiaries, schedule of, 231
  confidentiality, 230
  defined, 229
  economic advantages, 229
  paper work required, 231
  problems with, 230–231
  Schedule of Beneficial Interests, 231
  taxation and, 230–231
  tax filings, 231
  third parties and, 231
  as title holder, 229
Medicaid:
  asset protection from, 39, 156
  qualification requirements, 199–200
  special child benefits, 163
  spending down, 200
  third-party recovery, 202
  trust protection from, see
      Medicaid-qualifying trusts
Medicaid-qualifying trusts:
  asset transfers, 204
  beneficiaries, selection of, 203
  case study example, 202
  distributions, 203
  drawbacks, 201–202
  incomplete gifts technique, 90
  language of, 202–203
  provisions:
    generally, 203
    sample, 206
  purpose of, 8, 117, 200–201
  spendthrift provision, 203
  sprinkle trusts, 202
  structure of, 202–204
  tax considerations, 204
Medicare, special child benefits, 163

"Merger," avoidance of, 5
Minor children's trusts, see Children's trusts
Miscellaneous provisions of trusts:
  distributions:
    boiler plate provisions, 73
    generally, 80–83
  information included in, 16
Multiple trusts:
  under living trusts, 123–124, 130
  tax treatment of, 244–245
  throwback rules, 256
  under wills, 100

Name selection, 12
Noncitizen spouse:
  credit provision for, 147
  qualified domestic trusts (Q-DOTs),
    147–148
  sample provisions, 151
  special gift tax rule, 147
Nonmarital partners:
  confidentiality, 156
  contribution documentation, 155
  gift and estate concerns, 155
  irrevocable trusts and, 154–156
  joint tenancy with right of survivorship,
    154–155
  living trusts and, 120
  property title, structure of, 153
  revocable trusts, 156
  tax problems of, 153–154
  zero-tax planning, unavailability of,
    154–155

Partial transfers, reason for, 33
Partnership interest:
  sample assignment of, 32
  transfer of, 27
Per stirpes, defined, 82
Perpetuities, rule against, 80–81, 143
Personal property, transfer of, 27
Personal residence trusts, 184
"Person under disability," defined, 82
Pooled-income fund, 174
Pour-over will:
  asset transfer and, 21
  confidentiality, lack of, 121
  date of trust, 13
  living trusts and, 124, 127, 129
  probate and, 114
  purpose of, 9
  sample provision, 37
Power of appointment, 8
Power of attorney:
  coordination with, 9
  defined, 6, 119
Prenuptial agreement, irrevocable trusts
    and, 76
Principal, defined, 81
Principal distribution, general provisions
    regarding, 15–16. See also Distribution of
    income and principal

Privacy, advantage of, 7. See also Confidentiality
Probate:
  ancillary, 22
  asset transfer and, 21
  avoidance of, 39, 116
  cost of:
    generally, 113–114
    reduction in, 115–116
  creditor's rights and, 117
  estate, see Probate estate
  legal fees incurred, 115
Probate estate:
  defined, 92
  insurance proceeds and, 207

Qualified domestic trusts (Q-DOTs):
  income and principal distribution
    provisions, 15
  purpose of, 147–148
Qualified Subchapter S Trusts (QSSTs):
  assets, types of, 238
  beneficiaries, 228
  income and principal distribution
    provisions, 15
  requirements of, 27, 227–228
  sample provisions, 237–238
  savings clause, 238
  special election qualification:
    requirement, 228–229
    sample, 239
  trustee powers, 227
  use of, 226–228
Qualified Terminable Interest Property Trusts
    (Q-TIPs):
  advantage of, 146
  charitable remainder giving and, 173
  estate tax marital deduction, 70, 146
  as generation-skipping tax-exemption
    trusts, 101
  income and principal distribution
    provisions, 15
  revocable living trusts and, 40, 132
  sprinkle power, 72
  unlimited gift deduction, 70
  unlimited marital deduction, 102

Real estate transfer:
  costs of, 24–25, 113
  deed and, 23
  gift deed, 25
  property tax reassessment, 26
  quit claim, 25
  taxation of, 26
Recordkeeping:
  inadequate, 256
  significance of, 27, 116, 120, 123
Remaindermen, defined, 182
Revocability:
  asset transfer and, 24
  defined, 8, 141
  flexibility and, 39
  tax issues and, 243

Revocable living trusts:
  asset protection and, 194
  co-trustees, 194
  distributions:
    control over, 69
    sample provisions, 74
  establishment of, 7
  key element of, 141
  real estate transfer, 26
  taxes:
    considerations, 69–70, 243
    treatment by, 227
  trustees, sample provisions regarding, 62
Revocable trust(s):
  grantor as trustee of, 44
  living trusts, *see* Revocable living trusts
  personal taxation advantages, 44
  provision stating, 39–40
  purposes of, 39
  sample clause, 40
  termination of, 263–264
  See also Revocable living trusts

Sale of property:
  distributions to beneficiaries, 259–260
  quick sales, special tax rules for, 260–261
  tax basis determination, 257–259
Sample clauses:
  Beneficiary's Annual Demand Power, 50–51
  Declaration of Trust, 12
  Distribution of Trust Estate When Amount
    Is Less Than Specified Sum, 266
  Irrevocable Trust, 40
  Limitations on Trustee's Discretionary
    Authority, 49
  Limited Annual $5,000/5 Percent Right of
    Withdrawal, 49–50
  Revocable Trust, 40
  Trust Assets, 22
  Trustee Provisions, 58–66
Schedule of Beneficial Interests, 231
S corporation(s):
  defined, 225–226
  qualified subchapter S trusts (QSSTs), *see*
    Qualified Subchapter S Trusts (QSSTs)
  stock as gifts, 90
  tax treatment of, 225–226
Second-to-die insurance:
  compound interest, 209
  defined, 2208
  marital deduction, use of, 208–209
Section 2503(b) Trusts:
  income-only trusts, 159–160
  sample Minor's Trust provision, 166
  special trusts for minor children,
    161–162
Securities, transfer of, 26
Settlor, defined, 4
Signature lines:
  as building block, 16
  sample page, 20
Signature page, sample, 20

Simple trusts:
  beneficiaries, taxation of, 250
  tax treatment of, 247
  termination and, 267
Social Security, special child benefits, 163
Special child trusts:
  disinheritance and, 163
  life insurance trusts, 164
  resource allocation, 163–164
  trustee, powers and provisions, 164–165
Spendthrift provisions:
  asset protection and, 192
  Medicaid-qualifying trusts, 203
  primary use, 135
Spouse(s):
  asset transfer to, 191–192
  as beneficiary and trustee, 48–49
  charitable gifts to, 172–173
  trusts designed for:
    marital deduction and, 145–146
    noncitizen spouse, *see* Noncitizen spouse
    See also Credit Shelter Trusts; Qualified
      Terminable Interest Property Trusts
      (Q-TIP Trusts)
Sprinkle power, utilization of, 71–72, 76,
  98, 159
Sprinkle trusts:
  defined, 8
  Medicaid-qualifying trusts and, 202
Standby trusts:
  defined, 5, 13
  formation of, 5
Stock power(s):
  sample, 35
  transfer of, 26–27
Successor trustee(s):
  charitable remainder trusts, 177
  children's trusts and, 158
  grantor's rights and powers and, 44
  living trusts and, 119, 123
  role of, 14
  selection of, 56
Supplemental Security Income (SSI):
  qualification for, 199
  special child benefits, 163

Tax adviser, professional advice regarding:
  federal/state gift tax return, filing of, 30
  generation-skipping transfer tax, 183
  gift and estate tax planning and, 93, 96
  qualified subchapter S trust (QSST)
    elections, 225–227
  valuation rules, 96
Tax identification number, need for, 13, 26, 113
Taxable estate, defined, 92
Taxation:
  calendar year, 245
  deductions and losses:
    complex trusts, 247, 249
    generally, 245–247
    simple trusts, 247–249
  filing requirements, 245

Taxation *(Continued)*
  income:
    calculation, 244, 250
    determination as, 244–245
    distributable net income (DNI), *see*
      Distributable net income (DNI)
    tax-exempt, 246
  multiple trust rules, 244–245
  tax basis, capital gains and losses, 257–259,
    261
  See also specific types of trusts
Termination:
  deferral of, 266
  general release and indemnification,
    sample, 272–273
  irrevocable trusts, 41, 264–265
  reasons for, generally, 263
  revocable trusts, 263–264
  sample clauses, 266–267
  tax consequences, 267–268
  trust agreement terms, 265–267
  windup period, 267
Testamentary trusts:
  asset transfer, selection of, 25
  establishment of, 7
  grantor's rights and powers, 39
Third-parties, indemnification of, 80
Throwback rules:
  accumulation distribution calculation,
    253–254
  defined, 252–253
  exception to, 256
  shortcut calculation, 252, 255–256
  tax calculation steps, 255–256
  total deemed distribution, 254–255
Title insurance policy, required purchase of,
  25, 113
Title transfer, 13
Transfer agent, securities transfer and, 26
Trust(s):
  advantages of, 6–7
  boiler plate provisions, 14, 57, 73
  building blocks, *see* Building blocks
  defined, 3–7
  categorization factors, 7–8
  overall planning, 8–9, 125–126, 211
  purpose of, 3, 8
  selection of, 9–10
  tax treatment, *see* Taxation
  termination of, *see* Termination
  See also specific types of trusts
Trust accounting:
  cover page, 269
  defined, 268
  disclosures in, 269–271
  fiduciary accounting, 268–269
  final accounting:
    inclusions in, 269–271
    review of, 271
  IRS audit, 270
  liability and, 268–269
  summary, 269

  trustees and, sample provisions, 59–60
  vs. tax reporting rules, 269
Trust agreement:
  flexibility in, 266
  trustees, provisions regarding:
    exoneration from liability, 56–57
    sample, 58–66
    trustee fees, 56
  termination provisions, 265–267
  voting stock and, 224–245, 233–236
Trust estate, defined, 82
Trust planning, voting trusts and, 225
Trust property, defined, 4–5
Trust res, defined, 4
Trustee(s):
  alternates, 14, 54, 58
  authority of, sample provisions, 61–62
  as beneficiary, 48, 71
  characteristics, desirable, 54–55
  children's trusts, administration of, 64,
    164–165
  commissions:
    charitable remainder trusts, 178
    disclosure of, 270
    generally, 43
    living trusts, 116
  decision-making, sample provision,
    61–62
  defined, 5, 82
  distributions:
    administrative powers, 70
    discretionary powers, 71
    living trusts and, 118
    sample provisions, 64
    sprinkle power, 71–72, 76
  fees:
    deductibility, 243, 246
    disclosure of, 270
    generally, 43
  grantor as, 44–45
  institution as, 56
  liability, exoneration from, 56–57, 61
  living trusts and, 125
  naming of, 13–14, 54, 58
  removal of, 43
  resignation of, sample provision, 58–59
  rights, obligations and powers:
    compensation rights, 56, 116
    distributions, *see* Trustee(s), distributions
    generally, 8, 14–15
    investment decisions, power designation
      sample guidelines, 67
    sample provisions, 59–66
    statement of, need for, 63
    trust documents stating, 56
  sample trustee provisions, 58–66
  selection of:
    charitable remainder trusts, 170
    duration of trust and, 56
    generally, 53–54
    legal/tax considerations, 55
    personal note regarding, 54

special child trusts and, 164–165
spouse as, 45, 53
successor, role of, 14
tax basis, adjusted, 257
termination of, sample provisions, 59, 66
See also Co-trustee(s); Successor trustee(s)
Trustor, defined, 4

Unanimous Written Consent of All
    Shareholders and Directors, 223
Undistributed net income, defined, 253
Unfunded trusts, defined, 21
Uniform Gift (or Transfers) to Minors Act,
    children's trusts and, 158
Uniform Gifts to Minors Act, children's trusts
    and, 158–159
Unitrusts:
    grantor-retained, *see* Grantor-Retained
        Unitrusts (GRUTs)
    charitable remainder trusts and, 167–168
Unlimited marital deduction:
    estate tax planning and, 91
    noncitizen spouse and, 147
    Q-TIP trusts and, 102, 146
    terminable interest and, 145

Voting trusts:
    beneficiaries, 233
    corporate resolution authorizing
        participation in, sample, 232
    defined, 221
    divorce and, 222–223
    process of, 223–224
    purposes of, 8, 221
    trust agreement for:
        duration of, 233
        inclusions in, 224–225
        sample, 233–236
    trustee selection, 223–224
    trust planning, effect on, 225
    uses of, 222
    validity of, 223

Will(s):
    multiple trusts under, 100
    need for, 114
    pour-over, *see* Pour-over will
    testamentary trusts and, 7, 25
Windup period, 267